D0992191

EARLY RECOLLECTIONS

Early Recollections

Their Use in Diagnosis
and Psychotherapy

Compiled and Edited by

HARRY A. OLSON, Ph.D.

Psychologist in Private Practice, Reisterstown, Maryland
Part-time Faculty, The Johns Hopkins University
Baltimore, Maryland
Visiting Professor, Adler-Dreikurs Institute of Human Relations
Bowie State College, Bowie, Maryland

With a Foreword by

Raymond J. Corsini, Ph.D.
Psychologist in Private Practice, Honolulu, Hawaii
Formerly Editor, Journal of Individual Psychology

WITHDRAWN

CHARLES C THOMAS · PUBLISHER
Springfield · Illinois · U.S.A.

Published and Distributed Throughout the World by
CHARLES C THOMAS • PUBLISHER
Bannerstone House
301-327 East Lawrence Avenue, Springfield, Illinois, U.S.A.

With THOMAS BOOKS *careful attention is given to all details of manufacturing and design. It is the Publisher's desire to present books that are satisfactory as to their physical qualities and artistic possibilities and appropriate for their particular use.* THOMAS BOOKS *will be true to those laws of quality that assure a good name and good will.*

Printed in the United States of America
W-2

Library of Congress Cataloging in Publication Data
Olson, Harry A.
Main entry under title:
Early recollections.
    Bibliography: p. 358
    Includes index.
    1. Mental illness—Diagnosis—Addresses, essays,
lectures. 2. Recollection (Psychology)—Addresses,
essays, lectures. 3. Psychotherapy—Addresses, essays,
lectures. I. Olson, Harry A., 1944-
[DNLM: 1. Memory—Collected works. 2. Psychoanalytic
interpretation—Collected works. 3. Psychoanalytic
therapy—Collected works. WM460.5.M5 E12]
RC469.E22   616.8'914   78-17725
ISBN 0-398-03826-0

". . . Adler's routine request for a first memory was actually the first approach toward the *projective-*test method now so widely used. . . . His first memory technique was not only unique as a quasi-test device but at its inception unique in the theory that loosely governed conscious production may be used *systematically* to reveal deep personality trends."

RUTH L. MUNROE
Schools of Psychoanalytic Thought
New York, Dryden, 1955, 428-429

*This book is gratefully
dedicated to*

Hal McAbee

and

Harold Mosak,

*colleagues and friends
who have made significant
contributions to my personal and
professional development.*

CONTRIBUTORS

Lucy K. Ackerknecht, Ph.D.—Director, Western Institute for Research and Training in Humanics; Professor of Psychology, John F. Kennedy University, Orinda, California.

Alfred Adler, M.D. (Deceased)—Psychiatrist, author, and lecturer; founder of the theory of individual psychology.

Heinz L. Ansbacher, Ph.D.—Professor emeritus of psychology, University of Vermont, Burlington, Vermont; author, editor.

Paul Brodsky (Deceased)—Former child psychologist and teacher; former director, Sunset Play Corner Day Program, Los Angeles, California.

Du-Fay Der, Ph.D.—Assistant professor, Department of Counseling Psychology, Faculty of Education, University of British Columbia, Vancouver, British Columbia, Canada.

Don Dinkmeyer, Ph.D.—Adjunct professor, Nova University, Fort Lauderdale, Florida; President, Communication and Motivation Training Institute, Inc., Coral Springs, Florida.

Daniel G. Eckstein, Ph.D.—Assistant professor, Department of Behavioral Sciences, College of Education, Louisana Tech University, Ruston, Louisiana.

Frederic Feichtinger, M.D. (Deceased)—Former associate professor of clinical psychiatry, Dorm State Medical Center, State University of New York, Brooklyn, New York. Student and colleague of Alfred Adler.

Norbert Freedman, Ph.D.—Psychologist, New York, New York.

Joseph Friedman, Ph.D. — Instructor, University of Pennsylvania, Philadelphia, Pennsylvania; psychologist in private practice.

Janet S. Greene, Ph.D.—Diplomate in Clinical Psychology, ABPP, New York, New York.

Carolyn W. Ilgenfritz, R.N., M.S.—Clinical specialist in psychiatric nursing, Walter P. Carter Center, Baltimore, Maryland.

Barbara Janoe, A.B.—Artist, teacher, and author, Vancouver, Washington.

Ed Janoe, M.Ed.—Marriage and family counselor; Director, Family and Life Enrichment Service, Vancouver; Faculty, Clark College, Vancouver, Washington.

Asya L. Kadis (Deceased)—Founder of the Group Psychotherapy Department, Postgraduate Center for Psychotherapy, New York; Former assistant professor of psychiatry, Downstate Medical Center, State University of New York, Brooklyn, New York.

Marc King, Ph.D.—Coordinator of group services, Personal Development and Life Planning Center; assistant professor, Bowling Green State University, Bowling Green, Ohio.

Richard Royal Kopp, Ph.D.—Coordinator of Theoretical Curriculum and Instruction, California School of Professional Psychology, Los Angeles; Assistant director of training, Mid-Valley Community Mental Health Council, Inc., Durante, California.

Sofie Lazarsfeld, Ph.D. (Deceased)—Formerly private practitioner, Vienna, Paris, New York; author.

Daniel I. Malamud, Ph.D.—Adjunct associate professor, New York University, New York; Private practice, New York, New York.

Guy J. Manaster, Ph.D.—Associate professor, Department of Educational Psychology, University of Texas, Austin, Texas.

Harold V. McAbee, Ed.D.—Dean of the Graduate School and Director, Adler-Dreikurs Institute of Human Relations, Bowie State College, Bowie, Maryland.

Norma Lou McAbee, B.A.—Art therapist; visiting associate professor, Bowie State College, Bowie, Maryland.

William H. McKelvie, Ed.D.—Associate professor, Adler-Dreikurs Institute of Human Relations, Bowie State College, Bowie, Maryland; psychologist in private practict, Silver Spring, Maryland.

Patrick L. Morris, Ed.M.—Counselor, Northwest Baltimore Community Corporation, Baltimore; visiting assistant professor, Adler-Dreikurs Institute, Bowie State College, Bowie, Maryland.

Harold H. Mosak, Ph.D.—Diplomate in clinical psychology, ABPP; Private practice, author, and lecturer; Chairman, Board of Directors, Alfred Adler Institute, Chicago, Illinois.

Hertha Orgler—Author, biographer and student of Alfred Adler, London, England.

Helene Papanek, M.D.—Psychiatrist in private practice; Director, Alfred Adler Institute, New York; Lecturer, Postgraduate Center for Psychotherapy, New York, New York.

Franz Plewa (Deceased)—Former worker, Boys' Town, Nebraska.

George W. Rogers, Jr., Ed.D.—Director of testing and psychological services and assistant professor of psychology, Northern Kentucky University, Highland Heights, Kentucky.

Paul Rom—Founder and editor, **Individual Psychology Newsletter,** London, England.

Harold M. Schiffman, Ph.D.—Professor, Department of Psychology, Duke University, Durham, North Carolina.

Jane Taylor, Ph.D.—Psychologist in private practice, Washington, **D.C.**

Paul Thatcher, LL.B.—Attorney, Ogden, Utah.

Robert G. Willhite, M.S.W., A.C.S.W.—Psychotherapist in private practice, Willhite and Associates, Minneapolis, Minnesota.

FOREWORD

Psychology as a science seeks to understand generalized and individual human behavior for a variety of purposes: the pure pleasure of knowledge, for prediction, for control. To achieve this knowledge, to be able to predict and to be able to control, inferences must be made, to the effect that: "People under certain circumstances will . . ." or "Oscar is likely to . . ." or "If Helen is treated in this way she should. . . ."

Now, how can we predict others? Certainly, the best of all ways is long-term intimate knowledge. Knowing a person for a long time in a variety of situations surely seems the best way of understanding and predicting people's behavior. And yet, we have knowledge of individuals who know each other quite well, for instance, parents who have known their children since birth, who will admit that they "never would have thought . . ." or "just can't believe . . ." when they hear of some behavior of their own offspring.

It is possible to divide the other methods for understanding into three rough categories: (a) procedures that call for observation of the person in action, such as an interview, (b) procedures in which the individual is expected to give direct on-paper information about himself, such as in questionnaires, and (c) the so-called projective tests in which the person gives information about himself but does not know what he is giving, such as on the inkblot (Rorschach) test. For the purpose of this foreword, we exclude unscientific means such as astrology, numerology, palm-reading, tea-leaf readings, and the like.

Professional therapists, such as psychoanalysts, use a variety of procedures, ranging from color selection to diaries. Among the better known methods are free association (calling off words when a series of words are given as stimuli), the Thematic Apperception Test (making up stories to a series of drawings), and the analysis of dreams. However, some people (and I am one

of them) having used a good many of these procedures believe
that the very best method for understanding a person in depth
is the analysis of early recollections, the subject of this book.

An early recollection is nothing but a unitary early memory,
an event or closely connected series of events that one recalls,
such as:

> I was about four. My mother and I were in a park near our house.
> Mother sat on a bench and told me to go and play. Then she called
> me, and I went over to her. She opened her purse and pulled out a
> small pie. I was surprised: where had she gotten the pie, and I was
> surprised to see such a small pie. She divided the pie in half and we
> ate the pie. It was an apple pie.

This incident recalled by a man in his mid-sixties as his earliest
memory, an event that occurred more than sixty years ago, must
have some symbolic significance. Why out of the tens of thousands of possible incidents that he could have recalled from the
first five or six years of his life should he recall this particular
one? What meaning can it have? What does it tell about that
person? Why has he recalled this one?

The analysis of early recollections, originally suggested by
Dr. Alfred Adler, the founder of the school of psychology known
as Individual Psychology, is the first of the projective techniques,
and, in my judgment and possibly in the judgment of Dr. Olson
and the other contributors of this book, is the best of all such
predictive techniques known. I have used projective techniques
for some thirty-five years—the Rorschach, Free-Association, the
TAT, as well as some lesser known procedures—but in the past
twenty years, since being trained in their use by Dr. Rudolf
Dreikurs, a close associate of Dr. Adler, I have used early recollections as practically my only projective technique. It has ele-
gance, power, and subtlety. When properly employed its predictive abilities are uncanny. It is the purest of all projective
techniques, needs no stopwatch (as in the case of Free Association) or materials (as in the case of the Rorschach or TAT) and
cannot be done incorrectly, even though it is possible that the
interpretations made, while rarely wrong even when done by a
neophyte, can be insufficient.

This book covers the whole gamut of the subject of early

recollections: the theory, the technique, the practice, and offers both the experienced and inexperienced clinician, as well as the seeker of pure knowledge, a thorough course in the subject. The clever addition of a series of early recollections such as the one included here, with their interpretations by experienced Adlerian clinicians, should make this a do-it-yourself volume of rare usefulness.

Dr. Olson and his associates have prepared a meaningful collaboration of everything you may want to know about this powerful and efficient technique, which can be so helpful in shortening the time that is needed to perform successful psychotherapy. I wish to make the statement that anyone who practices in-depth counseling and psychotherapy who does not understand the theory and technique of early recollections is missing a most important tool in his armamentarium of clinical devices.

RAYMOND J. CORSINI, PH.D.

PREFACE

T HE USE OF early recollections, or ERs, in diagnosis and psychotherapy is a highly potent technique which opens to the therapist
the perceptual frame of reference, or private logic, of the client:
the way he construes and interprets his experiences in the world
and the attitudinal base which serves to form his current behavior.
ERs when correctly interpreted often reveal very quickly the
basic core of one's personality, or life-style, and suggest important, bedrock themes with which the therapist must currently
deal in treating the client.

Early recollections were used as a tool by both Sigmund Freud
and Alfred Adler and their followers, although the meaning and
interpretations they derived differed. Freudians, referring to
ERs as screen memories, see the ER as a concealing device to
cover latent or repressed material. Adlerians, on the other hand,
see ERs as revealing the person's central life-style themes. Unfortunately, ER interpretation has been bypassed in many psychiatry, psychology, and mental health training programs, so that
most mental health professionals are not aware of the utility
and potency of this technique.

The literature on ERs is growing. There are about 100 articles
to date dealing with ERs specifically. It is the purpose of this
book to bring together for the first time under one cover seminal
papers on ERs for the practitioner and researcher. Papers were
chosen from the existing periodical literature to cover the topic
both in breadth and depth, from the standpoints of background
theory and of practice. A criterion for selection was the presence
and quality of actual clinical examples in the body of the paper.
Gaps in the periodical literature have been filled by papers
especially written for this book. In addition, the reader practice
section provides actual client ERs for the reader to interpret,
followed by the interpretations made by the client's therapist.
The annotated bibliography provides reviews of almost every

other article specifically dealing with ERs which does not appear reproduced in this book. The result is a book which can serve as a manual for the use of ERs in diagnosis and therapy and a compendium of the available ER literature.

I wish to gratefully acknowledge the encouragement of Ray Corsini who enthusiastically supported my efforts and provided the foreword to this book. I also wish to thank the contributors of invited papers, without whose cooperation the book could not have been as complete as it is, and the authors of reprinted articles and the editors of the journals in which they appeared for their kind permission to reproduce these papers. Special appreciation is due to my wife, Carol, who bore the brunt of most of the manuscript typing and preparation and who was willing to share me with this project.

H.A.O.

CONTENTS

SECTION I.
THEORY AND BACKGROUND

SECTION II.
EARLY RECOLLECTIONS AS A PROJECTIVE TECHNIQUE

SECTION III.
TECHNIQUES OF INTERPRETATION

SECTION IV.
USE OF EARLY RECOLLECTIONS IN PSYCHOTHERAPY

SECTION V.
CLINICAL PAPERS

SECTION VI.
CASE STUDIES

EARLY RECOLLECTIONS

SECTION I

THEORY AND BACKGROUND

INTRODUCTION

Ansbacher's paper heads this section, and indeed the book, because even though old (1947) it provides a clear, basic discussion of the dynamics of recall, which is necessary for the understanding of early recollections (ERs). In addition, Ansbacher compares and contrasts the two major theories on recollections—Freudian and Adlerian.

The Adlerian aproach to ERs is expanded in the paper by Adler and the selection by Plewa. These three papers, then, set the stage for the rest of the book, which deals with the clinical application of ERs.

CHAPTER 1

ADLER'S PLACE TODAY IN THE PSYCHOLOGY OF MEMORY*

Heinz L. Ansbacher

Introduction

T HE PROGRESS OF science is characterized by the formulation of theories on the basis of controlled or uncontrolled observations. The theory suggests further controlled observations which in turn lead to its confirmation, modification, or rejection. The present paper is concerned with Alfred Adler's theory of memory and its position today in the light of subsequent research. Adler's views relate specifically to (1) the dynamics of recall in general and (2) the significance of earliest childhood recollections. This is in accord with his interest in the idiographic rather than the nomothetic problems of psychology, i.e., the problems concerned with the understanding of some particular event in a particular individual rather than those concerned with the finding of general laws[4] (p. 22). We shall see that Adler's views have stood the test of later investigations.

For our discussion it will be desirable to contrast Adler's views with those of Freud because the confusion of their theories today is great. It has become quite general usage to call any form of depth-psychology psychoanalysis, including Adler's Individual Psychology; such usage is comparable to the error often committed by primitive minds of calling any camera a Kodak®, any refrigerator a Frigidaire®. The result is that statements such as the following from a recent college textbook of applied psychology can be found: "One of the benefits that has come from

---

* Reprinted by permission from the *Journal of Personality*, 1947, *15*, 197-207. Copyright 1947 by Duke University Press.

psychoanalysis sponsored by Freud, Jung, Adler, and others, is the emphasis placed on the pervasiveness of sex"[7] (p. 106).

The Dynamics of Recall

On the general mechanism of recall Adler wrote:

> The functions of memory . . . are dominated by the necessity of adaptation. Without memories it would be impossible to exercise any precaution for the future. We may deduce that all recollections have an unconscious purpose within themselves. They are not fortuitous phenomena, but speak clearly the language of encouragement and warning. There are no indifferent or nonsensical recollections. . . . We remember those events whose recollection is important for a specific psychic tendency [attitude], because these recollections further an important underlying movement. We forget likewise all those events which detract from the fulfillment of a plan. . . . Every memory is dominated by the goal idea which directs the personality-as-a-whole[1] (pp. 48-49).

The implications of this statement are clear. If our tendency is to move towards an object, the recollections will be encouraging; if the underlying attitude is one of withdrawal, the recollections will sound a warning. Thus pleasant or unpleasant, positively or negatively toned memories may dominate the scene, depending entirely on the situation. This is expressed further in the following:

> Out of the incalculable number of impressions which meet an individual, he chooses to remember only those which he feels, however darkly, to have a bearing on his situation. Thus his memories represent his "Story of My Life"; a story he repeats to himself to warn him or comfort him, to keep him concentrated on his goal, to prepare him, by means of past experiences, to meet the future with an already tested style of action. The use of memories to stabilize a mood can be plainly seen in everyday life. If a man suffers a defeat and is discouraged by it, he recalls previous instances of defeat. . . . When he is cheerful and courageous, he selects quite other memories. . . . Memories thus serve much the same purpose as dreams. A melancholic could not remain melancholic if he remembered his good moments and his successes. . . . Memories can never run counter to the style of life[2] (pp. 73-74).

This view is quite divergent from Freud's. Although Freud very definitely appreciated that the "child no less than the adult retains in memory what is important"[14] (p. 178), he was from the start more interested in forgetting than in remembering and postulated that "the forgetting in all cases is proved to be founded on a motive of displeasure"[16] (p. 96).* This is the theory of the repression of the unpleasant which "is the pillar upon which the edifice of psychoanalysis rests"[15] (p. 939). Freud's contention was tested by psychological research in many dozens of studies, as surveyed by Meltzer,[20] Cason,[8] Gilbert,[17] and Barrett.[5] Most of the studies showed that the majority of subjects tended to forget the unpleasant, but a number of questions remained unanswered. Among these the most important one to our way of thinking was: "What individual differences . . . are correlated with the tendency of some individuals to forget the unpleasant more than others?"[17] (p. 33). According to Adler, of course, the pleasant-versus-unpleasant issue is the outcome of a faulty formulation of the problem; depending on the individual case, unpleasant memories might be very necessary while pleasant ones might be disturbing. The entire issue needed redirection of emphasis as expressed by Meltzer, who realized that pleasant and unpleasant memories must be correlated with other significant measurable factors[20] (p. 137).

The problem was reformulated in 1938 by Barrett, who, on the basis of very careful experimental research, offered the following theory: "A prevailing attitude, which is pleasant for most of the individuals, is in part responsible for the relatively better memory of the pleasant items of experience, as reported in some current investigations. When circumstances are such as to foster

---

* To be sure, Freud eventually went beyond the pleasure principle by introducing the life and death instincts, the purpose of the former being the maintenance of life of the individual and species. But these concepts have remained enigmatic to psychologists ever since they were proposed. Symonds[22] (p. 31 n.) in his recent book states that he could find no evidence for these instincts as psychological forces. We believe that this conclusion is based on the most careful and sincere investigation of all possible evidence. Among psychoanaysts as well the concept of the death instinct seems still to be offering difficulties. For example, Simmel[21] replaces Freud's dualism with new theoretical constructs. He finds our lives governed by an erotic instinct of love with the ultimate aim of preserving the race, and a destructive devouring instinct of hatred, with the aim of preserving the self. This departure from Freud would seem to be a moderate approximation to Adler's "social interest" and "striving for superiority."

an unpleasant frame of mind, one would expect more unpleasant items to be remembered"⁵ (p. 53). The following may serve as an example of Barrett's type of work. She read to 30 subjects in individual sessions a statement such as "He didn't mean to make work for his wife, but time and time again he'd tramp across the newly scrubbed floors in his muddy boots." This was followed by the reading of the 10 adjectives: *honest, cruel, perverse, responsible, truthful, thoughtless, congenial, impudent, dependable, discourteous.* Eighteen to forty-eight hours later 29 of the 30 subjects recalled more unpleasant adjectives, the one remaining subject recalling an equal number of pleasant and unpleasant adjectives. The subjects had had no knowledge that there was to be a memory experiment following the reading of the statement and the adjectives.

In 1941 Edwards formulated practically the same hypothesis independently. He said: "Experiences which harmonize with an existing frame of reference will tend to be learned and remembered better than experiences which conflict with the same frame of reference"¹² (p. 36)¹³. His evidence came from the field of social psychology. He compared, for example, the retention of pro- and anti-New Deal material for subjects with pro- and anti-New Deal attitudes and found in all cases significantly greater recall for material compatible with the subject's attitudes than for material which was incompatible. Edwards goes on to discuss the Freudian theory of recall and to show that Freud himself was not as dogmatic regarding the hedonic theory of recall as the experimentalists have taken him to be. Freud limited his theory of repression by stating "the defense against painful associations plays a certain part but is far from explaining everything"¹⁴ (p. 68); and he was also well aware of the fact that often "it is just that which is painful which it is hard to forget." But Freud's resolution of this apparent contradiction does not take us far when he says: "Evidence of one particular tendency does not in the least preclude its opposite; there is room for both of them. The material questions are: How do these opposites stand to one another and what effects proceed from one of them and what from the other?"¹⁴ (p. 68). We feel that the research psychologists cannot be blamed for having first tackled those aspects on which

Freud expressed himself definitely, leaving aside those on which he offered no clear solution.

A third line of research which is relevant here is represented by the classical experimental study on memory by Bartlett.[6] In the many thousands of cases of remembering which he collected, he found that literal recall was altogether very rare. "Remembering appears to be far more decisively an affair of construction rather than one of mere reproduction"[6] (p. 205). "The construction that is effected is the sort of construction that would justify the observer's 'attitude.' Attitude . . . is . . . very largely a matter of feeling, or affect. We say that it is characterized by doubt, hesitation, surprise, astonishment, confidence, dislike, repulsion and so on. . . . The recall is then a construction, made largely on the basis of this attitude, and its general effect is that of a justification of the attitude"[6] (pp. 206-207). From this Bartlett concludes: What we remember is "apt to take on a peculiarity of some kind which, in any given case, expresses the temperament, or the character, of the person who effects the recall"[6] (p. 213). The final paragraph of Bartlett's work describes memory as a tool for the attainment of certain ends, much as Adler might have done. "I have regarded memory as one achievement in the line of the ceaseless struggle to master and enjoy a world full of variety and rapid change. Memory . . . is one with the age-old acquisition of distance senses, and with the development of constructive imagination and constructive thought where at length we find the most complete release from the narrowness of presented time and place"[6] (p. 314).

Last but not least the important experiments of the 1920's by Lewin and Zeigarnik[23] and other Gestalt psychologists must be mentioned here. These led Köhler to the conclusion that reproduction is restricted mainly to those cases "in which it has a value with respect to the actual total field and its dynamical development as a functional whole"[18] (p. 343).

The four more or less independent series of research just outlined are all in accordance with Adler and lead to the conclusion that today Adler's theory of the dynamics of recall can be considered a basically well-established fact and that more and more evidence seems to be piling up in its confirmation.

The Significance of Earliest Childhood Recollections

Adler's view on earliest recollections is expressed succinctly in the following:

> Early recollections have special significance. . . . They show the style of life in its origins and in its simplest expressions. . . . What is of most value about them is that they represent the individual's judgment, "Even in childhood, I was such and such a person," or, "Even in childhood, I found the world like this." Most illuminating of all is . . . the earliest incident he can recall. The first memory will show the individual's fundamental view of life; his first satisfactory crystallization of his attitude.

The earliest recollections offer the following two advantages for personality assessment: (1) "In the main, people are perfectly willing to discuss their first memories. They take them as mere facts, and do not realize the meaning hidden in them." (2) The compression and simplicity of first memories "allows us to use them for mass investigations. . . . It is comparatively indifferent whether the memories are accurate or inaccurate"[2] (pp. 74-75).

As in the case of general recall, Freud's view on the present point differed from Adler's by accentuating the negative. He was interested in amnesia of childhood, by which he meant "that the first years of life, up to the age of five, six, or eight, have not left the same traces in memory as our later experiences." Although there are exceptions, "it is incomparably more common for the opposite, a blank in memory, to be found." Such amnesia tends to result from the repression of infantile sexual impulses, and it is "a regular task in psycho-analytic treatment to fill in the blanks in infantile memories." Yet in spite of infantile amnesia "certain clearly retained recollections emerge." These appear "often so banal and meaningless in themselves that we can only ask ourselves in amazement why just this particular detail has escaped oblivion. . . . That what is important is represented (by the process of condensation and, more especially, of displacement) in memory by something apparently trivial. For this reason I have called these childhood recollections *screen memories*"[14] (pp. 177-178). "The 'childhood reminiscences' of individuals altogether advance to the significance of 'concealing [or screen] memories' "[16] (p. 65). "The meagre childish recollections which people have always, long before analysis, consciously preserved, can be falsified . . . or at least can contain a generous admixture of truth and falsehood. . . . Phantasy and reality are to be treated alike and . . . it is . . . of no account whether the childhood experiences under consideration belong to one class or to the other"[14] (pp. 321-322). These concealing or screen memories can be interpreted only in the light of a complete psychoanalysis. "Owing to the previously discussed nature of the relations of the childhood reminiscences to later life, it becomes extraordinarily difficult to report such examples. For, in order to attach the value of the concealing memory to an infantile reminiscence, it would be often necessary to present the entire life-history of the person concerned"[16] (p. 65).

In comparing Adler and Freud we may say that (1) they agree (a) in ascribing importance to the early childhood recollections, (b) in considering it comparatively immaterial whether the early childhood memories correspond to actual fact or not. (2) They disagree in that (a) Adler sees no particular difficulty in their interpretation whereas Freud does; (b) Adler considers the earliest incident one can recall as particularly illuminating, which Freud never pointed out; (c) Freud stresses infantile amnesia, which Adler never mentions, and is primarily interested in those infantile experiences that come to the fore only during a psychoanalysis.

Research in childhood memories has been undertaken since 1895, as pointed out in a review by Dudycha and Dudycha[11] which covers the literature up to 1940. No further reports of studies in this field have become known since then. The papers were interested primarily in accuracy of the memories, average age of earliest memories, sex differences, sense modalities represented in the memories, emotions attached to the memories, relation of age of earliest memory to intelligence and language development, and racial differences. Several studies were related to the hedonic tone of the earliest memories and led to conclusions similar to those reported for hedonic tone and recall in general. The common characteristic for practically all these studies was that they took memory per se, separately from attitudes and personality, and were satisfied with making some

contribution to general developmental psychology, but did not'
tackle the problem of the significance of the memories for the
individual who produced them.

Only two published studies have dealt with early recollections
in relation to dynamic factors of individual personalities, and
both aimed at the testing of certain implications from Freudian
theory. The first study, by Crook and Harden[10] was designed
to test the hypothesis that infantile amnesia is positively correlated with neuroticism. Since, according to Freud, the childhood screen memories are in themselves quite meaningless, the
authors could well dispense with having the content of the
memories noted. They merely required the subjects to indicate
the number of their memories before the age of six by marking
crosses on a chart. The chart listed the various age levels up to
six, and the crosses were to be placed opposite the age level to
which the memory could be assigned; thus the earliest age for
any memory of an individual could also be determined. A relatively small number of crosses and a late earliest memory were
taken as an indication of amnesia, hence of repression, hence of
neuroticism. When the authors correlated number of memories
and age of earliest memory with scores on the Pressey X-O test
of neuroticism, they actually did find that the more emotionally
stable an individual is, "the greater the number of memories
he retains from the first six years of his life, and the earlier the
age from which he retains the first memory." However, the
number of subjects was only 19 and the correlations were statistically not reliable. Therefore Child[9] repeated the study with 290
college students. Although his correlations pointed toward confirmation of the original assumptions, they were very small and
did not deviate significantly from zero, so that Child concludes
that "no significant association obtains between the purported
measures of degree of infantile amnesia and of degree of neuroticism." But Child believed that the original assumptions were
dubious deductions from psychoanalytic theory and that therefore "the findings may not be taken at present as evidence against
any psychoanalytic postulates."

Although specifically suggested by Adler[2] (p. 75), no research
based on the Adlerian theory of earliest recollections is known

to us. We began such a study a year ago; the work is still in progress, but first results from 271 male college students are available. The procedure consisted of two parts: (1) A simple questionnaire was administered, the main item of which was the completion of the statement: "My earliest childhood recollection is. . . ." The preceding instructions stressed to write down the earliest incident that comes to mind and not to worry whether this is actually the earliest memory or not. (2) The first 25 items from the Maslow Security-Insecurity Test[19] were administered. The test is designed to fit the following definitions of insecurity: feeling of rejection, of isolation, uniqueness; perception of the world as dangerous, of other human beings as essentially bad; feelings of threat, mistrust, shame, guilt; tendency to pessimism, unhappiness. Security is defined as: feeling of being liked, belonging, safety, friendliness, calm; perception of the world as pleasant, of other human beings as essentially good; tendency toward optimism, happiness, self-acceptance; "social interest" in the Adlerian sense.

The specific purpose of the study was to see if any relationship could be established between security scores and certain types of earliest memories. The findings are, in brief:

(I) Subjects who remember themselves as participating in group activities, as being active in general, as being treated kindly by others (88 subjects, 33% of the total group) have more frequently high security scores than not.

(II) Subjects who remember themselves as cut off from the larger group, as getting or losing prestige, as having done something bad; or who remember others receiving kindness and attention, or suffering harm, or inflicting harm on one another (54 subjects, 20% of the total group) practically always have low security scores.

(III) Recollections of sickness, accidents, interference from other people are not related to security feeling, but tend to occur more frequently in subjects in the middle of the security range than in those near either extreme (83 subjects, 30% of the group). A small number of miscellaneous recollections are included here.

(IV) Recollections of inactivity, contemplation, fear, and of witnessing disaster (46 subjects, 17% of the group) are of ambiguous significance in that they are found slightly more often with very high or very low rather than with middle-range security scores.

Contrary to expectations, recollections of receiving presents, a subgroup of 17 cases, were practically always found among the upper 40% of security scores and were thus included in Group I. Some examples are: "When my father gave me and my brother a watch chain"; "When my father gave me a pony"; "My mother had bought me a new pair of shoes"; "Getting a train for Christmas"; "A lady came up and handed me a little toy dog." Apparently such recollections signify a generalized attitude of "People are good to me, the world is a relatively good place."

Another somewhat unexpected finding is the relationship to security scores of recollections concerned with harm suffered by others. There were only five recollections in this subgroup, but all were found among the lower 40% in security. They are: "When my brother broke his arm"; "An accident my mother encountered"; "Seeing my sister fall and cut her leg"; "My older brother fell from the attic"; "Seeing a window cleaner fall from the third floor." Such recollections apparently stand as a warning that "the world is dangerous, and I better stay on the side lines lest I also be drawn into the maelstrom." The groups and subgroups which emerged from this study are, by and large, in amazing agreement with some indications given by Adler,[3] although the present author was not aware of Adler's suggested categories at the time he developed his own.

This study by no means exhausts the significance of earliest recollections. Clinical examination of each case would undoubtedly uncover a wealth of further relationships, as would also greater refinement of our categories. But the study does show that even relatively crude means such as ours yield quantitative results from a normal population, which are basically in accord with the Adlerian theory of early recollections. On the other hand, if childhood memories were "concealing," in the Freudian sense, it is not likely that any relationships could have been demonstrated, inasmuch as "concealing" memories are in themselves quite meaningless, being symbols for infantile repressions which, in turn, can be uncovered only during a thorough psychoanalysis.

Summary

In an attempt to find Alfred Adler's place today in the psychology of memory we have arrived at the following conclusions:

1. His view that it is underlying attitudes (or goals, as he expressed it) which largely determine individual recall has been substantiated by extensive important research.

2. His view that early childhood recollections are particularly expressive of an individual's basic attitude toward life has been tentatively substantiated by some preliminary research.

3. By contrast, Freudian theory regarding the same problems, tied in firmly as it is with the concept of repression, stands today without sound support from research data, in spite of a great deal of effort on the part of academic psychologists.

As an additional, summarizing comment, we may say that Adler was able to formulate these partial theories from his basic holistic view of the individual, a view which is increasingly being shared by all biological and social sciences.

References

1. Adler, A. *Understanding Human Nature*. New York: Greenberg, 1927.
2. Adler, A. *What Life Should Mean to You*. Boston: Little, Brown & Co., 1931.
3. Adler, A. Erste Kindheitserinnerungen (First childhood recollections). *Int. J. Indiv.-Psychol.*, 1933, *11*, 81-90.
4. Allport, G. W. *Personality: A Psychological Interpretation*. New York: Henry Holt & Co., 1937.
5. Barrett, D. M. Memory in relation to hedonic tone. *Arch. Psychol.*, 1938, no. 223, 61.
6. Bartlett, F. C. *Remembering: A Study in Experimental and Social Psychology*. Cambridge, England: Cambridge University Press, 1932.
7. Berrien, F. K. *Practical Psychology*. New York: Macmillan Co., 1944.
8. Cason, H. The learning and retention of pleasant and unpleasant activities. *Arch. Psychol.*, 1932, no. 134, 96.
9. Child, I. L. The relation between measures of infantile amnesia and of neuroticism. *J. Abnorm. Soc. Psychol.*, 1940, *35*, 453-456.
10. Crook, M. N. and Harden, L. A quantitative investigation of early memories. *J. Soc. Psychol.*, 1931, *2*, 252-255.
11. Dudycha, G. J. and Dudycha, M. M. Childhood memories: A review of the literature. *Psychol. Bull.*, 1941, *38*, 668-682.

12. Edwards, A. L. Political frames of reference as a factor influencing recognition. *J. Abnorm. Soc. Psychol.*, 1941, *36*, 34-50.

13. Edwards, A. L. The retention of affective experiences; a criticism and restatement of the problem. *Psychol. Rev.*, 1942, *49*, 43-53.

14. Freud, S. *A General Introduction to Psychoanalysis.* New York: Liveright, 1935.

15. Freud, S. The history of the psychoanalytic movement. In *The Basic Writings of Sigmund Freud.* New York: Modern Library, 1938. Pp. 931-977.

16. Freud, S. Psychopathology of everyday life. In *The Basic Writings of Sigmund Freud.* New York: Modern Library, 1938. Pp. 33-178.

17. Gilbert, G. M. The new status of experimental studies on the relationship of feeling to memory. *Psychol. Bull.*, 1938, *35*, 26-35.

18. Köhler, W. *Gestalt Psychology.* New York: Liveright, 1929.

19. Maslow, A. H., Hirsh, E., Stein, M., and Honigmann, I. A clinically derived test for measuring psychological security-insecurity. *J. Gen. Psychol.*, 1945, *33*, 21-41.

20. Meltzer, H. The present status of experimental studies on the relationship of feeling to memory. *Psychol. Rev.*, 1930, *37*, 124-139.

21. Simmel, E. Self-preservation and the death instinct. *Psychoanal. Quart.*, 1944, *13*, 160-185.

22. Symonds, P. M. *The Dynamics of Human Adjustment.* New York: Appleton-Century, 1946.

23. Zeigarnik, B. Über das Behalten von erledigten und unerledigten Handlungen (The retention of completed and incompleted activities). *Psychol. Forsch.*, 1927, *9*, 1-85.

CHAPTER 2

THE SIGNIFICANCE AND DEVELOPMENT OF EARLY RECOLLECTIONS: TWO SELECTIONS

SIGNIFICANCE OF EARLY RECOLLECTIONS[*]

Alfred Adler

T HE DISCOVERY OF the significance of early recollections is one
of the most important findings of Individual Psychology. It has
demonstrated the *purposiveness* in the choice of what is longest
remembered, though the memory itself is quite conscious or
the recollection is easily brought out upon inquiry. Rightly understood, these conscious memories give us glimpses of depths just
as profound as do those which are more or less suddenly recalled
during treatment.

We do not, of coure, believe that all early recollections are
correct records of actual facts. Many are even fancied, and
most perhaps are changed or distorted at a time later than that
in which the events are supposed to have occurred; but this
does not diminish their significance. What is altered or imagined
is also expressive of the patient's goal, and although there is a
difference between the work of fantasy and that of memory,
we can safely make use of both by relating them to our knowledge of other factors. Their worth and meaning, however, cannot be rightly estimated until we relate them to the total style
of life of the individual in question, and recognize their unity
with his main line of striving towards a goal of superiority.

In recollections dating from the first four or five years we
find chiefly fragments of the prototype of the individual's life-
style, or useful hints as to why his life-plan was elaborated into

[*] Reprinted by permission from the *International Journal of Individual Psychology*, 1937, 3 (4), 283-287. Sidney M. Roth, Publisher, Editor in English.

17

its own particular form. Here also we may gather the surest indications of self-training to overcome the deficiencies felt in the early environment or organic difficulties. In many cases, signs of the person's degree of activity, of his courage and social feeling are also evident in the early recollections. Owing to the great number of spoiled children who come under treatment, we find that the mother is rarely absent from the earliest remembrance; indeed, if the life-style is one of a pampered child, the guess that the patient will recall something about his mother is usually correct. If the mother does not appear in the early recollections that, too, may have a certain significance; it may, for one thing, indicate a feeling of having been neglected by her. However, he will never have understood the meaning of his early remembrances. In answer to my question he may, for instance, simply say, "I was sitting in a room playing with a toy, and my mother was sitting close to me." He regards a recollection as if it were a thing by itself and as if it had no significance; he never thinks of its coherence in the whole structure of his psychic life. Unfortunately many psychologists do the same.

To estimate its meaning we have to relate the early pattern of perception to all we can discover of the individual's present attitude until we find how the one clearly mirrors the other. In the example just given we begin to see this correlation when we learn that the patient suffers from anxiety when alone. The interest in being connected with the mother may appear even in the form of fictitious remembrances, as in the case of the patient who said to me, "You will not believe me, but I can remember being born, and my mother holding me in her arms."

Very often the earliest memory of a spoiled child refers to its dispossession by the birth of a younger brother or sister. These recollections which record the feeling of being dispossessed vary from slight and innocent reminiscences, such as, "I recollect when my younger sister was born," to instances highly significant of the particular attitude of the patient. A woman once told me, "I remember having to watch my younger sister, who was lying on a table. She was restless and threw off the coverlets. I wanted to adjust them and I pulled them away from her, whereupon she fell and was hurt." This woman was forty-five when she came to me; at school, in marriage, and throughout life she had felt herself disregarded, just as in her first childhood when she had felt herself dethroned. A similar attitude, even more expressive of suspicion and mistrust, was expressed by a man who said, "I was going to market with my mother and little brother. Suddenly it began to rain, and my mother took me up in her arms, and then remembering that I was the elder, she put me down and took up my younger brother." Successful as he was in his life, this man distrusted everybody, especially women.

A student thirty years of age came to me in trouble because he could not face his examinations. He was in such a state of strain that he could neither sleep nor concentrate. The symptoms indicate his lack of preparation and of courage, and his age shows the distance at which he stood from the solution of the problem of occupation. He had no friends and had never fallen in love, because of his lack of social adjustment; and his sexuality was expressed in masturbation and nocturnal emissions. His earliest memory was of lying in a cot, looking round at the wallpaper and curtains. This recollection reflects the isolation of his later life, and also his interest in visual activity. He was astigmatic, and was striving to compensate for this organic deficiency. [We must remember, however, that any function which is strongly developed but which is not also related to a fair degree of social interest may disturb the harmony of life.] For instance, to watch is really a worthwhile activity, but when the patient barricades himself against all other activities and wants only to gratify his eyes all day, it is possible for watching to become a compulsion-neurosis. Some people are interested primarily in seeing. But there are only a few positions in which interest in seeing is the chief one to be employed. Even those positions cannot be found by a person who is socially maladjusted. This patient, as we have seen, had not been a real fellow man to anyone, so that he had found no use for his peculiar interest.

The earliest remembrances not infrequently disclose an interest in movement, such as: traveling, running, motoring, or jumping. So far as we can see this is often characteristic of individuals who encounter difficulties when they find it necessary to begin work in sedentary occupations. I found this in the case of a man of twenty-five, the oldest son of a very religious family, who was brought to me because of misbehavior. He was disobedient, idle, and a liar, and he had contracted debts and stolen. His sister, three years younger than himself, was a familiar type—striving, capable, and well-educated, an easy winner in the race with him. His misconduct began with his adolescence, and I am aware that many psychologists would ascribe it to some sort of emotional "flare-up" caused by the growth of the sexual glands—a theory which might seem all the more plausible in this case because of the existence of premature and mischievous sexual relations, as is found in many other similar cases. But we ask: Why should the perfectly natural period of puberty be the cause of a crisis and of a moral disaster in this case but not in another—not in the sister's case, for example? We answer: Because the sister was in a more favorable position. The brother's situation was one which we know, from experience of very many cases, to be one of special danger. Furthermore, when we go more deeply into the history of this case, we find that he wanted always to be first, in every situation, and that adolescence did· not create any change in this young man's style of life. Before that time the boy had gradually been losing hope of being "first" in a life of social usefulness, and the more hopeless he grew there, the more he had wandered into the easier ways of useless compensation.

This young man's earliest remembrance gives a clear hint of his great interest in motor activity and in movement in general. It was: "I was running round the whole day in a kiddy car." After treatment, when he was improved, he was taken back into his father's office, but he did not find the sedentary life there to his liking. He finally adapted himself to life as a traveling salesman.

Many first remembrances are concerned with situations of danger, and they are usually told by persons with whom the use of fears is an important factor in the style of life. A married woman once came to ask me why she was terrified whenever she passed a pharmacy. Some years previously she had spent a long time in a sanatorium undergoing treatment for tuberculosis, and a few months before I saw her a specialist had pronounced her cured, entirely healthy, and fit to have children. Shortly after this plenary absolution by the doctor she began to suffer from her obsession. The connection is obvious. The pharmacy was a warning reminder of her illness, an employment of the past in order to make the future seem ominous. She was connecting the possibility of having a child with danger to her health. Though she and her husband had agreed that they wanted a child, her behavior clearly showed her secret opposition. Her secret objection was stronger than any reasonable and common sense logic which said that for her there really was now no danger in bearing children. The doctor, as a medical expert, could minimize the danger to her health, but he could not remove the symptom of fear. In this as in many similar cases we know in advance that the real reasons for the symptoms are deeply rooted, and are only to be found if we can discover the most important strivings in the style of life.

Seldom is it true that resistance to having children is based upon *objective* fears of childbirth or illness. In this case it was easy to discover that the woman had been a pampered child who, herself, wanted to be in the center of the stage. Such women do not wish to bring a little rival on to the scene, and they argue against it with every variety of reason and unreason. This woman had trained herself perfectly to be on the lookout for danger, and to perceive opportunities for taking the center of attention. Asked for her earliest recollection she said, "I was playing before our little house on the outskirts of the town, and my mother was terrified when she saw me jumping on the boards that covered the well."

A student of philosophy came to consult me about his erythrophobia. From earliest childhood he had been teased because he blushed so easily, and for the past two months this had so much increased that he was afraid to go to a restaurant, to attend his lectures, or even to go out of his room. I found that he was about to take an examination. He was a faint-hearted man, timid and bashful, and whether he was visiting in society, working, or in company with a girl, in all situations alike he suffered from feelings of tension. His blushing had recently worried him more, and he began to use it as a pretext for retreat from life. From childhood this man had had a strong antipathy towards his mother, who, he felt, was partial to his younger brother. He had lived in the greatest competition with his brother; and he now no longer believed that he, himself, could achieve any success if he went on. Here is his earliest remembrance: "When I was five years old I went out with my three-year-old brother. My parents were much excited when they found we had left the house, because there was a lake near by, and they were afraid that we had fallen into it. When we returned I was slapped." I understood this to mean that he did not like his home, where he felt that he was slighted, and this opinion was corroborated when he added, "I was slapped, but not my brother." But the discovery that he had been in a dangerous situation had no less impressed him, and this was reflected in his present behavior, which was dominated by his guiding idea—not to go out, not to venture too far. Such persons often feel as though life were a trap.

It is easy to imagine this patient's painful experience when in company of a girl. We can understand how he put his blushing between himself and women, thus did not allow himself to come into a relationship with any of them. In this way he avoided coming into a situation where he ran the risk of losing out to another man. He always feared other men would be preferred to him, as he felt his mother had preferred his brother.

When rightly understood in relation to the rest of an individual's life, his early recollections are found always to have a bearing on the central interests of that person's life. Early recollections give us hints and clues which are most valuable to follow when attempting the task of finding the direction of a person's striving. They are most helpful in revealing what one regards as values to be aimed for and what one senses as dangers to be avoided. They help us to see the kind of world which a particular person feels he is living in, and the ways he early found of meeting that world. They illuminate the origins of the style of life. The basic attitudes which have guided an individual throughout his life and which prevail, likewise, in his present situation, are reflected in those fragments which he has selected to epitomize his feeling about life, and to cherish in his memory as reminders. He has preserved these as his early recollections.

THE MEANING OF CHILDHOOD RECOLLECTIONS*

FRANZ PLEWA

Inquiry into the *meaning* of any psychic expression is justified only if one accepts wholly the fundamental viewpoint of Individual Psychology, which holds that the personality is a unity, striving towards a goal which relates it to the community. To consider psychic processes as separated from the individual, to see them as self-active units which perpetrate a kind of despotism over the whole, leads, at best, to forcing the psyche into abstruse theories and to losing one's self in a labyrinth of more or less ingenious conjectures about one's own inner world. From the Individual Psychological viewpoint of the *unity of the personality*, it might appear, at first, unjustified to emphasize any special phase of psychic life by isolating it for special discussions. For out of these discussions the idea might arise that by appearing to give the *part* more than its share of importance, we seem to destroy the conception of the *whole*, i.e., the unity of the personality.

But in this case, the consideration of the personality is like the consideration of a machine. While ordinarily one is concerned only with the performance and output of a machine, there are times when one must examine a cog or screw in order to determine how it fits the whole mechanism and wherein it contributes to performance and output. But the entire meaning and significance of the cog or screw, is dependent upon its participation as a necessary part of the whole machine. A person without knowledge of machinery, looking at an isolated screw, would find it merely a piece of metal of certain peculiar shape, whose usage could be variously interpreted according to the background and the imagination of the beholder. But to the expert mechanician the shape of the screw would have a definite significance. He could give many correct hints as to its function and application because he would be capable of reconstructing, mentally, the whole machine to which such a cog or screw might belong. It might even be possible for him to recognize, in

* Reprinted by permission from the *International Journal of Individual Psychology*, 1935, *1* (1), 88-101 (excerpt, pp. 88-90). Sidney M. Roth, Publisher, Editor in English.

general, the kind of work of which such a machine would be capable.

Naturally, we must not carry this metaphor too far. But we can say that with man, as with the machine, it is the performance, the outer visible effect, which is decisive. Only from that can one conclude whether or not the function of the part belongs rightly to the whole—whether or not it fits the whole. The machine, however, was built for a definite purpose—a purpose outside of itself. And in case the machine does not function properly, many times it is only necessary to change a single part in order to make it do its work. Here our metaphor fails us— for with man a different element enters. Man, himself, creates his goal and his purpose, which the machine does not; and seen from this wholly personal goal of man's, all his psychic processes are right and full of meaning. Nevertheless, these psychic processes appear as authentic work only when one observes how the individual moves in relation to the world and its tasks. One can recognize and assert that an individual's psychic apparatus works correctly, or incorrectly, for the community, and that its function is meaningless or significant to the community, always according to whether or not it contributes to the advancement of the community. To resume the metaphor of the machine for a moment: When we recognize the life-structure as mistaken in any given case, we must not imagine that, as with the machine, it is only one part that needs to be changed or repaired, for, as I have pointed out, man creates his self-purpose and forms his psychic processes according to it. From the perspective of the community, this purpose may prove to be incorrect. It is not, however, the single step which is at fault in the psychic structure by which the individual achieves his goal. It is the purpose itself which is mistaken. But in using the metaphor of the machine, my purpose was to illumine one special realm of psychic movement without danger of losing sight of the unity of the personality.

One of the first discoveries of Individual Psychology was that the goal of every human being is set in the first years of child-hood, and that therefore the whole direction of movement is then determined. So the entire process takes place before the period of logical judgment. It proceeds under the determining influence of the child's interpretation of himself and his world and that world's attitude to him. Certainly there proceeds constantly in the child a groping, fumbling search for the way of least resistance, a trial and retrial of circumstances favorable to his greatest possible personal profit. Therefore, how far the outer world, the community, is successful in winning a child to cooperation, depends only in part on its attitude to the child. But the personal conception, the opinion of the child, the attitude the child himself takes, plays the predominating part. If the child, having been encouraged by success in any one direction, believes *that* direction to be the right way for his striving, he will cling to it and fortify it with every possible experience. The child selects an experience, or an impression, and re-shapes it, until the disturbing elements are eliminated, and then engraves this impression on his soul, as on the tablets of the law. It becomes then the first strong fortification that justifies his psychic movement. Over and over again the child will seek such supports. He will cling to these supports, which all show the same tendency. That tendency is to advance positively the particular *leit-motif* of the child. All other impressions will be creatively re-formed, or simply forgotten.

Adler has said that experiences are devoured, digested and assimilated in order to make them suitable to the general life-tendency of the individual. Therefore, the first life-recollection does not contain objective truth, but has been subjectively colored and molded. The first recollection is already tendentious. One can almost call it a kind of "handwriting on the wall," the characters of which point out to the person a definite direction which he himself has determined. Therefore, the first recollections acquire a very special significance because in them can be seen the individual's whole conception of life, his apperception of life's problems, his whole psychic movement. One can perhaps deduce from early recollections something of past experience, of tragedies, inhibitions, successes—even certain characteristics. In these early recollections, too, the fate of the individual is foreshadowed. In a way, they "prophesy" whether he can stand the difficulties of life, whether his life-style is durably built, or whether in it there is a weak link likely to give way under a burden. All these things are inherent in a first recollection. It is no wonder then, that in the outbreak of a neurosis, we so frequently see in the situation a repetition of the situation pictured in the first recollection. Such recollections have usually become a sort of warning signal for the individual. They are symbols of a defeat which he wants to avoid in the future.

This leads us for a moment to the consideration of a peculiar characteristic of memory. Perhaps nothing is lost out of the experience of the individual. But at times he allows things to disappear from his consciousness. He does this because these things are of no use to him in his immediate situation. Since, in his uncertainty in any given situation, he can comprehend himself and his relation to that situation only allegorically (with an "as if"), he compares the situation with an occurrence in his distant past. In this allegorical picture he assumes a definite attitude, which allows him to go forward as victor. Therefore, it is understandable that recollections frequently change, often seem entirely forgotten; or that certain ones which have long seemed forgotten, reappear. When the allegory of a recollection is understood, the parallel between the momentary attitude of the individual and the recollection he produces can always be recognized.

EARLY RECOLLECTIONS AS A PROJECTIVE TECHNIQUE

INTRODUCTION

K̲OPP AND D̲ER lead this section with a discussion of assessment from a humanistic perspective. They not only use ERs to demonstrate this but also present a sentence-by-sentence interpretation technique which bears similarity to the Willhite technique (Section III).

The Kadis, Greene, and Freeman study demonstrates the integration of ERs into a projective process by comparing ER results to TAT stories and indicates the relationship between these two techniques.

Taylor reviews, integrates, and summarizes the results of several studies dealing with ERs as a projective technique.

Rogers has reported only the second study (November 1977) to have been published to this editor's knowledge using ERs to predict nonclinical performance. Rogers has attempted to demonstrate a relationship between ERs and college achievement. The first study, by Burnell and Solomon, reviewed in the Annotated Bibliography, demonstrated that ERs, used clinically, could predict success in Air Force basic training. These studies imply the validity of the application of ERs to industrial/management assessment.

CHAPTER 3

HUMANISTIC PSYCHOLOGICAL ASSESSMENT IN PSYCHOTHERAPY

RICHARD ROYAL KOPP AND DU-FAY DER

T HIS PAPER PRESENTS a humanistic approach to assessment in contrast to psychometric diagnosis. A humanistic model of knowing a person is discussed. An illustration of assessing early recollections in psychotherapy as a method which implements this humanistic knowing of a person is provided.

The Diagnostic and Assessment Process

To better understand their clients, psychologists and psychiatrists usually employ two basic methods of evaluation: psychometric diagnosis and humanistic psychological assessment. The diagnostic process is primarily characteristic of the medical model. The purpose is to provide data about the etiology of the illness and to predict the course of the illness. When the cause is discovered, a treatment procedure is chosen (Coleman, 1964; Ullman and Krasner, 1969). Psychometric diagnosis is also used to reveal in what manner the individual differs from the norm. The individual therefore is typed, scaled, and categorized (Allport, 1937, 1961; Brown, 1972; Rosenzweig, 1949). Employed in such a manner, the diagnostic process often emphasizes the negative and unhealthy experiences of the individual (Brown, 1972; Craddick, 1972).

In contrast to psychometric diagnosis, humanistic psychological assessment focuses on the individual as a unit. By viewing the individual as a whole, the humanistic assessment process takes into account one's strengths, weaknesses, joys, sorrows, and strivings. The emphasis is on the person—one's values and beliefs and how one functions in life. In other words, we assess

29

a person's phenomenological stance toward life—one's perception of oneself, life, and the world and one's personal life goals. Thus, to fully understand an individual humanistically, we must tune-in to that person's internal world of meanings (Brown, 1972; Maslow, 1966; Rogers, 1951, 1964; Stein, 1972). This paper will show how early recollections can be used to develop empathic contact with a client based on a humanistic understanding of the client.

A Humanistic Model of Knowing a Person

Various humanistic psychologists and psychiatrists have written about the process of knowing or understanding a person. For example, Adler proposes that to understand a person, we must view that individual as a unique and indivisible entity. Also, we must try to understand empathically a person's internal world of meanings by thinking, acting, and feeling as if we were the other person (Adler, 1956, 1958; Ford and Urban, 1965; Stein, 1972). As Adler (1958) suggests, "We must be able to see with his eyes and listen with his ears" (p. 72). Maslow (1966) also states that in order to know a person he would approach that individual as unique, and the sole member of his class. He further suggests that, "By far the best way we have to learn what people are like is to get them, one way or another, to tell us, whether directly or by question and answer or by free association, to which we simply listen, or indirectly by covert communications, paintings, dreams, stories, gestures, etc.—which we can interpret" (p. 12). It is in a truly therapeutic and growth relationship where this interpersonal knowing of a person becomes evident. Rogers (1964) differentiates interpersonal or phenomenological knowing from subjective and objective knowing. In subjective knowing one directs one's capacity for empathy toward oneself, while in objective knowing the knower's capacity for empathy is directed toward a reference group. In between these two modes of knowing is interpersonal or phenomenological knowing whereby the direction of the empathy is toward the other person.

Assessment of Early Recollections as a Method of Humanistic Knowing

One method of implementing this humanistic knowing of a person from a subjective, phenomenological perspective described by Maslow (1966), Rogers (1964), and Adler (1956, 1958) is an assessment process based on early recollections (ERs) or early memories. Adlerian psychologists and psychiatrists (Adler, 1947, 1925, 1937; Kopp and Dinkmeyer, 1975; Mosak, 1958; Mosak and Kopp, 1973; Papanek, 1972) have used this method in a therapeutic relationship for many years. Guidelines for collecting ERs have been presented by Kopp (1972), Kopp and Dinkmeyer (1975), and Mosak (1958). From the Adlerian perspective, ERs are those events, experiences, and episodes one selectively remembers that are consistent with one's current perception of oneself, the world, and significant others. These ERs provide support and confirmation of the one's subjective framework which aids one in choosing adaptive behaviors that help move one towards security, success, search for meaning, and self-actualization (Adler, 1956, 1958; Kelly, 1963; Kopp and Dinkmeyer, 1975; Mosak, 1958; Mosak and Kopp, 1973). Because ERs reflect one's present internal reality and one's approach to life, an assessment based on them would provide an excellent tool of understanding a client's private world of meaning. By sharing the hypotheses and expressing an interest in what the client experiences as true, early in the therapeutic relationship, the therapist can quickly develop rapport and demonstrate empathic understanding of the client. This process stimulates mutual respect and encourages the client to become an active and valued participant in the therapeutic process.

Early Recollections: An Example of Humanistic Assessment in Psychotherapy

The client (C) who offered these ERs is a bright, attractive, thirty-year-old, married, female graduate student. Each sentence in the following ERs is numbered in order to illustrate the interplay between the therapist's hypotheses and C's reactions.

Early Recollection "A"

Age about four years. "(1) My sister Kathy and I were out on the sidewalk in front of the house playing catch. (2) The ball we were playing with was a pink and white hard plastic ball. (3) Kathy had thrown the ball at me while she was looking at something off to her side. (4) I called her as I started to throw the ball back. (5) As the ball left my hand I realized with horror that she wasn't paying attention to me and that the ball would probably hit her. (6) I called again. (7) She was turning toward me as the ball hit her in the face. (8) I think it hit her in the face. (9) I remember her coming at me and screaming at me. (10) She may have hit me also. (11) She kept accusing me of having hit her deliberately. (12) I remember telling her it was an accident, (13) and then looking into her face as she was screaming at me and realizing I was never going to be able to convince her that I hadn't meant to hit her. (14) I decided arguing with her wouldn't do any good. (15) I just looked at her with a feeling of hopelessness, realizing that I couldn't change her mind. Two points in this memory stand out the most: the feeling of horror I had when I had just let go of the ball and I realized Kathy wasn't looking; and looking at Kathy as she was screaming at me and realizing she would never believe it was an accident."

ASSESSMENT OF ER "A":

(1) play catch—Hypothesis: C involved in cooperative activity with a female peer. C takes an active stance.

(2) pink and white and hard—Hypothesis: Attention to color and tactile mode. C has artistic interests.

(3) background—Hypothesis: Kathy isn't doing what she should—not the "right" way. What will happen when others don't do what they should? C looking ahead and interacts actively.

(4) called—Hypothesis: C warns through verbal communication.

(5) wasn't paying attention—Hypothesis: People pay dearly when they don't pay attention and/or don't play the game the right way. What was happening? (Getting

hit.) Why? (Because she wasn't looking.) This is an example of a metaphor for not doing the "right" or appropriate thing.
Hypothesis: C reflects, thinks, and draws conclusions and makes predictions. C will tend to make this a mode of interacting with the world.

(6) another warning.
(7) prediction confirmed—Hypothesis: C's fear is realized.
(8) She is not sure so it is not part of the ER. Her "I think" indicates it's not important to her as she remembers it.
(9) I'm assaulted and attacked—Hypothesis: C uses auditory mode which may indicate she is a sensual person who experiences the world through sight, thought and hearing.
(10) not part of ER—see (8) above.
(11) accusing—Hypothesis: C feels accused of being malicious.
(12) explaining—Hypothesis: C responds by explaining to Kathy that the accusation is inappropriate.
(13) unable to convince her—Hypothesis: C feels it's no use— there is no hope of her getting through to Kathy—she'll never understand and see it "my way." Process is observant, and conclusion, again and again concerning a hopeless outcome. Fatalistic (never!).
(14) decided—Hypothesis: C makes decisions and alters her behavior in living with her observations and conclusions.
(15) feeling of hopelessness—Hypothesis: C feels powerless and unable to influence others.

C's Reactions to Assessment of ER "A":

(1) "Yes, I'm always actively involved sometimes I wish I could just sit back and let things happen."
(3) "Being concerned about the "right" way to do things has always been very much a part of me—too much a part of me. Trying to shed rigid excessively high standards for myself and others is something I've been consciously working on for about 10 years now."
(5) "Reflection is automatic to me and yes I do draw conclusions and make predictions all the time. Often I've wished I could erase the predictions and conclusions that so easily come to my awareness."

(13) "Fatalistic (never). Oh, yes . . . It is only recently that I have begun to come to terms with my pessimism. I think one of the ways I protected myself from this awareness was to continuously be mobilized with the determination 'not to give up!' "

(14) "Yes—change comes easily for me. In fact when I think back over the last ten years and see how I have evolved as a person I am amazed."

(15) "This has only applied to what others think of or feel toward me in a personal way. I haven't doubted my ability to succeed academically or professionally. As a young child I believed that if I made up my mind to do something, I probably would be able to do it—within reason."

Early Recollection "B"

Age seven years. "(1) I was recovering from a bad case of the chicken pox. (2) My body has been covered with sores which I was determined not to scratch because I didn't want any scars. (3) There were only a couple of scales left. (4) I was riding my bike or roller skating—I'm not sure which. (5) Anyway, the thing I remember was how good the cool air felt blowing against my face. (6) Some hair was in my eye. (7) And as I brushed it away I knocked off both of the big scabs on the side of my face. (8) I remember feeling the scabs come off and (9) being very upset and angry. (10) Upset because I knew I'd have scars and (11) angry because I had worked so hard not to scratch them and now all that work was to no avail. The outstanding part was the feeling of the scabs pulling away from the skin and being angry and realizing I would have scars."

ASSESSMENT OF ER "B":

(1) background
(2) background—fighting a battle or struggle with her own temptation.
(3) background—C was almost successful.
(4) memory begins (because the actual imagery and action begins). moving along on wheels—Hypothesis: C enjoys independent activity which requires balance.

(5) tactile mode—Hypothesis: C likes to experience things (sensually). C feels that this is the way life *should* be. (Because she likes it. Things one mentions as "likes" in ERs typically indicates ideals: The way life, I, and others should be.) C wants to move freely through life—experiencing nature and the elements—freedom of movement—independence from others are the central themes.

(6) a problem presents itself—Hypothesis: C is saying, "When I can't see where I'm going, I am in trouble and sometimes I block my own vision of things."

(7) solve problem—Hypothesis: C says "My attempts to solve my problems are disastrous."

(8) attention to detail—Hypothesis: C may be tactile/sensual in nature.

(9) upset and angry—Hypothesis: Negative emotions in ERs indicate a basic fear or indicate a situation which is expected in life and which the person seeks to avoid in life.

(10) scars—Hypothesis: C's attention to looks—shows awareness of how others see her and may be a potential embarassment.

(11) work to no avail—Hypothesis: C's basic fear that in spite of all my efforts, I will fail. C feels that "When my resolve is high and I am vibrant I can pursue the goals I set for myself. But when one drops one's guard or is distracted (as Kathy was in ER "A") disaster strikes and all is lost. Never let your guard down."

C's REACTIONS TO ASSESSMENT OF ER "B":

(2) "I don't do this as much anymore; however, there was a time . . . "

(5) "Freedom of movement and fully experiencing life are the values which really fit, independence from others not as much."

(6) "Yes, this is related to the first part of ER "A"—this fear complicates my life. (Several years ago I realized how the urgency to know exactly what I was doing and where I was going, controlled much of what I did. I

am more comfortable with myself now.) I hope to come to an acceptance of life that will enable me to relax even more and allow myself to simply evolve."

(7) "Personal emotional problems—yes. Functional problems—no."

(9) "I don't understand this—I need clarification on what the basic fear is."

(10) "Yes."

(11) ". . . fail . . . yes—in finding happiness." "Never let your guard down. Right on! However, it's been slowly coming down the last several years."

Summary

From the assessment of the ERs, we could identify values and attitudes that are facilitating or inhibiting with C's growth toward self-actualization.

GROWTH FACILITATING ATTITUDES: C enjoys freedom of movement and fully experiencing life; she takes an active, involved stance with others, especially of the female sex; and she reflects, draws conclusions, and makes predictions before acting and is able to alter her behavior.

GROWTH INHIBITING ATTITUDES: C tends to set high standards for herself and tries to live up to others' and self's high expectations; in certain situations, she has expectations that she is fighting a losing battle because things will not turn out well; and in order to gain control, she must not let her guard down and she must also know where she is going or what she is doing.

The Assessment Process

In assessing an ER, the memory is separated into action units. Each action unit is assessed to distinguish the background (i.e. setting) from the actual memory (i.e. when the client can visualize the incident). Then the sequence of action units is assessed.

The rationale for the assessment of ERs is based upon Adler's view that early memories are selective and these retained recollections reflect one's approach to life in the present (Adler, 1958; Kopp and Dinkmeyer, 1975; Mosak, 1958). From ERs the therapist is therefore able to hypothesize upon the client's basic beliefs, values, and attitudes. Corrective feedback from the client will provide the therapist a more empathic understanding of the client's subject world of meaning.

Discussion

Using ERs as a method of humanistic assessment in psychotherapy provides several distinct advantages. From the ERs, the therapist hypothesizes on the client's internal world of meanings. This understanding of the client is tested by the client's reactions. Feedback from the client will assist the therapist in obtaining a more accurate interpersonal knowing of the client's internal frame of reference. Incorrect hypotheses are just as important as accurate ones since the client's feedback may take these hypotheses further to provide better therapist-client contact. The use of ERs during the early stages of therapy will provide the therapist the opportunity early to obtain a phenomenological understanding of the client. This may shorten therapy in certain cases. ERs used in this manner encourage the client to take an active, involved part in psychotherapy.

References

1. Adler, A. *The practice and theory individual psychology* (*1920*). Totowa, N. J.: Littlefield, Adams, 1969.
2. Adler, A. How I chose my career. *Individual Psychology Bulletin,* 1947, *6,* 9-11.
3. Adler, A. The significance of early recollections. *International Journal of Individual Psychology,* 1937, *3,* 283-287.
4. Adler, A. *The individual psychology of Alfred Adler.* Edited by H. L. and R. A. Ansbacher. New York: Basic Books, 1956.
5. Adler, A. *What life should mean to you* (*1931*). New York: Capricorn Books, 1958.
6. Adler, A. *The science of living.* New York: Greenberg, 1929.
7. Allport, G. W. *Personality: A psychological interpretation.* New York: Holt, 1937.
8. Allport, G. W. *Pattern and growth in personality.* New York: Holt, Rinehart & Winston, 1961.
9. Brown, E. C. Assessment from a humanistic perspective. *Psychotherapy: Theory, Research and Practice,* 1972, *9,* 103-106.
10. Coleman, J. C. *Abnormal psychology and modern life.* Glenview: Scott, Foresman, 1964.

11. Craddick, R. A. Humanistic assessment: A reply to Brown. *Psychotherapy: Theory, Research and Practice*, 1972, 9, 107-110.
12. Ford, D. H. and Urban, H. B. *Systems of psychotherapy: A comparative study.* New York: John Wiley & Sons, 1965.
13. Kelly, G. *A theory of personality: The psychology of personal constructs.* New York: W. W. Norton, 1963.
14. Kopp, R. R. *The subjective frame of reference and selective memory.* Unpublished doctoral dissertation, University of Chicago, 1972.
15. Kopp, R. R. and Dinkmeyer, D. Early recollections in life style assessment and counselling. *The School Counselor*, 1975, 23, 22-27.
16. Maslow, A. H. *The psychology of science: A reconnaissance.* New York: Harper and Row, 1966.
17. Mosak, H. H. Early recollections as a projective technique. *Journal of Projective Techniques*, 1958, 22, 302-322.
18. Mosak, H. H. and Kopp, R. R. The early recollections of Adler, Freud, and Jung. *Journal of Individual Psychology.* 1973, 29, 157-166.
19. Papanek, H. The use of early recollections in psychotherapy. *Journal of Individual Psychology*, 1972, 28 (2), 169-176.
20. Rogers, C. *Client-centered therapy: Its current practice, implications and theory.* Boston: Houghton Mifflin, 1965.
21. Rogers, C. Toward a science of the person. In T. W. Wann (Ed.), *Behaviorism and phenomenology: Contrasting bases for modern psychology.* Chicago: The University of Chicago Press, 1964.
22. Rosenzweig, S. with Kagan, K. *Psychodiagnosis.* New York: Grune and Stratton, 1949.
23. Stein, J. *Effective personality: A humanistic approach.* Belmont: Brooks-Cole, 1972.
24. Ullman, L. P. and Krasner, L. *A psychological approach to abnormal behavior.* Englewood Cliffs: Prentice-Hall, 1969.

CHAPTER 4

EARLY CHILDHOOD RECOLLECTIONS— AN INTEGRATIVE TECHNIQUE OF PERSONALITY TEST DATA*

ASYA L. KADIS, JANET S. GREENE, AND NORBERT FREEDMAN

Introduction

THE REPORT GIVEN by a person about his past life lends itself to an approach from various angles. One might be: What effect did the stated event have upon his later development? Another question might doubt the actuality of the reported happenings. (The recollection might have been preferred as a cloak under which the person sought to hide.) A third approach, the one used in this paper, is to regard the recollections as a perceptual act, a selective view taken from the vantage point of the person's life situation at the present, upon the acts and roles of himself and those with whom he early associated.

From this point of view, episodes in which a person remembers himself acting—perhaps succeeding, failing, breaking rules, or obeying—are perceptions which are likely to be consistent with his other views regarding himself and others. As such they may be looked upon as important data relating to his conduct in his present life situation.

This approach was first formulated by Alfred Adler (2):

"Early recollections," Adler said, "are most helpful in revealing what one regards as values to be aimed for, and what one senses as dangers to be avoided. They help us to see the kind of world which a particular person feels he is living in, and the ways he early found of meeting that world. The basic attitudes

* Reprinted by permission from the *American Journal of Individual Psychology*, 1952, 53, *10*, 31-42.

which have guided an individual throughout his life, and which prevail like in his present situation, are reflected in these fragments . . ." (1).

The purpose of the present study is to show how "early childhood recollections," henceforth called ECR, are data which will aid the examiner in integrating and making more meaningful the information derived from projective material. Projective material may present the examiner with a highly diverse set of attitudes, needs, and anxieties. A general problem arises: in defining which of these attitudes is relevant in terms of the subject's conduct or functioning. Thus, a distinction here used is between functioning traits to be observed in the subject's conduct and latent traits which may be projected in a test which, however, are not directly accessible to observation of behavior.

In clinical experience, we found that "early childhood recollections" make possible the prediction of functioning traits; they thus act as a point of relevance to organized projective material. Some of the theoretical reasons for this supposition will be outlined.

(1) The subject of a recollection is always the self, and the attitudes expressed are likely to bear an intimate relation to the "I." In much projective material the perplexing questions are raised: Does the individual's attitude aim at himself, a peer, or an elder? Does he refer to a real or ideal image? On the other hand, the problem of defining the subject of identification usually does not occur with recollections. It thus appears that as an image relating to the self, we are dealing with an image *focal* to the *subject's perceptual* field.

(2) In content ECR deals with a person's primary group, his parents, parent substitutes, and siblings, and the way he early responded to challenging situations in this group. If we accept the notion that family attitudes tend to generalize as to other human relationships, childhood recollections should permit specific *predictions* of the way a person pursues his goals and relates to others.

An assumption underlying the present study, then, is that childhood recollections represent a *focal image* of the individual's perceptual field which is *predictive* of the way he pursues his goals and relates to others. This assumption leads us to expect better prediction of functioning traits when a knowledge of ECR is added to other projective material. Our major hypothesis, therefore, is that a knowledge of ECR improves prediction of functioning traits specifically in two areas of the subject's activities:

(*a*) pursuing a task, to be called *approach* category;
(*b*) relating to elders, to be called *authority* category.

Procedure

The raw data consists of three sets of material for each of twenty female high school (private) students, aged 14 to 17.

(1) Summary descriptions by two teachers (one homeroom teacher) both well acquainted with the students. These were drawn up at the end of the school year. Each teacher was instructed to describe the students' (*a*) manner of approach to school tasks, and (*b*) the relationship to staff with whom there was also a good deal of extracurricular contact.

(2) Ten stories, written by the students in response to ten Thematic Apperception Test cards, which were projected on a screen.

(3) Finally, students were asked to write the earliest episode they could remember when they were little girls and the earliest episodes relating to their mothers and fathers.

Three judges were then asked to rate on both the *approach* and *authority* categories, the teachers' conduct descriptions, the Thematic Apperception Test (TAT) data without a knowledge of ECR, and finally ECR which was then added to the TAT protocol.

This procedure of adding ECR to TAT was employed (*a*) to make the method consistent with clinical practice, where ECR is never used alone as integrative technique, (*b*) to emphasize that ECR and TAT are not independent of each other. (*c*) This procedure also seems appropriate to provide an answer to the general question of this paper: "What does ECR contribute to the prediction of functioning traits, not already predicted by other projective tests, such as the TAT."

Each judge thus had three separate checks for each subject: one derived from teachers' conduct notes, one from TAT and one from ECR. The checks derived from teachers' reports served as criteria for the prediction of functioning traits. TAT checks were matched against conduct checks, as were ECR checks, and it was determined whether the latter significantly increases prediction of conduct or the functioning trait.

Method of Scoring

Seven items were contained in the approach category, and will be cited as examples:

1. Pursuing a goal with initiative
2. Pursuing a goal by setting own rules, disregarding barriers
3. Pursuing a goal by employing evasive, fictitious, or gratuitous means
4. Pursuing a goal compliantly; doing no more than situation demands
5. Passive resistance, complies using a minimum of effort, begrudgingly and with hostility
6. Works without confidence in own aspiration, doubt, depression, inner resignation
7. Unscorable*

The first three items in the list relate to an active approach, the second three to a passive approach. Similar items were established for the *authority* category (see appendix). Rules for scoring were arranged, so that there could only be one check per subject for each of the three groups of data. Sample responses for TAT and ECR taken from an exploratory pilot study were selected to guide the scorers in their decisions (see appendix).

For the TAT, each card was scored separately and the judges were asked to assign one master check to the total protocol. (Thus we had ten card checks and one master check for each TAT protocol.) The master check was not necessarily in the category of highest frequency of checks, but was based on

---

* "Unscorable" checks only appeared for single TAT cards (see below), but never for TAT master checks, ECR, or criterion checks.

scorer's clinical judgment. It was guided by factors such as mood, outcome of plot, and degree of affective involvement. Only actions emanating from the hero (who was defined for each card) were considered to contribute to at least one of the items in the categories (appendix).

For ECR, inferences were made similar to those made for TAT. Each of the judges, all of whom were experienced clinicians, had at least one year of practice in making ECR interpretations. Judges were asked to focus on type of action, which subject remembers himself as *doing*, beginning and outcome of episode, affect associated. A sample interpretation will be given. One of the girls reported, "When I was four, I made a terrible racket on Sunday morning when I wanted to try out my new bike and my parents wanted to sleep." The inference was drawn that the girl maintained an image in which she did what she wanted to do, irrespective of parental sanctions. It is predictive of item two in the *approach* category: "Pursuing a goal according to one's own rules." A response that would represent the corresponding item for the TAT would be, "The boy is supposed to play the violin, but doesn't feel like it when he sees the gang play baseball —he's disgusted and breaks the bow."

Results

Basic data of the study consist of three ratings on each subject made by the three judges independently.

1. Rating on teacher's report
2. Rating of TAT only
3. Rating of ECR

An answer to the problem of the present study may be approached by comparing correct matchings between ratings based on TAT on the one hand and teachers' reports on the other. An analysis of the *approach* category in Table 4-I, shows that of the 20 cases there was correct matching between the scores from TAT and criterion (teachers' reports) to the extent of 10, 8, and 8 cases for each of the three judges. This was increased to 17, 16, and 16 cases when ECR was added. All Chi Squares, used* here as a measure of change, showed values larger than the .05 level of significance.

TABLE 4-I

CORRECT MATCHING WITH CRITERIA FOR APPROACH
AND AUTHORITY CATEGORIES

Judges 1, 2, 3—(based on sample of 20 cases)

| | Approach | | | | Authority | |
	TAT	ECR	X^2†		TAT	ECR	X^2†
Judge							
1	10	17	5.14		10	14	1.6
2	8	16	4.08		8	15	4.0
3	8	16	6.13		9	15	3.13

† Values exceeding the .05 level of significance underlined.

Table 4-I also presents the corresponding data for the *authority* category. Correct matching between TAT and the criterion was 10, 8, and 9 cases for each of the three judges. This was increased to 14, 15, and 15 when ECR was added. One of the Chi Squares here reached a level larger than the .05 level of significance, while the other two improvements, though small, were in the expected direction.

The effect of adding ECR may be shown in another way— more specifically as to the degree which judges agreed with themselves on the various ratings made in the study. (Table 4-II) For the *approach* and *authority* categories, in 9 and 8 cases out of the 20 (40% and 45%), all three judges agreed with reference to TAT checks. Addition of ECR raised the agreement to 13 cases or 65% of the sample for both categories. Further investigation of the agreement for the criterion ratings, teachers' reports, revealed that in 16 and 15 cases, 80% and 75% of the sample for

---

* The formula used: *Chi Square* $= \dfrac{[(A - D) - 1]^2}{(A + D)}$, No. 86a McNemar (4); 'A,' representing the number of cases where ECR *only* matched correctly with criterion, and 'D,' the number of cases where TAT only matched correctly. Recognizing that TAT and ECR (used with knowledge of TAT) are not independent of each other, we seek here to eliminate those cases where *both or neither* ECR and TAT matched correctly.

approach and *authority* categories, the checks for all three judges coincided.

TABLE 4-II

NUMBER AND PERCENT OF AGREEMENT FOR ALL THREE
JUDGES, FOR ECR, TAT, AND CONDUCT RATINGS,
APPROACH AND AUTHORITY CATEGORIES
(based on sample of 20 cases)

	TAT		ECR		CONDUCT	
	N	%	N	%	N	%
Approach	9	45	13	65	16	80
Authority	8	40	13	65	15	75

Discussion

The results then support the hypothesis that recollections lead to more accurate prediction of functioning traits. Our observation that much of the projective material is not directly expressed in conduct is quite consistent with other studies, for example, those found in Sanford's *Harvard Growth Study* (7). Also, to our knowledge, the authors of the TAT never intended stresses, needs, or themes to have direct reflection in the individual's conduct (5).

In this particular study, ECR aims to clarify and integrate TAT material. For instance, a qualitative examination of our cases, in which judges failed to predict the criterion on the TAT but succeeded with the ECR, illuminates the relationship between ECR and TAT. Five out of six judgments on the *approach* category overestimated an anxiety reaction. They showed doubt, resignation, and depression where the functioning attitudes were compliance, or even rebellion. The girl whose first memory was reported earlier as disturbing her parents by wanting to try out her new bike brings out themes in her TAT such as loneliness, desolation, weakness, and frustration—all passive in content. Her behavior reports, on the other hand show her to be a good organizer, with insistence on handling decisions her own way. Her key word, say her teachers, is "I object"—all active in behavior.

The girl then presents the picture of rebellious functioning, as revealed by behavior and recollections, with an underlying depressive tone. Without denying the importance of such latent feelings, we may ask—How does she handle them? The functioning traits define this for us. The point may be clarified if we think of functioning and latent traits as having a relation of figure and ground. The meaning of the ground or latent trait is dependent on the figure or functioning trait. A depressive tone subordinated to the life-style—the aggressive pursuit of a goal and human relationships—has a meaning very different from a depressive tone subordinated to a life-style of fright and immobilization. A specific value of ECR is that when it is integrated with other test material, it clarifies for the observer the way in which the subject acts upon his latent trends.

The theoretical relationship between ECR and TAT is further clarified if we note that in 9 out of 11 cases in which a judge's master score failed to correspond with the criterion, the functioning trait was checked on at least one of the ten TAT cards. The difficulty for a judge to select the correct category out of ten cards is revealed if we focus on the disagreement among the TAT cards; that is, the scatter of checks over a number of categories ranged from 2 to 5 per subject out of a possible 6 categories relating to "approach." The mean was 3.78.

The fact that ECR would select from these three or four possible responses reinforces the original assumption of ECR as a focal image which organizes data with references to functioning level. The increased agreement among judges when ECR is added is consistent with this view, if agreement is used as an index of understanding. We may say that ECR makes accessible to the external observer the structure of the subject's perceptual field.

From a practical point of view, there may be developed many other tests using different concepts to achieve similar ends. Aside from being test data, ECR has important theoretical attributes. As an instance of memory, ECR involves time (6) and is likely to be a persistent focal image. It is this persistence over time that led to the assumption by Adler that recollections are a signpost of life style.

Summary and Conclusions

This is an exploratory study and we are aware of important gaps in the data; but the same propositions regarding recollections can be tested by still other methods. A few of the many questions that suggest themselves may be stated.

Basic to the idea of a persistent focal image is continuity over time. Will recollections from the same subject, representing different periods of his childhood result in identical inferences? Furthermore, is it possible to spell out more precisely the cues that lead to interpretation and prediction of a recollection in this or another category? Finally, in what areas of functioning is prediction by ECR most adequate?

(1) To restate some of the major conclusions, we noted that recollections, viewed as perceptions of the past, are predictions of present conduct, specifically in the way a subject pursues a goal and relates to others.

(2) Finally, by predicting conduct, recollections enable the observer to distinguish between characteristics which are functioning and those which are latent, thus organizing projective material around a point of relevance.

As such, ECR presents itself to be of value both in a practical testing situation and with reference to personality theory.

APPENDIX

Prior to presentation of the three sets of raw data, each judge was presented with the following instructions:

Instruction to Judges

A. *Rating Criterion*

Attached are summary descriptions of the conduct of 20 high school girls as given by two teachers (one homeroom) at the end of the school year. In terms of these descriptions, ask yourself, "How would she handle a challenging task?" Then, try to place her in one of the six categories under "approach." Next, ask yourself, "How would this girl relate to an elder or superior?" Try to place her in one of the four categories under "authority."

If none of the categories seem to apply, place her in an unscorable category. Use the examples cited in Column II to guide you in your decisions.

B. TAT Ratings

Attached are 20 TAT protocols, each consisting of the stories of 10 TAT cards. For each TAT card ask yourself, "How would this girl handle a challenging task?" Try to place her under one of the six categories under "approach." Next, ask yourself, "How would this girl relate to an elder or superior?" Try to place her into one of the four categories under "authority." If none of the categories apply place her in an unscorable category. Use the examples cited in Column III to guide you in your decisions.

Note: (i) For each card only actions emanating from hero are scorable responses. Heroes are arbitrarily defined as follows:

TAT Cards

1. Boy	7GF. Child
2. Girl	9GF. Woman at right
3BM. Boy	11. _____
3GF. Woman	12F. Young woman
4. Woman	16. _____

(ii) After you finish scoring all ten cards in the protocol, assign a master score by placing a circle in the category of your choice. These factors will determine a master score:

(a) Frequency of checks
(b) Emphasis of affect
(c) Emphasis and ending of plot

C. ECR Ratings

Attached to each TAT protocol, you will find a statement by the 20 girls (*a*) relating to the earliest recollections of themselves and (*b*) their mothers and fathers. Ask yourself for each statement, "How would this girl handle a challenging task?" Try to place her into one of the six categories under "approach." Next, ask yourself, "How would this girl handle a relationship to an elder or superior?" Try to place her into one of the four categories under "authority." If none of the categories apply, place her into an unscorable category. Use examples cited in Column IV to guide your decisions.

Note: These factors should be considered in your scoring:
(i) Only consider actions emanating from the subject as she remembers herself.
(ii) Focus on the beginning and outcome of the episode recalled.
(iii) Affect associated with it.

References

1. Adler, A. "The Significance of Early Childhood Recollections." *Int. Journal of Ind. Psych.* 1937, III, 4, p. 286.
2. Ansbacher, H. L. "Adler's Place Today in the Psychology of Memory." *Ind. Psych. Bull.* 1947, 6, 32-40.
3. Dudycha, G. J. and Dudycha, M. M. "Childhood Memories, A Review of the Literature." *Psych. Bull.* 1941, 38, 668-682.
4. McNemar, Quinn. *Psychological Statistics.* John Wiley, New York, 1949.
5. Murray, Henry A. and staff. *Thematic Apperception Test Manual.* Harvard University Printing Office, Cambridge, Mass., 1940.
6. Oppenheimer, Oscar. "I and Time—a Study in Memory." *Psych. Rev.* 1947, 54, 222-228.
7. Sanford, R. Nevitt. "Personality Patterns in School Children" in Barker, Kounin and Wright, *Child Behavior and Development*, McGraw-Hill, New York, 1943, 567-590.

APPROACH—SAMPLE RESPONSES DRAWN FROM:

I. Category	II. Teacher's Reports (Conduct Notes)	III. TAT	IV. ECR
1. Pursuing goal with initiative.	She has reading difficulties, but persists in trying to read—has made great improvements. She won't take no for an answer.	(3BM) The boy lost his home, but he'll help build a new one that's even prettier.	It was a stormy day. It was my first hike. I walked all the way and we went swimming.
2. Pursuing goal regardless of barriers.	She decides what the homework will be. When she couldn't change the class plan, she decided to carry on alone.	(16) They had a fine time: a feast of venison; when they're through they will rob a rich bishop and maybe give the money to the poor.	I remember I put my fist through my grandfather's newspaper when I wanted him to see my new doll.
3. Pursuing goal by fictitious gratuitous means—"scheming."	She plays one against the other to get what she wants. She takes her material from obscure and obsolete books and presents it as her own.	(1) He hated this practicing. Then he got an idea. "Mom, can I go to the store for you?" "Why, you sweet boy."	I had some candy and Dad wanted to buy it from me for a dollar; I decided to sell it because I knew Dad would give me the candy anyway.
4. Pursuing goals as means of security.	Does good work, but quotes me verbatim. She recopies work at least three times so that it is as perfect as any paper can be.	(2) She clutches her books and goes off to school. She knows she will be able to help her parents if she studies hard.	I broke the dish, cried and asked Mother to pardon me. She told me she still loved me and I stopped crying. I would sit on Ma's lap while she was reading.
5. Complies, by doing minimum under protest. Passive opposition.	She says "yes," but I always feel she does "no." She does her work in the last minute, or when she expects a reprimand, or is practically forced to.	(1) His mother told him, to go on practicing, or else. He's now practicing, and every so often doodles on his paper—then goes on again.	I hated carrots; I just could not swallow them, and stored them in the side of my mouth. Dad was a good horseman. But he's pushed riding on to me and so I don't like it.
6. Depression, resignation, doubt.	I do this because that's all I can do. Refused to go to prom saying, "I never have any fun anyway."	(12F) The woman has been wanting to go to work. No food for 7 days. With her son killed, she will aimlessly work in the walls she calls her home.	Standing at the end of the deck looking into the water. Then I fell in, and I remember feeling the bubbles going up and down. I was lying in the crib on the porch; it was unbearably hot.

AUTHORITY—SAMPLE RESPONSES* DRAWN FROM:

I. Category	II. Teacher's Reports (Conduct Notes)	III. TAT	IV. ECR
1. Complete acceptance of authority relationship; empathy and positive identification.	She does what I want even before I ask her to do it.	(7GF) She wants to listen to what her tutor was saying. How else could she grow up to be Daddy's little lady?	Father used to swing me around by the hands and I loved it. Mother told me I should not sleep with my head dug into the pillow. I turned my head, it was uncomfortable, but I do not recall since then having slept the other way.
2. Denying a relationship by indirection. (Ridicule, derogation, suspicion, criticism.)	She would bring in bits of information and offer them to correct me, to show where I made an error.	(7GF) Mother is reading the Bible, and she is closing her eyes to take the wisdom in small measure.	I remember lying in bed with my mother, wondering why she said "Yes," for "Yes."
3. Denying a relationship by open break.	"I won't let you mess into my business." Refused to write her autobiography because she felt "the teacher had no right to personal and family information."	(1) His mother wants him to practice. But he sees the boys downstairs and breaks the bow and smashes the violin.	My father used to punish me when all my friends were around. Mother and I got into the subway and it was very crowded. She told me to get off at 86th St. She did—I didn't, and I waved to her as the train left the station.
4. Denying a relationship by aloofness; the avoidance of involvement.	She is holding all the teachers at arm's length. She goes from advisor to advisor, but hardly ever listens to what they have to say.	(12F) The voice of the old woman warned her not to marry. She smiled to herself, stared and gave no answer.	I was careful with the new china. Though I tried not to, I broke the cup. Father punished me, and I felt it was very unfair. I didn't cry or say anything, I can't remember my mother's face when she was bending over my crib.

* All examples have been abbreviated.

CHAPTER 5

EARLY RECOLLECTIONS AS A PROJECTIVE TECHNIQUE: A REVIEW OF SOME RECENT VALIDATION STUDIES*

JANE A. TAYLOR

Mosak (1958) REVIEWED much of the literature dealing with early childhood recollections (ERs) and discussed the interpretation and application of ERs as a projective technique according to the theory of Adler's Individual Psychology. This article examines some of the more recent research directly related to the projective use of ERs.

According to Adler (1937) a person's

> early recollections are found always to have a bearing on the central interests of that person's life. Early recollections give us hints and clues which are most valuable to follow when attempting the task of finding the direction of a person's striving. They are most helpful in revealing what one regards as values to be aimed for and what one senses as dangers to be avoided. They help us to see the kind of world which a particular person feels he is living in, and the ways he really found of meeting that world. They illuminate the origins of the style of life. The basic attitudes which have guided an individual throughout his life and which prevail, likewise, in his present situation, are reflected in those fragments which he has selected to epitomize his feeling about life, and to cherish in his memory as reminders. He has preserved these as his early recollections (p. 287).

Thus, whatever a person may select to remember from his childhood is related to the individual's present fundamental view of life and can be used projectively to assist in understanding his repetitive behavior patterns, his evaluation of himself and his

* Reprinted by permission from the *Journal of Individual Psychology*, 1975, *31*, 1, 213-218.

world, and his role in the world (Kadis, 1958; Mosak, 1958, 1965). Since Adler first discussed his view of the significant role of ERs, little interest had been shown among therapists and counselors outside of Adlerian circles regarding the diagnostic/projective usefulness of ERs until the last fifteen years. Prior interest in ERs generally seemed to be according to Freud's (1956) beliefs about ERs being concealing memories rather than Adler's (1937) view that ERs are revealing memories—though both men felt that the memory is selective.

M. G. Lieberman (1957) reported a study designed to test the hypothesis that there is a significant correspondence between the material revealed in ERs and other projective data. Her sample was composed of eleven psychotic and eleven non-psychotic females who were each administered a full test battery consisting of the Wechsler-Bellevue, Rorschach, Bender-Gestalt, and House-Tree-Person drawings. Each subject's ERs were also solicited and the following questions asked: What is the earliest incident that you can remember in which your mother was involved? your father?" The subject's ERs were then given to the experimenter along with the ages of the subjects. The experimenter wrote reports on each subject based only on her memories while the staff psychologist composed reports based on the findings of the test battery. The two reports for each subject were then compared using a checklist of descriptive items to evaluate personality traits (such as Perception of the Environment: Threatening Physically, Threatening Emotionally, or Friendly). Each item, according to Lieberman, was previously chosen and then specifically defined in order to eliminate as much ambiguity as possible. Though Lieberman's sample was small, she obtained significant results in terms of the presence of more agreement than disagreement in relation to the type of material revealed in the psychological reports based on a projective test battery as compared to the reports based on the ERs ($t = .65$, $P < .001$). She also found a significant correlation ($r = .66$, $P < .001$) between the amount of information elicited from ERs and that obtained from the psychological report though, of course, more information was obtained from the psychological report. Thus, Lieberman concluded that ERs may serve as a rapid valuable sample of the type of data likely to be obtained from the longer time consuming projective test battery examinations. Differences in memory content distribution between the psychotic and nonpsychotic groups were noted though no statistical analysis was done because of the small sample size.

In another attempt to validate the projective use of the ER technique, McMarter, Tomkins, and Schiffman (1961) examined the use of ER characteristics to predict performance on a variety of the Tomkins-Horn Picture Arrangement Test scales. The Tomkins-Horn protocols of 75 male university students were compared to predicted Tomkins-Horn performances estimated from each subject's ER. The authors concluded that results obtained from the comparison indicated ERs to be a valid method of personality appraisal specifically in the areas of degree of activity, including work, and social interest. The authors were not able to validate ER prediction of optimism-pessimism.

Based on the assumption that the ERs of a patient should bear some relationship to his current neurotic symptoms, the ERs should be of diagnostic value according to Jackson and Sechrest (1962). This assumption is essentially the same as the one on which the two preceding studies were based. In this study the authors examined the following hypotheses:

1. ERs of patients suffering from anxiety reaction will show obvious fear.
2. Depressed patients will give memories of abandonment.
3. Obsessive-compulsive patients will recall strong prohibitions.
4. The ERs of patients with gastrointestinal disorders, such as ulcers and colitis, will concern gastrointestinal distress.

The results reported by the authors indicate that though the absolute frequencies of the themes were too low to have import for differential diagnosis, more than the other groups the ERs of anxiety neurotics were characterized by themes of fear, depressed patients by themes of abandonment, and gastrointestinal sufferers by themes of gastrointestinal distress—these findings are in accord with hypotheses 1, 3, and 4. Jackson and Sechrest also reported finding that themes of sex were more frequent among the obsessive-compulsives, and themes of illness, accident, and trauma were more frequent among the anxiety neurotics and gastrointestinal sufferers and the group of normals who were included for comparison purposes. In conclusion, the authors found that the neurotics as a whole had more unpleasant ERs than the normal group; however, the four neurotic categories did not differ significantly among themselves in the pleasantness of their ERs.

Hypothesizing that (a) experiences of success and failure will not significantly influence ERs, although they will influence Thematic Apperception Test (TAT) stories, and (b) experiences of hostility and friendliness will not significantly influence ERs, although they will significantly influence TAT stories, Hedvig (1963) conducted two experiments and analyzed the results for thematic content of the ERs and TAT stories. In order to test the hypotheses, 360 subjects were randomly assigned to one of twelve experimental conditions which were: ERs or TAT stories written by subjects (1) after experience of success, failure, or neutral experience (a total of six conditions), or (2) after experience of friendliness, hostility, or neutral experience (a total of six conditions). Analyses of variance of pleasantness ratings assigned by subjects to TAT stories and ERs indicated no significant differences as a result of the major experimental conditions. The χ^2 analysis of the thematic content for the success-failure experiment showed that only the need-achievement theme significantly differentiated the various experimental conditions for the TAT stories; the experimental conditions did not differentiate the ER groups. In the friendliness-hostility experiment, thematic analysis showed significant differences in the TAT groups for hostility and aggression, and unhappiness; no significant thematic differences were found between the ER groups. Hedvig concluded that she had at least partially confirmed her hypotheses that experiences of success-failure and friendliness-hostility significantly influence TAT stories but not ERs. She felt that this demonstrated greater stability of ERs than TAT stories.

E. D. Ferguson (1964) published an article dealing with her research on the use of ERs for assessing life-styles and diagnosing psychopathology. She demonstrated that life-style summaries based on ERs are reliably communicable to a wide range of professional workers by having ten clinicians (Adlerian, eclectic, Freudian) match life-style summaries written by three of the Adlerian clinicians on the basis of ERs collected from 30 subjects (10 psychotics, 10 neurotics, 10 normals) to ER records. Of the total number of matchings attempted by the clinicians, all but one were found to be significantly better than chance. In terms of the ability of the clinicians to make valid diagnoses of psychopathology from ERs none were able to make diagnoses better than chance. Ferguson suggested this inability to make accurate diagnoses of psychopathology on the basis of ERs can be explained by the fact that on the whole Adlerians consider knowledge of life-style insufficient to make such predictions; that is, Adlerians feel that only the interaction of a given life-style with a given set of environmental circumstances (a crisis, for example) leads to psychopathology (p. 410), not the life-style alone.

Hedvig (1965) reported a study investigating the extent to which three Adlerian clinicians could determine from the ERs of 51 elementary and high school students whether they had been diagnosed by a clinical team as cases of psychoneurosis or as cases of adjustment reaction, conduct disturbance. When the data were subjected to χ^2 analysis, the combined results were significant at the .001 level of confidence, though taken separately, the abilities of the judges individually differed widely. When the diagnoses of the judges were correlated, the highest correlation was only .11, even though the correlations computed between the diagnoses of each of the three clinicians with those of the clinic were .70, .32, and .08, the first two of which were found to be significant at the .01 and .05 levels of confidence. Hedvig's results indicate that on the basis of ERs alone, experienced Adlerian clinicians can make accurate diagnostic judgments only to a limited extent—and that appears to be dependent upon the ability of the individual clinician. Her findings do suggest the usefulness of ERs as part of a battery of projective tests or as an aid in the formulation of an individual life style.

Summary

Since the publication of Mosak's (1958) article, interest in the projective usefulness of ERs has grown among therapists and counselors. Six articles specifically dealing with attempts to establish the validity and reliability of the diagnostic/projective use of ERs have been summarized here. The results of these articles lend support to the use of the ER as a diagnostic/projective technique in that:

1. ERs may serve as a rapid, valuable sample of the type of data likely to be obtained from the longer time consuming projective test battery examinations (Lieberman, 1957; Hedvig, 1965).

2. ERs may serve as a valid method of personality appraisal, specifically in the areas of degree of activity, including work, and social interest (McCarter, Tomkins, and Schiffman, 1961).

3. There appear to be some thematic differences among ERs produced by subjects diagnosed as belonging to several neurotic categories (Jackson and Sechrest, 1962).

4. There is evidence to suggest that ERs are not influenced by situations of success or failure, hostility or friendliness, and thus are more stable than TAT stories which do appear to be influenced by such situations (Hedvig, 1963).

5. Life-style summaries based on ERs are reliably communicable to a wide range of professional workers (Ferguson, 1964). On the other hand, however, information obtained from ERs only does not appear to be adequate for valid diagnosis of psychopathology for most clinicians (Ferguson, 1964; Hedvig, 1965) nor for the prediction of optimism-pessimism (McCarter, Tomkins, and Schiffman, 1961).

The results of these studies are far from conclusive, but they are encouraging. It is hoped that during the next decade, we will see the appearance of more conclusive evidence in support of what seems to be a valuable clinical tool.

References

Adler, A. Significance of early recollections. *International Journal of Individual Psychology,* 1937, 3, 283-287.

Ferguson, E. D. The use of early recollections for assessing life style and diagnosing psychopathology. *Journal of Projective Techniques and Personality Assessment,* 1964, 28, 403-412.

Freud, S. *Psychopathology in everyday life*. (A. A. Brill, translator). New York: The New American Library, 1956.

Hedvig, E. B. Stability of early recollections and thematic apperception stories. *Journal of Individual Psychology*, 1963, *19*, 49-54.

Hedvig, E. B. Childhood and early recollections as basis for diagnosis. *Journal of Individual Psychology*, 1965, *21*, 187-188.

Jackson, M. and Sechrest, L. Early recollections in four neurotic diagnostic categories. *Journal of Individual Psychology*, 1962, *18*, 52-56.

Kadis, A. L. Early childhood recollections as aids in group psychotherapy. *Journal of Individual Psychology*, 1958, *14*, 182-187.

Lieberman, M. G. Childhood memories as a projective technique. *Journal of Projective Techniques and Personality Assessment*, 1957, *21*, 32-36.

McCarter, R. E., Tomkins, S. S., and Schiffman, H. M. Early recollections as predictors of the Tomkins-Horn Picture Arrangement Test performance. *Journal of Individual Psychology*, 1961, *17*, 177-180.

Mosak, H. Early recollections as a projective technique. *Journal of Projective Techniques and Personality Assessment*, 1958, *22*, 302-311.

Mosak, H. Predicting the relationship to the psychotherapist from early recollections. *Journal of Individual Psychology*, 1965, *21*, 77-81.

CHAPTER 6

EARLY RECOLLECTIONS AND COLLEGE ACHIEVEMENT*

GEORGE W. ROGERS, JR.

ALFRED ADLER STATED in 1937 that an individual's
early recollections are found always to have a bearing on the
central interests of that person's life. Early recollections give us
hints and clues which are most valuable to follow when attempting
the task of finding the direction of a person's striving. They are
most helpful in revealing what one regards as values to be aimed
for and what one senses as dangers to be avoided. They help us
to see the kind of world which a particular person feels he is living
in, and the ways he really found of meeting that world. They
illuminate the origins of the style of life. The basic attitudes which
have guided an individual throughout his life and which prevail,
likewise, in his present situation, are reflected in those fragments
which he has selected to epitomize his feeling about life, and to
cherish in his memory as reminders. He has preserved these as his
early recollections. (p. 287)

Therefore, what an individual chooses to remember from his
childhood is related to his present view of life and can be used
to understand his repetitive behavior patterns, his evaluation of
himself and his world, and his role in the world (Adler, 1931;
Kadis, 1958; Mosak, 1958, 1965; Taylor, 1975). Following this
reasoning, this study was undertaken to explore the relationships,
if any, between the manifest content of early recollections (ERs)
and college achievement, which will be defined as grade point
averages (GPAs). Because ERs are fluid and do change Eckstein,

* Appreciation is expressed to Dr. James McKenney and Ms. Debbie Rowe,
both of Northern Kentucky University, for their assistance in the preparation of
this study. Reprinted by permission from the *Journal of Individual Psychology*,
1977, *33*, 2, 233-239.

1976; Nikelly, 1971), this study utilized grade point averages just for the semester during which the ERs were obtained.

Method

Sample

Written ERs were obtained from 97 students enrolled in three introductory psychology classes during the first week of a 16-week semester. The ages of the students ranged from 17 to 54 years, with a mean age of 21.55 years. The sample included 75 freshmen, 6 sophomores, 7 juniors, and 7 seniors.

Procedures

Each student was asked to produce five written ERs, but obviously some produced less. The mean number of ERs was 3.88. ERs were then independently scored by two scorers using the *Manaster-Perryman Manifest Content Early Recollection Scoring Manual* (Manaster and Perryman, 1974). A reliability

TABLE 6-I

MEAN VALUES OF 97 CASES OF ERs SCORED WITH
THE MANASTER-PERRYMAN SCORING SYSTEM

CHARACTERS	X		
Mother	1.40	Auditory	.10
Father	1.13	Motor	.55
Siblings	1.13		
Other family members	.63	SETTING	X
Nonfamily members	1.42	School	.58
Group	.50	Hospital	.24
Animal	.13	Inside the home	1.59
Other	.12	Outside in neighborhood	.91
THEMES	X	Traveling	.13
Birth	.04	Inside home of non-family	
Death	.20	member	.05
Illness/Injury	1.00	Away from home or	
Punishment	.44	neighborhood	.58
Misdeeds	.93	Unclear	.05
Givingness	.07	Others	.07
Mastery	.67		
Mutuality	.40	ACTIVE-PASSIVE	X
Attention-getting	1.25	Active	2.86
New situation causing		Passive	.92
excitement	1.30		
Anxiety-provoking situation	1.60	CONTROL	X
Open hostility	.47	Internal	2.28
Other	.36	External	1.53
		AFFECT	X
CONCERN WITH DETAIL	X	Positive	1.47
		Negative	2.18
Visual	1.14	Neutral	.21

test with the ERs of 10 randomly selected students resulted in a 91% level of agreement between the two scorers. This scoring system allows one to analyze ERs across 42 different variables which are subsumed under the broad categories of: (a) Characters (persons mentioned in the ER); (b) Themes (what the memory is about); (c) Concern with detail; (d) Setting (where the situation remembered took place); (e) Active-Passive (if the person initiates action or is acted upon); (f) Control (responsibility for what happened in the ER); and (g) Affect (overall feeling tone of the ER).

Scores for each variable of this study were tallied on either a presence or absence basis across the five possible ERs, and scores for each variable totaled over a student's five ERs given was also included as a score from 0 to 5. The number of ERs given was also included as an independent variable in the statistical analysis to see if this alone would be a major contributor to the variability of GPA.

At the completion of the semester, the grade point averages (a 4-point system was used) of each student for that semester were obtained. GPAs ranged from 0 to 4, with a mean of 2.31. GPAs were fairly evenly divided into three distinct groups: 31 students had obtained GPAs between 0 and 1.99; 34 had GPAs between 2 and 2.99; and 32 had GPAs between 3.00 and 4.00.

Statistical Analysis

The data were analyzed by means of a Stepwise Multiple Regression (SPSS computer program, Nie, Hull, Jenkins, Steinbrenner, and Bent, 1975). This procedure allows the researcher to isolate a subset of predictor variables that will yield an optimal prediction equation with as few terms as possible. For this study, the variable that explained the greatest amount of variance in the dependent variable (GPA) was first extracted. Next the variable that explained the greatest amount of variance in conjunction with the first was extracted, and so on. The statistical criterion established in the parameters section of the program was $F = .05$. Table 6-II is a summary of the multiple regression analysis including: (a) Multiple R; (b) R^2 (amount of variation in GPA as explained by the independent variables); and (c) Simple R (the correlation between each individual independent variable and GPA). Twenty-eight variables are presented in this table.

TABLE 6-II

SUMMARY TABLE

Variable	Multiple R	R^2	Simple R
Active-Passive (Active)	.57	.32	.57
Setting (Travel)	.65	.42	—.34
Setting (Outside in neighborhood)	.69	.47	—.11
Concern with Detail (Auditory)	.71	.50	—.04
Setting (Inside home)	.72	.52	.33
Themes (Exciting situation)	.74	.54	—.07
Characters (Siblings)	.75	.56	—.15
Concern with Detail (Motor)	.76	.58	—.20
Control (Internal)	.77	.59	.55
Number of ERs	.77	.60	.39
Control (External)	.79	.62	—.27
Characters (Group)	.80	.63	—.07
Themes (Birth)	.80	.65	—.01
Characters (Nonfamily)	.81	.66	.07
Characters (Animal)	.82	.67	.02
Themes (Other)	.82	.68	.23
Affect (Positive)	.83	.68	.22
Setting (Away from home)	.83	.69	—.07
Themes (Misdeeds)	.84	.70	—.06
Characters (Other)	.84	.71	.13
Characters (Mother)	.85	.72	.28
Themes (Illness/Injury)	.85	.73	—.004
Setting (School)	.86	.73	.11
Setting (Other)	.86	.74	—.15
Affect (Neutral)	.86	.74	—.04
Setting (Unclear)	.86	.75	—.21
Themes (Mastery)	.87	.75	.36
Characters (Other family)	.87	.75	.13

TABLE 6-III

SELECTED STATISTICS FROM THE STEPWISE
MULTIPLE REGRESSION

Multiple R	.71		
R^2	.50		
Standard error	.82		

Independent Variables		B	Beta
Active-Passive (Active)		.43	.63
Setting (Travel)		—.94	—.31
Setting (Outside in neighborhood)		—.25	—.23
Concern with Detail (Auditory)		—.59	—.18
Constant		1.49	

Results

Twenty-six variables account for 75% of the variance in GPA, making for a very unwieldy prediction equation. However, only four variables (a) Active-Passive (Active); (b) Setting (Travel);

(c) Setting (Outside in neighborhood); and (d) Concern with Detail (Auditory) in combination account for 50% of the variance in the dependent variable GPA. Variable Active-Passive (Active) correlates fairly high with GPA and alone accounts for one third of the variance in GPA. In order to produce a simple and manageable prediction equation, attention will be focused on these four aforementioned variables. Selected statistics for them are presented in Table 6-III. Using these, the prediction equation for GPA would be

Y = 1.49 + .43 (the number of Active responses) −.94 (the number of Travel responses) −.25 (the number of Outside in neighborhood responses) −.59 (the number of Auditory responses)

The standard error of estimate for this equation, though, would be ±.82, indicating that, on the average, predicted GPAs would deviate from actual GPAs by ±.82 points.

Discussion

The prediction equation derived from this pilot study is certainly not a significant development, particularly when the predicted GPA can deviate from actual performance by ±.82 points, yet still be statistically accurate. However, there do seem to be some rather interesting findings which point to the idea that the potential relationships between ERs and college performance should be investigated further. The fairly high positive correlation of the variable Active-Passive (Active) with GPA points to a strong relationship between high achievement and a tendency to act rather than to be acted upon. In other words, the high achiever in college would tend to believe that he has some control over his destiny and is not totally dependent upon the actions or decisions of others. In addition, this tendency to take action seems to be coupled with a weak trend to recall a minimal amount of traveling experiences or experiences external to the home. The other variables used in the prediction equation—Outside in Neighborhood and Auditory—do not easily lend themselves to interpretation because of their negligible correlations.

Perusing Table 6-II again, one can see other variables which have relatively high simple Rs but which are not as important statistically in explaining the variance in GPA. Setting (Inside the home), Control (Internal), the Number of ERs, and Themes (Mastery) are variables which should also be considered. The high positive correlation between GPA and Control (Internal) indicates a strong relationship between high academic accomplishments and a tendency to feel responsible for one's destiny. For these students, situational outcomes are not automatically viewed as being dependent on luck or chance or others' influence or desires. Also, high achievers tended to be more productive when asked to recall ERs. Students with low GPAs produced fewer ERs than did students with high GPAs. In addition, those with high GPAs produced more ERs relating to themes focusing on mastery or attempts at mastery of their personal skills, of others, or of their environments. Finally, the results regarding Setting (Inside the Home) are supportive of the data previously discussed relating to experiences of travel or experiences external to the home.

A more expansive study is planned and further research should be undertaken in this area utilizing not only the Manaster-Perryman scoring system but also such other systems as that by Altman (1973). This study does point out the great difficulty experienced when one attempts to predict academic performance with a single instrument, a situation subject to numerous internal and external pressures. Yet there do seem to be some personality factors related to ERs which may assist in this prediction process.

References

Adler, A. *What life should mean to you.* Boston: Little, Brown & Co., 1931.

Adler, A. Significance of early recollections. *International Journal of Individual Psychology,* 1937, *3,* 283-287.

Altman, K. *The relationship between social interest dimensions of early recollections and selected counselor variables.* Unpublished doctoral dissertation, University of South Carolina, 1973.

Eckstein, D. G. Early recollection changes after counseling: A case study. *Journal of Individual Psychology,* 1976, *32,* 212-223.

Kadis, A. L. Early childhood recollections as aids in group psychotherapy. *Journal of Individual Psychology,* 1958, *14,* 182-187.

Manaster, G. J. and Perryman, T. B. Early recollections and occupational choice. *Journal of Individual Psychology,* 1974, *30,* 232-237.

Mosak, H. Early recollections as a projective technique. *Journal of Projective Techniques and Personality Assessment*, 1958, *22*, 302-311.

Mosak, H. Predicting the relationship to the psychotherapist from early recollections. *Journal of Individual Psychology*, 1965, *21*, 77-81.

Nie, N. H., Hull, C. H., Jenkins, J. G., Steinbrenner, K., and Bent, D. H. *Statistical package for the social sciences* (2nd ed.). New York: McGraw-Hill, 1975.

Nikelly, A. (Ed.), *Techniques for behavior change*. Springfield: Thomas, 1971.

Taylor, J. A. Early recollections as a projective technique: A review of some recent validation studies. *Journal of Individual Psychology*, 1975, *31*, 213-218.

SECTION III

TECHNIQUES OF INTERPRETATION

INTRODUCTION

Olson's "Techniques of Interpretation," which was written for this book, attempts to provide basic information and fill some of the current gaps in the literature regarding process and technique of ER interpretation. This paper supplies a foundation for the papers which follow.

Ackerknecht's paper expands on the ideas presented in Olson's paper, indicating further interpretation concerns with specific examples.

Brodsky's paper describes six vital considerations in a well-rounded ER interpretation and supports these with clinical material. Some of his inferences go beyond the data provided and, to the degree to which they do, those guesses must be regarded as tentative even though his style would lead the reader to assume his guesses are facts. Also, it is important to note the different use Brodsky and Mosak (in Olson's "Techniques") make of other persons in the ERs. Brodsky uses the ER to focus upon specific relations during the subject's early development, whereas Mosak views specific persons mentioned in the ER as prototypes of more general relations, e.g., with men, women, authority figures, or people in general.

Willhite has developed an extensive and effective analytic process based on ERs and involving identifying feelings and guided imagery to reconstruct the ER. This process helps delineate current behavior and game set-up patterns for clients which can then become targets of therapeutic intervention.

Morris's paper expands on the Willhite process, and serves as a companion piece. Morris puts greater emphasis on the Focus (Vivid), Feeling, Reason for Feeling, and "I Want" statement.

67

The McAbees have developed a technique involving drawing the earliest recollection. While they did not invent the technique, they have refined it into a meaningful tool and are the first, in the editor's knowledge, to publish a systematic description and guideline for the technique.

Kadis and Lazarsfeld take ER interpretation one step farther, introducing the concept of images in the early memory. They discuss the similarities and differences of ERs and images and provide guidelines for obtaining and interpreting them.

Olson's "To Score or Not to Score," written for this book, reviews and describes some of the current scoring systems and discusses the nature, benefits, and cautions of the scoring of ERs. The reader is referred to the few available scoring manuals and systems and is informed as to where they can be procured.

CHAPTER 7

TECHNIQUES OF INTERPRETATION

HARRY A. OLSON

ONE OF THE WEAKER areas of the overall ER literature is the insufficiency of specific *how-to* information, i.e. techniques and considerations in interpretation. The purpose of this chapter and the ones following is to help fill this gap. Since this chapter was written for this book, it purposely omits material covered in the other papers included in this section. The reader is encouraged to study all of the papers in this section in the order presented.

Childhood dreams, especially recurring ones, are interpreted in the same manner as ERs, so much of what follows for ERs can be applied to childhood dreams as well. Adult dreams are different, having a much more current focus in terms of present concerns of the dreamer.

Techniques for Obtaining Early Recollections

The actual words used in the instructions are not critical, provided that the directions do not bias the recollection. It is important that the client be free to produce any ER that comes to mind. An example of bias would be, "Tell me about your first day of school." There is nothing wrong with asking such a question, but in the collection of ERs that question would restrict the client's range of responses. It is vital that the client have free rein to respond, not limited in terms of age or context.

I use the following instructions, their significance will be discussed later: "I would like you to go back in your memory and describe in detail the earliest incident you can remember." At this point the client will usually supply an incident, and the recollection is written verbatim. If he does not volunteer it, I will ask the client's age. Occasionally a client will hesitate and ask what I mean. This is noteworthy because it is a relatively rare occurrence and may imply that the client is guarded or unsure, wanting to be on safe ground before proceeding. He may also have an exaggerated need to be exact, correct, or to please.

When the client stops talking, I usually ask, "Is there anything else you can tell me about this incident?" This is done to elicit more details, particularly when the ER is vague or underdetailed. I then ask, "What part stands out most vividly as you recall this incident?" I call this the *Vivid* and write it verbatim following the ER, set off by (V). Next I ask, "What feelings did you recall having then?" These are written, following the (V) statements, and set off with (F). At any point thus far, I will probe for more detail if the response is vague or apparently insufficient. Finally I ask the client, "Suppose you could change anything at all about the recollection, what would you change?" These comments are written down after the symbol (C). This completes my questioning to obtain one ER. I usually obtain five to eight ERs and use ER retrieval as a standard technique during the first two interviews with every new client.

There is a rationale for presenting the instructions in this way. What we desire to elicit is the private logic, or the attitudinal bias and frame of reference of the client. We need to know this in full detail. The recollection alone, without the Vivid, Feelings, and sometimes the Change statements are often insufficient. Dreikurs (1952) stressed the importance of obtaining sufficient details in the ER proper:

> The details which the patient remembers are of utmost importance. Without them, the recollection may be utterly insignificant, or its significance may be completely distorted. For example: A patient remembers a big flood at the age of three; men were working to repair some damage. Without details this meant little. It took prodding to get the details of the recollection: Patient, held by mother, was looking out of a third floor window, watching the big men working below. This is revealing. The little child who needs protection, and, compensating for his being small, in a dangerous

world of strong men looks down on the strong who do the "dirty" work. (This was his basic personality pattern.)*

Without inquiring further, however, even a well-detailed ER may still be insufficient for complete interpretation. An ER is like a message of warning or encouragement from the past, reconstructed to be made consonant with the client's present outlook on life. Thus there is one or more central themes to the ER. The Vivid will often pinpoint that central theme, and in the Vivid and Feelings the real issue is frequently made manifest. An analogy would be a camera with an adjustable lens. The photographer adjusts the lens to produce the effect he desires. If he turns the focus ring one way, objects in the distance will fade into a blur while objects up close stand out in sharp relief. Likewise, if he turns the ring in the other direction, near objects will be fuzzy while a distant object will be prominent. So it is when the client recreates an ER. As Kopp and Der point out (in Chapter 3), not all material in the ER necessarily constitutes the central focus but may be included to set the stage. Consider the following ER:

I was four and in the hospital having my tonsils out. The aftermath of the operation hurt a great deal. My parents were not there, but there were several other children on the ward that I played with.

There are several possible main themes: parents, pain, and pals. All are important or they would not be included in the memory, but which is the central focus? What is the client really saying? Suppose the Vivid is the following:

(V) The fun I had playing with blocks with the other children.

This would indicate a person who takes pain and setbacks in stride. For him every cloud has a silver lining and he will make the best out of it via his friendly and cooperative involvement with others.

Suppose, however, the above ER had this Vivid:

---

* Note Dreikurs's symbolic interpretation of height. This will be discussed in further detail later.

(V) The pain, the awful raspiness in my throat. To add insult to injury, the pain was compounded by my parents leaving me.

Note that, given the same ER proper, the mood and meaning shift with the Vivid. This ER bespeaks a person who is impressed by pain and feels entitled to support, and possible service, from those around him. Social activities (play with other children) may be used to cover pain and avoid loneliness. Thus, the Vivid often provides the clue as to how the ER should be interpreted.

Next comes the Feelings. Without digressing into a discussion of the psychology of emotion, we can say that the person creates those feelings which suit his purpose at the time. Dreikurs (Verger and Camp, 1970) indicated that knowing the feelings is a main interpretive clue. Feelings reflect how the client interpreted the event. Continuing our example and using the first Vivid—"The fun I had playing with blocks with the other children"—suppose the feelings were the following:

(F) Happy, enjoying myself with the other children.
This would reinforce the *silver lining* interpretation made earlier. Pain is eclipsed into active social involvement. Suppose, however, the feelings were as follows:

(F) Angry at my parents, they left me.
Here the tone changes. This person nurses his anger deeply even though on the surface he is enjoying himself with the other children. In fact, he stifles the anger and goes along with daily activities.

Up to this point, we have dealt with the ER as it has been reconstructed. When we come to the *Change* area, we are asking the client to rewrite the script, so to speak, and the results are significant. Answers to the Change question usually reflect some ego-ideal or preferred outcome. As such, the Change statement can be a barometer of change of ideals, identifications, or patterns in the client during the course of therapy. Also, however, they can be used to further spell out private logic. Examine this ER:

Age ten—I was breaking into a house with my brother and his friends. The cops caught us and locked us up over night. Next day, my Mom and Pop were notified and they came to get me out.

(V) Getting caught and having to spend the night in jail.
(F) Scared. I didn't know if I'd ever get out.
(C) I never would have broken into the house.

We can guess here that the client may be on the way to rehabilitation, but suppose the client said the following:
(C) I'd never have gotten caught.

Notice how the whole recollection now has a different shift in
emphasis. Rather than help keep the client on the straight-and-
narrow, it supports the use of greater cunning in future mischief
and a desire to evade accountability for one's actions.

Basic Considerations for Interpretation

Whatever the client says is significant. There are two basic
contributors in the production of ERs. The first is memory itself
with its distortions over time.* The second is the language chosen
to express the recollection. Memory brings the incident to mind
with richness, often with visual as well as auditory recall, and
may even include a recall of olfactory, gustatory, and tactile
sensations. To communicate this private experience requires
translation into language, which truncates the experience and
robs it of some of its original richness. As interpreters, it is
important for us to know *for what purpose* the client remembers
this particular event and expresses it *in just this way*. The
individual distorts memory via exaggerations, omissions, and
minimizations in favor of his current biases, needs, and approach
to life. He emphasizes or remembers that which supports his
current behavior and private logic, and minimizes or forgets that
which is not useful or in conflict with it (Mosak, 1958). Thus
memory contributes to the individual's self-fulfilling prophecy. It
does not matter whether the material presented is factual.

Several issues are then raised by way of interpretation. First,
it is important to distinguish between a recollection, a report
(Mosak, 1958), and a family story. A recollection, according
to Mosak, is a one-time event which can be described as such,
whereas a report is a summary statement of two or more incidents.

---

* For a discussion of memory as reconstruction, see Ansbacher, Chapter 1
in this book.

These are combined together to form a general statement, while the specific details are lost. Thus, they have less interpretive significance because of the lessened detail (Mosak, 1958). A statement such as "We used to . . ." or "I always . . ." is a typical opening line for a report. An example of a report would be, "Everyday Johnnie and I walked to school together." A recollection, however, would be, "Johnnie and I were walking to school together one day. He tripped over a crack in the sidewalk, but I grabbed his arm and prevented his fall."

A family story is an incident regarding one or more members which is handed down over the years as family lore. It may even be reinforced by photographs. Such stories are implanted in the memories of most people to some degree and may be even more removed from remembered personal experience than a report. Often a client will say, "I'm not sure I actually remember this, because . . ." or "I've only been told about it" or "I have only seen the photos." Often, then, there may be a felt sense of unreality or unsuredness about the family story. Since the story is about the client, but told to the client by others, the crucial issue is whether the client has incorporated the story in his mind as his own, i.e. if he really believes it happened. If this is so, the story would count as a recollection. If the client *disowns* the story, i.e. he cannot remember it happening to him or is not sure if it happened, its projective value is significantly lessened. Whether real or not, if the client incorporates the incident, it is *real for him*, and it is perceptual reality, not objective reality, which concerns us in ER interpretation.

The distinctions between a recollection, report, or family story are not always clear, but Mosak (1958) suggests a solution. If the client can *visualize* the event in his mind, it counts as a recollection, even if it is a family story. Recollections can be visualized, reports cannot because of their absence of detail and their summary, conglomerate nature. In unsure cases the client may be asked to close his eyes and visualize the incident, reporting on the details as he visualizes them. Mosak considers all remembered material as significant but only interprets recollections (distinguished from reports and family stories by the criterion of visualizability) projectively. Having the client visualize can be used to check whether the material presented is an actual recollection, and also to help produce recollections in a client who seems to be producing only reports.

Assuming a concept of holism, which is fundamental to Adlerian psychology, everything produced by the individual is consistent with the life-style and underlying goals of the person (Mosak, 1958). Thus, contradictions between ERs are more apparent than real, and they can be resolved through interpretation. This does not mean that all ERs must have the same theme, but rather there can be many manifestations of the personality which are revealed via ERs. Yet they all must reflect the unity of the personality in some measure. A task of the interpreter is to find the common line between the divergent points brought out within and/or between ERs (Dreikurs, 1965), or at least reconcile apparently opposed inconsistencies within the entire context. Sometimes the contradiction may be that under one set of circumstances the client acts in one way and when circumstances change, the client behaves differently (Mosak, 1958). Therefore it is important not only to interpret *within* a given ER but also across ERs, looking for consistent themes and divergences, in order to put the entire puzzle together. Mosak (1958) warns that it is hazardous to generalize about the total personality from just one ER and that sequence analysis of additional ERs almost invariably adds new nuances and conditions, rounding out the total picture.

Who is in the ER is an important consideration, as the presence or absence of others and their roles often reflect the extent and quality of the social sphere and the type of role the individual himself takes in life. In the ER cited earlier in this chapter about the persons walking to school, the client took a helper role (preventing his friend's fall). We could guess that this is a person who takes quick action to assist others in trouble. Consider the following ER:

I was lying in a hammock looking up at the sky. No one else was around.

The five other recollections produced by this client were equally devoid of people. This ER was produced by a schizoid individual, and quite often the recollections of self-bound, schizoid, schizophrenic, and borderline persons are devoid of other people or the interpersonal interactions are hostile, hurtful, or at best neutral (Friedman and Shiffman, Chapter 28). We would also guess that our schizoid client would be a visual type—he focuses upon looking, he observes rather than participates. In fact, he does fancy himself a critic of society and refuses to involve himself in "cheap" or "mundane" tasks such as holding a job or interacting with people, most of whom he considers phoney.

Following Mosak (1958), I interpret the specific others in the ER as prototypes of classes of people. For instance, a sister may represent a peer female or a woman in general, a mother, father, or specific teacher could be interpreted as an authority figure. This view makes sense in that ERs themselves are prototypical. The specific incident is used to reinforce for the client a general "truth" or point of view about life, others, and/or self, and serves as a guide for present and future thinking and action.*

Adler himself provided a list of nine considerations for ER interpretation:

1. Much comes to light through the choice of presentation of a "we" or "I" situation.
2. Much also comes to light from the mention of the mother.
3. Recollections of a stay in the country with the mother, as well as the mention of certain persons like the mother, the father, or the grandparents in a friendly atmosphere, often show not only a preference for these persons who evidently pampered the child, but also the exclusion of others.
4. The recollection of the birth of a brother or sister reveals the situation of dethronement.
5. The recollection of the first visit to the kindergarten or school shows the great impression produced by new situations.
6. Recollections of dangers and accidents, as well as of corporal and other punishments, disclose the exaggerated tendency to keep in mind particularly the hostile side of life.
7. The recollection of sickness or death often is linked with a fear of these dangers and occasionally with the attempt to become better equipped to meet them, possibly as a doctor or a nurse.

---

* The reader is referred to the Brodsky article, Chapter 9, which differs from Mosak's position. Brodsky views ERs as a method of reconstructing specific relationship paradigms from the formative years.

8. Recollections of misdeeds, thefts, and sexual misdemeanors which have been committed usually point to a great effort to keep them from occurring again.

9. Occasionally one learns also of other interests, such as visual, auditory, or motor, which may give occasion to uncover failure in school and a mistaken occupational choice, and indicate an occupation which corresponds better to the preparation for life (Ansbacher and Ansbacher, 1956).

Reviewing some of Adler's points, the choice of a "we" or "I" situation (point 1) would reflect the boundaries and character of the social sphere as suggested above, as well as the degree and method of cooperation. The relationship with mother (point 2) is the primary relationship in infancy and the early years. If mother is absent in the ER but was present in reality, it usually suggests a painful or traumatic relationship. Recollections of the type mentioned in point eight might also reflect normalcy of and interest in mischievous or criminal behavior in the life of the person. As Verger and Camp (1970) observe, Adler's points are suggestive and have not been empirically proved. They are clinical helps which might in some cases be inaccurate. The crucial determiner is the manifest content of the ER itself. General guidelines can only be considered as hints. In the final analysis the guide to accuracy is the client himself. Does he see the ER interpretation as fitting him? Does it make sense? The best interpretations bring an "ah-hah" response from the client.

Another consideration is the innocuousness versus the dramatic nature of the ER content. Innocuous memories tend to be more significant in understanding the person than dramatic ones (Mosak, 1958). Compare the two ERs that follow:

1. I was sitting on the floor watching TV when my sister came up and hit me on the head with the feather pillow.

2. Jim and I were playing on the seventh level of an open, high-rise parking lot. Jim bet he could walk the outer wall. He climbed up on the wall, took a few steps, and then slipped and fell to the ground. He was killed instantly.

Many would say the second ER is more significant because it is traumatic. For our purposes, that is precisely why it is *less* significant. Almost anyone who would have experienced the second ER would remember it. Very traumatic events tend to etch themselves on the mind. More significant, therefore, is the first ER. Why, after all these years, would a person, when asked for one memory, choose *that* one, unless it held very special significance for him.

Finally, the ER portrays the client's basic unconscious attitudes toward life, not necessarily just overt behavior (Mosak, 1958). As such it reveals the *modus vivendi*, the style of viewing the world, not the *modus operandi*, the method of operation. As Mosak indicates, one can behave in many different ways given a particular outlook. If one holds that the world is dangerous, one may withdraw, become obsessive-compulsive, become anxious, or even court danger. Thus it is not always easy to predict overt behavior from the ERs. Often, however, behavioral paradigms are provided in ERs.

Techniques for Interpretation

As with other projectives, the interpretation of ERs is an exercise in empathy. The clinician must put himself in the client's shoes and savor the experience. It is extremely important in interpreting ERs to remember that it is the client's, not our, perceptual reality with which we deal. The client is the expert for his own experience. We therefore must work to avoid biasing our interpretations with our own ideas and values, or jumping to conclusions which are not supported by the data. Yet it is also important to be active in the interpretation process. Guessing is at the heart of the techniques that follow. The interpreter should guess freely, not restricting himself to only one right answer.

To interpret correctly, we must make a generalization from the data. The ER is a specific incident which usually reflects one or more general principles in the client's perceptual/interpretive schema. We wish to find the generality, yet to make unfounded conclusions is as inappropriate as to not move beyond the ER itself to the principle. To illustrate, examine this ER from a young woman.

Age five—I was standing in the dining room. My father came home and brought me a surprise. I couldn't wait to open the box. It was a doll I wanted. I was overjoyed. Father often brought me things.

(V) Father coming home with the surprise.

(F) Happy. Loving my father.

It would be correct to interpret that this lady enjoys surprises, that she is curious, that she feels loved and special, and that these two feelings are extremely important to her. She was probably spoiled (in that she chose *this* memory and also stated, "Father often brought me things" and that she reported no direct show of appreciation to father). We might even guess that she feels that people *should* bring her things, be in her service. It would be incorrect on the basis of this ER, however, to assume that this lady is *dependent* on her father or on males. Such may be the case, but *this* ER neither supports nor rejects this conclusion. The dependency theme per se is not present here, although it may come out in subsequent ERs. With such an ER, however, dependency could be suspected.

In approaching an ER, it is helpful first to analyse it thematically, i.e. find the general message or focus, and then to review it for specific details. Consider the following:

Age four—I was playing in the backyard. The ragman came up the alley. When he got to our fence, he called me over to him. I was scared and didn't go. Then he came in the yard after me. I ran into the house to tell Mama. She came out and chased him away.

(V) The ragman coming into the yard.

(F) Frightened, panicky.

The main themes which are reflected here are "men are dangerous," and "when I feel in trouble I run for help." Exploring the details we find that this is probably an active girl (playing) and that she relies on those stronger to get her out of scrapes. She will choose a *Mama*. Here is a young lady who feels she needs the help and support of women because she feels small and inadequate in the hostile world of men.

Take another example from the same client:
Age six—My sister and I were outside. She was in the next
block. A man came by and offered her some candy. I told
her hundreds of times not to accept candy. I ran to tell
mother. Two boys came along and chased the man away.
(V) The man offering candy to my sister.
(F) Scared for her.

Thematically, the same themes arise again, "men are dangerous,"
"run to bigger women for help." This repetition of themes tends
to reinforce these views as central ones to her life-style. Looking
at details we find that again men make aggressive advances. The
client may find her sense of superiority through moralizing and
being right ("I told her hundreds of times . . ." which is not
necessary but parenthetical to the story. Therefore, it must be
significant). Also, she cares for others, feels for them, and acts
to aid them. But how do we reconcile the two male roles? Males
both threaten and save in this recollection. When considering
the details, we find that it is a *man* who threatens, but *boys* who
save. In fact this client married a "boy," a man slightly younger
than she from another culture, who was so passive and afraid
that he would plead with her not to leave him in the apartment
alone when she would go out shopping. It is clear that men
scare her intensely and she can only feel safe with "boys."

Sometimes it is difficult to "get into" a recollection, to draw
conclusions. Mosak (workshop presentations) demonstrates a
method he calls the Headline Technique. He suggests treating
the ER as if it were a news story. The interpreter's task becomes
writing a title for the ER that, as a newspaper title, summarizes
the essence of the story. An example for the previous ER would
be "Man accosts sister. Little girl runs for help." The title
captures the central themes. The interpreter can deal with the
details from here.

I have developed a technique called the Motto Technique.
A motto is a truism or philosophy stated succinctly which is to
serve as a guide for living. ERs serve unconsciously as examples
of life principles which the client has developed. They may or
may not be accurate or realistic but the client acts as if they
were true. The Motto Technique attempts to enunciate the

guiding principle embedded in the ER simply by constructing a motto for the ER, of which the ER is reflective. For example, in the above ER a motto might be, "Men are dangerous—watch out!" or "You can't be too careful where men are concerned."

Another technique I have developed is the Bottom Line Technique. Adlerians often describe the life-style of the client as an attempt to complete the following formula:

I am:＿＿(self-concept)＿＿＿＿＿＿
The world is:＿＿(world view)＿＿＿＿

＿＿＿＿＿＿＿＿＿＿＿＿＿＿＿＿＿＿
Therefore:＿＿＿＿＿＿＿＿＿＿＿＿

The Bottom Line Technique focuses on the "Therefore," the end results or conclusions implied in or represented by the ER, to which the client has arrived and which underlie his behavior. In the same ER example, the bottom line might be "I need protection (from men)." or "Men are dangerous." or "I can't handle threatening situations myself."

The statements generated by these techniques are powerful ones, all the more so because they are succinct. Such statements, when told to the clients in those words, often bring out "ah-hah!" recognitions. When I use ERs, I usually give direct feedback to the client right away and usually in the first person—e.g. "You seem to be saying, 'Men are dangerous.'" or "Could it be that you're saying, 'I can't handle men on my own'?" When doing a life-style, I write the ER interpretations out in succinct first person or declarative statements such as those above. Presenting the interpretations in that manner is more poignant than using the second or third person. If, however, the client is too disturbed to handle the interpretations, they are held for later use.

Robert Powers (in workshop presentations) advocates closing one's eyes and trying to empathically relive the client's ER in your own mind, trying to intuit how the client must have felt, interpreted the situation, and responded. While this may not be an interpretation technique per se, it is the best one for seeing with the client's eyes and hearing with his ears.

It is important also to look not only for principles but for behavioral patterns which may emerge in the ER. In the example we have been using, the client not only draws a conclusion (men are dangerous), but also takes action (she runs for help to more effective people). It must be remembered, also, that the whole context of the recollection must be considered in interpretation and that the whole may modify significantly the conclusions derived from the parts.

References

1. Ansbacher, H. L. and Ansbacher, R. (Eds.) *The individual psychology of Alfred Adler*. New York: Basic Books, 1956, p. 354.
2. Dreikurs, R. The holistic approach: Two points on a line. *Education, Guidance, Psychodynamics*. Proceedings of the Conference of the Individual Psychology Association of Chicago. St. Joseph's Hospital, Chicago. November 13, 1965.
3. Dreikurs, R. The psychological interview in medicine. In R. Dreikurs. *Psychodynamics, psychotherapy, and counseling*. Chicago: Alfred Adler Institute, 1970, p. 143.
4. Mosak, H. H. Early Recollections as a projective technique. *J. Proj. Tech.*, 1958, 22, 302-311.
5. Verger, D. M. and Camp, W. L. Early recollections of the present. *J. Counsel. Psychol.*, 1970, 17 (6), 510-515.

CHAPTER 8

NEW ASPECTS OF EARLY RECOLLECTIONS (ERs) AS A DIAGNOSTIC AND THERAPEUTIC DEVICE*

LUCY K. ACKERKNECHT

EARLY RECOLLECTIONS (ERs) refer to specific events that a person believes to have taken place within the first few years of his life. The individual unconsciously selects, distorts, or invents memories to fit his underlying mood, purpose, and interest. In 1907 Adler held that a person has an active part in what he remembers, and in 1911 he dealt with a particular case for the first time (Ansbacher, 1973). Later he said: "There are no chance memories: out of the incalculable number of impressions which meet an individual he chooses to remember only those which he feels, however darkly, to have bearing on his situation. Thus his memories represent 'a story of my life'; a story he repeats to himself to warn him or comfort him, to keep him concentrated on his goal and to prepare him by means of past experiences so that he will meet the future with an already tested style of action" (Adler, 1958, p. 73).

It is not all-important that the present first memory or earliest recollection is indeed the first one, or that the ER describes the actual past event. An ER may be considered a creative construction of the individual. Ansbacher (1973, pp. 135-145) states: A recollection as a purposeful construction was quite at variance from Freud's concept of early memories as screens of traumatic sexual experience." Mosak and Kopp (1973, pp. 157-166) dealt at some length with these differences, while analyzing first memories of Adler, Freud, and Jung.

* Reprinted by permission from the *Individual Psychologist*, 1976, 13, 2, 44-54.

When asking for early recollections, one insists on specific events. It is not advisable to record early history at this point of a life-style analysis. Early history reports frequently start with: "I used to . . .," or "When I was small, I had a habit of . . .," etc. ERs begin with: "One time . . .," "It happened when I was small . . .," or with similar specifics. The ERs are briefly recorded together with the approximate age at which the event is believed to have taken place. At times, ERs are quite involved. Then the analyst asks for the highlight or most important aspect of the ER. He also inquires about, and records, the emotion or emotions accompanying the memory.

ERs are one of the most essential parts of an Adlerian life style analysis and, among other things, uncover the life fiction or goal of superiority of which the individual is not totally, or not at all, aware. A psychological life-style analysis, used by Individual Psychologists since the early twenties, corresponds to a psychological or psychiatric diagnostic interview or simply to an attempt of understanding the whole person, body, soul, and mind, in his social and ecological environment. Techniques of life-style analyses, developed by Adler, have been refined in recent years by Dreikurs (1967, pp. 95-102), the author (1974, p. 40), and others (Manaster and Perryman, 1974, p. 237).

This paper deals specifically with early recollections. ERs are valuable because they reflect the person's present-day attitudes and intentions. These intentions may be conscious but more often are unconscious, that is: A person is only half aware or not aware at all of his final or fictitious goals. Basic attitudes are largely influenced by a person's subjective opinions about himself and others. These opinions, attitudes, and goals are unified into a life-style in early childhood. Adler's contention was that the life-style was formed and firmed up by the very young child (Adler, 1930, p. 81). He also maintained that the very earliest recollection reveals to the experienced clinician the essence of a person's personality.

For many years in my clinical and teaching practice I have experimented with ERs in hundreds of cases and have come to the following conclusions:

1. While one memory can give us some understanding of a person's functioning and social interaction, more early recollec-

tions offer more specific information on a person's life-style. The author has found seven to be an optimal number. Papanek recommends five to ten ERs (Papanek, 1972).

A 47-year-old minister with three children remembers as his earliest recollection

> riding in a dark, closed-up car on the way to his grandparents. He then sees himself climbing steps. Above are standing grandpa and grandma. The highlight is the movement toward the beloved grandparents; and the feeling is happiness.

This memory tells us about striving, the goal being to reach the loving, protecting, and possibly indulging grandparents. To achieve this goal the minister has to exclude the rest of the world.

> In the second memory the somewhat older child (age 3-4) is sitting with the family in church. He leaves his seat to go and sit under the pulpit from which his grandfather is preaching. The feeling still is a good one.

The subject leaves the family pew to profit from someone else's "fame" in order to feel more significant himself. The feeling of smallness was not as strongly expressed in the first memory. In it there were only he and his goal. In the second recollection he has to leave "the human community" and sneak under the pulpit to partake in personal superiority.

> In the third memory (age 5) he tells about the upstairs neighbor, who "spoiled us, my brother and me." The neighbor played Santa Claus. Mother told the neighbor that we had done something wrong. Very shortly after this, Santa Claus knew of this. The feeling was amazement.

The new life-style aspect introduced in ER 3 is intellectual curiosity.

> ER 4 (age 5-6) tells about his parents leaving the house, and the brothers screaming and fussing terribly despite grandma's presence. The feeling is disappointment and frustration at parents' leaving.

Here we suspect an added life-style trait of attempts at willful dominance over others.

ER 5 took place at the same time. The community nurse came to visit mother. It was very cold and the streets were icy. The nurse had woolen socks slipped over her shoes. "I was amazed."
This, again, shows intellectual curiosity.
At ER 6 the subject was 6 years old and remembers his first day in school. (Following an old custom, parents, when picking up their children from school, bring them some sweets packed in a very special container.) The subject received his sweets in just an ordinary bag. He was disappointed.

This expresses his present-day attitude of "the world is unjust to me."

In the seventh memory, at the same age, he received a boy scout uniform and proudly showed it off in the street.
He tries to obtain self-worth feelings through outward appearance but also through group identification—a positive note.

The first memory shows that the subject is striving to reach a high goal of being loved, protected, and possibly indulged. The goal is difficult to reach, and the outside world has to be excluded. Memories two to seven show up the present-day life-style aspects: The feelings of smallness and insignificance which tend to be compensated by his partaking in someone else's fame or superiority. One also learns about the search for knowledge and understanding, about willful dominance over others, a feeling of being treated unjustly and another attempt to attain self-worth feelings, this time through outward appearance and group identification.
2. The first two or three memories often represent the present-day attitudes and intentions. The next two or three show a developmental trend, while the last one or two of the seven ERs usually reflect a process of social maturing and increased cooperativeness.

A 47-year-old school principal, married, one child, his first memory at age 2 that he was in bed with a cold and was not allowed to play outdoors, where he heard others playing. Barefooted, he jumped out of the window in order to join the playing. He had felt unjustly confined.

Apparently, the unjust treatment was more important as a feeling aspect than the risk he took in doing something about it.

ER 2 (age 4-5) informs us about the subject's playing with his 10 months older cousin. "We dug holes into the sand and put marbles into them." He did the rough work while the cousin specialized in precision work. This annoyed him. He pushed the cousin and, in turn, was beaten up by the cousin's older brother, whereupon the subject tried to kick the older brother. Again, he felt unjustly treated, this time because he had had to do all the rough work.

The theme is the same as in ER 1: I am treated unjustly and am taken advantage of, and my defensive kicking back is unsuccessful.

ER 3 took place at age 4. "We visited grandma and grandpa. Someone put three large spoonfuls of salt, instead of sugar, into my coffee. Everybody tried to make me drink it. Then grandpa tried it, spit it out, and swore about its taste. He then comforted the little one." The feeling is extreme frustration.

The theme still is "the world is unjust to me, and I am taken advantage of because I am small and therewith handicapped." (The subject is, indeed, small, several inches shorter than his wife.)

In the fourth ER the boy is already 7 or 8 years old. His brother had annoyed him and, upon that, he struck out with a fork and injured his brother. He felt guilty and was then especially nice to this older brother. Feelings: annoyance and guilt.

The new development in ER 4 is the subject's being successful in his attempt to deal with a situation of injustice, although through a negative act, which he tries to rectify by feelings of guilt.

As ER 5 he remembers (age 5) that he had taught himself to swim without the knowledge of his parents. When later his mother took him to a pool, he swam out to the middle and screamed: "Help, I'm drowning." Mother paled in panic and tried to save him. She fell sick afterwards. The feeling was pride of achievement, not a power struggle, he recalled.

As in ER 4, a change in his development is observed which now is even more pronounced. Smallness is overcompensated by extraordinary achievement which had to be dramatized.

As ER 6 (age 6), the subject remembers having defended a boy younger than himself by beating up his aggressors.

This shows us in which direction he is moving. He has more feelings of self-worth now; some social interest is showing and this time not in its pseudoform: guilt. We still notice some slight overcompensation; "Small as I am, I am yet able to beat up other children."

In the seventh memory (age 6-7) he plays on the ice with other children. One boy breaks into the ice. The subject rescues him. The feeling is pride.

The theme is much like in ER 6: growing social interest and feelings of self-worth.

The first three memories represent present-day attitudes. In the case above they show feelings of unjust treatment and frustration. The next two show a development trend. Feelings of inferiority and of unjust treatment are compensated and over-compensated by bold action combined with guilt-feelings and regret. The last two memories represent the growing social feelings in the attempt to help and defend others. Not clear is whether these acts were performed out of genuine social feeling or for self-glorification. It may be assumed that a combination of both motives was the case.

3. If a person of at least average or normal intelligence cannot produce any early recollections before the age of 6 or 7, this may represent a resistance toward the interviewer, but more often it indicates that the reality of the early years of this person's life does not agree with the subjective or fictional character of a person's life history on which his life-style is based.

A 46-year-old divorced social worker, working in a large industrial firm in a very competitive situation, was married for eight years. She has no children. In her

Earliest recollection (age 7) she overheard her maternal grandmother saying: "Father doesn't pay enough attention to the girl." The feeling was sadness.

The basic life-style aspect, communicated by this memory, is: "I am unloved, rejected."

The second memory, somewhat earlier, was introduced with the following remark: "but this was something positive." The bishop had visited the school and the girl had been allowed to recite a poem. The feeling was great pride.

She seems to be saying that only if she performs as an exceptional person can she get recognition.

ER 3 (at the same age of 6-7) is introduced by: "Do you want to hear this one too?" At the annual carnival and rifle match she had been picked as "rifle queen." It had been wonderful.

Here again, recognition was experienced only through being someone very exceptional and being personally superior to all the others.

In ER 4 she is already 14 years old. In the Christmas play she is playing Mary. During the dress rehearsal her long veil is pulling a pile of hay after her. She was embarrassed.

Again, the girl plays the main role but is now greatly embarrassed. Nothing has been learned as yet of her emotional relationship to her family, except in memory one, where her father is not supposed to pay enough attention to her. She feels rejected by her family and can gain recognition and fame only by playing extraordinary top roles in the outside world.

In memory 5 she is 15 years old and belongs to a scout-leader group. The boys are making fun of her because she blushes so easily. They think this is cute. She felt so embarrassed she could have killed them.

Again she belongs to the top group in the outside world and feels special through her blushing.

Had one stopped at this point, he could have assumed that she really had been an unloved, unimportant member of her family and had not felt that she belonged. Her present attitude as reflected by these memories is still: "I can not belong to any group unless I am the most important person in the group." But, according to prior observations, the assumption at this time is that she most probably is a woman who had been greatly pampered by all of her family during her early years and cannot bear remembering this indulging family climate because it does not fit into her self-pitying and striving for exceptionality lifestyle. In most cases of unconscious avoidance of preschool memories, ER 6 and 7 would carry on the same theme. Here, however, a breakthrough is happening.

In ER 6 the subject suddenly remembered something that happened in her third year. She even recognizes her resistance to this early memory by stating: "This one I have kept secret from you." She remembered that she went to the beautiful home of her grandparents and her aunt. She stayed there until her sister was born. She then added that up to age 12 she was going home only on the weekends and that she had been much pampered at both places. Her sister then had been very jealous that she had not been allowed to stay with her grandparents as well.

The subject was a sixth semester student in Individual Psychology and probably therefore was able to face her pampered life-style at this point.

In memory 7 she was between 8 and 9 years old. "I remember how I had others wait on me. I sent a girl out to buy a notebook for me."

This memory underlies the demanding life-style of a pampered child.

It seems that in this case, as in a number of parallel cases, her early life-style was: indulgence, special care, and more than average attention paid to a pretty little girl by parents, grandparents, and aunt alike. The child developed an insatiable need for special attention which in adult life she still feels is due her. Her means to strive for this unattainable goal are largely exceptional performance. She is fighting an unbelievably hard and losing battle. Recognition of early childhood reality helps to re-experience love and warmth and social interest and can help a person to set more realistic goals.

4. It has been suggested that a person's ERs change, and the emotional coloring of the ERs change, in accordance with life-style changes during therapy. In longitudinal studies, when ER recordings are made at intervals of six months or a year over a number of years, not only can general changes be noticed, but also specific problem areas not yet cleared up can be identified.

Back to the memories of the 47-year-old school principal, which are recorded under Statement 2. Two years after he gave his first memories, the following ERs were recorded:

ER 1 (age 4). It was in the winter. Father and I were shoveling snow. Then we packed the snow down. After that we sat inside. Father smoked his pipe. It was very pleasant and relaxed.

This memory shows the person's development and maturity. In ER 1—first set—he was sick, was unjustly confined, and was seeking companionship. Set 2 reflects an attitude of cooperation and satisfaction.

In ER 2 (age 2) father had found a dog and had brought him home to the boy. The dog became his most valued possession. He took a piece of rope, tied the dog and took him for a walk. "The neighbor child was jealous," he stated, "I didn't seem to understand."

The dog was something he could control, and this was what he remembered: leading him and making him follow. In the therapeutic session following this recording, too much manipulation was identified as the problem that he would still have to work on.

ER 3 (4 to 5 years old) is a variation of ER 2, Set 1: We played marbles in the yard. The holes had to be hard. My cousin did the fine work while I had to do the rough job because my cousin was not strong enough for that. Then we played. My cousin wanted new rules. The others did not want to play any more. That stopped it, and we were disappointed. First all had wanted to play and then came the disappointment.

The new aspect in this second set is that the subject, although a person of rather small size, feels stronger than his ten months older cousin. His self-image has changed in those two years. Self-worth feeling has increased. This ER of the second set tells of group activity even though it was in a certain way disappointing. Attempts at group cooperation were there, but the subject felt frustrated because he could neither manipulate the group nor assume successful leadership.

ER 4 (age 5). We, fifteen to twenty boys, played in the street. The street was wet from rain. We had played soccer. The subject was happy and went home. There was a stranger in the house who had told mother that he had thrown mud on his jacket. The subject knew nothing about the mud incident and mother believed him. He was very happy that mother trusted him.

He felt unjustly treated in the first two ERs of Set 2. In ER 3, he felt extreme frustration and had a conflict with his brother in ER 4. In Set 2, twenty children are playing happily, which is a reflection of his much improved relationship with his co-workers. He feels trusted by his mother, which reflects an improved relationship with his wife.

ER 5 (4 years old). The little boy visits grandma. He was sick and stayed overnight. Mother's two youngest sisters, aged 2 and 12, were also there. He relates: "I shared the bed with my 12-year-old aunt. I snuggled up to her. This gave me such a beautiful feeling that at first I could not fall asleep. Then I fell asleep anyhow. It was too bad."
This too shows a vastly improved relationship with his wife.

The progress the subject has made during the two-year interval is very clearly reflected in the second set of memories. The first ER set reflects an initial attitude of "I can belong only if I am more miserable and more unjustly treated than the others." To overcome this attitude—still in the first set—he attempts courageous acts such as sticking a fork into his brother, teaching himself to swim, and scaring his mother to death. This leads to the development of being a hero, defending the underdog, and rescuing the drowning. In Set No. 2 a much more cooperative life-style is showing. He still is coping with the problem of control but has come a long way towards developing communal feelings and towards a much more equal and affectionate relationship with his wife.

5. Instant attitudinal changes are reflected in changed early recollections.

In one of the psychological life-style analysis classes, a student (in his early forties) volunteered to be "the case." He had brought a special pillow along, probably to elevate himself and make his performance more impressive. He said that he had participated in many California groups of one kind or another (mostly of the "fad" variety). He had taken them very seriously. He was also familiar with the production of his Alpha brain waves. His life history reflected a subjective memory of extreme suffering. He claimed to have been born in a rural U.S. southern state to an unwed mother, sired by an unknown father, "dumped" at birth in an orphanage, picked up from it by a "paranoid" grandmother (not related to him), and to having been raised and exploited by her. This "paranoid" grandmother later took in also his mother and his mother's later husband. He recalled having been sent out into the streets by "those people" to sell candy bars so that they could buy groceries. This sad story he had told in all his previous groups and thus had achieved his specific goal of personal superiority by having everybody feel extremely sorry for him. What a tremendously great guy he would be had he not had to suffer from all those tragic circumstances! Making himself so miserable was a high price to pay for the attainment of his goal.

In his ER 1 (age 1) he stated: I was standing in my crib, hanging on to the bars, jumping up and down, crying desperately for water. It was very hot. My stepfather came but, instead of bringing me water, he brutally beat me with a brush.

Further recollections expressed a similar "poor me" life-style aspect. He was confronted with his goal to be very special and a superior "showman." Recommendations for change were made and a protocol of the class session was recorded.

One week later, the protocol was read and the student was asked about his thoughts and feelings concerning the last week's session. He started retelling his sad story but was stopped, and it was suggested that his early life could not have been all that bad, that the "grandmother" must have had some kindness in her heart to take into her home an abandoned infant and later the infant's mother and stepfather, and that possibly his mother and "grandmother" had competed for his favors and had indulged and spoiled him. The subject then showed a clear recognition reflex and began to substantiate this hypothesis, seeing his early life now in a completely new light. At this point he was again asked to tell his first memory. He stated that he had told it already and that everybody in the group knew it. Upon insistence though he produced the following:

ER 1 age 1). I was in my crib, standing, holding on to the bars, and jumping up and down happily.

The whole class recognized the change and reacted with amusement. The student wondered what was going on. When told of the difference between these two memories, he denied it and could be convinced only by having reread the previous week's recording, which he had heard just a little earlier.

This incident shows the great sensitivity of ERs in reflecting even temporary attitudinal changes.

Another example of ER changes is the case of a 49-year-old medical consultant, married, with three teenage children. He presented his case in an Adlerian Psychotherapeutic Marathon. He remembered the following:

(Age 3) It was back home, at the northern coast of Germany. My father was a veterinarian. I was placed in a black crib, the feeling was bad. Then he added: I was sad because I did not like the countryside there and liked it much better with my grandparents in the mountains.

After one hour of concentrated therapeutic group work, in which he had temporarily succeeded in changing his negative attitude toward his parents and had recognized the indulgence he had experienced from his grandparents, he was asked to tell his earliest recollections again. He told the following:

I was 3 years old and put to bed at my grandparents' house in the mounutains. The crib was brown. I felt very good because I was the center of attention.

The negative feelings about his parents were no longer dominant. Not only the countryside but even the color of the crib had changed, in a pleasant way. Obviously, the subject had not changed his pampered life-style. (It takes years to change a life-style.) But for the moment he had changed his negative blaming attitude toward his parents and the world in general.

6. It may be of considerable therapeutic value to show the patient that his line of development, as reflected in his first seven ERs, points toward increasing maturity and social interest.

The patient can be shown that he is engaged in finding his true self, which may be better than he had thought it to be. Also the pointing out of growing social interest and progress in cooperation is a genuine encouragement and of prime importance in any therapeutic work.

This maturation trend, however slightly it may be reflected in the early recollection series, is helpful also in establishing a cooperative and socially equal relationship between therapist and patient and counselor and counselee. An early resistance, known as transference in other schools of psychology, can be reduced or eliminated, if the patient is able to recognize in his early memory reflections that he already has started work on his problems; and therewith the therapist needs not be the Almighty. He has already started to change, and further changes will come about through his and the therapist's cooperative endeavor.

It is advisable to record the seven first recollections as early as possible in the diagnostic therapeutic session in order to fixate the initial emotional state of the patient. ER recordings can then be repeated at three months, six months and twelve months intervals to indicate emotional growth or therapeutic progress.

It is recommended that interpretation of ERs not begin during the recording time. However, if the last two recollections indicate positive development, this should be pointed out to the patient, as stated above under Point 6.

A tentative life-style analysis may start after the first seven memories are recorded, and its results can be communicated to the patient if he can handle them at this time. As a rule, this procedure is followed mostly in therapy groups and in marathons, where mini-life-style analyses are done for less severe cases. In individual therapy, and especially with the very neurotic or psychotic patients, the therapist usually keeps his insights to himself until much later and proceeds with further aspects of life-style analysis.

Themes running through early recollections, such as repeated references to "riding in the back seat," "being the chosen one," or "sitting in elevated places," lend themselves as excellent mirrors reflecting the patient's present attitudes and intentions.

The interpretation of early recollections can not be taken lightly. Mistakes can easily be made before one has the total life-style picture. ER interpretation should be acceptable to the patient and evaluated and tested over and over again by further diagnostic material.

References

Ackerknecht, L. K. Il Ruolo dell'analisi dello stile di vita nelle maratone Adleriane. *Rivista di Psicologia Individuale*, 1974, p. 2.

Adler, A. *Understanding human nature.* New York: Greenberg Publisher, 1930.

Adler, A. *What life should mean to you.* New York: Capricorn Books, 1958.

Ansbacher, H. L. Adler's interpretation of early recollections: Historical account. *Journal of Individual Psychology*, 1973, 29.

Dreikurs, R. *Psychodynamics, psychotherapy and counseling.* Chicago: Alfred Adler Institute of Chicago, 1967.

Manaster, G. J. and Perryman, T. B. Early recollections and occupational choice. *Journal of Individual Psychology*, 1974, 20.

Mosak, H. H. and Kopp, R. R. The early recollections of Adler, Freud and Jung. *Journal of Individual Psychology*, 1973, 29.

Papenek, H. The use of early recollections in psychotherapy. *Journal of Individual Psychology*, 1972, 28.

CHAPTER 9

THE DIAGNOSTIC IMPORTANCE OF EARLY RECOLLECTIONS*

PAUL BRODSKY

T HE CLINICAL EXPERIENCE of the psychologist has amply demonstrated that early recollections are furnishing most important diagnostic clues in analyzing character and personality structure. Alfred Adler observes in his *What Life Should Mean to You,* "The memories of early childhood are especially useful in showing how long-standing is the individual's own peculiar approach to life, and in giving the circumstances in which he first crystallized his life attitude."

In his early recollections an individual reveals his conclusions about his relations to the outside world on the basis of his experiences at the time at which he places these memories. Since the individual arrives at these conclusions on the basis of his own interpretations and these interpretations are frequently unnoticed or misunderstood by his surroundings, they prove to be very valuable signposts in determining his psychic make-up or style of life. The individual's conclusions about life, his picture of the outside world, result from his evaluations of many factors in their varying relations; however, in early childhood, these factors are primarily concerned with the immediate surroundings. Therefore, an individual betrays in his early memories, his true concept of his environment, particularly as it concerns his human relationships.

It is not necessary that the individual should actually experience what he purports to recollect. His "memory" may be something he was told about himself, or it may be quite fictional.

* Reprinted by permission from *American Journal of Psychotherapy,* 1952, 6, 484-493.

To the analyst, however, it offers a two-fold diagnostic lead: (1) It emphasizes the importance of the age to which the individual refers his recollection and (2) the fact that he has selected a particular recollection as real proves that for some reason it must have impressed itself upon his mind. The psychic function of this memory is to serve as a guide for approaching the problems of life. Thus an individual's concept of life manifests itself as unformulated pattern in his selection of memories as well as in his complaints and symptoms at the time he produces the recollections. In fact, the selective character of these memories becomes more significant as fresh recollections are produced in accordance with a changing approach towards life. In short, out of the vast storage of childhood memories, only those are recalled which can serve as a justification of the individual's specific approach to life at the time they were reproduced.

In the course of therapy, the changes in attitude as revealed by hitherto unrecalled memories often prove very helpful to the analyst in recognizing progress. In evaluating early recollections, the analyst must always focus his attention upon the relationship of the patient to his surroundings and to the role which he elects to assign to himself. In observing how the patient undertakes to produce these highly indicative early recollections, the therapist will find it very useful to keep in mind the following diagnostic criteria: (1) The patient's approach to the task of reproducing recollections. (2) Indications of organ inferiorities and emotional tendencies. (3) The role the patient assigns to himself in the reproduced recollection. (4) The locale of the recollection. (5) The role assigned by the patient to his mother, father, and/or any other member of the family. (6) The role assigned to other people.

With these general principles in mind we shall demonstrate on hand of two case histories the usefulness of our approach.

The first case is that of W., a twelve-year-old boy, interviewed by the therapist before he discussed the situation with the parents. His earliest recollection in his own words was as follows: "At Yosemite I saw a deer in the snow. That is all. I must have been very little. It is sort of blurred in my memory."

This recollection can be broken down into three separate

entities: (a) "At Yosemite I saw a deer in the snow. That is all." (b) "I must have been very little." (c) "It is sort of blurred in my memory." Applying the six diagnostic considerations mentioned above, let us see what we can make of this recollection:

(1) *The patient's approach.* W. produces the memory readily, talking very rapidly in a rather flippant way with little movement of his lips. He tries to give himself an air of "bigness." He appears unconcerned about revealing his memory; as he "drops" it in parts he leaves it to the therapist to pick up the fragments. His tendency to give no more than asked for is shown in his remark "that is all." In this light, the apparent need to volunteer the closing sentence, "it is sort of blurred in my memory," becomes particularly significant. It is as if to forestall any suggestion to elaborate on the recollection.

From his manner of approach we can tentatively conclude that W. is cooperative on his own terms only, that is, when he sees a chance to become the center of interest. We suspect that he rarely finishes anything, that he leaves it to others to pick up after him. He hides his self-consciousness behind a mask of self-assurance but is cautious about revealing himself.

(2) *Indications of organ inferiorities and emotional tendencies.* The memory begins with a visual impression but continues with a reference to W.'s small size. Although for the small child vision is the foremost means of contact with the outer world, a visual impression related in an early recollection assumes particular significance. A child with normal vision will take the effortless use of his eyes for granted as in contrast to a child who, because of some visual impairment, has to put more effort into seeing what others see. Consequently in recollections with a predominant visual impression the existence of a possible inferiority in the visual sphere may betray itself. In our case this suspicion is further strengthened by the use of the word "blurred," a term which describes a visual impression.

While we must be careful not to read into the "recollection" anything that is not furnished by the patient, we must constantly be on the lookout for the more subtle indicators of emotional experiences because they are by their very nature less subject to formulation at the moment of experiencing them, to say nothing of being more prone to being withheld at the time of reproduction.

With regard to emotional tendencies we can, at the moment, discover nothing in the recollection that indicates a deviation from what is considered to be normal. W. saw a deer in the snow. Using the most common educational patterns in fostering desirable feelings the rare sight of animals in the snow in this part of the country has been associated in the child with feelings of friendliness and "cuteness."

However, when we consider W.'s allusion to his size ("I must have been very little"), we realize that it might be a definite clue to his personality structure. Awaiting more corroborative evidence, we may suspect that W. interprets "bigness" merely as a condition for maintaining his prestige in a world of adults. Perhaps he views the time when he was small as a time when he enjoyed a dominant position and was the center of interest particularly when he was on vacation with his family or others and away from the accustomed home milieu. At the time he produces the memory, however, this situation belongs to the past, a lost paradise. It seems that here is a pampered child, possibly an only child, and a child already so discouraged by the difficulties of growing up that he postulates "bigness" as a goal for overcoming his painful feelings of inferiority. True enough, he may be small for his age, and his physical constitution may not be up to par. However, he appears somehow anxious to achieve superiority without being yet ready to function on his age level, lest failure should be experienced by him as loss in personal value.

(3) *The patient's own role.* W. appears to be an onlooker, since in his recollection no active participation is indicated. All he does is see a deer. If, as seems likely, his formula for dealing adequately with his environment is "I am so small that I cannot do anything by myself," he will, in all probability, develop that kind of aggressive passivity which forces others to do their utmost to make him do the least. Hence his normal feeling of inferiority becomes greatly exaggerated and he now tends to restrict his field of action.

(4) *Locale of the recollection.* The fact that some interesting event outside his home is produced can be taken as an indication

that W.'s home experience was not a satisfactory one. Apparently, he feels more "at home" away from home even in his memory. While traveling, he feels himself more the center of the adult's care. It would be important to find out with whom he took the trip. If he is a pampered child, as we suspect, he will prefer a situation in which less demands will be made upon him, such as a trip. At the same time the closeness of traveling with those in whose care he was will provide a feeling of security and protection.

(5) *Role assigned to mother, father, and other members of the family.* It will be noted that no member of the child's family appears in the recollection. This fact strengthens our suspicion that W.'s relations to his family are not good. This can, of course also indicate, that perhaps there is no family, that W. is an orphan, etc. but the trip to Yosemite National Park at an early age makes that rather unlikely. Yet even if there were no parents, one should expect to find some indications as to the relations to those with whom he traveled if these relations had been experienced by him as being friendly. Quite probably there has been some failure on the part of the parents to help W. to realize the reciprocity in human relations. Since he came to think of care, attention, and pampering as something to which he was entitled to, he was quite unprepared to relate himself properly to others. Being over-protected he could not tolerate any change in the atmosphere that surrounded him without deep disturbance. Instead of being ready to accept the functions and responsibilities of his age level his emotional response to any diminution in care and attention is one of resentment at being let down by "deserters."

(6) *Role assigned to other people.* Assuming that W. had been taken on this trip by people who were not members of his family, they, too, do not appear in his recollection. Although W., as any other child, has enough contact with other people during the routine life of his family, he hardly takes notice of them. He speaks only about himself. It seems, to him, people are important only insofar as they provide something for him. He takes it for granted to find himself on the receiving end. His strong tendency towards self-centeredness and to staying

away from life is further indicated by the fact that the only living thing worth remembering is an animal, the deer in the snow.

If our hypothesis is correct we may expect W. to be very cautious in his social relations. Not being prepared to give, to be of value and service to others, he will always be found to receive and to expect to be given. To share, to cooperate, to consider the rights of others will be quite difficult for him. He will prefer the company of people older than himself who are willing to make allowances for him, rather than risk contact with his own age group which will expect him to share their interests and to cooperate.

Summary: W. appears to be an only child. He has an inferiority of his visual track and probably is below his age level in size and weight. He has probably been overprotected since he shows signs of pampering. He is too discouraged to assume an active attitude in dealing with the problems of life on his age level and, consequently, feels insecure. Contributive to this insecurity is probably an unharmonious home atmosphere. He tries to achieve security by maintaining a strong dependency on his surroundings. While this gives him a feeling of superiority, he thereby avoids meeting problems on his own and escapes to be confronted with his limitations which he evaluates as inferiorities.

Outline of case history. Interviews with the parents and case study reveal the following facts: W. was an only child. He was wanted by his mother more than by his father; mother was very emotional during pregnancy. The birth was a forceps birth with no injuries. W. was nursed until age four months; he used to fall asleep during nursing and had to be awakened. During the first fourteen months the baby suffered from colds and diarrhoea. X-ray pictures show a difference in the attachment of the hips of about half an inch. W. complains about pains in his left ankle when running. At age of two the right eye "turned in"; at four years W. is given glasses and a patch for corrective training. At the age of six an eye doctor considers the condition as incorrigible with possible blindness at the age of twenty-five. At seven he has a tonsillectomy. At present W. has to undergo eye exercises, he attends a posture class and has to exercise his feet.

During the first year of the child the parents separated and rejoined. Father given to drinking brutalized the family until, under therapy, he gave up drinking and became a devoted father and husband. Mother, however, cannot completely shake off some fear of him. Father has definite concepts about his child's responsibilities, is more definite in his expectations and very down to earth. Mother intellectually overambitious tries to dominate her husband by her power of reasoning. She is rather lenient to the child and tends to rationalize his behavior. Mother's left eye is affected with ulcus serpens, vision on both eyes impaired.

The three keep constantly close together; one parent rarely going out without the other. If at all possible, the child is always with them. If left alone, he is resentful and keeps track of where the parents go. The parents complain about the boy being untidy and uncooperative. He does not mind and is disrespectful to parents and unfriendly to others. Some difficulties with conduct at school, negligence with home work and frequency in losing things are also pointed out in the complaints of W.'s parents.

W. is irritated by his parents' frequent arguments with one another. He likes to watch college boys playing ball and to get stray balls for them. He likes to go window shopping by himself. His hobby is carrier pigeons. He also likes to draw and to cook.

In the light of the facts in the case history the personality picture as deducted from his recollection appears to be quite correct, although a deductive diagnosis from a single recollection should always be a tentative one.

As above demonstrated, a single recollection can successfully be used to establish an individual's personality structure. However, the analysis of two or more memories, given at the same time, will prove of inestimable value in corroborating findings. Since the recollections usually show a striking similarity in their main content they may further reveal the purposiveness in helping the individual to uphold his concept of his role in life. Analyzing each recollection along the lines suggested, the conclusions of each will serve to support the findings of the others and thus provide a reliable check on the overall analysis.

In presenting the second case history the author will postpone to give his conclusions as based on the analysis of the patient's early recollections. He will limit himself to stating the main elements while leaving it to the trained observer to see in these elements the problems with which the patient finds herself confronted while attempting to meet the problems imposed upon her by her home situation.

It must be kept in mind that the therapist has to understand each patient as a singular psychophysical unit which developed out of the interplay between the particular individual and the particular environment of his childhood. It is this singularity of each personality which makes it impossible for the Adlerian school of thought to accept any psychological "type" or "category." With that in mind it will be understandable that the validity of the analyst's interpretations of the main elements in the recollection will depend on how closely they correspond with the patient's own interpretations at the time these elements are produced. In order to present more dramatically the relation between the patient's interpretation of her experiences and the validity of the interpretation in the analysis of the memories we shall first look at the case history given in the form of complaints and information by the parents and the patient:

Complaints of the parents: Even when she was a little baby, her mother could not keep her in her crib. She runs around with the wrong kind of people. She stays out until past midnight. Her boyfriends are much older and of the wrong kind. She is disrespectful towards her parents, especially towards her mother. She attempted to run away from home. She is getting into troubles with the school because the teachers are not good. Father states, that in in his opinion, his wife's inability to have a child is due to her frigidity.

Complaints of the child: Her parents treat her like a baby. Father and mother are trying to exercise too tight a control over everything she does. They continually check up on her friends, causing the latter to withdraw from her. They do not allow her to go out and have fun. She says: "I am afraid of father and hate mother. Why can't I like my parents and like to be home as the other girls do?" She is afraid of staying alone. At the age of eight when left in care of some friends of her parents, while they went to a party, the friend's grown-up son tried three times to seduce her. While in quarantine with a severe case of measles her parents had a fine time leaving her in care of an "old woman." The child was an only child, adopted at the age of five months; she had been informed about her adoption.

The patient in question, a girl, aged fifteen produced during the first interview three early recollections:

First recollection: "My mother told me things. She told me, when I was two or three years old I had a strep infection; put in the hospital they thought I was going to die. They had to safety-pin me down to the bed: I walked down the hall, wanted to go home, with the mattress pinned to me."

Second recollection: "When I was four or five, boys lived up the street; we used to fight. They tied me to a tree and bashed my head against the tree. They all cried when I left for S. I was six or seven years at that time."

Third recollection: "Probably age four or five. Remembers making ashtrays in kindergarten at S.

Now let us break down these recollections into their main elements and indicate their meaning:

Main elements	*Meaning*
First recollection:	
Her mother is the principle	"My mother told me things." counterpart opposite whom she plays her role in life.
". . . put in the hospital they thought I was going to die."	Misinterpreting her placement in the hospital she feels put out when in danger. She registered her serious condition as a means to experience importance to her parents.

"They had to safety-pin me down to the bed. I walked down the hall wanted to go home with the mattress pinned to me."

They can not do that to her: keeping her from home. The hospital was a real shock to her: the parents who deserted her and the others who tried to hold her back. No one can be trusted. Yet again she experiences others getting worried, as she walks down the hall; she might get worse.

Second recollection:

"Boys lived up the street; we used to fight."

She meets the other sex in competition. It is important for her to prove to be as good as they are, possibly superior.

"They tied me to a tree and bashed my head against the tree."

Being tied up is the worst that can happen to her; it means to get hurt. Others, boys, are out to get you, beware. My folks are not here when I am in danger. They better watch out for me; I might get hurt.

"They all cried when I left."

She again believes to be of importance to those whom she accuses of treating her wrongly. When she is gone they begin to worry about her.

Third recollection:

"Remember making ashtrays in kindergarten at S."

Again it is not home she remembers. She is sent away to kindergarten. If they treated her right she could do things all right, she could be a good girl.

By merely placing the main elements of the recollections in juxtaposition to their meaning according to the patient's concepts, one can easily obtain a picture of her personality structure with considerable verisimilitude. Of course, this preliminary sketch will have to be filled in into full portraiture in the course of subsequent interviews. Nevertheless using only the clues provided by the three recollections, one can confidently expect ample confirmation of the preliminary conclusions.

The patient is struggling for security. She is afflicted with greatly disturbed parent relations and tied up with her mother in a bitter fight for dominance. She is disturbed about her sex role and will produce symptoms of a strong "masculine protest." Distrusting other people she uses the threat of getting hurt (physically or emotionally) to make her parents watch over her as a means of domination. She overevaluates her own importance in order to achieve a fictitious sense of values rather than being prepared to gain recogniiton through constructive means, of which, however, she is capable. Her goal is superiority by making herself "precious." Her style of life is characterized by running away from the problems she finds herself confronted with instead of facing them. She uses the threat "to get hurt" as a tool to assure herself the closeness of her parents. As she needs people to accomplish her goal, she will appear to be "outgoing" though in reality she is completely self-centered.

In conclusion it can be said that in the analysis of early recollections we have singular means to approach the dynamics of an individual's character development. As the memories give us important clues for the understanding of an individual's relations to his surroundings they help reveal his total personality and his concept of life.

Bibliography

1. Adler, Alfred: *The Science of Living.* Garden City Publishing Co., Garden City, N.Y., 1929.
2. Adler, Alfred: *What Life Should Mean to You.* Grossett and Dunlap, New York, N.Y., 1931.
3. Adler, Alfred: *Social Interest: A Challenge to Mankind,* 3rd ed. Translated by John Linton, M.A. and Richard Vaughan Latimer, Trend and Co., Ltd., Plymouth, 1945.
4. Wexberg, L. Erwin: *Individual Psychology.* Translation, Cosmopolitan Book Corp., N.Y., 1931.

CHAPTER 10

"THE WILLHITE": A CREATIVE EXTENSION OF THE EARLY RECOLLECTION PROCESS*

ROBERT G. WILLHITE

Fantasy is but another creative faculty of the soul . . . Just as the projection of certain memories into the sharp focus of consciousness, or the erection of the bizarre super-structures of the imagination, fantasy and day-dreaming are to be considered part of the creative activity of the soul. (Adler, 1927, p. 57)

EACH OF US HAS no doubt had occasion when the interpretation of an Early Recollection did not flow smoothly or, despite best efforts, the client could not (or would not) comprehend the interpretation. I found myself facing such a situation in 1975 while working with an anxious, self-doubting client, Gil. He had not given me a well-defined overall feeling for the Early Recollection, and I was stuck; I couldn't get him to accept my explanation. In an attempt to clarify the meaning for him, I went to the board and wrote out the recollection verbatim and broke it into logical segments, thus:

1. I am playing catch with my father on the front lawn.
2. It's a very soft ball—a big padded ball.
3. We are throwing it back and forth.
4. I realize he's not having fun.
5. He's teaching me. He's looking down on me. That's the reason he's doing this.

---

* Reproduced by permission of Willhite and Associates.

6. It's his responsibility to make me better.
7. I don't know how to be better.
   [Overall feeling:]
8. I'll never be able to do it well enough.

To my chagrin, he still did not grasp my explanation. Since he was elaborating about how life is for him, it occurred to me to ask him how he wished life would be, and I wrote these statements in a second vertical column, opposite to those of the original recollection. Because I knew the way situations worked out for him were consistent with the original recollection—not the revised story in the second column—I assumed that the revised recollection represented his self-ideal, while the original memory was consistent with his self-concept. What I now had on the board was:

Self-Concept	*Self-Ideal*
1. I am playing catch with my father on the front lawn.	I am playing catch with my father on the front lawn.
2. It's a very soft ball—a big padded ball.	We're throwing the ball back and forth.
3. We are throwing it back and forth.	He throws the ball to me and I fumble it.
4. I realize he's not having fun.	I run after it, pick it up and throw it back to him.
5. He's teaching me. He's looking down on me. That's the reason he's doing this.	We're laughing and having a good time.
6. It's his responsibility to make me better.	We start talking about things.
7. I don't know how to be better.	He's listening to me.
[Overall feeling:]	[Overall feeling:]
8. I'll never be able to do it well enough.	Loved.

Returning to the original Early Recollection (the *Self-Concept*), I had Gil tell me the emotions appropriate to each of the frames. Then I had him imagine what emotions would be involved in the idealized story in the second column (the *Self-Ideal*). By this means I was able to tune into what feelings and emotions he would use in the *Self-Ideal* to affect change. Recall that the original memory and the *Self-Ideal* were written opposite one another; therefore it was quickly evident at what point he would have to create different emotions in order to avoid the pattern shown in the Early Recollection.

Self-Concept	*Self-Ideal*
1. I am playing catch with my father on the front lawn.	I am playing catch with my father on the front lawn.
(Apprehensive, Nervous)	(Joyful, Warm)
2. It's a very soft ball—a big padded ball.	We're throwing the ball back and forth.
("A Fact")	(Caring, Closeness, Warmth, Trust)
3. We are throwing it back and forth.	He throws the ball to me and I fumble it.
(Fear, Anticipation of What Is Going To Happen Next)	(Disappointed, Frustrated, Impatient)
4. I realize he's not having fun.	I run after it, pick it up and throw it back to him.
(Fear, Confusion, Concerned)	(Confident, Proud, Energized)
5. He's teaching me. He's looking down on me. That's the reason he's doing this.	We're laughing and having a good time.
(Inferior, Small, Tight)	(Accepted, Elated, Energized)
6. It's his responsibility to make me better.	We start talking about things.
("A Fact")	(Warm, Worthy, Trust)
7. I don't know how to be better.	He's listening to me.

(H e l p l e s s, Abandoned,   (Understood, Content)
Lonely, Inadequate)
[Overall feeling:]   [Overall feeling:]
8. (I'll Never Be Able To Do   (Loved.)
It Well Enough.)

Since that day two years ago, I have used this same basic technique—which has come to be known as "The Willhite"—with hundreds of clients. Out of this experience I have developed some refinements which help the client to quickly grasp the hidden logic and his/her unique psychological modus operandi.

I always have the client dictate the *Self-Ideal* frame by frame (comparing it to the *Self-Concept* while doing so) so that each column has the same number of action-emotion components. This format prevents the client from skipping over those portions which are indicative of anxiety and/or denial. At the conclusion of the Early Recollection the client gives me a word or phrase which is descriptive of the overall feeling of the memory. I also get an overall feeling to write in as the last frame of the *Self-Ideal*, so that the two are graphically analogous. I number the frames for convenience.

Although the original Early Recollection (the *Self-Concept*) is not to be changed in any way, I instruct the client that he/she is free to add or delete emotions as I am writing it on the blackboard. The *Self-Ideal* (revised Early Recollection) can also be reworked. It is often a bit of a struggle for the client to develop the *Self-Ideal* fantasy and it is necessary to encourage him/her to be innovative and flexible.

One simple and useful therapeutic tool is my "Feelings List." This is a piece of paper on which I have listed about 150 emotions, plus a section briefly describing commonly used defenses. A person who is highly defended, or who comes from a family which had a "no-talk rule," or who is experienced in behavior-oriented therapy may sincerely not know how to identify specific feelings or emotions. I have the list available for the client to refer to during our sessions. The person who is searching for a descriptive word for a feeling will skim the list and will consider only those words which are consistent and appropriate; words that are irrelevant will be disregarded.

Before the emotional component is added to the Early Recollection I instruct the client that if one of the thought-units does not elicit any emotion whatever it will be called "a fact." Other words may be used by the client which are essentially equivalent to no recalled emotion—such as "confused," "blah," or "bored."

When the client uses "a fact" or an equivalent term in place of an emotion, it is a tip-off that this is precisely the point at which he/she is blocking. At that moment in the past the person probably could not identify what the feelings were. His/her subsequent behavior was a cover-up act, making it impossible for others to know what the feelings really were. The client deceives himself/herself and others at the same time, which feeds into and amplifies the self-delusion.

When working with "The Willhite" it is important for the therapist to record everything the client says from the beginning of the recollection to the end. The inclusion of supposedly objective explanations, parenthetical information, distracting phrases, etc. is crucial to a correct and poignant analysis. It is precisely this apparently inconsequential data which often reveals where the client is repressing, blocking, or resisting getting in touch with his/her feelings. In so many instances these nervous or distracting comments directly precede a painful part of the memory—softening its impact and easing the pain. This may also mark the point at which the person unconsciously decided to skew the interactional process by using his/her emotions as a manipulative tool. When reviewing the emotional sequence with the client, I spend some time trying to get him/her in touch with what the feeling really was at that point.

I explain to the client that where "a fact" or other non-emotion word is inserted in place of an actual emotion that at that moment in the episode he/she was probably behaving in such a way that he/she could not identify what the feelings were. The conscious picks up that as no feeling; therefore, the frame gets labeled "a fact" or some such innocuous term. Now I help the client search more deeply for a believable feeling and reconstruct the episode. He/she is then able to realize that this part of the memory has been purposively discounted or repressed.

The next step of "The Willhite" is to list just the emotional sequence on the blackboard. This graphically illustrates in a terse and easily comprehensible form his/her personal interactional style and perception of life. I explain to the client that this is an emotional set-up which he/she has created—leading to a self-fulfilling prophecy that invariably confirms one's expectations about life. A quick reading of the sequence of emotions reveals the psychodynamics which the client typically employs toward the outcome of relationships, and I can pinpoint where the negative or pathological attitude and accompanying behavior is first manifested. (This is invariably near the beginning of the Early Recollection of a troubled person.) I explain that this emotional set-up—and the progession of events which ensues—is designed to confirm one's expectations about life. The client nearly always responds to this with quick recognition —that "Aha!" response which is a prelude to opening up to insight and change.

Returning to Gil's case, the emotional sequence for the *Self-Concept* reads:

1. Apprehensive, Nervous
2. "A Fact"
3. Fear, Anticipation of What Is Going to Happen Next
4. Fear, Confusion, Concerned
5. Inferior, Small, Tight
6. "A Fact"
7. Helpless, Abandoned, Lonely, Inadequate [Overall Feeling]
8. I'll Never Be Able To Do It Well Enough.

The emotional sequence is typical for Gil; this theme—and variations on it—appears repeatedly in his life. Without being cognizant of it he sets himself up for the same denouement in a variety of guises—"I'll never be able to do it well enough."

I teach clients that emotions are not random physical events nor merely responses to environmental stimuli, but rather that they are a vital force which can be harnessed and used to enhance relationships and realize positive personal goals. A clear understanding of emotions is a prerequisite to putting new feelings onto behavior patterns. By discovering and affirming various emotions people can become responsible for controlling their behavior.

I actively work to change the pattern of emotions which were employed to reach and reinforce the conclusion of the *Self-Concept*. That change requires (in addition to the client's willingness to work) a therapeutic intervention—i.e. information, insight, retraining, accurate feedback, and an opportunity to practice the new behaviors in a safe environment.

At this point it is very helpful to have the client describe a current interactional problem with which he/she is having dfficulty. Going beyond the statement of the problem, the client also describes how he/she imagines the episode will unfold and what the conclusion will be. As with the *Self-Concept* (the original Early Recollection) and the *Self-Ideal* (the revised Early Recollection), I write the client's description out word for word (on paper), separating it into thought-units, and add the emotions appropriate to each unit. Now the client has revealed in detail how his/her private logic is going to be put to work to reach a negative or unhealthy outcome. I then transfer the current problem to the blackboard. I do not, however, write it out literally as I did for the *Self-Concept* and the *Self-Ideal*. In order to expose the underlying pattern I fit the episode into a format involving the same number of frames as the *Self-Concept* and the *Self-Ideal*. This usually involves compressing the data. Occasionally there is an apparent gap in the sequence; I simply ask the client to fill it in for me. This rather arbitrary reconstruction of the current example (which I call the *Private-Logic-At-Work*) is necessary; most clients are more verbal about current events (*Private-Logic-At-Work*) than about memories (*Self-Concept*) or possible alternatives (*Self-Ideal*).

When we compare the *Private-Logic-At-Work* sequence to

the *Self-Concept* it is usually remarkably analogous. Because the *Self-Concept* is a prototype for the private logic, the dysfunctional pattern persists. The client is again drawn down into the familiar transaction and unhappy conclusion. He/she sincerely believes in the inevitability of the outcome which speciously "proves" that the private logic is unalterable.

Let's take a look at Gil's *Private-Logic-At-Work* (which was adjusted somewhat to make it fit the pre-existing eight-frame format, p. 116).

Interpretation of "The Willhite"

Self-Concept

The *Self-Concept*—Gil's original Early Recollection—shows that he has strong feelings of inadequacy but does not know how he sets himself up to carry off the pattern. The Early Recollection, with the feelings inserted, is a revelation of how the process is set up.

The first step in the analysis is to look at the end—because the last frame or two will state, usually quite literally, the person's goal in life and his/her basic perception of what life is like. Knowing this makes it easier to comprehend the private logic which is employed to attain this goal while subtly disguising the mechanics involved. The Early Recollection gives us a candid glimpse of the person's personality with the underpinnings laid bare. Remember that behavior has two purposes: (1) to achieve the goal per se and (2) to hide the interactional mechanics sufficiently so that the person's private logic—erroneous as it may be—is left intact. Gil's intended goal is to avoid taking responsibility and to justify that avoidance. This goal is obvious from the feelings in Frame 7—"helpless, abandoned, lonely, inadequate"—and from the succinctly stated conclusion in Frame 8—"I'll never be able to do it well enough." Since these are Gil's own words he is not in a position to deny their validity as part of his behavior pattern. Notice that the last two frames of the *Private-Logic-At-Work* (center column), which is a description of a current relationship, highlights the same conclusion. Gil's private logic—seemingly so fragile—is

Self-Concept	Private-Logic-At-Work	Self-Ideal
1. I am playing catch with my father on the front lawn.	I TRY TO KEEP A DIALOGUE GOING WITH MY WIFE WHEN I REALLY DON'T WANT TO.	I am playing catch with my father on the front lawn.
(apprehensive, nervous)	(WORTHWHILE; PUTTING MYSELF FORWARD)*	(joyful, warm)
2. It's a very soft ball – a big padded ball.	I TRY TO BE CORRECT – TO SAY SOMETHING CORRECT SO SHE CAN'T ARGUE WITH ME.	We're throwing the ball back and forth.
("a fact")	(ANTICIPATING TROUBLE)	(caring, closeness, warmth, trust)
3. We are throwing it back and forth.	SHE WINS BY CHANGING THE ISSUE.	He throws the ball to me and I fumble it.
(fear, anticipation of what is next)	(ANGER, FRUSTRATION, BETRAYED, VULNERABLE)	(disappointed, frustrated, impatient)
4. I realize he's not having fun.	I REALIZE I AM GOING TO LOSE.	I run after it, pick it up, and throw it back to him.
(fear, confusion, concerned)	(APPREHENSION, FEAR, CONFUSED)	(confident, proud, energized)
5. He's teaching me. He's looking down on me. That's the reason he's doing this.	I SENSE THE FUTILITY OF THE DISCUSSION.	We're laughing and having a good time.
(inferior, small, tight)	(DESPAIR, INADEQUATE)	(accepted, elated, energized)
6. It's his responsibility to make me better.	SHE SEEMS TO HAVE A CORNER ON IRREFUTABLE TRUTH.	We start talking about things.
("a fact")	(FRUSTRATED, ANGRY)	(warm, worthy, trust)
7. I don't know how to be better.	I WANT TO LEAVE.	He's listening to me.
(helpless, abandoned, lonely, inadequate)	(USELESS, INADEQUATE)	(understood, content)
8. (Overall feeling:) (I'll never be able to do it well enough.)	(OVERALL FEELING:) (SHE ALWAYS WINS – ABANDONED, LONELY)	(Overall feeling:) (loved)

* The apparently inconsistent feeling in this frame
is explained in the following interpretation.

iron-clad; this design is the "scarlet thread" which keeps appearing in his life. Other memories and current relationships will also unwittingly fall into this same pattern unchallenged, since Gil unconsciously engineers the outcome. Compare this with the outcome Gil fantasizes in Frames 7 and 8 of the *Self-Ideal* (third column)—to be content, understood, and loved.

Returning to the *Self-Concept,* we see that he enters the interaction with an apprehensive and nervous feeling (Frame 1), probably because he sees the other person (his father in this case) as awesome and overwhelming. We know that he does not deal with the feelings because he inserts the mundane sentence, "It's a very soft ball." When I asked him to identify a feeling or emotion for this sentence he could not, to him it was merely "a fact." I have found that whenever "a fact" appears in the emotional sequence it shows precisely where the person is not in touch with his/her feelings; it can also be an indication of which specific feelings the person is afraid to express. In this case, the position of the "fact" tells me that Gil does not deal with his apprehension and fear of not being able to measure up—products of his low self-esteem. This was the hunch I played, and he confirmed it with a recognition response. I can now show Gil how—by not dealing with his fear—he is setting himself up to fail.

Frame 3 of the *Self-Concept* shows what happens even when the other person cooperates; Gil still shows apprehension and fear about what is going to happen next. Gil's attitude, "I'll never be able to do it well enough," supports the low self-esteem. Gil is putting himself down by elevating his father; father is elevated by Gil's rationalization in Frame 4 that father is not having fun. This further supports his feelings of inadequacy. The first four frames show how Gil has carefully set up this process—filtering the action through his predetermined perceptions about life—so that it appears to be someone else's fault (father's) that he feels inadequate.

Frame 5 reinforces his low self-worth with the statement, "He's teaching me. He's looking down on me." The feelings associated with this frame—inferior and small—clearly feed into the intended goal. Since this is now an absolute for Gil he carries his self-deception one step further by making the whole thing father's responsibility (Frame 6). Since the feeling of inadequacy is so strong Gil won't take responsibility for it himself; rather he assigns the responsibility to his father. This frame was labeled "a fact"; Gil had no awareness of an accompanying emotion. We can conjecture that he doesn't dare confront the person he is so dependent on, probably because of fear of losing the relationship. The "fact" no doubt also covers his anger which he must desperately conceal and deny.

Frames 7 and 8 show the total emotional bankruptcy with the declaration, "I don't know how to be better." The feelings of helplessness, loneliness, inadequacy, and abandonment now potentiate the low self-esteem, and also reinforce the fear that if he asserts himself he will be rejected or abandoned. "I'll never be able to do it well enough" (Frame 9) is his erroneous conviction about life.

The *Self-Concept* as a whole reveals the self-fulfilling behavior pattern in detail; Gil has an opportunity to learn by examining the step-by-step process.

Private-Logic-at-Work

In the *Private-Logic-at-Work* sequence (center column) we analyze a specific on-going situation with which the client is having difficulty. In Gil's case we see how his persistent low self-concept colors his relationship with his wife. Gil—not his wife—initiates the attitudes and concommitant behaviors which will once again confirm his belief about life: He doesn't measure up, but it's someone else's fault.

In Frame 1 he takes the lead in the interaction—"I try to keep a dialogue going with my wife when I really don't want to. He has now shown us how he controls the opening gambit with his negative attitude; the self-fulfilling prophecy is already set in motion. The feelings he states for this frame, "worthwhile; putting myself forward," indicate he is not consciously aware of the apprehension and nervousness indicated in the recollection; he is denying these very discomforting stirrings by using the defense of false feeling of worthiness. He carries this self-delusion into Frame 2 and sets himself up by "trying to be correct" so she can't argue with him. This defensiveness is an effort to protect himself from the feelings of inadequacy which are threatening to surface. The emotion he states is "anticipating trouble." One can guess at this point that he will emerge' from this encounter in a one-down position. He does not deny his feelings quite as vigorously in this instance as he did in Frame 2 of the *Self-Concept,* which was "a fact." This observation can be used to help Gil gain insight into how he sets himself up for another failure.

Next (Frame 3), "She wins by changing the issue." This is the ploy by which he deceives himself into believing that his wife is responsible for the impending interactional disaster. How artfully this fits into Gil's goal in life—avoidance of responsibility and justification for that avoidance. His feelings here of anger, frustration, betrayal, and vulnerabiilty combine to set the stage for Frame 4: the apprehension and fear of realizing that he is going to lose. His confusion is a device to smoke-screen his emotional bankruptcy. In Frame 5 he "senses the futility" (with supporting feelings of despair and inadequacy) and gives up any power he might have had when he says, "She seems to have a corner on irrefutable truth." His frustration and anger are more out front here than in the *Self-Concept* where this frame was labeled "a fact." Nonetheless, at this point he is self-victimized and can do very little about it. His only recourse (as he perceives the situation) is to leave, which he expresses a desire to do in Frame 7. This is the feeling of uselessness and inadequacy that Gil promotes leading to a "such is life" conclusion of: "Others always win, and I am abandoned and left to feel lonely." This is consistent with Frame 8 of the *Self-Concept—*"I'll never be able to do it well enough." Many times a client is not consciously aware of this progression, but with this method he/she becomes aware of the subtle ways in which the progression is predetermined by the fictive goal. The *Self-Concept* revealed by the Early Recollection and the life story revealed by the private logic are analogous because they are based on the biased perceptions the person has learned and nurtured.

Self-Ideal

The feelings of the *Self-Ideal* form a different pattern than those of the *Self-Concept* and *Private-Logic-at-Work*, yet they are still within the framework of the person's potential for interacting. This set-up has also been created by the client and is available to get him out of the self-fulfilling emotional bind. Gil's *Self-Ideal* shows—via his fantasy about how he would like life to be—how he would be willing to consider modifying his behavior to reach a better conclusion.

Sometimes people have the perception that in order for life to be different for them, others have to change. This is particularly true of the person who has chosen the victim role; he feels that no matter what he does "they" will keep him from succeeding. In Gil's case he is still willing to risk playing catch with his father (Frame 1), indicating he is willing to try to do somethng different with the relationship. The significant difference is that Gil has chosen a joyful, warm feeling to replace the feelings of nervousness and apprehension of the *Self-Concept*. This in itself initiates a shift in the pattern of behavior, setting him up for what he wishes for—caring, closeness, warmth, and trust (Frame 2). This attitude is an appropriate one and can lead to his fantasized goal—to be loved (Frame 8).

The key to the behavior change is the identification of the emotions or feelings involved; when Gil gets in touch with these he can volitionally alter his behavior pattern. It is this identification of feelings permitting the shift to new behaviors which is the strength of the Willhite method. I have found that people don't change until they are given alternatives backed up by feelings that are consistent with their private logic.

Frame 3 of the *Self-Ideal* shows Gil still flirting with failure, but just having been fortified with caring, closeness, warmth, and trust (Frame 2), he can now respond to fumbling the ball appropriately with disappointment, impatience, and frustration. This is quite different from the corresponding feelings in Frame 3 of the *Self-Concept*—fear, anticipation of what is going to happen next. The disappointment of fumbling the ball, however, opens up the opportunity for him to run after it and throw it back to his father (Frame 4). Here Gil assumes the courage to take a risk. With the feelings of confidence, pride, and being energized, he has now set into motion the new pattern of behavior which facilitates change.

Now he is faced with considering a new conclusion as a result of his efforts. Many times a client wishes to stop in the construction of his/her story at this point but to allow him/her to do so would overlook handling the feelings and emotions in the remaining frames; in both the *Self-Concept* and the *Private-Logic-at-Work* these are devastating. By being forced to fill in all the open frames Gil has to create a new ending for the story—and so he continues. In Frame 5 both he and his father are laughing and having a good time; this reinforces feeling accepted, elated, and energized. Frame 6 shows Gil sharing equally again—"We start talking about things." The feelings of warm, worthy, and trust fortify this behavior and allow him to progress in Frame 7 to entertain the notion that someone would want to listen to him. And this leads to feelings of being understood and contentment.

The overall feeling of the *Self-Ideal* is that of being loved. The way Gil got there was by counting himself as an equal and being able to risk trusting and being close (Frame 2). The task of therapy now becomes an effort to encourage Gil to factualize the fantasy of the *Self-Ideal* by deliberately creating the emotions that were identified.

As a therapist my goal is, of course, to disrupt that sequence which leads to dysfunctional behavior by changing the conclusion about life. By using the information the client has provided for the *Self-Ideal* it is clear just how (and how much) the client is willing to change. And it is clear how the pattern of emotions must be altered in order to effect a new and more desirable outcome.

The Early Recollection, in addition to being a diagnostic aid for the therapist, contains within itself the seeds of a dynamic phenomenological process, therapeutic in and of itself, and made possible by the creative use of fantasy on the part of the client.

I have found this method to be an excellent tool for uncovering psychological mechanisms as well as an opportunity to become closely involved with the client in a situation where he/she is comfortable, interested, and relatively nondefensive. A meaningful, therapist-client interaction is the most effective way of building trust and effecting change.

Inherent in this process is a belief in the creative potential of human beings, with the opportunity for expressing that creativity given the client through the fantasy of the *Self-Ideal*. Related to this is implied faith in the ability of the client to change, to take charge of and be responsible for his/her own life, with the therapist providing encouragement. "The Willhite" is an exercise in change, an experiential introduction to the therapeutic mode.

As an Adlerian psychotherapist I subscribe, of course, to an ideographic philosophy based on the following axioms:

1. All behavior is purposive and goal-oriented.
2. We use emotions and specific emotional sequences creatively to facilitate reaching personal goals.
3. Motivations may be on an unconscious level and may effectively hide the person's goals from consciousness.
4. Behavior and life-style are determined by and consistent with each person's unique system of private logic.
5. Differential behaviors comprise and reinforce the life-style, and the life-style in turn ostensibly substantiates one's private logic.
6. Behaviors, life-style, and private logic—in concert as they must by definition be—can occlude a person's awareness of alternative possibilities.
7. This lack of awareness confirms the private logic and leads to delusions and self-fulfilling prophecies.

In order for the client to change, he/she must acknowledge the dysfunctional behavior which prior to the Early Recollection demonstration may not have been available to him/her consciously—thus protecting the hidden private logic mechanisms. The first step of the therapeutic change process is an experiential awareness of behavior patterns.

Since the possibilities for change have been stated by the client—not just arbitrarily imposed by the therapist—he/she is more readily willing to accept the responsibility for trying out the new behaviors and to work on developing appropriate emotional response patterns. He/she has provided every word on which the interpretation is based; therefore he/she must accept that the sequence is accurate and take responsibility for it. Even in the revised Recollection—the *Self-Ideal*—I explain that he/she could not possibly have given me data which was beyond the scope of the private logic.

In the following example, given to me by a passive and responsibility-dodging woman, Alice, notice the consistency between the *Self-Concept* and the *Private-Logic-at-Work* when she portrayed her unsatisfactory sexual relationship. By using the data drawn from the *Self-Ideal* I was able to help her develop appropriate alternative attitudes and behaviors which resulted in a more positive and fulfilling outcome. (p. 124.)

Interpretation of "The Willhite"

Self-Concept

The *Self-Concept* column shows how Alice gets herself into the helpless position (Frame 6) which is her interactional goal. In Frame 1, her brother is sick. From the onset she is an observer of the action; distance is set up. She reacts to the situation by feeling lonely and scared. The function of describing the illness—spinal meningitis—in Frame 2 is to repeat the emotion of scared and add the feelings of trapped and overwhelmed. It is interesting what she does with these feelings in Frame 3. The denial and covering up of her feelings is obvious; she takes the feelings of loneliness, fear, trapped, and being overwhelmed and then boldly states, "It doesn't bother me."

After experiencing her brother's movement away from her, she looks for support and closeness from her mother. Again she finds no solace because her mother is in the bedroom crying (Frames 4 and 5) and Alice is again left alone emotionally. She is sad, sorrowful, and hurt, but again this is denied: ". . . but I don't want anyone to know." As long as Alice skillfully denies her feelings—as she does in Frames 3 and 5—she can logically conclude, "I can't do anything to change the situation." The resulting feeling is one of helplessness—but remember she

Self-Concept	Private-Logic-at-Work	Self-Ideal
1. My brother was sick.	My husband and I have a sex problem.	My brother is well.
(lonely, scared)	(cheated, lonely)	(content, relaxed)
2. He had spinal meningitis.	He doesn't initiate any action, and I figure, "To Hell with you, buddy, I don't need it either."	He is outside playing.
(scared, trapped, overwhelmed)	(rejecting, defiant, irritated, proud)	(relief — he's not bothering me)
3. They came with an ambulance and took him away.	I don't give any ground; he doesn't give any ground. A stand-off.	His friends come over to play with him.
(It doesn't bother me.)	(It doesn't bother me.)	(pleased, happy)
4. Mother was in the bedroom sitting in a chair.	I can get all the attention I need from work.	Mother is cooking dinner.
(sad, sorrowful)	(sad, sorrowful)	(satisfied, warm)
5. She was crying. I didn't want to see her cry.	I won't show him I'm hurt, by damn!	She is laughing and talking: I am laughing and talking with her.
(hurt — but I don't want anyone to know.)	(mad, angry, hurt)	(joy, fulfilled)
6. (Overall feeling:) I can't do anything to change the situation.	(Overall feeling:) I can't do anything about it.	(Overall feeling:) I am involved.
(helpless)	(helpless)	(warm, close)

has gone through a cleverly designed five-step process to get there.

Private-Logic-at-Work

The private logic story parallels the *Self-Concept*; there is the same step-by-step progression toward Alice's preconceived conclusion of "such is life." She starts out in Frame 1 stating that she and her husband have a sex problem. The emotional response—cheated, lonely—is a dead giveaway to how she will conclude her story. Whenever she gets this feeling with someone she finds a way to withdraw and emotionally isolate herself. She does this in Frame 2 by blaming him for not initiating any action; she says "To hell with you, Buddy, I don't need it either." This is her way of building her road to helplessness because of the accompanying feelings of rejection, defiance, irritation, and pride. Pride is probably the emotion she uses to justify the others, and it also allows her to drive these painful feelings underground. Note in Frame 3 she follows on course by saying, "It doesn't bother me," in response to the phrase, "I don't give any ground; he doesn't give any ground—a standoff."

Again, according to the plan of the *Self-Concept,* Alice turns her attentions elsewhere to find solace (Frame 4). She says, "I can get all the attention I want from work." The feelings, however, sadness and sorrow, belie this statement. She must now deal with these feelings—and again she follows her pre-ordained path by covering them over: "I won't show him I'm hurt, by damn!" This is the denial of the mad, angry, hurt feelings and leads her to her personal conviction of "I can't do anything about it." The resultant emotion is, once again, helplessness.

Self-Ideal

The *Self-Ideal* reveals to what extent Alice is willing to consider changing her style of life. It also helps her identify what feelings and emotions she will need to make the new behavior believable. In the *Self-Ideal* Alice reveals that even in fantasy she chooses to promote her distance from others. In the first frame we see that brother is well, and she feels content and relaxed. The therapist could well speculate that she will construct the fantasy so he will pay attention to her—but, as we see in Frame 2, this is not the case. Alice places him outside playing and expresses relief that he is not bothering her. This shows her inability or unwillingness to get close. It could mean that she sees males as too threatening to get close to; she may have a need to maneuver them out of the picture because the thought of a close relationship is too threatening.

This is a good example showing why the therapist—no matter what his/her guess might be—should not interfere with the client in constructing his/her own logical fantasy process.

The distancing is even more clearly revealed in Frame 3 where she has her brother's friends come over to play with him so she gets off the hook from having to be too close and still does not have to take the blame or responsibility for it. In this case she feels pleased and happy. The story follows her pattern —for at the end of Frame 3 she has completed one relationship transaction and immediately turns to another to find satisfaction. She is perfectly free to continue the single relationship with her brother, yet she chose to switch the focus to mother. Alice still maintains her lack of intimacy by having mother cooking dinner; she feels satisfied and warm (Frame 4). Frame 5 finds mother laughing and talking, and Alice is laughing and talking with her—yet one still gets the impression of distance, even though the emotional component reads, "joy, fulfilled." In Frame 6 Alice sees herself as involved and feels warm and close—but she has accomplished this with minimal or no risk to herself. This method of analysis gives the therapist this expanded data to work with—and is also a warning that Alice is not willing to take risks in intimacy, while at the same time she will complain long and loud that the significant others are not intimate with her.

The therapeutic intervention in this case can well be made by contrasting Frame 2 of the *Private-Logic-at-Work* with Frame 2 of the *Self-Ideal*. The former reads, "He doesn't initiate any (sexual) action," and the feeling is "rejection"—the latter reads, "relief—he's not bothering me." She needs to be faced with this discrepancy and to realize that her alternatives are to either risk getting close to a male to find pleasure and happiness, or to decide it is too risky and then she will intentionally promote distance in the relationship. When she does this she must realize her own responsibility for the decision and accept that she still can be okay. Maybe then she can stop blaming others; thus feeling rejected and irritated, and stop the denial—"It doesn't bother me."

It is helpful when analyzing an Early Recollection (or any

column of "The Willhite") to gain a better perspective on the client's private logic by being aware of the overall pattern of the event. Each memory contains the following data:

1. The setting;
2. The person's place/position in the setting (e.g. involved, a spectator, on the firing of the action, etc.);
3. The person's perception of what is happening;
4. The sequence of events;
5. The person's private predetermined (often unconscious) goal;
6. The overall feeling or conclusion—one's personal view of the world—"such is life."

In Alice's Early Recollection these six factors are:

1. *The Setting*—"My brother was sick." Here we see Alice setting up illness as a distance-producing device and the accompanying feelings confirm it—lonely and scared.
2. *Place/Position*—Here Alice is very much a spectator all the way. Everything is observed and there is absolutely no interaction and no direct involvement on her part. This is another way she has of promoting her helplessness.
3. *Person's Perception of What is Happening*—Alice sees all of the things happening to her brother, but also becomes acutely aware of her mother's reaction and is aware of the fact that she cannot do anything about her mother's crying.
4. *Sequence of Events*—Alice is immobilized and helpless to change the outcome. *He* has spinal meningitis; *they* come with the ambulance; *she* was crying. There was nothing poor Alice could do (so she thought) to change the course of fate.

5. *Person's Private Goal*—In Alice's case this is to avoid risk-taking; she accomplishes this goal by believing she is helpless and by creating interpersonal distance.
6. *Conclusion*—"I can't do anything to change the situation."

The *Self-Concept* represents the past, and the *Self-Ideal* speaks to the future; nonetheless, we must focus on the present pain, problems, hopes, fears, motivations, strengths, and weaknesses. Using this process—"The Willhite"—the client is able to existentially experience the possibilities of change. Notice that specific emotions and feelings are identified which, when embodied in new believable behavior patterns, can reveal to the client a new perspective on how life can be. This is the encouragement factor that is so essential in the growth process. This extended Early Recollection technique helps to clearly pinpoint and identify erroneous attitudes so that the client is consciously aware of the new growth direction.

Since trying out new responses and behaviors in real-life situations does not always lead to the predicted and hoped-for conclusion, I encourage the client with the advice that he/she is responsible only for making the effort—not for the outcome.

Another way I encourage the client is by helping him/her risk developing a fantasy for the *Self-Ideal*—a risk which challenges the old dysfunctional behavior. As the client becomes excited about the prospect of defying his/her own mistaken opinion of life, he/she takes on the responsibility of making the new behavior functional and believable. The therapist and client work closely in this process, promoting trust, cooperation, and respect. The client can readily see that it is through his/her own creative powers that new behavior evolves. He/she can take charge of his/her life; one's past experiences need not prophesy doom but rather challenge one's ingenuity and imagination. At this point the client recognizes that there are alternatives—choices—and with choices comes the freedom to choose. "The past is dead, he is free to be happy and to give pleasure to others," a quotation I find very meaningful and which I believe is in the spirit of Adler, but for which I cannot find the source.

Summary

"The Willhite" process is holistic because its individual parts —the *Self-Concept*, the current *Private-Logic-at-Work*, and the *Self-Ideal*—contribute to a whole which is dynamic, flexible, and synergistic. The chronological realities of past, present, and future merge into a viable, mutable experience which denies none of these realities but is more than all of them.

The process is compatible with the tradition of brief psycho-therapy, which quickly gets to the heart of the matter, presenting the client with a recognizable picture of his/her behavior and a blueprint for change which he/she has designed.

In order for the client to change, he/she must acknowledge the dysfunctional behavior which prior to the Early Recollection demonstration may not have been available to him/her con-sciously—thus protecting the hidden private logic mechanisms. The first step of the therapeutic change process is an experiential awareness of behavior patterns.

Emotions are created—on an unconscious level—which are consistent with the private logic and which serve to reinforce it. The early memories which a person retains are retained precisely because they serve as a statement of one's private logic and goals. It is my belief, however, that the Early Recol-lection reveals not only the private logic and goals but also the *emotions* a person uses to give impetus to the logical sequence leading to the preordained conclusion.

"The Willhite" adds a new dimension to therapy by allow-ing for much more involvement on the part of the client. It establishes a much clearer and better defined contract between the client and the therapist.

There are several unique features of "The Willhite" which extend and enhance the usefulness of the Early Recollection process:

First, by having the client specify which emotion(s) are appropriate to each segment of the recollection it is revealed what sequence of emotions he/she employs to confirm the private logic—that sense of "such is life." The person whose behavior is dysfunctional tends to utilize the same general pattern over and over again in problem solving.

Second, in addition to the original recollection I have the client reconstruct the episode the way he/she would like to have had it happen; this is called the *Self-Ideal*.

Third, by developing the *Private-Logic-at-Work* section the client has an opportunity to discover the bottleneck of his/her psyche and can consider the alternatives suggested in the *Self-Ideal*—since this is consistent with the person's system of private logic.

Finally, "The Willhite" creatively uses fantasy as a vehicle for making the transition from diagnosis to treatment. Indeed, it serves as the catalyst for a process which, I believe, exemplifies Ansbacher's statement: "There is in Adlerian therapy no sharp distinction between diagnosis and treatment" (Ansbacher, 1972, p. 141).

References

Adler, A. *Understanding Human Nature.* New York: Greenberg, 1927.

Ansbacher, H. L. Adlerian psychology: The tradition of brief psychotherapy. *Journal of Individual Psychology,* 1972, *28,* 2, 137-151.

CHAPTER 11

STRUCTURED EARLY RECOLLECTIONS

Patrick L. Morris

After having been exposed to a method of using early recollections (ERs) in counseling via a demonstration during an Adler-Driekurs Institute workshop, I have found an aspect of this technique most useful in pinpointing and facilitating insight into functional problems. This method was developed by a social worker from the Midwest, Bob Wilhite, in the course of his counseling experience. In brief, this technique brings together his beliefs or scripts (in the Original), values or goals (in the Ideal) and current strategies (in the Current Event). Using Wilhite's lateral format with the progression developed by Mosak, Shulman and Gushurst, a clear display of the dynamics of the ER can be demonstrated. A detailed example is the most appropriate means of demonstrating the process (see ER display). The following is a step-by-step description of the Structured Early Recollection process followed by a discussion of the content of the sample ER.

SER Process

In eliciting the ER, the most readily available ER is pursued, in the case of several being available, select the most vividly prominent. (It is suggested that the facilitator listen to the complete ER before attempting to write in order to isolate the ER from memory information.) The manifest content of the ER is noted using the exact wording of the client (see Figure 11-1).

Original Elements of the SER

AGE: The age is noted and the client is asked general feelings about this period of life. (The answer is not pursued as to the

	E.R.	CURRENT SITUATION	RESTRUCTURED E.R.
	HOW LIFE IS (HAS TO BE)	HOW I LIVE	HOW LIFE SHOULD BE (IDEAL)
AGE	8	23	any age
SITUATION	Sitting in *my* tree on the highest branch which would hold my weight — cherry tree — I could watch tree blossoms, cherries ripen — this was my favorite of several trees. I am looking out from the best viewpoint, eating cherries.	In mountains of Pennsylvania in cabin with good friend — very wild and rustic with warm and genuine people.	I would like to be in the mountains or by the ocean, some secluded, natural setting. On a mountain, being self-sufficient.
FOCUS	Looking out, eating cherries	Being in the situation	Seeing the terrain
FEELING	Good, enjoyable	Good — contented	Contented
REASON FOR FEELING	Felt good to be alone with thoughts	I felt natural — a part of . . .	Being part of the natural surroundings
"I WANT" STATEMENT	I want time to myself	I want my place to be content	I want to be part of the natural order of things
FACILITATORS	"Ideal" situation	"Ideal" situation	"Ideal" situation

Figure 11-1.

specifics of this period of life, simply the general memory of feeling.)

AGE: 8

The relatively late age of the most prominent ER reflects several possibilities: first, that change in location, social setting, parental setting, school, etc. necessitated the development of new strategies in place of or beyond those strategies developed earlier that would be reflected in earlier recollection (during ages 1 to 5); second, that later embellishments on basic schemata which had proved "successful" during childhood are not succeeding in producing the desired results in adulthood.

SITUATION: The sequence of the event is listed in the exact words of the client. (It is common for what qualifies as two ERs to exist in one overall sequence of events and it is necessary to treat each of them separately.) The client's meaning in using certain "loaded" or possibly "loaded" words or phrases should be *briefly* clarified.

SITUATION: SITTING IN MY TREE ON THE HIGHEST BRANCH WHICH WOULD HOLD MY WEIGHT—CHERRY TREE—I COULD WATCH TREE BLOSSOMS, CHERRIES RIPEN—THIS WAS MY FAVORITE OF SEVERAL TREES. I AM LOOKING OUT FROM THE BEST VIEWPOINT, EATING CHERRIES.

In examining the manifest content of the ER, it would appear that personal superiority or aloofness were the dominant points to be noted in this ER.

FOCUS: Determining the focus gives impetus to the ER. The focus of the ER is that situation or event which elicits the affect of the ER and is that aspect of content which is most vivid.

FOCUS: Looking out eating cherries

With the emphasis not on the highest branch *or* my tree *the likelihood that personal superiority is the theme of the* er *is lessened. The elements of the focus are situations which exist.*

FEELING: The immediate emotional response to the focus event/situation is identified by listing key words. Most responses use key emotional words such as "scared" or "happy." Many responses will contain cognitive or quasi-emotional words such as "curious." These should be reflected to the client until appropriate (meaningful to the client) clearly emotional words are found. When several are given, seek the most prominent and note it.

FEELING: Good-enjoyable

These emotions in this context reflect the moderately intense feelings associated with the individual's understanding of normative situations. More intense emotions (i.e. elation, terror) would reflect disruptions of this normative view.

REASON FOR FEELING: The reason for the feeling, in conjunction with the focus, will begin to show the true "theme" of the ER.

REASON FOR FEELING: Felt good to be alone with thoughts.

This expression of the reason for the feeling in the er *begins to clarify the theme. Self-acceptance and purposive time for self is indicated rather than a reactive, backing off from or aloofness to others (i.e. felt good to be beyond the reach of others).*

I WANT STATEMENT: The purpose of this aspect of the ER is to produce a statement of the client's theme as laid out in the ER: a statement in present, thematic terms which is consistent with the ER structure and how the client presently operates. It is often necessary for the facilitator to make this part of the

ER more clear by guessing the "I Want" statement with emphasis that it is a guess to be corrected by the client. The wording and structure of the statement should be reviewed and reworked until the client feels comfortable with the wording, structure and meaning.

I WANT STATEMENT: I WANT A TIME TO MYSELF.

The I WANT statement in conjunction with the feeling and reason for feeling demonstrates the active aspect of the individual's apperceptive schema or self-written "script." This particular I WANT statement reflects pursuit of self-esteem. The evaluation of the reflective "commonsense" reflected in the I WANT statement is central to the usefulness of this process. Had the I WANT statement been I WANT TO BE BEYOND REACH for instance, the element of personal superiority in reflection to social belonging could be reviewed.

FACILITATORS: The facilitator of the ER is the thematic element of the ER which "makes it work." It is possibly most readily seen as the basic element which, if removed, would reduce the ER to a simple memory.

FACILITATORS: IDEAL SITUATION

The removal of the special nature of the situation would reduce the ER to a memory of climbing trees in childhood. Different elements can be drawn for the facilitator—in this case, the external nature of the determination of "ideal."

This original element of the SER reflects what the individual has seen as viable options in pursuing the three parts of the structure of life: making human life permanent, successful overcoming of external difficulties and a stand towards the tasks of social life. In pursuing self-esteem and peace of mind, this individual is faced with roadblocks in that there is shown a mistaken belief that the desired goal/value is bound to the externally determined situation. The manifest content of the ER indicated that earlier situations had been perceived as cold or hostile, and personal aloofness was employed during that period. This is consistent with the appearance of a First Priority (Pew) of Moral Superiority.

Ideal Element of the SER

The second process in the Structured ER is to have the client reconstruct the ER step by step, taking each content or affect element and either preserving or changing each to form a new, "ideal" ER. A new "I Want Statement" and "Facilitator" for the newly constructed ER are formed from the new information. Simply stated, the task here is to help the client remake the ER to represent how this individual would like life to be.

AGE: ANY AGE.

(This nebulous answer may indicate that no particular period in childhood represented a time which enhanced this pursuit.)

SITUATION: I WOULD LIKE TO BE IN THE MOUNTAINS OR BY THE OCEAN, SOME SECLUDED, NATURAL SETTING. ON A MOUNTAIN, BEING SELF-SUFFICIENT.

The format of developing the ER step by step was altered here rather than the individual responding to changing each element (SITTING IN MY TREE, etc.) two changes were presented: First, the area or opportunity for this special place was vastly expanded from MY TREE to SOME SECLUDED, NATURAL SETTING. Second, BEING SELF-SUFFICIENT was added as an expansion of living off of the tree. In both, the key development is in the expansive nature of the changes.

FOCUS: SEEING THE TERRAIN.

Again the acceptance or change of the Original is not held to but the response seems to directly parallel that in the Original.

FEELING: CONTENTED.

The change from GOOD-ENJOYABLE to CONTENTED is significant in that contented reflects more of an internal sense of being as opposed to a evaluation or response (GOOD-ENJOYABLE) to a situation.

REASON FOR FEELING: BEING PART OF THE NATIVE SURROUNDINGS.

This point marks the first major change. The relationship of feeling good with one's thoughts and being part of is not only expansive but shows progression of the goals/values expressed in this ideal.

I WANT STATEMENT: I WANT TO BE PART OF THE NATURAL ORDER OF THINGS.

While this statement exudes belonging in the greater sense, the the lack of other people being noted to this point must be pursued later in the SER process.

FACILITATOR: IDEAL SITUATION.

The continuation of the theme is especially important at this point as a verification of continuity of the SER process due to the change in format with which the client felt more comfortable (in the situation and focus of the Ideal).

The broader scope of the Ideal and the lack of others in the ER to this point raises concern about self-esteem in relation to the overcoming of external difficulties (being part of the natural order) as they relate to self-worth.

Current Event Elements of the SER

The Current Event should be in the recent past (days or months) and be a situation which resembles the Original or Ideal in flow and emotion.

AGE: 23.

SITUATION: IN THE MOUNTAINS OF PENNSYLVANIA IN CABIN WITH GOOD FRIENDS—VERY WILD AND RUSTIC WITH WARM AND GENUINE PEOPLE.

The shift in emphasis from the physical surroundings to the interpersonal surroundings is significant. Here we see the direction that this individual has chosen. Rather than being committed to previous modes of finding peace of mind (being alone), the inclusion of others indicates that the current mode is moving more closely to the ideal than to previous beliefs.

FOCUS: BEING IN THE SITUATION.

The subtle shift from activity (looking, eating, seeing) indicated in both the Original and Ideal to "being" indicates a shift from external to internal focus of control (definition/determination of the ideal situation).

FEELING: GOOD-CONTENTED.

Here the writer (facilitator) failed to have the client identify the most prominent of the two emotions, this information could have been useful in verifying the previous reference to the relation of the Current Event and the Ideal.

REASON FOR FEELING: I FELT NATURAL—A PART OF . . .

The movement of the current strategy to employ more of the ideal is clearly indicated by the change from being alone to being "part of." The naturalness expressed here reflects resolution of esteem.

I WANT STATEMENT: I WANT MY PLACE TO BE CONTENT. *The obvious movement in present strategies reflected in the Current Event is in the direction of the Ideal. The contentedness expressed in the "I Want" statement together with the "Reason for Feeling" corresponds more to the Ideal, "being part of" (reflecting social feeling), than the concern with self-esteem expressed in the Original of the ER.*

SER As a Counseling Technique

The use of the SER as a counseling technique is more clearly demonstrated in Figure 11-2. In both the "I Want" statement and the "Facilitator," the Current Event reflects commitment to the beliefs (or scripts) reflected in the Original element of the ER (note arrows). This fatalism is extracting the price of the loss of self-direction. The counselor's guess underlined in the "Situation" area of the Current Event ("Why the hell did I go

	E.R.	CURRENT SITUATION	RESTRUCTURED E.R.
	HOW LIFE IS (HAS TO BE)	HOW I LIVE	HOW LIFE SHOULD BE (IDEAL)
AGE	4½ generally good time	24 (10 mos. ago)	4½ g.t.
SITUATION	At baby-sitter's in backyard playing walkway dividing two houses kids on other side started to go to kids (saw) kid on porch dropped board on my head knocked out 15 minutes babysitter put bandage on took me to doctor doctor sewed me up.	On Gay Street (me and husband) rec. activities in street walked past ping-pong table ball hit me in mouth stood for little while held my mouth (didn't see). WHY THE HELL DID I GO ALONG WITH THAT	Baby-sitter's backyard playing walkway kids on other side started to go to kids kid drops board off porch saw it coming down I move – board hits ground. ____ ____ ____
FOCUS	Saw board coming down couldn't move.	Hit in mouth.	Saw board coming down able to move.
FEELING	Terrified (So scared I couldn't move.)	Angry/embarrassed.	Little scared – not like before.
REASON FOR FEELING	Saw something bad was going to happen to me.	All those people and I'm the only one that got hit.	Saw something bad could happen to me.
"I WANT" STATEMENT	I want life to make sense, to be fair, to be predictable. (Life is off the wall.)	I want life not be unpredic-table.	I want to be able to deal with crisis situation.
FACILITATORS	When I am not able to control what happens to me.	Something I had no control over happened to me.	I would have input into what happens to me.

I have to give in to fate – I am not in control of my life.
I cannot control everything that happens to me – but I can control what I do about it.

Figure 11-2.

along with that?") touched the salient point: incongruence between the client's feelings of fatalism and the ideal rationalization of internal loci of control. It is necessary to demonstrate to the client that the possibility of a choice of responses exists, as opposed to an automatic reaction with no options (see notes at bottom). Discussion of possible options and their advantages and disadvantages can be helpful as practice for making choices in future "unpredictable" situations.

SER Evaluation

In evaluating the characteristics of the SER, six areas are examined. First, the Hierarchical Level of the involvement using the established terminology and categorization developed by Maslow (1962). The hierarchy of needs—physiological needs, safety, love and belonging, esteem and self-actualization—is a behaviorial barometer of social courage. The implication of a sequence of development is consistent with observation of approaches to the tasks of life. Movement in meeting a Life Task can be viewed as activity in the hierarchy. The second characteristic is Life Task. Determination of the Life Task in which the participant is "working" is clearly indicated in the Current Event in the SER. This perceived way of viewing and acting in this current situation reflects what Rogers (1961) refers to as the incongruence between how we act and how we feel. The SER shows this as the task area being met and the beliefs, accurate or mistaken, about "how life is"—as opposed to "how life should be"—on which one acts. The commitment to inaccurate or limiting beliefs often is reflected in the failure to adequately deal with the Current Event which is the Life Task area requiring development. The incongruence between behavior and affect in the Current Event is a reflection of the level of social courage. The third area of evaluation is the examination of the direction which the Current Event reflects: Discouragement when commitment is to beliefs which are inaccurate or unsuccessful in meeting the task, and social courage when movement shows beliefs and ideals are being ameliorated with common logic to meet the Life Task. The fourth area is Active/Passive modes. The determination of active or passive is based on Current Event activity or passivity in relation to the activity or passivity in the Original or Ideal elements of the ER towards which the current situation shows movement. The determination of the fifth element, Internal or External Control, is similarly derived from the direction of movement in facing the Current Event and the participant's perception of the motivation in attempting to resolve the task. Themes, the final area, is an attempt to identify the topical content across the three elements of the SER which facilitates the ER process.

Evaluation of Six Characteristics of SER (see Figure 11-2)

   I. Hierarchical Level
       Level II—Safety

The problem set in this ER centers on the "world as a dangerous place." Competence and confidence in meeting the problems of life are of primary concern as seen in "I want" statements. The unrealistic "I want" statement in the ER desiring life to make sense and be predictable is offset by the more realistic (common logic) ability to deal with crisis situations. Development of social courage is needed here as hierarchical competence is not achieved. This is demonstrated in the conformity of the "I want" statement of the current situation with that of the ER rather than the Ideal (which reflects common logic).

  II. Life Task
      Community

The information in the Current Event (note reason for "Feeling") indicates that personal perception of risk, vis-a-vis others (people on the street), is unclear and the concern with competence (in dealing with crisis situations) is more social than occupational. Therefore the life task is community rather than occupation (or intimacy).

  III. Social Courage
      Discouragement

The "I want" statements and "Facilitators" show decision in the Current Situation to reflect mistaken beliefs in the ER rather than the more realistic (common logic) elements of the Ideal ER (see arrows). This is the essence of the incongruence in the counselors guess (underlined in center) which the client felt permeated life.

IV.   Active/Passive Modes

Passive

The Current Event reflected repetition of established modes of coping, maintaining the incongruence.

V.   Internal or External Control

External

The Current Event reflects the ER in that the impetus for the action was external in both ("saw board coming down, couldn't move," "hit in mouth") rather than the Ideal of internal control ("able to move").

VI.   Theme

Victim of Life versus active participant in life.

References

Ansbacher, H. and Ansbacher, R. *Superiority and social interest*. New York: Viking Press, 1973.

Goss, A. and Moresko, T. Relation between a dimension of internal-external control and the MMPI with an alcoholic population. *Journal of Consulting and Clinical Psychology*, 1970, 34, 2, 189-192.

Lombardi, D. and Angers, W. First memories of drug addicts. *Individual Psychologist*, 1967, 5, 1, 7-13.

Manaster, G. and Perryman, T. Early recollections and occupational choice. *Journal of Individual Psychology*, 1974, 30, 2, 232-237.

Maslow, A. *Toward a psychology of being*. Toronto: D. Van Nostrand, Co., 1962.

Mosak, H., Shulman, B., and Gushurst, R. Reference is made to the early recollection structure and procedure developed by these Adlerians as presented in courses at the Adler-Driekurs Institute instructed by McAbee, H., Pew, W., and McKelvie, W. Original works by these Adlerians are available.

O'Connell, W. *Action therapy and Adlerian theory*. Chicago: Alfred Adler Institute, 1975.

Pew, W. and Dreikurs, R. Life style handbook. Hennipen County Court Services, Minn. Handout in course at the Adler-Dreikurs Institute, presently unavailable.

Rogers, D. *On becoming a person*. Boston: Mifflin, 1961.

Willhite, R. Reference is made to an early recollection process which develops into a view of life-style. The writer became aware of the process and employed one aspect of this process through contact with Gloria Lane, Wilmington, Delamare, at an Adler-Dreikurs Institute workshop.

CHAPTER 12

DRAW AN EARLY RECOLLECTION

Harold V. and Norma Lou McAbee

T HE VALUE OF interpreting early recollections (ERs) as an effective means of ascertaining a client's current attitudes toward the tasks of life is commonly accepted by Adlerian therapists (Adler, 1963). ERs are most generally elicited as a part of the interview schedule used to obtain the basic information needed for interpreting the client's life-style (Dreikurs, 1954). However, with the increasing use of the life-style assessment technique, therapists have been seeking innovative and more effective ways to shorten and refine the process. One promising development, originated and refined by the authors of this article, has been that of asking clients to draw their ERs. Some experience with this technique has indicated several particular advantages.

One impact of having the client draw an ER confirms the often quoted saying, "One picture is worth a thousand words." Using visual representation of a recollection is a many-faceted aid in recall and interpretation. What the client draws frequently gets right to the *scene* or *frame* that the counselor is looking for. It usually pinpoints the most cogent part of the ER and reduces extraneous verbiage that often clouds the real issue. The counselor can often circumvent the reluctance of the client to cooperate as they look at the drawing together.

The symbolism that is sometimes used by a client may escape the counselor who has not had art therapy training. However, this need not be a deterent to employing this technique. Since the client is the real authority, as the drawing is discussed, the use of symbolism will be explored. Frequently, the counselor will hit *goldmines* that might otherwise have taken a greater amount of time to elicit and interpret. Both client and counselor perceptions of a given situation can be greatly enhanced by using graphic representations of specific incidents. There is more intense involvement by the client while drawing because not only is the individual recalling in memory, but he is also *seeing*—reliving—the ER as it develops on the drawing board.

This process can also be a tension releaser as the client manipulates the drawing materials. It is recommended that the actual drawing should be done while standing so that the counselor has the additional advantage of observing the body language which is a valuable adjunct to the drawing process.

Encouraging the client toward more active participation in the counseling process is one of the most desirable results of the technique of drawing an ER. Utilizing the technique with groups is also valuable, using the creativeness of group members in assisting participants to gain insight into their basic attitudes afford an opportunity for the development of social interest in the therapeutic process. Also, the shock of recognition as the ER unfolds in the client-counselor discussion time frequently stimulates the client to assume more responsibility in assessing his mode of behavior.

It is commonly accepted by Adlerians that ERs will change during therapy as the client's basic outlook and attitudes change. Applying this technique periodically may very well demonstrate these changes, or lack of them, more dramatically or effectively than untold amounts of verbal dialogue. Not the least important facet of this new technique is that it provides a varied procedure for the therapist or counselor in eliciting and interpreting essential information from the client.

The procedure for using this technique is as follows. Once the counselor has established an effective working relationship with a client, he might ask for the client's cooperation in an experiment. The suggestion can be made that it might be helpful to both in understanding the client if he would be willing to draw an early recollection. Most adults are "willing to try" but will protest that they cannot draw. When assurance that artistic ability is given no consideration in this experiment and that only what the client says about the finished drawing is important, most become eager to participate. Usually this is sufficient. Should the client still appear uncomfortable or uncertain (that in itself is an indicator of the individual's lifestyle), the counselor can suggest that the persons and objects in the drawing can be identified by using symbols such as stick figures for people and geometric forms for objects. This situation, however, rarely occurs. When an anxious individual is given this option, he will usually avoid using the suggested symbols and draw, in a most revealing way, where the ER took place, who was present, the movement and symbolism involved, the time of the recollection, and the exact moment in the scene that was most vivid.

As an observer, the counselor should be as removed as possible, that is, not peering over the client's shoulder yet remaining within a friendly distance. Being aware of the intensity with which the drawing is approached, whether revisions are made, whether the client stops or even steps back and views what has been drawn, will give additional clues as to how involved the client was in the ER and how body movements become indicators of the life-style. Factors revealed may be perfectionism, insecurity, humor, courage, dependency, control, rebellion, and others.

Materials are minimal in both quantity and kind. Newsprint in eighteen by twenty-four inch size and a good variety of colors of felt tip pens is all that is required. The use of pencils should be avoided. Pencils are inhibiting because they are most often used to sketch and the client is apt to become concerned with artistic production. Pencils also have erasers which again is inhibiting because the client will erase and spend time getting a line just right. The focus then is misdirected upon *how well* the drawing is done rather than upon *what* is being portrayed. Felt tip pens are indelible, produce linear drawings, come in a great variety of colors, and the client can work very quickly, which is also desirable. If possible, it is advantageous to have the paper on an easel or taped to the wall so the client may stand while drawing. It is helpful to have a second or third sheet as a backer so the felt tip pen will not mark the wall if it bleeds through the original sheet. Another acceptable model is to have a lapboard of solid but lightweight wood on which the paper can be thumbtacked or taped. This reduces the size of paper to a twelve by eighteen inch dimension which is quite acceptable. Drawing any smaller with the suggested tools is not advisable. No time limit need be set since the client will stop when he has portrayed the scene. Drawing time is usually less than ten minutes.

While the drawing is in progress, the counselor will be observing some things such as body language, time spent on any particular part of the picture, and how the client approaches the assigned task. It is vital to be aware that no marks, person, or object is drawn that does not have meaning or purpose in the recollection. Elements, such as size of persons or objects, omission and/or exaggeration—particularly of the human figures —and sometimes use of color, reveal how the client views the important aspects of the recollection (Lowenfeld and Lambert, 1975). Even though use of specific colors may be an additional dimension in assessing the ER, the portrayal of the action of the event is more important. No observable difference has been found between using a variety of colored pens or a single color for the entire drawing.

Evidence of the value of art imagery in life-style assessment can best be illustrated by citing some examples. The line drawing done by Jean shows a beach scene which Jean recalls as a very special place for her. The people identified include Mother, seated in the chair on the sand, two playmates, and Jean. The two playmates are in the shallow area of the inlet. One child is floating while the other splashes in knee-deep water. Jean shows herself farther down the shore, away from Mother. Using an arrow to show what she most liked to do, Jean told how she would dive into the deep pool which was a forbidden area. She related how she and her playmates would splash about in the shallow water, but when Mother wasn't looking would run and dive into the pool. As she recalled this incident, she had an impish grin on her face, but stopped and became very serious as one of her basic attitudes toward life was revealed from the way she drew herself, her mother, and her playmates. Jean realized that she had used very heavy lines for her own figure, a little less intense ones in the drawing of Mother, and very pale

Figure 12-1.

lines for the two playmates. She became aware from this use of the felt tip pen that she had made herself the most important person in the drawing. Mother was of almost equal importance in her life as shown in the drawing. This use of the pen revealed to Jean how important and powerful she felt herself to be at age six. The counselor confronted Jean with comments such as, "Could it be that you are a person willing to take risks to do what you want to do although knowing that there is danger in doing so? Could it be that your need for excitement gives you courage to tackle problems and seek solutions even when those in authority are not in agreement with your forging ahead with your ideas?"

Jean's reaction was positive and verified that she did the same thing in her present work and life. She reinforced verbally what she discovered in the drawing, i.e. the relationship with her peer group and how she would wait for others to turn away and then take advantage of the opportunity to do as she pleased.

Jean was quick to become a participant in identifying her

own life-style via interpreting drawings of early recollections. This became a discovery and learning experience for her. She took the responsibility for assessing her own behavior and, in partnership with the counselor, expanded her understanding of herself.

Figure 12-2.

Another example, drawn by Sue, shows a tree house secured high in the branches of a large tree overhanging a stream used by canoeists. A swing is suspended from one of the high limbs. The two figures shown at the swing are the same children whose heads can be seen in the tree house. Sue told how she and one best friend would play on the swing and then climb into the tree house and wait for boaters to come down the stream. Access to the house was by a sturdy ladder. The tree house was well hidden and the girls would wait until a canoe was right under the tree and then they would scream in order to frighten the people below. Sue placed herself in the tree house farthest away from the stream. Her face is shown with a huge smiling mouth and the word "scream" is written above her head. The friend has no features on the head and is making no sound.

As Sue related this recollection she identified herself as a loner who always had just one friend, a person who was usually a follower and needed a friend. She was the one who did the choosing, seeking out the person she wanted to befriend. Her voice and facial expression were placid while telling about her drawing until she related the part about screaming. At this point she became very animated, her eyes sparkled, and she evidenced the excitement of frightening people without being seen or caught in this activity. Applying this ER to her adult life, it was suggested that Sue liked to stir things up, yet wanted to play it safe and protect that safe position by interacting with others in a covert manner. Sue confirmed the assessments both in her recognition reflexes and verbally. Sue now seems to understand that she continues to have a limited number of friends and that she seeks out people that she can lead and control. Although she likes excitement, she is always on the periphery and therefore need not accept responsibility for what happens. The safe position in the drawing is evidenced by access to the tree house by using a ladder. To climb up using the tree limbs would be too risky. The ladder afforded a quick getaway in case Sue and her friend were discovered. Another indication of her desire for safety is her positioning of herself at the far end of the tree house, away from the stream. Presently she finds that by being on the periphery, she can maintain her independence and usually is able to escape, to remain noninvolved.

Summary

Eliciting ERs via drawings has proved to be a valid approach in helping clients better understand some of their basic attitudes towards life. The visual representation aids recall and interpretation and usually pinpoints the most cogent aspect of the ER.

Drawing the early recollection requires the client's active participation in the therapeutic process. Opportunities for observing and interpreting the body language of the client are greatly multiplied. Utilizing this technique in groups also affords the opportunity for the development of social interest between the participants. The technique affords variety for the therapist in eliciting essential information and offers valid shortcuts to interpreting the life-style.

That the cost of supplies is minimal and that steps in the procedure are easily learned should encourage experimentation in the drawing of ERs by therapists and counselors everywhere.

References

1. Adler, A. *Superiority and Social Interest*. New York: Viking, 1963, p. 95.
2. Dreikurs, R. The medical interview. *Amer. J. Indiv. Psychol.* 1954, *10*, 99-122.
3. Lowenfeld, V. and Lambert, B. W. *Creative and Mental Growth*, 6th ed. New York: Macmillan, 1975, p. 203.

CHAPTER 13

THE RESPECTIVE ROLES OF "EARLIEST RECOLLECTIONS" AND "IMAGES"[*]

Asya L. Kadis and Sofie Lazarsfeld

The "Earliest" Recollections

W HILE PSYCHOANALYSIS concentrates upon the task (usually long and arduous) of reconstructing the crucial "earliest" experiences, Adler (1) has found new approaches to the pathogenic layers of neurosis; it is from his basic observations that the ensuing remarks are derived. Adler attached great importance for diagnosis, prognosis and treatment to *consciously retained earliest recollections,* those which have been selected from the individual's host of early memories and have been stored permanently in his mind. He pointed out that the retained early memories, though they are "surface" material, must be worthy of our attention because of their very selectivity. They are usually selected by the individual as "guide posts" which he is ready to follow. They may serve him as warnings, incentives and challenges; as such they may just as well lead the therapist in his search for the patient's basic neurotic pattern.

A child's "earliest recollections" are actually *interpretations* of his earliest experiences; the subjective picture of his immediate environment (his home circle) is the prototype of the whole outside world as he perceives it. To repeat a known but pertinent axiom: The infant-parent relationship is a determining factor not only in shaping the child's ego but also in shaping his identification patterns. He projects these relationships onto the world at large so that it becomes his "private world." He then

* Reprinted by permission from *The American Journal of Psychotherapy,* 1948, 2, 250-255.

deals with it on the basis of his "private logic" which he has
built up from his earliest experiences.

Early retained recollections, therefore, cannot be dismissed
on the score that they are sometimes mere "screen memories."
Even when they are substitutes, they still remain meaningful
in themselves, and the therapist may find them extremely useful.
Therefore, the therapist should not limit himself to asking,
"What experience was so important and so embarrassing that it
had to be screened?" It is rewarding to ponder also, *"For what
purpose* was this special experience, and not another, chosen
and retained as a screen memory?" As Adlerians, we approach
the problem of "screen recollections" or substitute recollections
with the aspect of *finality,* and this approach gives the substitute
recollections quite another psychological value.

The "Images"

We shall now introduce a new aspect and evaluation of
early retained memories, namely, the concept of "images." The
image portrays the memory of other individuals who have played
a part in the patient's early life. It adds another dimension to
the individual's drawing of his early environment and appears
indispensable to a complete understanding of his early
recollections.

"Images" differ from "recollections" in several ways. Free
recollections to be useful must be the very earliest recollections,
chronologically speaking. The image can date from any age,
as long as it is the earliest recollecton which the patient can
give of the person whose relationship to him is under scrutiny.

In acquiring these two types of impressions the techniques
of interrogation differ. No guiding questions are asked to bring
forth "earliest recollections"; one merely queries, "What is your
earliest recollection?" In soliciting "images," however, one must
specify and ask direct questions. To obtain a first image of a
father, mother or sibling, we must ask for it directly. This is
feasible, because images are not sought until the patient has
volunteered his "oldest recollections."

But the most important difference between images and
recollections is the different role the individual himself plays

in each. In recollections the individual usually plays the main role. In the image the individual sometimes does not participate at all, sometimes he may play a part, but not the main part. Thus the scene usually revolves around the important persons who comprised his infant world. The image provides also a first-rate picture of the individual's attitude to persons who, in the process of his growth, have become representatives of the society to which he had to adapt. Thus the images enable us to see the misconceptions, misinterpretations, basic hostilities, resentments, neglects, humiliations—real or imagined—which may have formed the core of the individual's fully developed neurosis.

Therapists may not be surprised to find the image often at variance with the "oldest recollection." This is so frequently the case that we have come to look upon it as an invaluable aid to the unveiling of disguised oldest recollections and to the understanding of the development of the patient's neurotic trends. The image taught us to be chary of accepting oldest recollections at their face value.

Case 1. The patient is a twenty-year-old girl. Her earliest recollection was that she was standing on a chair while her mother was fitting a dress on her. She has no recollection of her father. When we asked for images of the respective members of the family we found that it was the father who had been the main figure in the girl's neurosis; her description of him and her image of him were at opposite poles. The girl's first general description of the family background portrayed her father as a sweet, kindly person who read to her, played outdoor games with her and—this she emphasized—always was fair to her. Nowhere could we detect disharmony in her free recollections of her father. However, when we asked her for the very first image of her father, she described a tempestuous scene, in which she saw herself having tantrums and saw her father yelling that he would "cure her" of it. This brought forth another scene, when her father unjustly accused her of having stolen something, and employed very cruel means of forcing a confession from her.

After this exposure of the real picture of her father and her true relationship to him, she volunteered many other negative recollections, which were completely at odds with her first free description dealing with an artificial picture of her father relationship.

The young woman opened each session by fighting with the therapist. She did not want to submit to the therapy, just as she had never wanted to submit to her father. After she had won insight into her characteristic pattern, she made the following observation spontaneously: "You are absolutely right; I do start everything with a fight."

Why is this girl's oldest recollection not one of her father, who—as we learned later through her images—had played so important a role in her childhood? If the most important person appears to be absent from the patient's oldest recollections, we believe that the omission originates from a basic feeling of hostility towards the person involved. The child, in denying such persons a place within his memory, seeks to deny them their right to exist. As long as we keep someone in our memory, he exists; those we do not remember, do not exist—at least as far as we are concerned.*

The psychic mechanism in the above mentioned case is as follows: The child was torn between resentment of her father and her ethical standards which condemned antagonistic sentiments against parents. In order to live up to her ethical standards, she had to endow her father with the most cherished qualities a father could have: kindness, and above all, fairness. Indeed, he had to be invested with an exceptional virtue, since there was no genuine love and the lack had to be compensated. Simple love was not sufficient to compensate, nothing less than worship would suffice.

Case 2. We found a similar psychic mechanism in the case of C.O., where a sister played the decisive counterpart. When C.O. came to see the counsellor, she was sixteen years of age, the second child in the family constellation. Her first recollection did not include her sister at all. Later she spontaneously introduced her three years older sister as her "ideal." She described her as one who had always been very kind and good to her. She displayed a veritable sister worship.

Yet, when we proceeded to ask for the first image of her sister, she related: "I was to be a flower girl at my favorite aunt's wedding. The night before the wedding my sister clipped my hair off. I could not go to the wedding." With the airing of this recollection, there came forth, spontaneously, many other early childhood episodes where this sister had taken advantage of her.

We saw the basic problem of this adolescent girl was sibling rivalry of which she had been totally unaware. And as she was

---

* The child's banishing of her father from her memory corresponds to what is known as the hardest curse in the Jewish creed. The curse is visited upon persons who have committed an unforgivable sin: Their name never shall be mentioned, and they shall be cut out from memory. Heinrich Heine immortalized this curse in his famous poem "Nicht gedacht soll seiner werden" (May he not even be thought of).

unaware of this, she was equally unconscious of her pattern of projecting in her later life her sister relationship onto her relationship with others. Yet this is precisely what she did. Most people, and especially females whom she met, were endowed with the properties of this apparently deeply beloved sister who had cut off her curls: she was alert to everyone as potential enemies; she suspected they would take unfair advantage of her and harm her. She characterized herself in her social environment as follows: "I always think that my fellow classmates are out to hurt me in some way; I always think that they are 'sneaky' and that one ought not to trust them; but I am watching out."

From the time the first image of her sister was brought to the "speech-ripe" level (2), the girl herself showed signs of awakened perception, which matured steadily until she came to understand her basic problem: sibling rivalry covered up by compensatory worship.

Case 3. G.W., twenty years of age, complained that she felt herself shut off from other people. Social life to her was a duty rather than pleasure, and it was impossible for her to relax and enjoy herself. Life had to run exactly according to schedule and she dreaded anything that was unexpected or unknown to her. Her relationship with the opposite sex was disturbed, although she was attractive enough to be sought after by men.

She offered only a few early childhood recollections: one was about a pleasant walk with her father and a few others which were connected with various persons of her immediate environment. No free recollection included her mother. To all appearances, her current relationship to her mother seemed well balanced; she expressed admiration for her which was not exaggerated, and there was no sign of hostility.

However, when the young woman was asked for her first image of her mother, she suddenly remembered a scene where her mother was pacing the room in deep concern over the prolonged absence of her husband; the girl was in the room, but she was given no attention.

As in the foregoing cases, the recollections which came to the surface after the initial revelation revealed the same basic attitude: her mother took care of others, but neglected her. The girl's reminiscences unfolded a picture of jealousy, to which was added the feeling of guilt, for her ethics labelled jealousy as a despicable and forbidden attitude.

The girl followed the familiar device of pinning the responsibility for her "unethical" feelings upon her mother, whose neglect had given her cause to be jealous. Although her psychological situation paralleled that of the previous case, it did not lead to an overt compensatory worship. Instead, the girl attempted to rid herself of her negative feelings by another weapon of defense: she tried to freeze out all her emotions.

She believed she could purify herself of "unethical" feelings by completely shutting off her emotional dynamo, or at least controlling its activity. She attempted to transfer human ties from the emotional to the rational level by intellectualizing her relations with people. Her avowed aim was to be a "nice person"—kind to every one on the surface but safely withdrawn, as a protection against the development of emotional ties.

Fear of emotions and consequent shrinking from emotional situations is a familiar tendency among neurotics. In this case this fear was fortified by the patient's particularly high ethical standards. It went so far as to censor her relationship toward her own body, which she endeavored to keep free of any "indecent" sensation. The censorship was applied not only to sexual feelings. Emotions per se were to be outlawed. She felt they were indecent because they operated against human dignity. . . . Emotional restraint often derives from an impulse to escape from dangerous emotions. In this case the revealing image of the mother saved valuable time in finding out *what purpose* was served by her defense device of rejecting all emotion.

Conclusions

It is striking that the "oldest recollections" so often are in sharpest opposition to the "image" which is brought forth by direct questioning. No less stimulating is the fact that when such discrepancies occur, the free recollection is invariably positive, while the image of the same person is, as a rule, negative.

These findings reinforce Adler's suggestion the therapist should keep in mind the individual *against whom* the child may have chosen to hold an incident of his past. Our method has helped us to remove compensatory masquerades which would otherwise have misled us for a long while.

The frequency of discrepancies between free recollections and images led us to investigate whether the extent of the discrepancy might be in a direct proportion to the individual's inclination for developing certain neurotic trends. Our research confirmed this supposition. We found that the inability to maintain certain unpleasant attitudes invariably moved the maladjusted person to replace them by more agreeable ones. As the tendency to avoid difficulties by artificial means, instead of coping with them in reality, is at the bottom of most neurotic trends, it follows logically that the inclination to substitute pleasant though spurious recollections for true but unpleasant ones must grow in a direct proportion to the individual's inclination for developing neurotic trends.

Such findings become visible in varying degree upon the application of any uncovering therapy; but direct requests for images may shorten the time it takes to achieve an understanding of the basic problem.

Modern psychotherapy never has ceased seeking ways of shortening the length of the therapeutic procedure. We think that the concept of the image represents one of the short-cuts and that it may assume its well deserved place within modern psychotherapy.

Bibliography

1. Adler, Alfred: *Understanding Human Nature,* Translated by Walter B. Wolfe, Garden City Publ. Co., New York, 1927.
2. Froeschels, Emil: *The Human Race,* Philosophical Library, New York, 1947.

CHAPTER 14

TO SCORE OR NOT TO SCORE

HARRY A. OLSON

As CAN BE DEDUCED from the majority of the papers in this book, ERs are usually interpreted intuitively, idiosyncratically. The specific recollection or childhood dream is examined and certain interpretive conclusions are drawn based on the data presented in the ER and the theoretical bias of the interpreter. In other words, most often ERs are interpreted *clinically* and are not scored in any way. This method of approach is similar to sequence analysis of the Rorschach and content analysis of the TAT. Like Rorschach and TAT protocols, however, ERs are scorable, and a number of studies have made use of scoring techniques. What we usually find in the literature in this regard is not a *scoring* approach per se, in which ERs are assigned statistical values, but rather a pigeon-holing of ER data according to predetermined theoretical or structural categories. Manaster and Perryman (1974) developed a scoring manual including the variables they found in the research literature useful for analysing ERs and applied the manual to a study of occupational choice.* No statistical values are presented in their manual, nor have any been suggested in any other scoring approach of which this author is aware, except those of Wynne and Schaffzin and Kopp and Der. Scoring, then, usually refers to the presence/ absence or frequency of themes or other variables in the ER.

While scoring is primarily an effective research tool for bringing a statistical or quasi-statistical approach to idiosyncratic clinical material, the clinical use of a scoring system should not be overlooked. Levy and Griggs (1962) hold that scoring

---

* The manual is reprinted in its entirety in Appendix A. Their paper and the other papers cited in this chapter are reviewed in the Annotated Bibliography.

156

makes clinical prediction and interpretation more precise and that meaningful statements about a patient's major dynamics, defenses, and coping style can be made on the basis of knowing only the patient's sex and the ERs. They state:

> From our standpoint, at the center of an early memory there is one focal theme or frequently a configuration of themes. A theme in an early recollection captures an essential emotional state of the individual. The themes are viewed as holistic units for analysing early memories and are by and large of a precarious nature, tapping frequently significant portions of the underlying affects and trends of object relations. As the themes in a set of early memories change, they reflect the dynamic shifting in the synthetic function of the ego.

They developed a thematic-configurational approach and a scoring system based on multiple variations of three basic theme types: dependency-independency, destructive aggression-constructive aggression, and sexuality.† In the study cited in their article, they were able to match ER themes produced by the patient with independently retrieved data from the patient's therapist regarding central dynamics and defenses in 70 percent of the cases. They commented that the therapists reported use of massive denial by a large proportion of the patients for whom they were unable to make a successful match. Their reliability study showed that their success rate (80%) could be maintained. They concluded that while correspondence of ER themes and themes deduced in interviews by independent therapists was not exact, there was sufficient overlap to demonstrate that ERs are a significantly effective predictor of patient dynamics and conflicts.

There are several additional "scoring systems" described in the literature, most from the psychoanalytic approach. Perhaps the most extensive and definitive is the manifest content scoring manual developed and reported by Langs et al. (1960).* Their article demonstrates their use of the manual and provides a listing of the manual's major headings. Again, scoring is based

---

† The reader is referred to the Appendix of their article for a full description of their scoring variables with clinical examples of each.

* Langs, R. J. and Riser, M. F. A manual for the scoring of manifest content of the first memory and dreams. Available from the Archives of the Library of the Albert Einstein College of Medicine, New York, Catalog #150.L25, 1951, C 2.

on presence/absence or frequency of themes and other variables found in the manifest content of the ER. Mayman (1968), viewing ERs as screen memories, presents a system of classifying manifest content of ERs according to the psychoanalytic stages of psychosexual development and outlines this in a systematic table. His use of the psychosexual stages is a developmental one, emphasizing phases of growth rather than the narrowly instinctual meaning implied in Freudian id-psychology.

Wynne and Schaffzin (1965) produced a manual* which uses a system of categorizing the number and intensity of subjective feelings in the ER. The manual is based on Plutchik's theory of emotion which postulates eight basic emotional dimensions (four polar opposite pairs) which produce all of the experienced mixed emotions. This manual permits the scoring of intensity of feelings on each dimension from zero (absent) to nine (maximum). Three ERs are recorded and scores are summed over the three ERs for each dimension. Eight other scales were derived covering total affect, positive affect, negative affect, degree of conflict within each dimension, and total conflict. The system proved reliable.

In addition, Eckstein (1976) lists categories of an abbreviated scoring system. Kopp and Der, in their article on level of activity, describe a Role-Activity Scale and demonstrate its validity. For a fuller discussion see Eckstein's paper, included in this book (see Chapter 19).

In conclusion, it appears that most clinicians do not score ERs but that scoring, properly done, can be an added, but not essential, means of increasing predictive efficiency. None of the scoring systems of which this author is aware supply normative data, statistical correlations between manifest content and pathology or emotional health, or diagnosis. The idiosyncratic nature of ERs would make this extremely difficult but the works extant outlining manifest content variables and themes are a solid basis for this technique. In current clinical practice it is not necessary to have such a level of statistical prediction, as

---

* Available from ADI Auxiliary Publications Project, Photoduplication Service Library of Congress. Washington, D.C. 20540. Order Document No. 8634. The fees at the time Wynne's article was printed were $2.50 for photocopies, $1.75 for microfilm.

the clinical sophistication of the technique in the hands of an able therapist or diagnostician is sufficient to describe basic attitudes and dimensions essential to the understanding of the particular patient. Yet to develop nomothetic data to be used in conjunction with a basically ideographic technique would serve to significantly enhance the value of ER interpretation for some purposes. In the final analysis, however, the basic issue is the individual clinician's effectiveness and style in using ERs. For some, scoring would assist; for others, it would be a hinderance. The interested clinician may familiarize himself with the Manaster-Perryman manual or another system and experiment from there. Care must be taken to see that ER interpretation does not become a sensitive instrument mechanistically applied.

References

1. Eckstein, D. G. Early recollection changes after counseling: A case study. *J. Indiv. Psychol.* 1976, 32, 2, 212-223.
2. Kopp, R. R. and Der, D. F. Level of activity in adolescents' early recollections: A validity study. Unpublished research report (see Annotated Bibliography).
3. Langs, R. J., Rothenberg, M. B., Fishman, J. R. and Reiser, M. F. A method for the clinical and theoretical study of the earliest memory. *Arch. Gen. Psychiat.* 1960, 3, 523-534.
4. Levy, J. and Grigg, K. A. Early memories: Thematic-configurational analysis. *Arch. Gen Psychiat.* 1962, 7, 57-69.
5. Manaster, G. J. and Perryman, T. B. Early recollections and occupational choice. *J. Indiv. Psychol.* 1974, 30, 2, 232-237.
6. Mayman, M. Early memories and character structure. *J. Proj. Tech.* 1968, 32, 303-316.
7. Wynne, R. D. and Schaffzin, B. A technique for the analysis of affect in early memories. *Psychol. Rep.* 1965, 17, 933-934.

SECTION IV

USE OF EARLY RECOLLECTIONS
IN PSYCHOTHERAPY

INTRODUCTION

PAPANEK BEGINS THIS section with a general discussion of the use of ERs and their application in psychotherapy. Clinical examples are cited.

Kadis demonstrates and explains the utility of ERs in selecting patients for group therapy and in obtaining therapeutic material in the group.

Malamud expands on the group use of ERs, describing their use in self-awareness workshops. His technique is spelled out step by step and may be used by the reader verbatim.

Mosak discusses transference issues and the use of ERs in predicting what assets and difficulties the therapist might encounter in the relationship via an analysis of ERs. Case material is presented by way of example.

Eckstein deals with a cardinal issue which is overlooked in the research literature, the changes in ERs during and after therapy. A systematic study with clinical examples is presented. He also demonstrates the use of Altman and Quinn's Early Recollections Rating Scale.

Janoe and Janoe report in detail the technique they have developed to deal with uncomfortable feelings in the present through working with ERs.

Olson, following the Janoes' discussion, describes the retrieval and therapeutic use of ERs under hypnosis. A specific technique involving age regression is outlined and a case example is presented. The complete protocol for Olson's technique is presented in Appendix C.

The Janoes' second paper describes their technique and some

161

cautions in the use of ERs with children. Many Adlerians eschew using ERs with children, but the Janoes have found the technique highly useful.

Kopp and Dinkmeyer also discuss and demonstrate the use of ERs in the assessment and counseling of elementary school children.

McKelvie concludes this section with a discussion of how ERs may be used in vocational counseling.

CHAPTER 15

THE USE OF EARLY RECOLLECTIONS IN PSYCHOTHERAPY*

HELENE PAPANEK

M Y PAPER DEALS with only one technique of Adlerian psychotherapy. But it is an important one. The preceding speaker,
Dr. Kurt Adler (2), has referred to it in each of his cases.† It is
the use of early recollections (ERs). I want to clarify this
technique because sometimes there is some difficulty in understanding it. How is it that the Adlerian approach which, in
contrast to Freud, emphasizes the present purposes of symptoms
and present relationships of the grown-up and tends not to talk
much about the past, does stress ERs? The answer is, as I am
sure you have gathered from Dr. Adler's presentation, that our
use of ERs differs from that of other schools of thought. I shall
deal here with the Adlerian theoretical basis for the ER technique
and some psychotherapeutic applications of it.

An individual's life-style includes most importantly a cognitive framework which enables him to understand the world and
to select behavior which will advance him toward his goals of
safety, security, self-esteem, and success and will protect him
from insecurity, danger, and frustration. All this is more or less
"erroneous," depending on whether the individual is more neurotic or more healthy. Each child selects from his many experiences some which impress him deeply and which he makes the
landmarks of his cognitive map. We are not interested in the
forgotten, but in what is remembered in this way. It is as if

---

* Reprinted by permission from the *Journal of Individual Psychology*, 1972,
28, 2, 169-176.

† Paper read at the Fourth Brief Psychotherapy Conference, Chicago Medical
School, Chicago, March 24-25, 1972.

the individual would say to himself, "Because this or that happened to me, I should never again behave in a certain way," or, "This or that brought such desirable results that I will behave again in a similar way and thereby reap the same reward."

The ERs reflect the person's guidelines for his behavior. An incident may really have happened as it is remembered, or the individual's assumptions and explanations about it may have been added, or it may never have happened. The result is the same. The ER will reflect the individual's opinion of the world and himself and the path of behavior he has selected for himself to cope with a complicated world.

ERs understood in this way are of the greatest help in psychotherapy. Instead of meandering in the patient's so-called unconscious and hoping that so-called free association will bring valuable material to light, the therapist is enabled by the ERs to follow an active course, focused on important material, to understand the life-style. Such material also includes dreams, and observations of the patient's relationships to the therapist and others in his life, and the like. But ERs in particular help to focus quickly on crucial problems, the nature of the patient's or client's mistake about himself, his aspirations, and the world around him.

The first stage in establishing the therapeutic relationship and atmosphere should be given to questions about the patient's complaints and what brings him to therapy. At the same time there is opportunity to observe the patient's face, figure, the way he talks, thinks, and relates to us. As the next step the therapist shows his interest in ERs, and the patient is asked, "Think back as far as you can, and tell me your earliest memory from your childhood years." We differentiate between early memories and reports. We differentiate between early memories and reports. We do not want a report, a generalization of the person's life as a child, such as, "I had a happy childhood," or "My parents rejected me and I was always lonely." ERs are vivid concrete incidents with all the details and emotions attached to them. To quote Adler:

His memories are the reminders [the person] carries about with him of his own limits and of the meaning of circumstances. There are no "chance memories": out of the incalculable number of impressions which meet an individual, he chooses to remember only those which he feels, however darkly, to have a bearing on his situation. Thus his memories represent his "Story of My Life"; a story he repeats to himself to warn him or comfort him. . . . A depressed individual could not remain depressed if he remembered his good moments and his successes. He must say to himself, "All my life I was unfortunate," and select only those events which he can interpret as instances of his unhappy fate. Memories can never run counter to the style of life. If an individual's goal of superiority demands that he should feel, "Other people always humiliate me," he will choose for remembrance incidents which he can interpret as humiliations . . . The first memory will show his fundamental view of life, his first satisfactory crystallization of his attitude (I, p. 351).

These old memories are not reasons for present behavior. They are not causes; they do not determine present behavior. They are hints; they help to understand the guiding fiction; they indicate the movements towards a goal and what obstacles have to be overcome. Because we can use them sooner or later, I write them down, so as to be sure to remember them for later use.

But first a therapeutic atmosphere of mutual involvement must be established. The patient must be brought into a state where he likes to listen, where he wants to understand. Only then can he be influenced to live what he has understood. Insight is only useful in an atmosphere of trust and courage. After such an atmosphere has been established, the therapist must evaluate the next therapeutic steps: how to use his knowledge about the patient's difficulties, and how and when to confront him with the errors in his life-style based on childish apprehension and misunderstanding. The timing of these interpretations and confrontations differs from case to case.

Some therapists differentiate between emotional and intellectual insight. This seems to me a mistaken dichotomy. Insight becomes meaningful to the patient if it is accompanied by two discoveries: first, that his neurotic suffering has been unnecessary; ERs are chosen, voluntary landmarks in an environment obtruding itself and influencing his developing cognitive structuring; and second, that a more realistic, adequate understanding of his present-day environment gives him the opportunity for socially directed, rewarding, coping behavior.

The whole idea is that we can explain to the patient that even if all the past happened as he remembers it, he can still shape the present and the future, and he is not just a victim of his past. This view makes the patient much more hopeful, and optimistic about therapy.

Usually I ask a patient to recollect a series of from five to ten incidents, in one or two therapeutic sessions, although this many may not be necessary. Often a single ER can illustrate a life-style and bring therapeutic gain.

My first example will be one of a patient in whose case the interpretation of one ER brought immediate relief. Yet I do not think it easy to change a person's life-style and life goal by a very short course of therapy. But I do think that even a patient who has had a long previous therapy can gain new hope and a new outlook on his symptoms if he sees the connection between his early recollections and present-day sufferings. It seems that in my practice patients have frequently been in therapy previously, often for years, without any change for the better. Time and money run out and they want a more active approach, a so-called new therapy, although we consider our method quite an old one.

Sickness, the Price for Attention

This is the case of a 30-year-old divorcee who had been in treatment, elsewhere, for years, because of headaches. She is a very gifted person who publishes and illustrates children's books, has a good job, and is also a free-lance writer. Her headaches are so severe that she is sometimes unable to work, either for herself or where she is employed.

She told me the following in the second session. Her father had been a very busy general practitioner who spent most of his time in his office which was not in the home. The mother felt always very neglected and angry at the father's absences, and the mother, the patient, already when she was ten years old, and her younger brother, suspected that the father used his office to have an affair. So his neglect of the children was an important factor. Even when the children were sick he frequently said, "Ah, it's nothing serious," and didn't come home any earlier from his office.

But once when the patient was six years old she had a stomach ache, and the mother called the father up, and he came home and suspected appendicitis. He got upset and took her to the hospital himself. It turned out not to be appendicitis and the patient was not operated on; so she did not have that satisfaction in the hospital. But she did have the satisfaction of seeing her father upset and caring for her. When I asked her to describe the feeling of the memory, she said it was "exquisite." I found this very striking, because, you know, she vomited, had a stomach ache, and all the symptoms of a severe disease. But the care and the concern of her father made it an exquisite memory.

Now that was so striking that I told her right then, in the second session, that perhaps she feels being sick is the only way to get attention. Thereupon she reported in the next session that her headaches had diminished to a very great extent, and that she now understands the difference between me and her previous therapist. During the several years that she had worked with him, he had always explained her headaches as repressed anger and had suggested that each time she had a headache, she should find out at whom she was angry. It hadn't worked, she said. Though she believed in this interpretation, it seemed six-times-removed because it was so hard to find anybody at whom she really was angry. But my interpretation, that she wanted some-body to be nice to her, to show her concern or attention, seemed to be only once-removed. It still didn't strike her as the only true explanation, but it was somehow easier to accept that she really wanted somebody to be nice to her and that the disappoint-ment brought on the headaches. She was in a very good mood because she hadn't had any headaches during this week, whereas she used to have headaches at least three days a week, and she could work so much better now.

This of course does not mean that her life-style changed, which is still in many ways one of dependency, but it certainly gave her more hope to straighten out her other problems which she has with men and girl friends, and to feel in general, which I think is very important, that relying on others is not a very safe attitude. Though as a child she had to rely on others, now she could try to be self-reliant with her girl friends and with her boyfriend, to be more outspoken in her relationships, and not hope others would give her care and attention just because she is she.

Lack of Courage to Fight Openly

The second case, Ann, is a 36-year-old, very attractive woman who seemed extremely successful in her private and her professional life. With a master's degree in school psychology she had a very good position as an instructor at a college, and she is married to a man who is a professor of physiology at a medical school.

She had become terribly dissatisfied with her life, with her marriage, and with her situation at work. She found her husband dull, uninterested in her and much more involved in his work. She was afraid of groups.

What bothered her most was an older woman at the college who had been her friend and helpful in getting Ann her present job three years ago. Today this woman still had a fantastic hold over her, as she said, putting her in a very difficult position because the woman was very unpopular. Still, Ann felt she had to be grateful to her sponsor, take her side, and protect her, even when Ann did not like her at all, for which she was really angry at herself.

Besides these complaints Ann had started an affair at the college with a man whom in a way she did not respect. She felt he was proud of his affair with her and wanted to let people know about it. She became especially upset when he arranged to meet her with two other men in a coffee house with a large window where all four of them sat, so that everybody passing by could see them. When she became pregnant she did not know whether it was by her husband or this man, and had an abortion. So she went through a very terrible time and was extremely upset when she came to me. She had not been in therapy before and came to me now because she was, as she felt, in a crisis situation.

Ann recalled that when she was three years old she was afraid to talk to her parents. From there she went on to say that her father was shallow and empty and she did not respect him. Her mother was always angry at her father, delivering violent tirades. Once she threatened him with a knife and threw a cup at him. When the parents fought, Ann always felt guilty.

Her brother who is six years older was out of the house at that time, and she has not much contact with him now.

She felt at the mercy of her parents. At ten or eleven years of age she always had to be home after school, and could have no friends. She developed suicidal ideas at that age, wanting to drown herself; but she did not make any actual attempt. When she tried to rebel against her parents, she would feel guilty and apologize. Maybe it was to get away from home that she got married when she was twenty, although she had not really been in love with her husband.

According to Ann, her parents' oppression went so far as to not permit her to attend her own high school graduation although she had been nominated to be the valedictorian. Instead, she had to stay home to help her mother with her housework. When I expressed doubt that she had been to such an extent at the mercy of her parents, she said "Yes, you are right. You know, I was always called very sneaky." I replied that in this case she must have done many things behind her parents' back to justify this description.

Indeed, it seems she never had the courage for open rebellion. At the age of 15, when she was already very pretty and had many dates, she used to lie to her mother, telling her she was studying with a girl friend instead of admitting that she was with a date. When she was not permitted to read at night, she switched out the light and read with a flashlight.

It is the same pretense and lack of courage that becomes again evident in her relationships to the woman who had given her her job, whom she detested yet with whom she did not break relations; to her husband who she felt was cold and whom she only had the courage to deceive; and to the other man who she felt actually despised her yet with whom she continued her relationship.

Even in her relationship to me, she also had this pretense. For example, in the beginning of her treatment when she told me all the sad stories of her life, she cried profusely using up many paper tissues. Yet at the same time she insisted that she was not at all involved in the treatment.

I put it to her this way, after about 4 to 6 weeks: I told her that she considered herself a second-rate person who at best fights only in a sneaky way. She never feels entitled to a first-rate position. Rather she shapes her life to feel second-rate— in her marriage, at her work, and in the affair that she had. At no point does she fight openly for the position of a really first-rate person, nor does she fight like such a person.

This is quite incongruous with the fact that she was, after all, an extremely attractive woman, with dark curls and very good color; had a very good job, prestige, and many friends. Why should such a woman make herself so miserable?

This interpretation apparently opened new alternatives to her and offered her real encouragement. It made her very happy. She saw its relevance to her problems, past and present. Ann was now able to resolve in one day the relationship to the older woman by talking to her openly, telling her that she really does not want to be her friend any more and wants to make her own way, in another department. She put her affair with the other man on a new basis by telling him how much she had resented to be, as she felt, exhibited. Only with her husband does she still not know what to do: Should she be more open with him and dissolve the marriage? But this will also depend on whether he might change his job, and so on.

Concluding Comments

The ER technique has the special advantage that the data can be gathered in a group situation. The teacher, e.g., can ask a class of school children to write down their ERs and then read them. This will give her, with very little training, a very valuable insight into the children of her class.

ERs, both written and verbal, can also be used in group

therapy. For instance I asked a group of women of very low education, with psychosomatic symptoms, to write down their ERs. Not all of them could do this, but they could think about it; and some gave ERs verbally, which then prompted others who did not remember anything at first to relate their ERs.

I have used ERs furthermore to demonstrate Adlerian methods in a training institute which was not Adlerian. The trainees were psychologists, psychiatrists, and social workers who all had had so-called teaching analyses. I was supposed to demonstrate Adlerian techniques. So we started with ERs. The first one who remembered was a trainee physician. His ER was that his mother was sick. The doctor and his father were in her room with her. The door to this room was closed, so that the children including the speaker had to wait outside, anxious for the outcome of the mysterious happening inside. When telling his memory he suddenly exclaimed, "All my life I never wanted to feel excluded like that, to be kept in the dark when important things were happening. That's why I wanted to study medicine myself so that I would not be excluded, but know what is going on." This, then, was a recollection which had never come up in his many years of "classical" Freudian analysis, and which gave him now such an interesting insight into what motivated him, at least in part, in his choice of profession. Through this he also became aware of how angry and resentful he was because of being excluded, and he realized his whole ambitious attitude.

Returning in conclusion to psychotherapy, we may summarize. The uses of early recollections are (a) to help the therapist understand the patient's life-style, (b) to help the patient understand his own life-style, and thereby (c) to open for the patient the possibility of choosing more healthy behavior and gaining the courage to try out new, socially and individually more useful attitudes.

References

1. Adler, A. *The Individual Psychology of Alfred Adler.* Ed. by H. L. and Rowena R. Ansbacher. New York: Basic Books, 1956.
2. Adler, K. A. Techniques that shorten psychotherapy. *J. Indiv. Psychol.*, 1972, *28*, 155-168.

CHAPTER 16

EARLY CHILDHOOD RECOLLECTIONS AS AIDS IN GROUP PSYCHOTHERAPY*

ASYA L. KADIS

THE SIGNIFICANT ROLE of early childhood recollections and images (11), henceforth called ECR, first brought to light by Alfred Adler (3), has become more widely recognized within the past decade. According to Adler:

> Early recollections are most helpful in revealing what one regards as values to be aimed for, and what one senses as dangers to be avoided. They help us to see the kind of world which a particular person feels he is living in, and the ways he early found of meeting that world. . . . The basic attitudes which have guided an individual throughout his life, and which prevail likewise in his present situation, are reflected in these fragments (2, p. 287).

Adler compared ECR to the story of one's life (1). The individual repeats it to himself—as a warning or comfort in times of stress—to help him concentrate on his goal and/or to prepare him, by means of past experiences, to meet the future with an already tested style of action.

The recent literature sheds further light on this subject. Among the conclusions borne out by these studies are: (a) ECR frequently clarifies the central theme of the neurosis (7). (b) Certain differentiating elements are found in ECR between schizophrenic and neurotic patients (6). (c) ECR proves to be of value both in a practical testing situation and with reference to personality theory (10). (d) ECR serves as a check on other projective material (12). (e) The first memory often reveals

* Reprinted by permission from the *Journal of Individual Psychology*, 1957, *13*, 182-187.

"the organ of choice for the psychological expression of anxiety" (5).

Group psychotherapy affords a special opportunity to observe the significance and validity of ECR and its therapeutic implications as revealed in the "group family" constellation. In a therapeutic group setting where eight to ten individuals are trying to work out their problems, it is inevitable that each member will re-experience his entire network of relationships. While in individual therapy the patient's reactions are limited by the presence of only two persons, the therapist and himself, the group setting, which offers peers, older and younger members, both male and female, enables the patient to reexperience, with his "group family," relationships which mirror those of his nuclear family (8).

ECRs are actually interpretations of the earliest experiences of the individual; the subjective picture of his immediate environment, his home circle, is a prototype of the whole outside world as perceived by him. To repeat a well-known axiom: The child-parent relationship is a determining factor in shaping the child's ego, and with it his identification patterns. He projects these relationships onto the world at large so that it becomes his "private world," which he proceeds to deal with in terms of his "private logic" built up from his earliest experiences. His ECR reflects his life-style and constitutes a blueprint of his behavior.

In content, ECR deals with the individual's primary group —parents, parent substitutes, and siblings—and his early responses to challenging situations within this group. If we accept the concept that family attitudes tend in general to reflect other human relationships, ECR's should enable us to predict how a person will pursue his goals and relate to others in a "group family" setting. For this purpose, I have in recent years asked patients specifically to include with their ECR an *image* of the family as a whole.

The author's purpose is to show how ECR can aid the group psychotherapist in the initial treatment-planning interview, in launching a new group and in stress situations. It might often be of great value in answering the following pertinent questions with which each therapist is confronted. (a) Can the patient go immediately into a group? Does he need a short or long period of preparation, and what specific kind? (b) Does he need combined treatment? Or can he hold his own on a group level? (c) What is the patient's emotional capacity for relating to authority and the peer group? What is his dependency-independency status?

Planning of Treatment

The following cases illustrate how ECR helped the therapist in the choice of treatment, by enabling her to foresee a negative experience for the individual as well as for the group.

L. remembered: "I was standing on a chair. Mother was fitting a dress on me." Her description revealed, among other elements, that she still wanted an exclusive relationship with her mother, to have something "tailor-made" and to be "elevated." Although L. had four siblings, this was the only spontaneous recollection of her family.

This recollection was a warning that the patient would have a difficult time if plunged immediately into a group, for she would not have a "mother" devoted exclusively to her. The treatment-plan decided on was to work through L.'s need to be the sole love object of her mother which meant abandonment of the rest of her famly. After a year, first with individual and then with combined psychotherapy, the patient was ready to give up her quest for an exclusive mother-child relationship and slowly came to recognize how difficult it has been for her to accept the idea of sharing her mother with four siblings.

P., a man of 25, said: "I was waiting in the street for father. When I saw his car coming, I ran toward him with outstretched arms. He yelled angrily, 'Go back into the house and put on your coat.'" This early recollection showed in the initial interview that the patient would look on an authority figure as someone who would rebuke him, reprimand or even punish him, and that he would thus find it difficult to establish close rapport with the authority-parental figure, the therapist. It was as though the patient wore a warning sign: "Keep your distance. If I stretch out my hands to you, I know you will reject me."

It was decided that P. would have only a few individual sessions before entering a group, in the belief that he could establish good peer-level relationships, although he could not accept an authority-parent relationship. P., indeed, related to the peer group very rapidly and took a long time before he trusted and accepted friendliness from the psychotherapist. P.'s case presents a sharp contrast to that of L., who required a long period of combined treatment before she could accept the "group family" situation.

Progress of Treatment

When launching a new group, and the group still finds it difficult to bring forth meaningful material on its own, the therapist may ask the group for an ECR. Invariably, at least one member will volunteer. This evokes responses of sympathy and empathy from the other members, as well as their own ECRs. Both inter- and intra-communications are established, either on a verbal or nonverbal level.

In times of crisis of an individual patient during group therapy, the therapist should keep ECR in mind as an aid to understanding the deep-seated motivations underlying the patient's manifest behavior.

N., a 22-year-old girl, joined a new group with a very few individual sessions. In group meetings she was very dependent on the therapist, moving slowly and with great caution. After a few months the group began to meet once a week without the therapist, so-called alternate meetings. N. refused to attend these alternate meetings, using all kinds of alibis, and was about to leave the group when the therapist, in front of the group, brought out her first ECR. "I was left alone at home with my sister. We were jumping rope in the street. I fell down and cut my lip."

The patient's response was immediate. She said excitedly: "I never saw the connection before, but it's true I was never part of a gang. I guess I'm afraid that if mama is not around to watch me, I'll cut my lip again." At this point she looked around at the members, whose manner was both sympathetic and supportive though they had not joined in the discussion, and said: "I'll risk it this time." She joined alternate meetings, but her fear and anxiety continued for a long time.

The therapist may also be helped by ECR in predicting and

understanding certain behavior patterns during treatment which might otherwise be overlooked or misinterpreted.

D., a man of 27, gave the following ECR: "I was sitting on mother's lap. Father came and pulled me off." With the recollection in mind, the therapist was prepared for D.'s exhibitions of anger and hostility, followed by accusations, which occurred each time after he had established a friendly relationship with a girl in the group. The ECR made it easier for the therapist to understand the patient's testing and abusive behavior at the outset and to cope with it at a propitious moment therapeutically.

J., a young man, when asked initially for an ECR which would include a picture of the family as a whole, described himself sitting at a table with his immediate family and relatives —a much larger gathering than usual. A frightening silence ensued; there seemed to be neither relatedness nor communication. J. continued: "To this day I can't talk when there is company around the table. I can only talk in a one-to-one relationship." This patient was practically mute for over a year in the group. He became a so-called absorber and required prolonged combined treatment.

In addition to eliciting ECRs in the initial interview, the therapist may also call them up any time a patient exhibits emotionally charged, repetitive, and compulsive behavior, as in the following case.

F., a 35-year old man, became uncomfortable and fidgety and started to look for another seat, whenever he found himself sitting on a couch between two people. After this maneuver had been observed again and again, he was asked the reason for his restlessness in this situation. "I can never sit between two people," he replied. "Whenever I get in this spot, even in a restaurant or bar, I get completely paralyzed and unable to communicate." He associated this with his family constellation: "I was the middle one of three brothers and the smallest. People always thought I was the youngest child. I hated to be in the middle, and always felt that my two brothers squeezed me out. Even today I can't have a good time with both of them. It has to be one or the other."

At this point F. was asked to look back and attempt to recall a specific unbearable situation relating to his place in the family. After a few minutes of silence, he said: "Something comes to my mind that I haven't thought about since my childhood. There was a parade in our town, and I was watching, holding a hand of each brother. Suddenly someone yelled, 'Hey, you little one, get out in front.' I became frightened and started to cry." Thenceforth, he was able to elicit many other ECRs. He became increasingly better able to relate at the peer level, both within and outside of the group. He was finally able to say: "I know I'm not a small potato any more."

As individual members grow and mature during group therapy, they slowly give up the negative recollections that "justify" their anger with themselves and the world. They begin to elicit pleasant ECRs and are always astounded to realize how carefully and purposefully they hid these recollections from themselves in order to justify their actions. This confirms Paul Brodsky's statement that those memories are recalled which, at the time they are reproduced, serve to justify the individual's approach to life (4).

Summary

In group psychotherapy, the use of early childhood recollections (ECR) in the initial treatment planning interview can guide the therapist in placing the patient in the treatment set-up best suited to his needs. ECR can help the therapist to overcome resistances in the beginning of the group process by facilitating inter- and intra-personal communication in the group. During treatment proper, it can help the therapist and patient, as well as the group, to recognize the patient's style of life and his goals, and to clarify compulsive, repetitive, and irrational behavior. More extensive study will reveal even wider application of ECR as a projective diagnostic and prognostic technique.

References

1. Adler, A. *What life should mean to you.* New York: Grosset & Dunlap, 1931.
2. Adler, A. The significance of early childhood recollections. *Int. J. Indiv. Psychol.*, 1937, 3, 283-287.

3. Ansbacher, H. L. Adler's place today in the psychology of memory. *Indiv. Psychol. Bull.*, 1947, *6*, 32-40.
4. Brodsky, P. The diagnostic importance of early recollections. *Amer. J. Psychother.*, 1952, *6*, 484-493.
5. Eisenstein, V. and Ryerson, R. Psychodynamic significance of the first conscious memory. *Bull. Menninger Clinic*, 1951, *15*, 213-220.
6. Friedman, Alice. Early childhood memories of mental patients. *J. Child Psychiat.*, 1952, *2*, 266-269.
7. Greenacre, P. *Trauma, growth, and personality.* New York: Norton, 1952.
8. Kadis, A. L. Re-experiencing the family constellation in group psychotherapy. *Amer. J. Indiv. Psychol.*, 1956, *12*, 64-68.
9. Kadis, A. L. The alternate meeting in group psychotherapy. *Amer. J. Psychother.*, 1956, *10*, 275-291.
10. Kadis, A. L., Greene, J. S., and Freedman, N. Early childhood recollections—an integrative technique of personality test data. *Amer. J. Indiv. Psychol.*, 1953, *10*, 31-42.
11. Kadis, A. L. and Lazarsfeld, S. The respective roles of earliest recollections and images. *Amer. J. Psychother.*, 1948, *2*, 250-255.
12. Lieberman, Martha G. Childhood memories as a projective technique. *J. Proj. Tech.*, 1957, *21*, 32-36.

CHAPTER 17

THE USE OF EARLY CHILDHOOD
RECOLLECTIONS AS A TEACHING DEVICE[*]

DANIEL I. MALAMUD

E ARLY RECOLLECTIONS, regarded by Adler[1] as significant reflections of an individual's style of life, have been considered a projective technique," and found to be useful in educational and vocational guidance, in psychiatric screening, in providing clues to differential diagnosis, and in individual and group therapy.[4, 3, 2] The present paper describes the use of early memories as a device for introducing students to the following concepts: (1) the formative influence of early childhood experiences, especially those involving parent-child relationships, (2) unconscious motivation, and (3) the selective function of recall in terms of current attitudes, needs, and conflicts.

The early memory proceedings to be described were developed as part of the "Workshop in Self-Understanding," a 15-week adult education course at New York University which aims at extending the layman's understanding of himself and the shaping influences in his life.[5] In this course the leader introduces a variety of group "games" and exercises designed to excite the student's curiosity about himself; these procedures involve the group in classroom experiences which elicit sharp individual differences in response and provoke students to search out for themselves the personal significance of these differences.

The early memory procedure, in its essentials, may be summarized as follows: The leader asks each member to write out his very first memory. After introducing the notion that first memories may reflect a person's basic attitudes (both past and

---

[*] Reprinted by permission from the *Teaching Psychology Newsletter*, Skidmore College, June 1968, 8-10.

present) towards himself and others, and after giving examples of how memories may be analyzed, the leader requests members to write out interpretations of their memories on the other side of their sheets. The papers are then collected, and the leader chooses one to read to the group without revealing whose memory it is. After the group gives its reactions, he turns the memory over to the other side and reads the author's own interpretation. He then invites the writer to give his reaction to the group's speculations. This procedure is then repeated with as many memories of as many other members as possible.

The introduction of the early memory procedure is carefully timed for that moment in the life of the group when it appears to be in an optimal state of readiness, i.e., when the class atmosphere tends to be predominantly relaxed and accepting, when considerable rapport has developed between the group and the leader, and when members show signs of interest in the possibility that early childhood experiences can be important sources of clues for extending self-knowledge.

The leader's initial instructions to the group run along the following lines: "Please write out your very earliest childhood memory, the very first incident, experience, or image that you can recall. Report a memory which you can actually recall yourself, not one which was told to you by someone else and that you yourself can't remember. Include your approximate age at the time." Members usually require no more than five minutes for this task.

The leader collects the members' first memories at least a week in advance of the memory session so that he can look them over and select those to be read to the group. He decides upon a sequence of presentation which appears most likely to provide encouraging experiences to the group in its first fumbling efforts at memory analysis; memories which appear to be especially simple and easy to interpret and which have been given by the more articulate, insightful members are presented first. All the memories are typed and duplicated so that a copy can be distributed to each participant. Members find it helpful to be able to refer repeatedly to a memory in the course of analyzing and discussing it.

The leader opens the session on memories with a brief statement along the following lines: "A person's first memory, no matter how apparently trivial, must have some special significance to him in the sense that just this one is recalled as the first rather than innumerable other possible childhood experiences. While the first memory may reflect a person's perception of an event rather than the actual occurrence itself, one can often discover clues in the memory as to the kinds of situations he actually had to cope with in his family and the ways he learned to deal with these situations. Each memory probably contains some hidden self-message, slogan, or conclusion which is important in the recaller's current life. In short, a person's first memory may serve as a basis for forming questions and hypotheses about his past experiences, the conclusions he drew from these experiences about himself and others, and his current orientation to life."

The leader then presents a series of simple first memories (obtained from patients or members of other groups) and discusses with the group its speculations to each in turn. This practice period usually requires about thirty minutes. The leader instructs members to "listen" to each memory with their emotions as well as their minds, to be as aware as possible of the thoughts, feelings, and intuitions which occur to them as they review a memory, and to share these reactions with the group without worrying about whether or not they seem to be plausible, or even reasonable.

After presenting a sample memory, the leader guides the group in its explorations with such questions as the following: What feeling did you get as you listened to the memory? What seems to be the central theme of this memory? Why might this memory have stuck in the person's mind? What needs seems to be central here? What might his relationship with his parents have been like? What kind of difficulties might this child have had at home? How might he have tried to cope with these difficulties? What do you think this child might be learning about what he and other people are like? Can you detect any hidden message or slogan in this memory? What kinds of patterns might this person be carrying over into the present? Does anything seem to be omitted in this memory? What kind of a person might recall such a memory? What attitudes does this person have towards himself? How does he feel about people? What does he want from people? How does he try to get what he wants from people? What might this person's role be in this class?

The leader encourages the group to be alert to the positive qualities and strengths that may be implicit in a memory as well as to the recaller's problems and difficulties. If the group focuses exclusively on thematic content the leader draws its attention to the possible significance of such memory character- istics as setting, presence or absense of reported emotion, lan- guage and style of reporting, persons included or excluded, degree of activity or passivity, age of recall, and the emphasized sensory modality. He sometimes assists the group by drawing its atten- tion to some pertinent phrase or word whose possible significance may have been overlooked and asks what comes to mind about this phrase or that word. He accepts all interpretive possibilities offered by the group, but he emphasizes from time to time that its comments are guesses and that a single memory provides an insufficient basis for drawing any firm conclusions.

Once the group shows evidence of having "caught on" to the process of exploring memories, the leader asks each member to reexamine his own first memory in terms of what he has just learned and to write out on the reverse side of the sheet his impression as to what it may be expressing and revealing. At this point there are usually some members who still cannot see anything meaningful in their first memory; they are instructed to simply write out a statement to this effect on the other side. Following the completion of these instructions, the leader informs the group as to the procedural steps which he will follow. He suggests that those in the group who do not wish to participate in the next steps simply write "Do not read" at the top of their sheet. (Almost all students are eager to submit their memories to group analysis, and it is rare that anyone chooses not to participate.)

After collecting the papers the leader reads his own earliest recollection to the group, identifying it simply as coming from "somebody in our group." The members give their reactions to the memory quite freely. Many of their comments are usually penetrating. When the leader informs them that the memory is his, the group reacts with shocked surprise. He then proceeds to acknowledge the validity of this or that specific comment and adds some of his own insights which may have been overlooked. He thus sets an example of matter-of-fact frankness and openness, enabling others to explore their own memories with a greater degree of openness and relaxation than might otherwise be possible.

He then reads another first memory anonymously to the group. During the course of the group's explorations, he enters freely into the discussion with his own associations, speculations, and interpretative comments. When the group fails to do so, he directs their attention to those features in the memory which suggest positive qualities, assets, or talents. He is especially alert to comments which simply enumerate this or that negative trait or attitude in a way which arouse defensiveness in the member whose memory is being read. At such point, he encourages the group to regard the negative trait in terms of its dynamic meaning in the life of a child struggling to cope with problems confronting him. For example, in response to one memory, a student said, "This is a person who puts on a false face to people." The leader added quietly, "If this is so, perhaps as a child she felt a false face was necessary because she felt her real feelings would not be accepted or understood by her parents."

After the group has exhausted its speculations, the leader reads the recaller's own interpretation of his memory on the other side of the sheet. More often than not the self-interpretation corresponds to some of the main points made by the group. Frequently the group has raised possibilities which are omitted in the self-interpretation and vice versa; less common are flat disagreements between self-interpretation and group judgments. At appropriate points the leader states that the validity of the memory, the group's interpretation, and even the recallers self-interpretations are unknown and need to be regarded as tentative, that both the group's and the recaller's speculations, whether they agree or disagree, need to be regarded simply as hypotheses which may be useful in stimulating new avenues of self-exploration. He also points out that members' comments may sometimes be more of a reflection of their own attitudes than of the attitudes implied by the memory.

After reading the self-interpretation, the leader invites the anonymous author of the memory under consideration to give his reactions to the speculations that have been expressed, asking such questions as "What did you think of the comments made about your memory?" "Do you recall how you felt as you were listening to the members' comments?" "Were there any comments which struck you particularly in one way or another?" After the author has replied to these questions, the leader invites the group to give its reactions to the author's comments, and encourages the cross-discussion among the members that often develops spontaneously.

The above procedure may be varied in many ways depending upon the group's needs, structure, and size. Examples of such modifications follow:

1. The leader may ask for the three earliest memories, or the first three memories of mother, etc. The group then pays special attention to the possibility of repeated patterns in at least two of the three memories.

2. Each member, in turn, reports orally his earliest memory relevant to a particular theme, for example, "school," "illness," "punishment," "a birthday," "separation," etc. At the completion of this go-around the leader invites the members to share what similarities and differences they noticed in the various memories and to explore what the personal significance of these differences might be. For example, when the stimulus theme is "punishment" the members compared their memories in terms of the reason for the punishment, the punisher, the nature of the punishment, and the reaction to the punishment. The past and present significance of variations around each of these characteristics are discussed.

3. When only one session can be devoted to the memory experiment in a group that contains over twenty members, each member's memory can be discussed if in the first half of the session the leader follows the procedure out-

lined above, and if in the second half of the session the group is broken up into a number of buzz groups. Each small group meets in a different area in the classroom, selects a chairman who then proceeds to follow the example set by the leader, collecting the memories of the members and submitting each one at a time to the speculations of the group.

The early memory session usually provides a "surprise" experience for laymen, most of whom have never attached any special significance to their early memories. In this session they begin to see their memories with new eyes; they become at least somewhat aware what they remember is not a matter of accident, but is determined by selective inner factors of which they have been previously entirely unaware, or only dimly conscious at best. This shared experience heightens the members' appreciation for the formative significance of early childhood experiences in a way that is more personally meaningful than probably any lecture or text could be. Without any explicit point being made about it, members begin to realize the possibilities of viewing memories as symbols with implications that go beyond what is concretely stated.

The first memory procedure is usually effective in furthering the group's harmonious closeness and freedom of communication. Students whose behavior has been annoying or puzzling to others are often seen in a more sympathetic light once their memories have been discussed. Thus the first memory procedure proves to be an exercise in empathy as well as a stimulus to self-insight.

The first memory procedure has been especially useful in workshops with patients prior to their entrance into therapy. The experiment not only sensitizes patients to the value of exploring childhood experiences later in therapy, and adds to their confidence in their own interpretive capacities, but impresses them markedly with the perceptiveness of others in the group and with the possibility of receiving helpful insights from peers as well as from the authority, thus paving the way for a later acceptance of group therapy. Also, the leader may find that the patient's reaction to the memory procedure provides prognostic clues as to his capacity for future growth and response to therapy. The degree of resistance to recognizing meaningfulness in a memory, the degree to which this resistance is overcome during the session, the nature of the self-interpretation, the degree to which the patient can accept ideas different from his his own—all of these are clues to the patient's picture of himself, his degree of rigidity, and his readiness to introspect and think psychologically about himself.

In conclusion, the author's experiences have been consistent with the Adlerian view of early recollections as being readily accessible to meaningful interpretation. It appears that laymen as well as the trained professional can interpret memories in a meaningful way. Workshop experiences have also confirmed Adler's view that early memories possess numerous practical advantages: People are generally unaware of the hidden or explicit meaning of their memories, discuss them willingly, and their brevity and simplicity make them readily available for use in large groups.

References

1. Adler, A. "The significance of early recollections," *Int. J. Indivi. Psychol.*, 1937, *3*, 283-287.
2. Brodsky, P. "The diagnostic importance of early recollections," *Amer. J. Psychother.*, 1952, *6*, 484-493.
3. Ivimey, M. "Childhood memories in psychoanalysis," *Amer. J. Psychoanal*, 1950, *10*, 38-47.
4. Kadis, Asya, Greene, Janet S., and Freedman, N. "Early childhood recollections—an integrative technique of personality test data," *Amer. J. Indiv. Psychol.*, 1952, *10*, 31-42.
5. Malamud, D. I. and Machover, S. *Toward self-understanding: Group techniques in self-confrontation.* Springfield: Thomas, 1965.
6. Mosak, H. "Early recollections as a projective technique," *J. of Proj. Techniques*, 1958, *22*, 302-311.

CHAPTER 18

PREDICTING THE RELATIONSHIP TO THE PSYCHOTHERAPIST FROM EARLY RECOLLECTIONS*

HAROLD H. MOSAK

AN INDIVIDUAL ORDINARILY behaves in a self-consistent manner consonant with his life-style. In psychotherapy he brings this same life-style to the therapeutic situation. Thus, what the Freudians refer to as transference attitudes are merely the expression of general convictions the patient has come to hold with respect to himself and the world. In 1913 Adler wrote:

> I expect from the patient again and again the same attitude which he has shown in accordance with his life-plan toward the persons of his former environment, and still earlier toward his family. At the moment of the introduction to the physician and often even earlier, the patient has the same feelings toward him as toward important persons in general. The assumption that the transference of such feelings or that resistance begins later is a mere deception. In such cases the physician only recognizes them later (1, pp. 336-337).

In order to avoid this "later" recognition it would be helpful to the therapist if he could predict early in treatment the patient's attitudes, whether referring to these as transference or not.

Such a possibility exists in the use of early recollections which Adler suggested as one of "the most trustworthy approaches to the exploration of personality" (1, p. 327). He explains the rationale of the diagnostic value of early recollections as follows: "(The individual's) memories are the reminders he carries

---

* Reprinted by permission from the *Journal of Individual Psychology*, 1965, *21*, 1, 77-81, and from *On Purpose*, Chicago, Alfred Adler Institute, 1976.

about with him of his own limits and of the meaning of circumstances. There are no 'chance memories': out of the incalculable number of impressions which meet an individual, he chooses to remember only those which he feels, however darkly, to have a bearing on his situation" (1, p. 351).

Early recollections (ERs) permit the formulation of a thumbnail description of the individual's life-style. The method has been described in detail by the present writer (3). For a method of rapidly ascertaining antecedent information concerning the family atmosphere, which Adlerians find congenial in their understanding of the development of the life-style, the reader is referred to articles by Dreikurs (2) and Shulman (4).

Case 1

To illustrate, let us analyze the following ERs given by a man of 40 who has a history of poor interpersonal relations. He tries hard to be a "nice" guy but others treat him poorly in return. He cannot understand why this should be, but wants to discover the reason in psychotherapy.

1. I was lying on the floor listening to the radio while my parents and another couple were playing bridge. My father was running his hand over my aunt's leg. She pushed it away but my father put his hand on it again. I was angry with my father because he was wrong.

2. I fell down the stairs and landed on my head on a cement floor. I was conscious but insensible. My mother got excited and took me on the street car to my uncle's office. He was a dentist. I don't know why she took me to him.

3. This happened in first grade. I was a talker in school. This day the teacher was bawling out a kid and threatening to call his father. I said, "You always say it but never do it." She said, "What did you say?" I was scared but I repeated it. She marched me into a room with a lower grade. I was only trying to help her.

4. The maid took me home to her house and offered me beer. I hated it but drank it and didn't let on I didn't like it.

5. When I was seven, my mother was pregnant and my uncle and aunt took me out. They stopped somewhere because I had to go to the washroom. There were some puppies there, and I bent over to pet one, and the mother dog bit me in the behind. I screamed. My uncle laughed, took me into the restaurant, and

applied iodine in public. I hated him for making me a laughing stock.

6. My mother sent me to the store with a $10 bill in my pocket and told me not to take it out. I did and lost it. I came home and lied that two men had held me up. My mother called the police, and I crossed myself up. My father beat hell out of me with a strap.

7. My father took us for a ride in his new car. When we got in front of our house, I jumped out before the car stopped and the door was torn off the car when it hit a pole. If my father could have killed me, he would have.

Life-style

Since ERs are assumed to reflect an individual's current mode of perception, we may use these to discern several major trends in his personality. We note that in all his ERs someone does wrong, intentionally or otherwise. People are constantly spoiling things for each other. The patient does not exempt himself from this category of wrongdoers. However, even when he endeavors to do the right thing, he winds up hurt. He tries to please but ends up suffering. He always gets "the short end of the stick." We arrive at the picture of a hypercritical individual who finds fault with all of life including himself although he has better intentions than others do. He does not believe in the possibility of good human relations. Anticipating suffering inevitably, he is a thorough pessimist who at times goes looking for his own beatings.

Predictions

How might this person perceive and use the therapy situations? The therapist can formulate several tentative hypotheses. The patient might

1. be critical of therapy, the therapist, and his progress;

2. perceive the therapist as another person who will make him suffer;

3. attempt to provoke the therapist—not intentionally, of course, to make him (the patient) suffer; then he can be critical of the therapist and feel morally superior to him;

4. devote himself to the recitation of incidents, past and present, where others have abused him, humiliated him, and wronged him;

5. distrust the therapist and distrust the possibility of a good

human relationship with him;

6. try to ingratiate himself with the therapist and then be disappointed when the therapist fails to meet one of his implicit or explicit demands;

7. caught in a tight spot, attempt to lie his way out, but would probably do so clumsily since he expects to be found out;

8. fearing punishment and humiliation, withhold certain information from the therapist until he feels he can trust him with it.

Outcome

In the course of treatment, the patient's behavior confirmed several of the above hypotheses. He consistently inquired of the therapist whether therapy was *really* helping him (Hyp. 1). At other times he would attempt to ingratiate himself with the therapist by telling him that therapy had been helpful but that his wife and children really needed the treatment (Hyp. 6). He devoted most of the initial period of treatment to a recitation of how his mother abused him, how his wife and her family wronged him, how his children misbehaved, and how his employees took advantage of him (Hyp. 4). He withheld speaking of his own misdeeds until much later in treatment, and then with a sheepish grin since he was apprehensive that the therapist might disapprove of him (Hyp. 8). When he terminated treatment, he grudgingly admitted making some gains but was still focusing on the world's abuse of him (Hyp. 1 and 4).

Case 2

Occasionally the question as to whether a certain type of therapist is preferable for a particular patient assumes importance. Frequently we ask ourselves whether the patient might relate better to a male or female therapist, though there are differences of opinion as to how crucial a factor this may be. This decision is difficult to make at the initiation of therapeutic contact since we have so little reliable information about the patient at this time. Here again ERs can give us assistance.

The following ERs were given by a college student both of whose parents set excessive standards for him. His father was a man with questionable authority in his own family since the mother dominated him (and the son) through a self-sacrificing, martyrlike goodness. This domination of the patient was so thoroughly effective that when he, soon after beginning treatment, was dismissed from college for deliberately obtaining poor grades, he boasted gleefully to his therapist, "That's the first decision I ever made on my own in my whole life." His ERs were:

1. My tonsils were being taken out. I remember someone putting a mask over my face. A woman was saying something to me. I felt like the breath was being drawn out of me.

2. I was playing ball with my sister. I bent over a wire to get the ball and my sister pushed me over it. I fell on a board and cut my hand on some glass. All the neighbors were throwing down towels to put around the wound but it kept bleeding through.

3. The first day of kindergarten. Our collie dog was going blind; it would defecate in the back yard. I stepped in it but didn't know it. When I came to school, I noticed the odor, looked down at my shoe, and scraped it off. When leaving the room, the teacher asked me to help her clean up the floor.

4. I was walking to school with a girl. I asked her, "Will you be my girl friend and I'll be your boy friend?" She slapped me. I came home and didn't want to ever go to school again.

5. My grandmother died and it was my first funeral. Everyone was crying, and I thought it was silly, and I laughed.

6. I called a girl a "whore." She cried and told my mother. My mother asked whether I knew the meaning of the word. I pretended I knew and wouldn't tell.

Predictions

From this brief diagnostic material it was possible to guess the patient's possible attitudes toward a female therapist. Consistently the ERs depict a little boy being overwhelmed and hurt by women. In addition, in ER 3, he attempts to cover up the malodorous part of himself, but even in this instance, a woman finds him out. As in the previous illustration we can phrase several hypotheses which in this case involve predictions as to what might occur were this patient assigned to a woman therapist. The patient might

1. see a female therapist as a threatening, potentially overwhelming person;

2. take perverse pleasure if something adverse happens to his therapist;

3. provoke the therapist to see whether she makes trouble for him since he feels he is the victim of women;

4. attempt to cover up his deficiencies, his "sins," and his

"ignorance," at the same time expecting to be found out;

    5. make some "innocent" sexual advances to the therapist; and if "accused" of such behavior, attempt to leave therapy;

    6. devote much of his therapeutic time to elaborating upon the theme, "You can't do business with women."

Outcome

In this case, acting upon the clear indications of the ERs, the choice of a male therapist was made. Consequently, the negative predictions for a female therapist were not directly checked by the course of events in therapy. This did, however, support the general conclusions drawn from the ERs regarding the subject's life-style.

When the patient entered psychotherapy, he was unmarried and constantly involved with women with whom nothing worked out. His mother made life difficult for him and for his father. He dropped out of treatment and was performing successfully at a university when he married a willful and, by her own admission, "spoiled brat." They fought almost every day of their marriage. The patient returned to psychotherapy and the wife also sought treatment. Except for periods of discouragement when he gave full expression to his failure, he attempted to "look good" to the therapist, even resorting to lying to cover up his negative aspects.

Summary

Prediction of the probable attitudes of a client toward his therapist would prove of considerable assistance to the therapist, whatever his theoretical orientation, and in the choice of a therapist. Early recollections, when understood as suggested by Adler as representative of the individual's life-style and hence as reflecting his current mode of perception and attitudes, provide a means for such prediction. This is illustrated by two cases.

References

1. Adler, A. *The Individual Psychology of Alfred Adler.* H. L. and Rowena R. Ansbacher (Eds.) New York: Basic Books, 1956.
2. Dreikurs, R. The psychological interview in medicine. *Amer. J. Indiv. Psychol.,* 1952, *10,* 99-122.

3. Mosak, H. H. Early recollections as a projective technique. *J. Proj. Tech.*, 1958, *22*, 302-311.
4. Shulman, B. H. The family constellation in personality diagnosis. *J. Indiv. Psychol.*, 1962, *18*, 35-47.

CHAPTER 19

EARLY RECOLLECTION CHANGES AFTER COUNSELING: A CASE STUDY*

DANIEL G. ECKSTEIN

T HE SIGNIFICANCE OF early recollections is one of the most important discoveries of Individual Psychology (Adler, 1931; Mosak, 1969; Nikelly, 1971; Sonstegard, 1973). Adler (1931) described the significance of such recollections:

Among the psychological expressions, some of the most revealing are individual memories. His memories are reminders he carries about with him of his own limits and of the meaning of circumstances. There are no "chance memories"; out of the incalculable number of impressions which meet an individual, he chooses to remember only those which he feels, however darkly, to have a bearing on his situation. Thus, the memories represent his "story of my life," a story he repeats to himself to warn him or comfort him, to keep him concentrated on his goal, and to prepare him by means of past experience, so that he will meet the future with an already tested style of action. (p. 73)

A crucial Adlerian theoretical notion regarding ERs is that during the course of therapy either an entirely new set of memories will be recalled or the same "objective" recollection will be accompanied by a different "subjective" personal reaction. Dreikurs (1967) writes:

The final proof of the patient's satisfactory reorientation is the change in his basic mistakes, indicated by a change in his early recollections. If a significant improvement has taken place, new

* Reprinted by permission from the *Journal of Individual Psychology*, 1976, 32, 2, 212-223. The author gratefully acknowledges the permission of Catherine Altman and James Quinn to use the Early Recollections Rating Scale. The statistical assistance of Martha Bayes of the University of South Carolina was also invaluable.

incidents are recollected, reported recollections show significant changes or are in some cases completely forgotten. (p. 71)

In a similar manner, Nikelly (1971) has noted that "ERs will often change before and after therapy in the same way the client's attitudes about himself and toward life are altered after treatment or following an unusual phase in his life" (p. 59).

This report is an effort to critically evaluate ER changes in one individual following nine months of counseling. The author's "subjective" case notes will be complemented by "objective" naïve expert ER ratings in researching changes. Thus clinical impressions will be contrasted with a psychometric approach in examining ER changes.

Method

Jane, a 19-year-old freshman at a women's college, requested counseling in her second week of school. Since a specific concern involved conflicts with her roommate, the counselor suggested that a life-style analysis might be beneficial in providing some insights. After an exploratory relationship-building introductory session, life-style data (including ERs) was obtained. Upon sharing with her the life-style summary, the counselor met weekly with Jane for the balance of the nine-month academic year. At the final counseling session, Jane was asked to report her earliest childhood memories again. No reference was made to previous ERs.

Standardized pre- and post-ER instructions were: "Think back as far as you can, and tell me your earliest childhood memories." Jane reported eight recollections and one recurring dream on the pretest, and five recollections on the posttest nine months later.

The 14 pre- and post-ERs were randomly presented to raters with the following written instructions:

"Enclosed you will find the following:
—1 Early Recollections Rating Scale
—14 ER sheets containing either a dream or an ER
—A folded and stapled envelope to be opened *after* you have completed the 14 ER sheets

Would you please follow this standardized procedure in rating:

(1) Read and review the 'Instructions to Rater' sheet defining and describing the nine bi-polar variables.

(2) Rate each sheet containing an ER on the 1-7 scale. Consider each ER *independently;* they are *not* to be considered together.

(3) After completing your ratings, open the folded envelope and follow the appropriate directions."

The second sealed envelope contained both sets of ERs from the pre- and posttest. The raters received the following instructions: "Please read the entire set of early recollections and then make one general, global rating based on your total impression of all recollections. There is one sheet for each set of recollections. Please do not consult your previous ratings."

There was no indication that the ERs were from the same subject. It was thus possible to compare separate, isolated ratings with a general, global rating on all pre- and post-recollections.

Instrument

The Early Recollections Rating Scale (ERRS) was originally developed by Altman (1973) and later modified by Quinn (1973). It rates nine different basic attitudes, each variable being on a bipolar scale containing seven numerical categories. A score of 4 indicates a "neutral" or "average" rating. Higher scores reflect greater social interest. The nine bipolar ratings consisted of: A. Subject's Behavior Toward the Environment: (1) withdrawn-gregarious, (2) passive-active, (3) competitive-cooperative, (4) dependent-independent; and B. The Individual's Subjective Affect or Feeling of the Environment: (5) hostile-friendly, (6) rejected-accepted, (7) discouraged-self-confident, (8) depressed-cheerful, and (9) mistreated-befriended.

Altman (1973) obtained inter-rater reliabilities on the ERRS for the nine bi-polar variables ranging from .56 to .79, all significant beyond the .001 level of confidence. Six of the eight raters in the present study had participated in the Quinn and Altman studies. All eight raters were experienced practicing Adlerian psychologists.

In her study, Altman found five social interest scores significantly correlated with measures of empathy, including: benevolence-aggression, befriended-mistreated, friendly-threatening, acceptance-rejection, and cheerful-depressing. She also found that three attitudes, benevolence, befriended, and self-confidence, were the best predictors of empathy.

Using a modified version of the ERRS which had a revised definition for the competitive-cooperative scale, Quinn studied relationships between ERs, recidivism, and type of crime with prison inmates. He found no significant relationships between the ERs of recidivists and nonrecidivists who had committed crimes against people. Conversely, in crimes against property, recidivists scored significantly lower than nonrecidivists on the competitive-cooperative scale.

The present study utilized the modified Altman ERRS variables as used to investigate single ERs, and also included global ratings.

Statistical Procedure

Rater mean scores on all nine bipolar ERRS variables were obtained for each individual pre- and post-ER. Mean scores of the global ERs were computed as were the sum of all Behavior and Affect variables. Two-tailed parametric T-tests evaluated mean differences between the pre- and post-counseling ERs.

Case Study

Although neither the subject's life-style nor a comprehensive case history is considered necessary, a brief summary of the counseling follows. The counselor sought initially to *develop the relationship* including the Carkhuff (1969) core "rapport" dimensions of genuineness, empathy, positive regard, understanding, etc. The second phase of the relationship consisted of a *psychological investigation,* including the completion of the life-style summary. The Kuder Occupational Interest Survey, the Tennessee Self-Concept Scale, the 16 Personality Factors, and the Edwards Personal Preference Schedule were also administered. The third phase, the *interpretation,* disclosed results of the psychometric instruments coupled with clinical observatons to provide some insight for the client.

Jane, the youngest of five children (sister nine years older,

three brothers eight, five, and three years older, respectively),
described her childhood in the paradoxical way of "unhappy,
but happy"—"I often got frustrated when I tied knots in my
shoes, always wanting to do what my brothers and sisters were
doing; I was always younger, and couldn't keep up physically
or emotionally. I liked ballet, played with dolls a lot, and liked
to dance. I enjoyed drawing, but often got frustrated because
I couldn't do it well enough, so I quit drawing completely until
high school. I've always felt like the baby."

In relation to her siblings, Jane found her place by being
a hard worker, helping around the house, being a "pleaser,"
critical of self and others, wanting and receiving her own way,
sensitive and easily hurt, throwing temper tantrums, and by
being idealistic and materialistic. She was also the sibling most
spoiled by her parents, obtaining special attention, love, and
material possessions from them. Her main sibling competitors
appeared to be her sister and second brother who was five
years older than Jane.

The following life-style summary, what Dreikurs (1953)
called the "theme of life, with its endless variations" (p. 43)
was shared with Jane:

> *Life* is a mixture of happiness and fun (i.e., when I'm playing or
> receiving special attention and material possessions) coupled with
> equally frightening experiences (i.e., when I encounter a new, un-
> known situation or am forced to rely on my own abilities).
>
> *Others* should provide me help or comfort in crisis situations. I
> enjoy being with other people.
>
> I want to be grown-up, but often find new experiences both
> challenging and frightening, especially when I must rely on myself.
> At such times I have a tendency to give up and become discouraged.
>
> It is important for me to gain special attention and be number
> one, especially with males, and to have special things provided me.
> I expect to have things go my own way.
>
> I enjoy having fun mischievously, especially at the expense of
> bending the rules a bit.

Much time was spent discussing and revising the implications of the above life-style summary with Jane. The counselor
explained the life-style summary as a general outline which
Jane was encouraged to apply to specific situations supporting

or rejecting basic notions about life, others, and self. Much to Jane's surprise, the life-style did provide important insights, and a commitment for long-term weekly counseling was obtained.

The final phase of counseling provided a *re-orientation* based upon insight and encouragement. After Jane and the counselor agreed upon her basic life-style, she was led to become aware that her unique style worked to her advantage as well as to her disadvantage. By gaining insight and seeing her life-style in action, Jane realized not only what was happening, but also began to understand that *she* had the *choice* of whether to continue specific behaviors or to act in new ways. Specific "conflict" situations included Jane's trouble with her roommate, her dependency upon male approval, plus her tendency to lean upon others in crises.

Throughout the counseling sessions, Jane experienced growth and renewed confidence in her ability to cope with problems. There were several disappointing setbacks—times in which she felt that no progress was being made. Jane was particularly concerned about her intolerant attitude which frequently resulted in peer conflicts. Specific goals for her Thanksgiving and Christmas holidays focused on becoming more self-sufficient at home and in coping with her dependency on her boyfriend's approval. She was encouraged to "get in touch" and "ride-with" the frequent periods of depression, including writing detailed diaries about her feelings in such situations. Her "bullheaded intolerance" was also discussed, including role-playing specific desired behavioral changes.

In the spring Jane continued to expand her interests and began feeling better about her art abilities, her creativity, and herself as a woman. She became intensely involved in the women's rights movement and was more active in campus activities. Jane also moved from an "inward" self-exploration to an "outward" concern for others which culminated in volunteer work at a telephone crisis center. During the final two months of counseling, Jane's biweekly appointments focused mainly upon the continuing changes she was initiating spontaneously. The posttest life-style data collection was conducted during the last visit, nine months after her initial counseling session. In a letter written during the summer she stated a new interest in personal meditation and reflection, a desire to work with others, and her improving self-concept.

Specific Early Recollections

The following pre- and post-counseling ERs were evaluated by the eight raters.

Pre-Counseling ERs

1. Had a nap—mom put us in smock dresses—man behind us had been painting—I sat down in bucket of paint—he was nice about it, didn't get mad—took me to mom; she and dad laughed. He took turpentine and got it out. Felt: in shock—didn't realize what had done, put on other dress—better dread being brought back by Mr. French.

2. My father put me on my sister's two-wheeler—I didn't trust him— I was terrified—felt I was too young to do it. He then took me off, knew I was too scared. Later went back and pretended I was riding. Felt: scared—relieved when got off—most vivid—screaming and hanging onto Dad—he didn't understand how scared I was.

3. My sis dressed me up in costume—she took me into backyard: took pictures. I liked it because my hair was fixed like grand-mother's. My sister then put her jewelry on me. Felt: in my glory—neat.

4. Suzie's birthday. Mother telling me I got my way with sister— there were two skirts; my sister wanted to wear the crinoline: didn't want to wear apron—I ended up in crinoline, I didn't have to threaten her—used reason; put on for picture. She was irked, but she never said anything. Felt: slick that I had been able to reason with her and weird: had gotten my way outside home—in a social aspect.

5. Mom said could take ballet or go to kindergarten. I figured kindergarten would end in year. First day—had been downtown with mom. She said could start but I didn't have a ballet outfit. The teacher said I could dance on my feet. I walked into room—it was the biggest had ever seen. It scared and thrilled me—unbelievably big. Felt: liked it—thought neat—know would like ballet. But scared me because new and didn't know other girls.

6. Remember playing in crib—sis sang "Itsy Bitsy Yellow Polka Dot Bikini" stood up and "danced" to music—thought it was fun. I was supposed to be sleeping, but wasn't. Content to be there in room—content and playing. Felt: happy, having good time.

7. Laying in crib—had mobile over head—had favorite mobile—colors red, black, blue. Used to watch it. Thought: pretty, tried to reach them.

8. Scared in dark-bathroom—one time Mother told me if I'd go upstairs by myself—would be candy behind toilet. Didn't believe it —got aunt to go up—she said there was candy up there. I went up there—was scared, but bold—two (Three Musketeers) were there. From then on not afraid. Proud of Mother—hadn't told me lie.

9. Dreams:—witch came into my room—woke up screaming and crying. Mother said lot of times new house causes bad dreams. Felt: safe—went back to sleep.

Post-Counseling ERs

1. Me and brother Allan—I was interior decorator—he was drunk— while mom decorating Christmas tree, we were playing. Hilarious —mom laughing at us; had to quit decorating just to watch us. She would decorate top half and let us decorate bottom half of tree. While she decorated top we entertained ourselves. Felt: happy, having fun.

2. Playing Monopoly® with brothers—got caught for cheating—they threw me out of game—but I wasn't mad—thought it was funny. Felt: didn't really want to play; was bored, so that was my way of getting out of it.

3. When moved out of old house—sitting back of stationwagon—we were taking last things out of house—remember being glad moving, but didn't know why. Felt: alone, but not in bad way.

4. Had white sandals; wasn't supposed to go barefooted. Put plug in sink to wash feet. Must have left plug in sink and left water running. She came home—there was water all over. It was a mess. She cleaned it up, but didn't get mad at me. I was upset. She knew why I had been up there, but she never said anything. The next day the lady next door bought me pink flip-flops to wear and mom didn't say anything. Felt: Okay, happy—had wanted flip-flops all along.

5. Father was teaching me to ride a two-wheeler—screamed at top of lungs—he was trying to teach me to ride—I should have been more cooperative. Felt: knew wasn't hurting me, should have been more cooperative.

Results

Table 19-I shows the mean rater differences based on global ratings of the nine pre-counseling ERs compared to the five post-counseling ERs. Mean pre- and post-ratings for each of the specific ERRS bipolar variables are compared, as are the sums of the four Behavior and the five Affect scales. There are significant differences for eight of the eleven variables. Mean scores improved on the posttest for all variables, the most significant change occurring on the depressed-cheerful scale ($p <$ .001). Significant ($p < .01$) improvements were noted on the ER total score associated with behavior. Similar growth ($p <$ .01) was noted on the total affect score.

Table 19-II compares the ERRS variables for individual ERs on both pre- and posttests. The mean of the nine specific ERs comprised the pretest score, while the posttest averages were based on the five concluding ERs. The primary difference be-

TABLE 19-I

MEAN PRE AND POST GLOBAL EARLY RECOLLECTION RATINGS

Variable	Mean ($n=8$)	Standard Deviation	T Value	2-Tail Probability Level of Significance ($df=7$)
1. Withdrawn-Gregarious				
Pre	4.13	1.13	—2.38	.05
Post	5.38	0.74		
2. Passive-Active				
Pre	3.88	1.55	—2.11	NS
Post	5.25	0.71		
3. Competitive-Cooperative				
Pre	3.38	0.92	—2.37	.05
Post	4.38	1.20		
4. Dependent-Independent				
Pre	2.38	1.60	—3.63	.01
Post	4.63	1.51		
5. Hostile-Friendly				
Pre	3.13	0.64	—3.86	.01
Post	4.88	0.99		
6. Rejected-Accepted				
Pre	4.00	1.20	—1.93	NS
Post	5.25	1.17		
7. Discouraged-Self-confident				
Pre	3.25	0.89	—3.23	.01
Post	5.13	0.99		
8. Depressed-Cheerful				
Pre	3.38	0.92	—5.29	.001
Post	5.38	0.74		
9. Mistreated-Befriended				
Pre	4.12	1.25	—1.76	NS
Post	5.13	0.99		
Total Behavior (Variables 1-4)				
Pre	3.44	0.72	—4.10	.01
Post	4.91	0.76		
Total Affect (Variables 5-9)				
Pre	3.58	0.82	—3.23	.01
Post	5.15	0.93		

tween Table 19-I and Table 19-II is that the former results are based on global ratings of all ERs, whereas the latter scores are determined by specific ERs. Results of Table 19-II indicate that the separate ratings were less significant and more variable than global comparisons. Two of the four Behavior variables were significant ($p < .05$), while none of the five Affect variables differed significantly.

TABLE 19-II

MEAN PRE AND POST INDIVIDUAL EARLY RECOLLECTION RATINGS

Variable	Mean (n=9)	Standard Deviation	T Value	2-Tail Probability Level of Significance (df=8)
1. Withdrawn-Gregarious				
Pre	3.96	0.49	—1.79	NS
Post	4.36	0.68		
2. Passive-Active				
Pre	4.64	0.74	—0.46	NS
Post	4.76	0.30		
3. Competitive-Cooperative				
Pre	4.02	0.12	3.06	.05
Post	3.82	0.19		
4. Dependent-Independent				
Pre	3.70	1.11	—2.97	.05
Post	4.64	0.60		
5. Hostile-Friendly				
Pre	4.25	0.44	1.24	NS
Post	4.07	0.38		
6. Rejected-Accepted				
Pre	4.49	0.56	1.14	NS
Post	4.22	0.47		
7. Discouraged-Self-confident				
Pre	4.21	0.59	—1.33	NS
Post	4.56	0.88		
8. Depressed-Cheerful				
Pre	4.62	0.47	—0.33	NS
Post	4.69	0.78		
9. Mistreated-Befriended				
Pre	4.63	0.67	0.04	NS
Post	4.62	0.54		
Total Behavior (Variables 1-4)				
Pre	4.58	0.70	1.83	NS
Post	4.11	0.57		
Total Affect (Variables 5-9)				
Pre	4.69	0.84	2.02	NS
Post	4.27	0.66		

Discussion

The major finding of this case study is that early recollections do appear to change significantly as a result of long-term counseling or therapy. This finding should be viewed optimistically by members of the helping profession who are committed to the belief that attitudes and behaviors *can* and *do* change.

The significant differences between the two sets of early recollections should also lend additional validity to the use of early recollections in assessing counseling changes. The high inter-rater reliabilities lend support for the use of the Early Recollections Rating Scale in evaluating significant content themes. However, additional validity studies are recommended.

Another important finding is that global ratings appear to be more uniform and more significant than individual ER evaluations. Such results are consistent with the belief that "the whole is more than the sum of the parts."

Adler stressed that specific events must be considered with reference to the total context (Zusammenhang) of the whole individual. In 1930 he wrote:

> To deny the context (Zusammenhang) is like picking single notes to examine them for their significance, their meaning. A better understanding of this coherence is shown by Gestalt psychology which uses this metaphor frequently, as we do. The difference is only that we are not satisfied with the "Gestalt," as we prefer to say, with the "whole," when we refer all the notes to the melody. We are satisfied only when we have recognized in the melody the originator and his attitudes as well, for example Bach, "Bach's Life Style." (p. 205).

The results of this study would appear to confirm Adler's "global" emphasis.

It is also interesting to note the raters' reactions at the conclusion of the ER evaluations. Not realizing that the global recollections had been based upon the same subject, a frequent response was: "I thought the ERs were from two different people —one set was definitely more positive."

This pilot study attempted to validate empirically the notion that ERs do change as a result of counseling or therapy. This intensive single-individual case study gives evidence in the expected direction, and provides support for future multi-subject research with control groups.

References

Adler, A. Nochmals-die Einheit der Neurosen. *International Journal of Psychology,* 1930, *8,* 201-216.

Adler, A. *What life should mean to you.* Boston: Little, Brown, and Co., 1931.

Adler, A. Significance of early recollections. *International Journal of Individual Psychology,* 1937, *3,* 283-287.

Altman, K. The relationship between social interest dimensions of early recollections and selected counselor variables. Unpublished doctoral dissertation, University of South Carolina, 1973.

Carkhuff, R. *Helping & human relations.* New York: Holt, Rinehart and Winston, Inc., 1969.

Dreikurs, R. *Fundamentals of Adlerian psychology.* Chicago: Alfred Adler Institute, 1953.

Dreikurs, R. *Psychodynamics, psychotherapy and counseling.* Chicago: Alfred Adler Institute, 1967.

Mosak, H. Early recollections: Evaluation of some recent research. *Journal of Individual Psychology,* 1969, *2,* 56-59.

Nikelly, A. (Ed.). *Techniques for behavior change.* Springfield: Thomas, 1971.

Quinn, J. Predicting recidivism and type of crime from early recollections of prison inmates. Unpublished doctoral dissertation, University of South Carolina, 1973.

Sonstegard, M. Life style identification and assessment. *The Individual Psychologist,* 1973, *10,* 1-4.

CHAPTER 20

DEALING WITH FEELINGS VIA EARLY RECOLLECTIONS

ED JANOE
With BARBARA JANOE

$\mathbf{F}$OR SEVERAL YEARS now, I have been using a technique that helps people get rid of uncomfortable feelings. The technique is rooted in Adlerian-Dreikursian principles and relies heavily on the use of early memories. Its basis is in the linkage between our rational, bodily, and emotional selves, which are not to be thought of as different or separate *parts* of our selves so much as different *aspects* of the same self.*

A child may interpret a situation he experiences. He may at that time become aware of a feeling in a certain part of his body, probably a part or parts he is using in that particular situation. When he later experiences a similar situation, a similar feeling will result. This may be called *body memory.* It is how we learn many of our feelings, and feelings can be learned. If they are automatic responses to a given situation, we should all feel the same way in any set of circumstances, yet we know that is not the case. We all know of some people who find high places exhilarating and others who are terrified at the thought of them; we know of people who are paralyzed if they must speak before an audience and others who think best and speak most coherently when they are the center of attention of a large group of people. At our first experiences of these things we learned how to feel, and now our body responds to similar situations in that same way.

---

* For a more detailed discussion of this viewpoint, see Dreikurs, *Social Equality: The Challenge of Today.* Chicago: Henry Regnery Co., 1971; Chapter 3, "The Orchestration of Emotion, Mind, and Body."

Another part of this method is the use of the vicarious experience, one of the oldest educational principles. When a teacher gives a reading assignment, he is telling the student to experience something vicariously. The direction "Go back and relive it the way you would like it to have been" used in this method tells the client to experience something vicariously. Just as the former is a learning technique, so is the latter.

When I first began to use this method, I had no idea what I was doing. A number of years ago, when I was a school counselor in an elementary school, a fifth-grade girl came into my office complaining about a sick ache in her stomach whenever she had to read out loud before the class. Kids seem to have this fantastic faith in their teachers and counselors, and trust them to take care of things like that. We talked about the discomfort for a while, then she left, agreeing to come back in a week. When she came back, I asked her about the stomach-ache. "It's gone," she said matter-of-factly. "What happened when you had to read?" "I didn't have it," she said.

Not long after that, I was visited by a fourth-grade boy who said he had a "bad, black feeling" whenever he was doing math or when the principal watched him eat lunch. Again, I had him tell me about it, then he left, making an appointment to return in a week. When he came back he reported that the feeling was gone.

On the faculty of that same elementary school there was an attractive teacher in her late twenties or early thirties. She was single but not happily so. She was shy and withdrawn around men because, as she said, "I feel so fat and ugly." As I said, she was actually very attractive and had a nice figure, but she had a *fat and ugly* feeling and that feeling made her *act* fat and ugly. I asked her to tell me about the feeling much the same way as I had with the children. Several days later she approached me in the teachers' lounge and said, "You know that fat-ugly feeling? I haven't had it since our talk the other day."

Something was helping these people lose their uncomfortable feelings, so I began to analyze the process I had used as we discussed the feelings together. Basically, at this point the whole process had just three steps: One, to describe the last time they had the feeling; two, to tell me all they could about the feeling; and three, to describe the earliest time they remembered having that same feeling.

Finding that people were being helped with the technique and were becoming more comfortable with themselves, I determined to expand the process. Instead of the bare-bones technique I had arrived at, I began to ask about color and shape and texture and size and rhythm, and many of the questions I inserted seemed to work. They added a degree of tangibility to the feeling that helped the client arrive at the feeling and get rid of it that much faster.

Before describing the process, however, users of this technique should be cautioned against formulating their questions in such a way as to *lead* the client. As an example, I generally say, "What is it like?" or "It's like a what?" If I say, "What shape is it?" the subject tends to respond with round, square, oval, etc. and if I were to say, when they express confusion as to my meaning, "Is it like a ball or a knot?" the very sentence puts the ideas of *ball* or *knot* in their heads. I ask, "What is it made of?" Asking, "Is it metal?" or "Is it tar?" can lead an unclear image toward the substance mentioned.

Below, then, is an outline of the procedure. The client is asked to do the following: *

(1) Feel the feeling. Try to bring it into your body and feel it.
(2) Locate the feeling. Where in your body do you feel it?
(3) Describe the feeling.
   (a) What is it like? (form)
   (b) What is it made of? (texture)
   (c) What color is it?
   (d) What size is it?
   (e) Does it have a rhythm?
   (f) Is there anything else you notice about it?

---

* For a more thorough, slower-paced, illustrated version of this outline see Janoe and Janoe, *Dealing With Feeling,* Vancouver: Family and Life Enrichment Center, 1973.

("I don't know" or "It doesn't have that" is a perfectly good answer to any of the above.)

(4) Recall a recent time you had the feeling. Describe what happened.

(5) Have the feeling and go back in memory to a time when you were a child. Find a very early time that you had that feeling and tell me about it. (At this point sometimes a person will say he can't think of one. He is probably trying to find one that *fits*, one that seems relevant. I sometimes say, "Was there one you thought of right away but rejected because it didn't seem related?" If such is the case, that memory will be used.)

(6) Now have the feeling and go back to that time again, only this time do it the way you would *like* it to have been. You can make any changes you want. How would you like it to have happened?

(7) Now, go back and do the same thing with the recent time. Make it happen the way you would like it to.

(8) Now bring the feeling back and see how it feels.

We recently led a *Dealing With Feeling* workshop for a marriage enrichment center in our community. As we were about to begin, suddenly all the lights went out. We had blown a fuse. I took the opportunity to point out the similarity between a building's electrical system and our own *feelings* system. When a fuse blows, it is telling us something about the system— exposed wires, an overload—something that should not be. In the same way, our feelings tell us something about our world. Feelings are friendly. They tell us about our world and our relationship to the world, but so many of us have learned not to trust our feelings; in fact, not even to be aware of them. Feelings, in and of themselves, do not cause anyone embarrassment, do not get anyone in trouble. Rather, it is the behavior we display when we become aware of the feeling that causes the trouble.

How did we lose touch with our feelings? Why don't we trust them? When I was a small boy with three older brothers, I used to tag along with them on hikes. Usually after an hour or so I would begin to lag behind. They would say, "Hurry up, slow poke!" My response of, "But I'm tired!" was usually followed by the retort, "No, you're not! Come on!" Now, my brothers were second only to my mother and God in wisdom, and perhaps a little more authoritarian than He, so whom was I to believe? My feelings which told me I was tired, or my brothers who said I wasn't?

Again, walking beside my mother on a gravel path, I fell and skinned my knee. She held me and rocked me and comforted my sobs with, "There, there. It doesn't hurt, now, does it?" Whom should I believe? My feelings said my knee was hurting. My mother said it wasn't.

So it goes through life. "You don't want to do that." "You don't like that." "You're not cold." "Isn't this fun?" People we love, people we trust, people in authority are telling us things that don't agree with our feelings. And we *know* that these people are right! So we learn to distrust our feelings. We try not to feel them. We try to push them away. We very often find that feeling our feelings makes us very uncomfortable.

Following are some examples of the *Dealing With Feeling* process being used. Most of the examples were taken from transcripts of workshops and groups. Little has been added in the way of commentary, as the reader will easily interpret the material for himself.

> T (Therapist): So that's why we came to a workshop called *Dealing With Feeling*. What are some of those feelings that brought you here? What particular feeling would you like to work on?
> C1 (Client 1): Anxious.
> C2: Sad or down.
> C3: When I'm criticized.
> C4: Tension and stress.
> C5: Helplessness.
> C6: Inadequacy.
> C7: Left out.
> T: Okay, now, before we go to work on those very individual feelings, let's work together on one we all have. Think of a feeling that everyone in the room has at one time or another; one we all know the feeling of.

C: How about anger?

T: Does everyone know what anger feels like? Okay, anger. Now don't say anything out loud, but everyone think of where you feel it when you feel anger. When you are angry you feel it in your body—where? Now, let's go around the room and each person tell *where* he feels his angry feeling.

C1: In my stomach.

C2: My chest.

C3: Across my shoulders and back.

C4: In my arms.

C5: My jaws and teeth.

T: All right, we've located the feeling. Now tell me about it. What is it like? It's like a_____?

C1: An iron ball—hard and black.

C2: Steel bands around my chest.

C3: Like a yoke—very heavy.

C4: A thick cable.

C5: Like wires—hot wires tying my jaws shut.

T: Say, I thought we were all talking about the same feeling! Listen to these answers. When I say "anger," one of you imagines an iron ball in the stomach; one, steel bands around the chest; and another, hot wires through the jaw. And yet we say "anger" is *a* feeling and talk about it as if it felt the same to everyone. Now we find out each person has his own kind of angry feeling! Now, I want you to feel what your angry feeling feels like. Have the feeling and think of a recent time you felt the same way. Would you share that time with us?

C1: A few days ago when my kids wouldn't clean up their rooms or get started on their chores.

C3: Yesterday on the way to work this creep cut in front of me, and I had to swerve and almost got into an accident; and he didn't even notice!

T: Now have that same feeling, and go back younger. Go back till you're a little child. Have the feeling and look around and see what's happening, and tell me about it.

C2: I had a puppy and it got really sick, and while I was

at school my dad took it to the vet's and he had to put it to sleep.

C4: My little brother was in my room, and he got into my models, and he broke my favorite model, and Mother said he didn't know any better—he was only a baby! I wanted to hit him so bad! (This is the man who felt anger in his arms.)

  T: Now, I want you to go back to that same experience again, only this time make it happen the way you would like it to have happened. That little person we used to be had a very real learning experience, and he learned to feel a certain way in a certain situation. But you're not the same little person any more. You're larger and older, and maybe wiser, and you *may* choose to do something different this time.

C2: Well, my dad let me miss school and go with him to the vet's, and the vet explained how sick the dog was, but he said he'd try to help him. So he kept him there, oh, for about a week.

  T: Then what?

C2: I don't know if he got well or not. It doesn't matter now. The important thing is that I was in on what was happening.

C4: The baby goes to my room, and he can't get in because I have three large padlocks on the door. He cries and cries his head off because he knows I've outsmarted him!

  T: Did you hit him?

C4: I didn't need to. I didn't even want to.

  T: Now find the feeling again in your body. Let it in. How does it feel?

C4: It's gone.

C2: Well, it's not the same. It's something else.

C1: I feel pretty good. Like I'm worth something.

  T: You may have noticed that your early experiences had something in common. They were times when you felt helpless. Powerless. There was nothing you could do. So the little, helpless, powerless person that you were did something he *could* do. He got angry, I want to hypothesize that what we often call an *angry* feeling is really a feeling of helplessness. Now that you've found where you might have learned to feel that way, the you that you are now might choose to react differently.

At this point we went to work on those feelings each person had mentioned earlier, the feelings they especially want to work on. I will attempt briefly to summarize the feelings, the early memory, the revised early memory, and the change in the feeling. There is no way to measure accurately the degree of discomfort of an uncomfortable feeling. It is a purely subjective judgment used to indicate to me whether the feeling feels better or worse or the same. I usually say something like, "On a scale of zero to ten, with zero being neutral and ten being extremely uncomfortable, how would you rate this feeling?" It is not presented here as *proof* nor is it intended to be used in that way.

The *anxious* feeling was described by one person as being a throbbing, growing, elastic feeling in the pit of the stomach. She remembered standing at the door waiting for her father to come home because she wanted to eat dinner. Imagine a hungry little girl standing at the door wondering where Father is, why he isn't home yet. This produces anxiety. In the revised memory, she moved away from the door and went to play with her dolls until he came home. When asked to give a numerical value to the degree of discomfort, she said it went from about ten to five.

Sadness was described as a choking feeling in the throat. She remembered the death of a pet parakeet, at which time she was supposed to be brave and not cry. Wanting to cry and not being allowed to cry equals a sad feeling. In her revision she cried and then she felt better. She said the discomfort went from ten to five.

Being criticized was a numb tightness in the jaw. He remembered a time at age six when his father said, "I don't know if you'll ever amount to anything." He wanted to convince his father that he would, but didn't know how. Wanting to prove his value and not being able to say a word equalled a feeling of being criticized. He changed it to have his father tell him that he was all right. On the scale of one to ten, he gave the discomfort a fifteen and said it was reduced to three or four.

Tension was an all-over, sharp pressure inside the head. She recalled the day her baby brother was born. The doctor's teen-age son tried to dress her and got her all tangled up in her suspender-type garters. They were on all wrong but she was made to wear them anyway. Being harnessed up all wrong and having to function that way equalled tension. In her revision, she went to sleep and didn't wake up till her father came home and dressed her properly. She said the feeling went from a ten to an eight.

Inadequacy was a cannonball in the stomach. She recalled a time she was taking care of her children, and she felt she just couldn't do it right because she hadn't graduated from high school yet. Having children before her education was completed provided a feeling of inadequacy. She revised it so that she finished high school, worked a few years, then got married and had a family. She said the discomfort went from a ten to a five.

The *left out* feeling was described as a board across the back holding him immobile. He remembered standing on the walk watching his uncle, who had told him he could go along and then forgetting, drive away. A little boy being left behind equals a left out feeling. In his revision, he ran after the car and caught up. They opened the door and he got in. He said the feeling went from an eight to a two.

What we may have learned from these examples is that the body has memory, and our learned feelings are that memory. The child that we once were had an experience. The discomfort or the pleasure of that experience became lodged in our body's memory, and forever after a similar experience may cause a feeling in that same part of the body. I often tell of one client who feels hunger in her left leg. When she was very young, the cookie jar was kept on a high shelf. In order to reach it she had to pull out the bottom drawer, step up with her right foot, then lift her left leg way up, putting her knee on the counter, to climb up to where she could reach the cookies. Her behavior at that time had a purpose and her feeling now has the same purpose.

A younger person is subjected to an experience, and he interprets that experience. Whenever he recalls it after that, he recalls it in the light of his interpretation. If the person that he has become today could go back and relive that experience, he might find that his interpretation is now very different.

When using the technique in family counseling, it is usually best to begin by obtaining random early memories, before the client has mentioned anything about uncomfortable feelings. Two to six memories are requested, whatever is comfortable, and only the memories they wish to share. During later sessions, after more trust has developed, they will be willing to share more deeply.

In one recent marriage counseling session, the wife cited the following memory: "I'm about three. My mother gave me a black purse, and my brother and I fought over it."

Among the husband's early memories was, "I'm in the second grade, and I have the other second-grade bully, who also has a gang, up against the wall by the collar. I never had any trouble with him again."

One of the problems this couple has was that they "get into moods." When the wife was asked how much of the time she had this mood, she responded, "About 90 percent of the time."

Then the husband was asked about his mood. He indicated that he is usually in a good mood at work, but that she gets him in a bad one when he gets home. He is in a bad mood about 30 percent of the time at home.

Then the wife was asked where she felt the feeling. She replied, "It's a knot in my stomach that hurts." Further, after questioning, she indicated that it felt like it was made of lead, as big as a cantaloupe.

The husband's feeling was in his face. It was hot, red, and tingling. The wife was asked to have the lead-knot feeling and to go younger. At first no time came to mind.

T: What time came to mind when you were looking? Maybe one that you rejected because it didn't seem related.
C: When my brother took my purse.
T: What happened when he took the purse?
C: I cried and he got in trouble.
T: When you start to cry, where do you feel it?
C: In my stomach. Why it's that same feeling.

When the husband was asked when he felt the hot, red,

tingling face for the first time, he recalled the time that he had the kid up against the building.

In both their cases the feelings were purposeful. Her feeling caused her to cry, and when she cried someone would punish her assailant. His feeling caused his face to become red and swollen which frightened his adversaries. The two became aware of how they had been using their feelings, and two weeks later they reported that the moods were no longer a problem.

In a couples' group one evening, we were talking about feelings of jealousy. One woman in the group had been bothered by jealous feelings during the week and asked if she could work on the feeling there in the group. Here is a partial transcript of the session.

T: Try to bring the feeling back now. Bring it back and tell me where you feel the jealous feeling.

C: Hmmm. Cold, all over . . . cold and shivery. My feet. My feet are cold, and I feel shivery all over. My feet feel squishy.

T: Does it have a color?

C: It's dark—black or brown. Very dark.

T: All right. Have the feeling now. Bring it back and remember the last time you had that same feeling. (To the group: Oh, and while she's doing it, I'm going to write a word or two on this slip of paper, and we'll see later if it fits into her memory.) To client: Would you like to share it with us?

C: Yeah. When Jay left for work, I told him to be sure to come right home afterwards, so I was pretty sure he'd remember; then that night, 5:30 went past, then 6:00, then 7:00. (Laughing.) My feet were pretty squishy by then. Well, there was this girl where he works and she called once and, well. Well, anyway, he got home about 8:00 and, well, he didn't say anything. Didn't seem to want to talk. He just said nothing was wrong, and what was for dinner? Boy, I feel that way just thinking about it! All goose-pimply all over and about to cry.

T: Now have the feeling again and go back even further. Go back till you were very small. Have the feeling and go back until a memory comes to mind. A time when you had that feeling.

C: Okay. Mmmm. Way back. Okay, I'm in the woods and, Oh, God, it's getting dark and I'm lost. We were on a picnic or something, and now nobody else is there. I'm all alone and, and the ground is wet and, and squishy! I'm lost in the woods, and I'm all alone.

T: You're alone, and you're lost, and you're getting cold. Oh, incidentally, what did I write on that paper? (Handed it to someone in the group who read, "lost or alone.") Now go back to that first time you had the feeling. Go into it and re-experience it, only this time relive it exactly the way you wish it had happened.

C: Okay, I'm back in the woods and it's cold and damp, and then my father comes out from behind a tree and says, "I've got an idea! Let's build a campfire and get this party warmed up!" And then he gives me a hug and tells me to get the kindling and he'll get the wood.

T: And then . . .?

C: So we build the fire, and the rest of the family comes too, and we all sit around the fire, and it feels good, and we're all happy.

T: Now go back to the recent time, and do the same thing. Re-experience it as you would like it to have happened.

C: Okay. Let's see. I say, "Come right home." and Jay says, "Okay, I'll call if I can't." then the day goes by and at 5:00 Jay calls and says, "It looks like I'll have to be about an hour late. I'll be home about 6:00. Love ya!" And then, hmmm, then he gets home at 5:58! Surprise!

T: How's the feeling?

C: Feeling? I never had a chance to get it!

T: Can you bring it back?

C: Sure, just a minute. Hmmm. Well, I'm trying. I guess I just don't feel like it now.

In that same group, there was an example of a technique

that can be used when a person cannot readily arrive at an early memory. Again the feeling was jealousy, and the woman described it as being in her arms: "It's like my arms are made of jello. My upper arms. There's no strength in them. They're all trembly and wobbly." When it came to a recollection, however, her mind was blank. Knowing she was experienced in fantasy work, I tried the following:

> T: All right, then, don't think of a memory. Just have the feeling. Bring the feeling into your body. Experience it. Now, be yourself as a child, and have the feeling and tell me what's happening.
>
> C: Hmmm. (Pause) My, gosh, I've never . . . okay, well, I'm on roller skates, and I'm in back of an old ice truck trying to get some chips of ice out of the truck, when the truck starts up. I didn't have time to let go, so I'm holding on to the back of the truck with my arms bent, like this. (Demonstrates) And the truck goes and goes, and it's going faster than I want to, and I hold on tighter and tighter, and my arms begin to shake, and I'm afraid I'll fall off. Boy, that's the feeling, all right!
>
> T: Stick with it. See where it goes.
>
> C: Okay. Well, I'm afraid I'll fall and get hurt. I'm really tense. (Pause, then a deep breath.) So I relax. I don't let go, I just relax my arms. Straighten them out. (Pause) Wow! What a difference. This is fun! It's like water skiing. (Laughs) I can go back and forth. I can see where I'm going. I'm having fun. Boy, what a message, huh? Don't hold on so tight. Relax. It's more fun. Wow.

Below is a partial transcript of still another feeling we worked on.

> C: I get really uncomfortable in crowded places. Places with people jammed into them. I get a sort of panicky feeling, like I have to get out.
>
> T: Feel the feeling. Where is it?
>
> C: Well, it's in my head, mostly. In my nose. Behind my eyes and in my nose.
>
> T: Does it have a color?

C: It's dark, like black or brown, but every once in a while it seems red, then it's dark again. And all the time, up toward the top, it's like fireworks or fireflies. Like a lot of little sparkly explosions. Little flashing lights.

T: What is it like?

C: It's like there are wires pulled through my head and they're making all those little sparks, and then my nose is hot and numb and like it was filled with lead. And I can't breathe through it. It's so warm and stuffy and suffocating!

T: Now go back to a recent time you had the feeling.

C: Okay. Let me see. Oh, yeah. We're at the circus, and the circus is over, and we're leaving. We're going out through those tunnel places, and it's solid people, all smashed together. I can't see where I'm going and it seems like people are pushing in every direction. I can't find anyone I came with. And I try to keep smiling because I know we'll be out of the tunnel soon, but I'm really uncomfortable. I want to get away!

T: Now have the feeling some more and go back in time. Go back younger. Try to find a time when you're very young.

C: Okay. Let's see. Oh, I have it. I'm in a car with this other family. It's their car. I'm in the back seat with my friend, and somehow it seems full of other children. There must have been two or three others. The car is parked on the street; the parents must be in a store. It's on a business street. I bend down to pick something up off the floor, and "POW!" (This is the image I remember best.) I'm there on my hands and knees on the floor of the car, and there's confusion and scuffling going on all around me, and I see these flashing lights, and my whole face feels numb and then it feels wet and warm, and there's this red stuff all over the floor, and it doesn't sink in what has happened. My friend starts crying and says she's sorry, it was an accident, she didn't mean to, and I don't know what she's talking about. But I just stay there on my hands and knees on the floor and I feel very confused about what's happening. Then the mother comes out and comes to the car, and she helps me up and seems to try to clean me up a little. I see her dabbing at my dress with a big handkerchief. And through her, I figure out that my friend kicked me in the face and my nose is bleeding, and bleeding and bleeding! The mother puts my head back and gives me the handkerchief to hold over my nose, and every time I put up my head to see what's going on, she tells me to put it back again. And all I can think is, "Why doesn't this hurt? Why can't I feel it? Why is there so much blood and mess and fuss, and it doesn't even hurt?" That's all I remember. I don't know what happened next, or when I got home. I just remember being confused because the amount of blood and the degree of pain didn't seem to match.

T: Have the feeling again, and go back to that time, but with this difference. This time have it happen the way you would like it to have happened. You be the director, the producer, and all the actors. How would it be?

C: (Pause while she thinks.) Hey, that's funny! I had to change it. At first I just had us all sitting quietly in the car with our hands in our laps, and it was *boring!* So we started playing around, and I bent over to pick something up from the floor, and my friend kicked my nose with her knee (rather than her shoe) and it hurt! It hurt a lot. And I sat up quickly, and she said she was sorry and gave me a handkerchief because it was bleeding a little, so I dabbed at it and it stopped bleeding, and there was no fussing. And then her mother came and got in the car and we drove home.

T: How does it feel?

C: It's okay. It hurt a little, but it's okay. Part of the problem before was that it didn't hurt enough, and that things were out of control and I didn't know what was happening. Now everything is under control.

T: Now do the same thing with the more recent time at the circus.

C: Okay. We're at the circus and everyone is leaving. And

we see what a smash it is at the tunnel. So we decide to wait at our seats till the crowd thins out. We sit down again and really have an enjoyable conversation. We enjoy it so much that pretty soon the building is empty and they're starting to turn off the lights, so we get up and walk out through that empty tunnel. Our footsteps echo in the auditorium, and someone calls "Goodnight" to us. And we feel very peaceful and happy.

T: And the feeling? Bring it back.

C: Oh, I don't want to. This one is so much better!

Although the process does not seem logical, it actually is if one understands its basis. However, attempts to define it or explain why it works during counseling sessions seem to make the whole effect weaker, probably because they move the process from the feeling level to the intellectual level where people are talking *about* their feelings rather than *feeling* them. But for the sake of this discussion, let us briefly summarize a possible explanation of what happens during this process.

Long ago, usually in childhood, a person had an experience which he responded to directly. The part of his body which was involved stored the memory of this experence as a feeling. When he meets similar experiences in the future, his body responds with that same feeling, even though he may no longer be consciously aware of that earlier experience. Through the use of this method the person is helped to find that original experience that taught him how to feel under those circumstances, and to see how, usually, the feeling made very good sense at the time. Now, being aware of the source of that feeling, he can choose his response to the present situation. He may choose the same feeling, or he may find that another response is now more appropriate. He has discovered the purpose of his feeling.

It should be emphasized that the method is to be used with *learned feelings*. If there is any possibility that a feeling might have an organic cause, it should be checked out with a physician.

This method has been found to work in family counseling and in groups, with children and adults. In school counseling situations, it has been used to help children who experience discomfort while involved in a particular activity—reading before the class, doing math, in physical education class. (Remember the agony of choosing up teams and not getting chosen?) Many people report that they are now able to use the method themselves to get rid of their own uncomfortable feelings.

Reference

1. Janoe, E. and Janoe, B. *Dealing With Feeling*. Vancouver: Family and Life Enrichment Center. 1973.

CHAPTER 21

THE HYPNOTIC RETRIEVAL OF
EARLY RECOLLECTIONS

HARRY A. OLSON

W HEN SPEAKING OF early recollections and hypnosis, two related concepts come to mind: hypermnesia and age-regression. Hilgard (1965) states that there is:

> some evidence that the past is more available in hypnosis than in the ordinary waking state. Memories can be revived under hypnosis either directly, through the hypnotist's suggestion that the forgotten material can be recalled, or indirectly, through returning imaginatively to an earlier time, the old memories then arising through the reconstruction (or reliving) of these earlier events. The improvement of recall falls under the general category of *hypermnesia,* that is, heightened memory; the method of recall through reliving comes under the general category of *age-regression,* implying a return, in some sense or other, to an earlier time. Of course age-regression might occur even though no unforgotten material was recovered, and one might enjoy reliving an experience the details of which are still subject to recall, just as one may enjoy rereading a familiar book. (Italics Hilgard's, p. 164.)

The exploration of early experiences through hypnosis is not new. Psychoanalysts and others have done it for years for clinical and research purposes. It is not this author's intent to discuss here in detail the hypnotic phenomena involved but rather to suggest a hypnotherapeutic method for ER retrieval and recreation through age-regression.

Janoe, in the preceding paper, discusses the concept of feeling memory. We know that feelings are a fundamental and inescapable component of attitude and, as such, serve to create, recreate, and reinforce certain biases which inform and underly our behavior. Feelings spur us into action. We also know that one of the functions of ERs and dreams is to serve as a factory for emotion. We "remember" (actually we "reconstruct") an incident in a way which fits our particular biases. That incident is invested with feelings which serve, then, to motivate us into certain behaviors. Janoe also discusses and illustrates the fact that recreating the recollection in a new way often causes a change in the level or kind of feeling experienced. In both of his papers in this book, Janoe shows that recreation of the ER can lead to improved behavior. Willhite and Morris, in their papers in this book, also discuss ideal recreation of the ER, although their use is primarily for the purpose of understanding the life-style. It is this author's experience and opinion that the reconstruction of the ER as the client would have liked it to have been is not only diagnostically useful, but emotionally liberating, and that this effect can be achieved, possibly to a more heightened extent through hypnosis.

In regard to hypnotic age-regression, several considerations must be noted. First, age-regression is never complete. There is, rather, an "observing ego" process which is operative during age-regression (Hilgard, 1965) which, like an observing adult, is in touch with current reality, even when the regression seems real to the subject. As Hilgard indicates, such must be the case or else the hypnotist could no longer control the situation during regression and the "child" would not so easily "grow up" again at the hypnotist's suggestion. He states, "Here we have almost a multiple-personality type of dissociation between the regressed ego (that of the child) and the observing ego (that of the watching adult), both belonging to the hypnotized subject" (1965, p. 171). Even so, hypnosis is useful in developing heightened recall, bringing to mind details that were otherwise forgotten (Dorcus, 1960). Yet Stalnaker and Riddle (1932) suggest that when subjects recall information under hypnosis, they are often less concerned with accurate performance, making and accepting more errors in recall than they would accept when recalling the same information during the waking state. For our purposes, however, this latter finding is not important because of the biased nature of memory. We are more concerned with the outlook on life reflected in the ERs than with accuracy of the material presented. Also, subjects rarely regress completely to the target age, but usually go back to an age slightly more mature than the age supposedly represented by the subject (Hilgard, 1965). Even so, this should not interfere with the subject's ability to recall an ER under hypnosis. The conclusion, however, is that the degree of revivification and "reality" of the experience in hypnotic age-regression is an open question, but surely revivification is not as complete as popularly assumed (Hilgard, 1965).

Cautions are sometimes raised about age-regression if it were used to bring back deeply repressed material, and that on rare occasions, such revivification has apparently brought on psychotic reactions. It is highly unlikely, however, that age-regression by itself could produce such a dramatic response unless the reaction probably would have happened anyway under other circumstances. At any rate, the technique to be described here leaves the target age and incident to be recalled up to the client, so any risk is minimized.

Although age-regression in itself is of questionable therapeutic usefulness, it can be used in ER retrieval in order to intensify and clarify feelings when clients have difficulty defining or getting in touch with feelings in a waking state. Revivification, to the degree to which it takes place in hypnosis, has the potential to enlighten the therapist to the *gestalt* of the ER and aid in empathic understanding. The meaning of the ER itself and the "vivid" potentially becomes more overt to the degree that revivification is more involving for the client than a mere description. New connections between feeling and experience cited in the ER can be temporarily made through suggestion in hypnosis. It must be noted, however, that the same effects can be achieved without hypnosis in many cases, and that hypnosis is certainly unessential to the therapeutic use of ERs. The technique as presented here will most likely be primarily of interest to hypnotists who wish to use it in conjunction with a program of ongoing hypnotherapy, or when the client is particularly barren in producing ERs.

The protocol (see Appendix C for the actual wording) involves several hypnotic techniques. First, the client is hypnotized. The client, while remaining in the present, is asked to describe his earliest recollection in detail, defining the most vivid part and his feelings at the time as if it were a movie being shown on a screen. Next, he is regressed to the age he was when that ER supposedly took place. Rather than view the scene as a movie, he is asked to relive the incident and describe it as it is taking place, identifying again the most vivid part and his feelings. The therapist should record the client's statements verbatim. Any changes should be noted between the ER as described as a movie and the initial revivification described during the age-regression. Next, the client is asked to relive the ER a second time, this time changing it in any way he would like, and then describe the vivid part and feelings he experiences in this recreation. He is then brought back to the present, with an amnesia suggested for the original ER and the feelings attached, and it is suggested that his new creation (second revivification) be substituted for his initial ER. The purpose of the amnesia is to reinforce the new linkage of feeling to fantasized experience in the reconstructed ER. The amnesia accomplishes this by removing the initial ER from view, especially if it were imbued with negative feelings. Then the client is "awakened" with suggestions for increased well-being and sense of accomplishment. The earliest recollection is again elicited post-hypnotically to check on the process and determine results. Parts of this protocol may be used in guided imagery fashion without actual hypnotic induction.

Preliminary research was done using this technique according to the protocol as presented in Appendix C. Three subjects were used, all of whom were easily hypnotizable, scoring a three or better on Spiegel's Hypnotic Induction Profile. In all cases, Spiegel's eye-roll-arm-levitation induction technique was used and the subjects were induced into a state of deep relaxation before the ER protocol was administered.

All three subjects showed a number of results in common. First, the initial revivification brought out much more imagery detail than was present in the original statement of the recollection in terms of both feelings and content. In one case a whole new theme was reported at this point. The basic ERs were not substantially changed, but they were enlarged and elaborated.

The ER when revivified became more real and alive for the subject, and in the case of two subjects, speech patterns and inflections became more juvenile. Second, the initial ERs presented were all relatively pleasant ones.

The amnesia built into the protocol for (A) going back in time and (B) forgetting the original ER was only partially successful. All subjects recalled going back in time, but they were unable to recall the specific details of the process. No subjects made sweeping changes in the ER when given the opportunity in the second revivification. The changes, while diagnostically significant, were relatively minor in content, so that the initial recollection was so incorporated into the second revivification that to forget the original recollection was a logical inconsistency, akin to having a body with some additional skin but no skeletal or muscular structure. Had the changes between the first and second revivifications been more pronounced or the initial ERs more unpleasant, it is possible that the amnesia for the original ER could have been more effective.

Most important therapeutically, however, was the cognitive-affective linkage made between the original ER and the changes made in the second revivification. Post-hypnotic questioning revealed that all subjects incorporated the changes they made in the second revivification into the original ER so that the result was an amalgamation or juxtaposition of the two, with new or altered feelings attached. Subjectively, the subjects reported it as if the changes were always there but heretofore not recalled. This effect, while interesting, should not be surprising. Since "recall" is actually a process of reconstruction in the present, the cognitive process of developing and revivifying an original (recalled) ER and changing the ER, also in a context of revivification, are virtually identical. The subjective experience for the subject, however, can be quite powerful and potentially liberating. Much more research is needed before firm conclusions can be drawn.

Figure 21-1 compares the recollections given by one subject according to the four conditions identified above. It is the least detailed of the three sets of ERs but the most dramatic in its impact. While no new themes were initially added, there was expansion in the first revivification.

1st Recollection — Movie Screen

Age — infancy.	My mom is holding me and I'm sucking milk from her.
(Vivid)	Sensation of my mouth on her breast.
(Feelings)	Security.

1st Revivification with Age Regression

	I'm being held. I'm drinking milk from my mom's breast Maybe my right side is leaning against my mom and I feel held and I feel warm and cared for and I feel pleasure around my mouth.
(Vivid)	Feeling warm, loved.

2nd Revivification with Age Regression, with Changes

	I'll be in my crib and my dad and my mom are coming and they're holding me and loving me, and I don't have to drink milk in order to be held.
(Vivid)	Feeling close and loved.

Post-hypnotic Recall

	There are two conflicts now. I feel that I was picked up by my mother and father and that I was sucking at my mother's breast, but I do feel the additional one.

Figure 21-1.   ERs of one subject elicited according to the four hypnotic conditions of the retrieval protocol.

As was discovered later, the changes in the second revivification were very significant. In the post-hypnotic discussion, the client stated:

I felt tingly because of the warmth of my naked body as a little baby being held by my parents, and I don't have to be drinking milk to have their loving and I feel great because one of the things I always did was eat when I felt neglected and I always had a weight problem.

At first I felt I had to be drinking milk from my mom because she wasn't wearing any clothes from her waist up and I was close to her body, and it was warm and I was tingly because of the good feelings. Then my recollection changed so that I was in my crib and both my parents were paying attention to me. I was in the process of being picked up and they stroked my head, my shoulders, just stroked and cared for me, and I feel the same warmth and love, and security. The latter part was an addition. I never had that feeling before. I had the feeling that to be close, very close to their bodies, I'd have to be drinking milk, and then it was just my mom. My mom would only pay attention to me when I was drinking milk, otherwise I was left alone and was lonely.

(Operator: "How do you feel now?") I feel good. I was feeling the need around my mouth (during the age regression) to be sucking something physically and it went away when I stopped, when I changed to the recollection.

The subject reported a week later that the hypnotic experience had been powerful for her and that she learned that she could now be free from eating when lonely or neglected. She has, at least for the moment, altered her eating habits accordingly.

References

1. Dorcus, R. M. Recall under hypnosis of amnestic events. *Int. J. Clin. Exp. Hyp.* 1960, 7, 57-61.
2. Hilgard, E. R. *Hypnotic susceptibility.* New York: Harcourt, Brace & World, 1965, pp. 164-175.
3. Stalnaker, J. M. and Riddle, E. E. The effect of hypnosis on long delayed recall. *J. Gen. Psychol.*, 1932, 6, 429-440.

CHAPTER 22

USING EARLY RECOLLECTIONS WITH CHILDREN

Ed and Barbara Janoe

Dᴜʀɪɴɢ ᴍʏ ᴇᴀʀʟʏ counselor training, I was told more than once that the use of early recollections as a counseling tool was not effective with children and should not be used with them. That is a lesson that I did not learn well, for when I began counseling in elementary schools several years later, I found that early recollections were among my most useful tools.

I did encounter some difficulty, however. I often found that if a child shared an early memory with me and I immediately responded with questions—in other words, if we began to *work* on it right away—he seemed unable or unwilling to recall other memories later.

Therefore I developed the habit of being just a listener at first, and taking only enough notes to remind me of the memory later, but not taking the time to write down all that the child was saying. A by-product of this method was that rapport and trust seemed to develop much faster when the counselor was an interested listener than when he was a probing interrogator. The child felt that I was really interested in him. He was telling me something he remembered just the way he remembered it. There were no right or wrong statements, no judging of what took place. (I later found that the same method was equally effective with new groups of adults, leading to trust and warm feelings between group members.)

Occasionally a child's recollection will not seem complete or will not reveal a possible purpose for his remembering just this precise incident. In cases like this, I might say, "And then what happened?" For instance, a little girl whose memory

230

was that she fell down and hurt herself. "And then what happened?" "My mom picked me up and carried me in the house and gave me some chocolate ice cream."

People familiar with the use of early memories are aware that this tool, like the family constellation, is a way of discovering the client's life-style—his own private view of the world. What the counselor is looking for in the memories the child relates is not *Truth* with a capital *T*, but clues to the very personal logic of that child.

The first step, as in using early recollections with adults, is to look for recurring patterns. Perhaps three of five memories will say, "When I'm sick or hurt I get loved." or "Whenever I get something it gets taken away from me."

Following are early memories of three different children, all of whom share the same place in the family. Before these memories were shared, I had seen each of the children several times and had developed family constellations for each. As you read them, see if you can guess what their shared position is.

A. I was up on my top bunk and my dad came in and said, "Move your mattress and bedding to the lower bunk." Then he put my little sister's mattress on the top bunk, and she slept there while they painted her room.

B. I am on a hike with my dad and my brothers. We come to this flat place on the top of a hill and I can see everything for miles. Dad says "Hurry up! Let's go!" but I wanted to stay longer.

C. My brother was riding his trike on the sidewalk. I accidentally ran into him and he fell down and we had to take him to the hospital. I felt bad.

As I mentioned, I had developed family constellations for each of these children. I knew that each was an oldest, but not a *typical* oldest, and I knew that each was followed by a sibling who, again, was not the *typical* second or middle child. In a family constellation, the oldest child is most likely to be an achiever, a pleaser, and to do well in school. A typical second child may not be as successful in school. He is often described as ornery or naughty. In all three of these cases, the characteristics were reversed. These three oldest children were referred to me either because of learning difficulties or behavior problems. All were followed within two years by siblings who were good students and well behaved. I had hypothesized that each of these *oldests* might feel that he had been dethroned— that is pushed off his top spot by the sibling following him.

To me, the early memories I have described verified that hypothesis. In the first, the child had to move from the top to the bottom bunk. He lost his top place. In the second, he was on top and he liked it, and he had to move off. The third example was given in response to the question, "Do you remember when you lost your top spot?" He told about knocking his brother down and having to take him to the hospital, and then went on to describe all the special attention his brother got in the hospital and even at home afterwards.

As you can see by these examples, I did not establish the fact that these children had been dethroned on the basis of their memories alone. Further, I used the early memories to check out and validate a previously formed hypothesis—that of dethronement. After having obtained these recollections, I allowed the children to experience them again, this time vicariously, in a more satisfying way. I would say something like, "How would you like that to have happened instead of the way it did? Imagine you are back there and reexperience it the way you would like it to have been?"

After doing this the child almost always seems to feel better about the situation.*

See if you can guess why this child was in the counselor's office.

I was doing adding in numbers in the second grade. There was a whole page of adding. I had done all of them except three, and the teacher called time and picked up the papers, and I didn't get to finish.

This was an early memory of a child referred to be because of difficulty in math. I asked him, "What was your first memory about math or numbers?" He gave the response I just quoted after a long, thoughtful pause. "What sort of problems were you

---

* See Chapter 20, "Dealing with Feelings Via Early Recollection."

adding?" I asked. "Like 4+1, 3+2, 5+2, 2+6," he said. I wrote the problems on the board and said, "Okay, go and finish them." He did, and seemed to feel relieved. Reports from his teacher verified that after that he became more comfortable with math. Had we discovered the instant that he learned to dislike math?

A third-grade boy was referred to me because he was not progressing in reading. He was an oldest, followed by a sister one year younger and a younger brother. One of his memories was the following:

> When my sister was in first grade, one day she came home from school and she picked up my reading book and she read out of it as good as I could.

From then on, when he read he was very careful not to make any mistakes, which led to his becoming more and more tense and kept him from progressing. We could question whether this was when he learned to feel tense about reading.

I asked him, "Do you want to be not as good, as good, or better than your sister?" "Better than," he stated without hesitation. Later in our session, he said thoughtfully, "I'd like to read better than my sister, but I don't *have* to."

> This memory is from a second boy with an older brother. I had a dime and my brother had a nickel, and we traded. He told me he'd give me a bigger one if I'd give him my little one. I felt pretty good, so I went and told my mother, and she made us trade back. She said the nickel wasn't worth as much as the dime. Then I felt pretty dumb, 'cuz it was my brother.

Hearing this memory helped me understand how confusing the world probably was to this young man.

I have found early memories to be an extremely versatile tool when counseling children.

For the counselor who is familiar with the use of early memories with adults, a few simple changes make it usable with children. Where, with adults, it seems to work well to take a recollection, to examine it, to work on it, to draw some conclusions, and then to go on to another; for some reason, at least in my experience, that often seems to lead to a dead end with children. For use with children, I would suggest a more gradual development something like the following:

1. Be an interested listener when memories are first shared. Get as many memories as the child wishes to share (up to six or seven) without asking questions or offering any interpretation.
2. Take only enough notes to help recall the memory later. Leave space so details can be filled in.
3. Ask the child to go over the memories again. This time fill in more details.
4. If some recollections seem to need further development, encourage it by asking "Then what happened?"
5. Look for patterns which will allow you more insight into the life-style.

For the practitioner who has not used early memories at all, I would say go into it gradually, using only as much as you feel comfortable with. Remember to keep checking with the child. He is the one who can tell you if you're on the right track. Don't make the mistake of *telling* him what his memory means. Use "Could it be that . . .?" and "Do you feel that . . .?"

For practitioners skilled in the use of dreams, fantasies, or family constellation, here is another tool at least as valuable as those, and one which moves into central issues very quickly by pinpointing the private logic which underlies behavior.

CHAPTER 23

EARLY RECOLLECTIONS IN LIFE-STYLE ASSESSMENT AND COUNSELING*

RICHARD ROYAL KOPP AND DON DINKMEYER

T HE IDIOGRAPHIC APPROACH to assessment presented in this article is based on the Adlerian approach to life-style assessment (Ansbacher 1967; Ansbacher and Ansbacher 1964; Dreikurs 1967; Mosak 1958, 1971; Shulman 1973). The idiographic method focuses on the individual case or person, whereas the nomothetic method is designed to discover general laws which are true for groups of individuals. Life-style is defined as the characteristic patterns of an individual's responses. Thus, the idiographic approach identifies the uniqueness of the child.

As Adler (in Ansbacher and Ansbacher 1964) states, "The goal . . . with each individual is personal and unique. It depends upon the meaning he gives to life" (p. 181). Too much of the data available to the school counselor is nomothetic; that is, it is related to norms and averages and thus does not help the counselor understand the individual student.

Relevance of Life-Style Assessment to the School Counselor

Life-style assessment not only enables both the student and teacher to become aware of the student's goals, but it also points to specific changes. For example, if the student is especially motivated by the desire for attention, the teacher may be helped to find active and constructive ways in which the student can obtain attention by contributing to the group. With the student who seeks power and control, it may be possible to give that student leadership responsibilities in the school setting.

This approach to assessment is of particular value insofar

---

* Reprinted with permission from *The School Counselor*, 1975, *23*, *1*, 22-27. Copyright 1975, American Personnel and Guidance Association.

as it reveals the pattern of the individual. Instead of dealing with unrelated test scores and observations, the idiographic approach presents a holistic picture of the basic beliefs and motives of the student. As we become aware of these beliefs and motives, the individual's behavior makes sense and is also more readily modified.

Assessment Using Early Recollections

The rationale for using early recollections as an assessment tool is based on the idea that people remember only those events from early childhood that are consistent with their present view of themselves and the world (Adler 1958; Kelly 1963; Mayman 1968; Mosak 1958). In remembering and telling a specific incident, the person reconstructs in the present an experience he or she once had.

The person selects only certain events from the countless number of experiences that occurred during early life and emphasizes certain aspects of each memory while diminishing or omitting other details. Because it is a product of these selective and evaluative processes, the memory can thus be used as projective data from which we can infer the basic elements of the current life-style (i.e., beliefs and motives) that influenced and shaped the recollection as it is told to the interviewer.

Collecting Early Recollections

Mosak (1958) suggests guidelines that are useful for defining an early recollection. These include: (a) the use of only those memories that can be visualized (or vividly recalled) and that are described as single events; (b) omitting incidents (termed "reports") that happened many times and/or that are vague with respect to details of action, feeling, or the setting in which the memory takes place; and (c) using only those memories of experiences that occurred before the individual was eight years old.

Our experience indicates that an individual eight years of age and older can usually produce early recollections which are of value. Because the procedure is not common to the student's experience, it is essential to follow the guidelines for collecting recollections precisely.

Kopp (1972) developed a procedure for collecting early recollections in writing, thus enabling memories to be collected in groups. This procedure is standardized and can thus be used for research purposes. The format presented below, which is a verbal procedure, is derived from this written procedure and can be used by the counselor when collecting recollections in a personal interview.

> Think back as far as you can to the first thing you can remember . . . something that happened when you were very young (it should be before you were seven or eight years old). It can be anything at all—good or bad, important or unimportant—but it should be something you can describe as a one-time incident (something that happened only once), and it should be something you can remember very clearly or picture in your mind, like a scene. Now tell me about an incident or something that happened to you. Make sure that it is something you can picture, something specific, and something where you can remember a single time it happened.

As the student begins to tell the memory, listen for the visual and specific part of the memory. Some background details may be appropriate. Do not, however, spend too much time setting the stage with facts leading up to or surrounding the incident itself. Instead, concentrate on what actually happened.

Phrases such as "We were always . . .," "would always . . .," "used to . . .," or "would happen" suggest incidents that occurred repeatedly. Ask the student to choose one specific time which stands out more clearly than the others and tell what happened that one time. If one particular incident does not stand out over others, eliminate this event and choose a different early memory which can be described as a single incident.

Before moving on to the next memory, ask the following questions and write down the student's response:

> Do you remember how you felt at the time or what reaction you had to what was going on? (If so), please describe it. Why did you feel that way (or have that reaction)?
> Which part of the memory stands out most clearly from the rest—like if you had a snapshot of the memory, it would be the very instant that is most vivid and clear in your mind? How did you feel (what was your reaction) at that instant?

Our experience indicates that although we can begin to

see a student's basic beliefs and motivations in the first memory, the accuracy of these interpretations increases when they are based on additional memories. The counselor's assessment thus should be based on at least three memories. Typically, from three to six memories are collected.

Using Early Recollections in Counseling: An Example

Ernie, a second grader, was referred to the counselor because he drew nude pictures of women and showed them to his teacher. The teacher asked the counselor what to do.

In order to be able to help the teacher and Ernie, we must first understand the meaning of Ernie's behavior. Let's see how the following early recollections can help.

Recollection A: Age one year. "Once my dad came in from work and I just bit him on the knee. That was telling him 'hello.' He giggled when I did it. He picked me up and sat down beside me and my leg was under him—he did it on purpose. I told him to get off—I was mad at him. Biting him stands out most—I wanted to say 'hello' and I didn't know how to say anything then."

Interpretation. The counselor must first focus on the action sequence described in the memory. In this memory, the initial action sequence is: Dad comes in; Ernie bites dad on the knee; Dad giggles. Having identified the sequence, we next focus on the messages and metaphors that the action expresses.

We are struck by the inappropriate and even contradictory method of communication expressed in the action, and we can infer that (a) Ernie believes that he must do the unexpected in order to communicate with others and get their attention, (b) he wants to make contact, and (c) he wants to make an impression. Since we are regarding the memory as a metaphor that is indicative of a general pattern, "saying 'hello'" suggests a specific instance of a communication style between people. Similarly, this pattern probably applies to most of Ernie's relationships with others, although it may be especially characteristic of the way he relates to males.

An action sequence can also reveal the child's self-image, image of others, motivation, and typical behaviors. For example, the second action sequence—Dad picks up Ernie; Dad sits on

Ernie's leg (on purpose); Ernie tells him to get off—suggests that (a) Ernie sees himself as small (needing to be picked up); (b) Ernie perceives others (perhaps men especially) as pinning him down; and (c) when he is (or feels) pinned down, Ernie gets angry and will protest overtly, in effect telling others to get off his back (or his leg in this case!).

"Biting him" stands out most for Ernie, indicating the main motivational theme of this memory: He wants to make contact with and impress others. It also suggests that Ernie chooses inappropriate and aggressive methods for doing this, methods which will impress others. (The act of biting literally makes an impression!) Further, the memory suggests that Ernie chooses this method because he feels that he doesn't know how to get others to notice him through appropriate methods.

Having formulated these initial impressions from the first memory, we turn to the second recollection.

Recollection B: Age one year. "James (Ernie's brother) climbed up in the barbecue. I saw him get in and I got in and took a bath in it. James got the ashes in his hands and rubbed it all over my face and hair. As soon as my mom and dad came out to see what we were doing, I just took a bunch and threw it at my brother and he threw it at my mom and dad. They spanked him and sent him to bed. I thought it was funny because he got in trouble."

Interpretation. Early recollections can suggest the social role frequently played by a child. The initial action sequence in this memory is: James climbs in the barbecue; Ernie watches; Ernie also gets in; Ernie "takes a bath" in the barbecue ashes; James rubs Ernie with ashes. Ernie's role here is as an observer and willing follower when seeking mischievous fun. Note, however, that this memory suggests that Ernie has the ability to cooperate and join with others (peers) in an activity (albeit a mischievous one).

The remaining action sequence is: Mom and Dad come out; Ernie immediately throws ashes at his brother; his brother throws ashes at Mom and Dad; Mom and Dad spank James and put him to bed. The main significance of this sequence is that James gets punished while Ernie does not. Ernie emphasizes this part of the memory as the part that is most vivid for him. This emphasis suggests the following about Ernie's life-style: (a) He wants to have fun (motivational goal), but does so in mischievous ways (method of reaching the goal); and (b) Ernie prefers that others get into trouble while he escapes the consequences of his behavior (this doubles his pleasure and doubles his fun!). As with the first memory, this recollection suggests that Ernie sees communication between people in basically nonverbal and aggressive terms.

Note that the question of whether or not these events actually happened in the way Ernie remembers them is unimportant for our purposes. Since he selects these events and details from the uncountable number of experiences he had as a small child, what Ernie does tell us reflects the present way he sees himself in relation to the world and others and the current things that are important to him. This is the rationale which allows us to interpret the memories as we have.

Life-style summary. An important final step in the life-style assessment process as described by Adler (1935), Ansbacher (1967), Ansbacher and Ansbacher (1964), Dreikurs (1953). Shulman (1965, 1973), Mosak (1954), and Allen (1971) is formulating a summary that includes the basic elements of the life-style. The life-style consists of (a) beliefs about self, the world (life), and others; (b) motivation (goals, purposes, and intentions); and (c) the choice of behaviors designed to reach life goals. Also included in the summary is an assessment of strengths and weaknesses (i.e., beliefs, goals, or methods which facilitate or interfere with successful functioning and development).

We can summarize Ernie's life-style as follows:

Self-concept: I am small and sneaky.

World image: The world is a place to have fun and make mischief.

Image of others: Others (adults) are strong and powerful; they can overpower and punish me.

Motivational goals: I want to impress others to make mischief without having to pay the consequences, to defend myself when I feel pinned down.

Behavior for achieving the goals: I will do the unexpected, be sneaky and clever, protest when I'm overpowered.

Strengths: Ernie is bright and assertive; he is capable of enjoying life, wants the recognition of others, is able to cooperate, has a good sense of humor, and knows how to get a response from others.

Weaknesses: He overemphasizes mischief and surprise tactics as a method for getting others to notice him and probably doesn't believe he can impress others in more constructive ways; he overestimates the power of others and their intent to use that power against him; and he expects inconsistent and even contradictory messages from adults.

Drawing nude pictures is but one method of impressing others by being mischievous and doing the unexpected. We are likely to find additional instances of behaviors that fit this life-style pattern. The counselor can suggest to the teacher that the pictures be ignored (thus eliminating the desired payoff) and that attention be given to constructive behaviors. Ernie's strengths also suggest that he is capable of being a leader and thus should be given an opportunity to direct the class in some activity. By sharing the life-style summary with Ernie, the counselor is able to (a) formulate counseling objectives; (b) quickly develop rapport with Ernie by demonstrating that the counselor understands how Ernie sees himself, life, and others; and (c) focus immediately on the probable reasons for Ernie's present behavior.

References

Adler, A. The fundamental views of I.P. *International Journal of Individual Psychology*, 1935, *1*(1), 5-8.

Adler, A. *What life should mean to you.* New York: Capricorn Books, 1958. (Originally published 1931.)

Allen, T. (Ed.) *The Counseling Psychologist: Individual psychology*, 1971, *3*(1), (monograph).

Ansbacher, H. The life style: A historical and systematic review. *Journal of Individual Psychology*, 1967, *23*, 191-212.

Ansbacher, H. and Ansbacher, R. (Eds.) *The individual psychology of Alfred Adler.* New York: Harper Torchbooks, 1964.

Dreikurs, R. *Fundamentals of Adlerian psychology.* Chicago: Alfred Adler Institute, 1953.

Dreikurs, R. *Psychodynamics, psychotherapy, and counseling.* Chicago: Alfred Adler Institute, 1967.

Kelly, G. A. *A theory of personality: The psychology of personal constructs.* New York: W. W. Norton, 1963.

Kopp, R. R. The subjective frame of reference and selective memory. Unpublished doctoral dissertation, University of Chicago, 1972.

Mayman, M. Early memories and character structure. *Journal of Projective Technique and Personality Assessment,* 1968, *32*(4), 303-316.

Mosak, H. H. The psychological attitude in rehabilitation. *American Archives of Rehabilitation Therapy,* 1954, *2*(1), 9-10.

Mosak, H. H. Early recollections as a projective technique. *Journal of Projective Techniques,* 1958, *22,* 302-311.

Mosak, H. H. Lifestyle. In A. G. Nikelly (Ed.), *Techniques for behavior change: Applications of Adlerian theory.* Springfield: Thomas, 1971. Pp. 77-81.

Shulman, B. H. A comparison of Allport's and the Adlerian concepts of life style. *Individual Psychologist,* 1965, *3*(1), 14-21.

Shulman, B. H. *Contributions to individual psychology: selected papers.* Chicago: Alfred Adler Institute, 1973.

CHAPTER 24

CAREER COUNSELING WITH EARLY RECOLLECTIONS

WILLIAM H. McKELVIE

A YOUNG PATIENT OF Adler's had indicated a desire to be a gravedigger, and when asked why this occupation interested him, the young man answered, "Because I don't want to be the one who is buried. I want to bury others" (Adler, 1964, p. 147). Adler wrote that later the young man became a merchant who "buried" his competitors. Although he chose another occupation, the goal of his behavior remained the same; and when this goal was understood, the dynamics of the change from wanting to be gravedigger to becoming a merchant were immediately clear.

Individual Psychology (IP) focuses on the goals which individuals establish to guide their behavior. Understanding any behavior, including that of selecting a career, involves understanding the goal toward which the behavior is directed. In this chapter, a goal-oriented approach to career counseling will be presented. This will include a brief overview of the concept of work in IP, the function of goals in the selection of occupations, and the Goals-Obstacles-Strategies (GOS) model for counseling adults (McKelvie and Friedland, 1978). Finally, using the GOS model, the use of early recollections in career counseling will be illustrated.

Work and Individual Psychology

Adler emphasized the importance of work in his theory. He felt that the ability to cooperatively organize and divide labor was essential to the survival of the human race, and that each generation was confronted anew with the problems of utilizing the resources of the earth to survive and promote the human race. This survival and enhancement of the human community was an ongoing problem to which in every age "mankind has arrived at a certain level of solution, but it has always been necessary to strive for improvement and further accomplishments" (Ansbacher and Ansbacher, 1956, p. 131).

Work was one of three life tasks of community living that Adler felt each individual was compelled to face. (The other two life tasks were friendship and love.) As with the other two tasks of life, Adler felt that the solution to the challenges of work had an integral relation to the ability to cooperate; thus occupational problems were basically problems in cooperation.

Although developed over fifty years ago, Adler's views have a contemporary ring. The challenge of how we are to use the resources of the earth without at the same time fouling our nest is anticipated in Adler's comments regarding work. In a sense, we must learn to cooperate with our environment. Likewise the way we organize ourselves to divide the labor has grown progressively more complex. The most recent edition of the *Dictionary of Occupational Titles* (U.S. Government Printing Office, 1977) lists over 35,000 job descriptions. Within a decade, a significant portion of these jobs will no longer exist; a large number of new jobs will have been created; and the nature of the remaining jobs will have changed considerably. Technological advancements, political decisions, sociological movements, and economic trends will all interact in a complex melange to keep the job market in a continual state of flux. Previous generations have not faced the challenge of how to make such a complex system work, and each individual is faced with how he will find a place in such an imposing juggernaut.

Like it or not, we have the opportunity to make more choices regarding our vocational development than our parents did. Not only are there more jobs from which to choose, but also there is an increasing awareness of psychological freedom to make choices. Modern children do not feel as compelled to follow the desires of parents nor are they as psychologically bound by the dictates of social conventions as were previous generations. However, this new awareness of the freedom of choice also brings with it the additional burden of responsibility for one's destiny. Each person makes his own choices and will live with both the good and bad consequences of those choices. The excuse of having been driven or forced into any decision, be it of choosing a career or a mate, is not as tenable as it once was.

Goals and Occupational Choice

In IP, both the choice of an occupation and the actual performance on the job are seen as being basic functions of the life-style of an individual. Thus, individuals will select occupations that they feel will allow them to move toward major goals implicit in their life-styles. For example, Adler suggested that the fear of death often was an important impetus in the life-style. Adler (1964) indicated two basic ways in which a person could respond to the fear of death. One was to focus on procreation and, by leaving progeny, perpetuate the race. The other way to overcome death was to somehow influence the future. In the latter instance, Adler postulated that compensation for the fear of death had been the "ruling motive" in the lives of many who had made important contributions in the arts and sciences. Adler cited samples from the works of Horace, Heine, and Tolstoy to demonstrate the "power of death in their reflections" (Adler, 1964, p. 146). Adler also suggested that a traumatic early experience with death could lead to a desire to be a physician. Indeed, one of Adler's early remembrances was of lying in bed, extremely ill, and hearing a physician tell his father, "Your boy is lost" (Orgler, 1963, p. 1). Adler claimed that every physician that he had interviewed had at least one early memory concerning death.

In all workers Adler wrote, "The choice of the occupation is foreshadowed by some dominant interest of the psychic prototype. The development of this interest into concrete realization of work is a lengthy process of self-training in which the same idea adapts itself successively to various material possibilities" (Adler, 1964, p. 147-48). The idea that becomes the focal point for the individual's behavior is based on his conception of what needs to be done to move from a perceived minus feeling to a perceived plus feeling. Thus early in life, the individual selects and develops traits that are seen as having the best potential of allowing for successful movement from the felt minus to the felt plus. In IP, it is always assumed that the individual has the capacity to develop many more traits and skills than those currently manifested.

Goals-Obstacles-Strategies

The complexity of choices confronting individuals has led to a recent interest in adult counseling. McKelvie and Friedland (1978) have developed an approach to life planning and career counseling which is based in IP. Their model utilizes a Goals-Obstacles-Strategies (GOS) paradigm that helps individuals focus on what they wish to do with their life (their life goal); what they see as standing in their way (their obstacles); and how they cope with their obstacles in moving toward their life goals (their strategies). In the following cases the use of early recollections was a valuable source of information in helping the counselor and client clarify the paradigm.

Goals

The idea that there is a unique life goal which guides each individual's behavior is an integral concept in IP. Holism requires unity and in living beings unity can only be viewed from the standpoint of movement toward a single goal. In the GOS model, the life goal is defined as the subjectively established idea which is the focal point of all the individual's behavior. All of the constructs that form the life-style flow from the life goal. Because the life goal is formulated before we have command of the language, it is difficult to put into words. However, when an individual hears his life goal articulated, there is an immediate recognition reflex. In the GOS paradigm, the counselor begins by attempting to articulate the life goal. In the following example, an Early Recollection (ER) was used to help Rene focus on the goal of her behavior (to be important or noticed), and to focus on her current strategy (rebellion) which she used to move toward that goal. Then counseling focused on other more positive and less costly strategies of moving toward her goal.

Rene was fourteen years old and in violent rebellion against her parents and teachers. After listening to the various ingenious methods used by Rene to defeat those whom she felt were trying to boss her around, the counselor asked, "What would you do if there were no bosses in your life?" For an instant, Rene looked blankly at the counselor and then weakly responded, "I'd do whatever I wanted to do." The counselor then asked for an Early Recollection (ER), and Rene related the following:

> *Five years old:* "We went into a ritzy store where they sold decorated candy boxes. Mom and Dad told me to stay away from the candy boxes but I went over to look at them. While I was standing there, a little kid who was looking at a box dropped and broke it. He ran and I was left there and was blamed for breaking it. Mom and Dad didn't say anything but were terribly upset. They took me home and spanked me and stood me in the corner."
> *Focus:* "Dad spanking me; I can still remember every detail of the bedroom."
> *Feeling:* "Mad, because I had gotten spanked for something I didn't do." (As an afterthought—"Well, they had told me not to go over there.")

The counselor gave Rene the following interpretation: "The world is an unfair place where I am being abused for things I didn't do." Rene's recognition reflex indicated that this interpretation was on target. The counselor expanded the interpretation by guessing that Rene appeared to have organized her life around the idea that she was picked on—perhaps because she stood out from the others. In other words, her rebellion was a way of showing others and herself what a superior person she was. Without someone to rebel against, she would become "just another kid." This was explored briefly, and Rene commented that by being a rebel in school,, she saw herself as being sort of a representative for other students who "would not stand up to the teachers the way I do," and "It is really neat that when I walk into a classroom others will say, 'There's Rene; did you see what she did to Mrs._____?' "

The counselor agreed with Rene that by being a rebel, she had gained notoriety. When asked if this might be a goal that she had in life—to be important—Rene immediately responded,

"Yes, I want people to know I was here." The counselor proceeded to inquire as to what Rene planned to do in the future. She said that she would like to "go to Hollywood and make a movie." When asked what she might do if this fell through, she replied, "Open a real high-class boutique with nothing but the top-line stuff."

The counselor finished the session by returning to the question of what Rene would do if there were no bosses in her life. Rene agreed that being a rebel had been an easy way to achieve quick recognition. However, she had gotten into the position of being what Rudolf Dreikurs called a "reverse puppet" who, when the string to the right hand was pulled, would raise the left hand. Rene was not really her own woman but rather was responding mechanically in a reverse manner to the requests and demands of parents and teachers. The counselor asked Rene if she would be interested in beginning to take charge of her own life, and deciding for herself what kind of person she would like to be. She agreed that she would like to do so. For homework, Rene was asked to investigate what opportunities there might be for her to become involved in acting classes or working with a community theater group.

COMMENTS: In this session, the counselor used the ER to help Rene recognize that an integral part of the way she looked at the world revolved around the idea that she was the victim of unfair treatment. If the counselor had made the interpretation after being told about the current "atrocities" committed against her by parents and teachers, Rene would probably just have agreed, "Yes, that is reality." However, by using the ER to make this interpretation it was emphasized that the counselor and Rene were dealing with an *idea* that guided Rene's behavior. If no one was treating Rene unfairly, she would probably create a situation where someone would abuse her. Thus, the issue in counseling became not whether or not Rene was being treated fairly or unfairly, but rather the focus became what *she* wanted to do with her life. Rene joined a school drama club and her classroom behavior improved dramatically. The exploration of her career aspirations were used by the counselor to redirect Rene toward more productive behavior.

Obstacles

Movement toward any goal always involves obstacles. Many of these obstacles are objective in nature. For example, a goal of becoming a plumber involves overcoming obstacles in terms of the requirements that must be met, e.g. joining a union, serving an apprenticeship, etc. However, frequently it is the subjective obstacles that serve as the real impediment to choosing and developing a career plan. Subjective obstacles are ideas which hinder or limit movement. These subjective obstacles may be adopted from cultural concepts which limit the range of choices open to the individual, e.g. "Women are not capable of thinking logically." Other cultural concepts make the decision process difficult: "There is only one job in which I can find happiness." or "I will have only one chance to select a career." Other obstacles are products of the individual's private logic and have been called by others: irrational ideas (Ellis and Harper, 1961), negative nonsense (O'Connell, 1971), and mistaken ideas (Mosak and Dreikurs, 1973). These subjective obstacles are generally the "musts," "shoulds," and "onlys" which obstruct movement, e.g. "I'll try new things only when I'm sure of being the best."

These are the ideas that the counselor attempts to pinpoint because they are easiest to change. For example, a subjective idea can be changed by the individual simply by judging it to be incorrect; but it is not as simple to change the requirement of what one must do to become a plumber.

In the following, James had created an idea which completely immobilized him. Only after his idea had been articulated and reinterpreted could he begin focusing on his career aspirations.

James, a twenty-year-old college student, approached the counseling session in a state of high anxiety. He had recently been suspended from college because of his grades. He complained about total confusion as to what he wanted to do, and had made two suicide attempts. After several futile attempts to pinpoint the issue, the counselor asked for ERs. James related the following:

Four years old: "I was sitting on our front porch with my

brother (two years older). He told me that I was dumb; I hit him, Dad came out and shouted at us. I got in trouble for hitting him."

Focus: "Dad coming out the door, very angry."

Feeling: "Depressed, felt that I wanted to cry because I was put-upon."

The counselor immediately guessed that James felt that he could never do the right thing and that others were always criticizing him. James responded dramatically to this disclosure. He related growing up in a family where his macho father, a successful contractor, was always criticizing him, and his brilliant older brother was continually downgrading him. As is true in many similar instances, Mother compensated by pampering James. Thus, James grew up wallowing in self-pity, feeling that "if only I could be a real man, all of my problems would be solved." To James being a real man meant being able to stand up for himself and having others listen to him. He measured his manliness in every attribute and eventually became obsessed with his feeling that his penis was not large enough. Being better endowed, James reasoned, would lead to being a real man, and he inquired if the counselor knew of any surgical procedures which would enlarge his penis. The counselor immediately asked James how large his penis was; and with some ceremony looked up "penis" in *Human Sexuality* (McCary, 1973). Reading through the section, it was established that physically in every way, James fell into the normal category. It was then discussed with James that the obstacle hindering his movement was his idea that he was of worth only if he could measure up to being a real man; and he had concluded that he measured up only when he was equal to or better than the best or biggest individual he could find. In discussing this idea, James agreed. In locker room showers, he always picked out for comparison those who were clearly better endowed and ignored those who were "average." The counselor helped James recognize that he had selected penis size as a symbol to continually remind himself that his father was right—and he in fact would never measure up. By reminding himself of his inadequacy, James was also provided with an excuse for not trying and generally was able to find people who would feel sorry for him—in particular, Mother. The counselor and James discussed how James could begin measuring himself in ways in which he would come out in a more favorable light. Mosak's Test of Masculinity (Mosak, 1977) was suggested as a way that James could prove that he was a "real" man. This simple test involves standing in front of a mirror and if the reflection indicates anything hanging between the legs, the individual is proudly certified as being masculine. (A similar Test for Feminity is also available.) James was encouraged to use this test whenever he doubted that he was a real man. It was also recommended that James buy a ruler and every time he started discouraging himself through comparison with others, he could look at the ruler and remind himself, "I do measure up."

Future counseling sessions centered around exploring some of James's doubts and questions about his own masculinity. This issue was currently of far greater importance to him than was his career planning. After this was placed in perspective and James began to feel comfortable with his sexuality, the focus turned to developing a career plan.

COMMENT: In this session, the counselor needed immediate information to help James cope with his anxiety. The ER helped the counselor understand James's private logic, and this in turn led to James feeling understood. This feeling helped him share for the first time his concern about his penis size, and the counselor could focus on the primary obstacle that kept James from coping with life—his feeling of not measuring up. As sessions progressed, James realized that his fears and questions regarding masculinity were shared by many other men. With this realization, James relaxed and began to turn his attention to his career problems. He saw how many of his academic problems were created by his fear of not measuring up. For example, frequently he would become "bored" and not be able to apply himself to his studies. The counselor pointed out that this also provided an excuse for his poor grades—"I'd do better if I could find something that interested me." Counseling with James, as it should be with all clients, was a process of encouragement, and he finally developed enough confidence to begin taking courses at a local junior college. He eventually returned to college as a full-time student.

Strategies

All of us in our lives are continually confronted with questions. From the GOS standpoint, a question consists of a goal (What do I want to move toward?) and an obstacle (What stands in the way of reaching my goal?). We develop strategies to answer our questions. A strategy is a pattern of behavior that we feel will help us move toward our goal. Thus, in any counseling session we always begin with an answer. The answer is what the client is currently doing. Usually the client seeks counseling because he is not happy with his current answer to the question. Initially, the counselor attempts to pinpoint the question being asked by the client and then moves to explore alternate answers.

In the following case, Martin's question was, "How can I be the center of attention when others will not give me special treatment?" Martin's answer had been to show people how "smart" he was. He was unhappy because others responded to his efforts to demonstrate his superiority by sabotaging his work.

Martin was a twenty-seven-year-old civil rights attorney. He was highly successful in the courtroom, but his relationships with his associates were a disaster. Attorneys with whom he worked avoided him, and he often thought that they tried to sabotage his work, even though to have done so would have been detrimental to their own interests.

The counselor asked for several specific examples of the above, and it became clear that Martin's life goal centered around being the center of attention and the obstacles he encountered stemmed from the idea that people should treat him in a special way. When these observations were disclosed to Martin, he concurred that they made sense. The counselor suggested that a life-style assessment be completed in order to help Martin become aware of both the ideas that guided him and those that created obstacles for him. The following ERs obtained during the interview were helpful in understanding the strategies Martin used.

Four or five years old: "Mom sent me in to get Father up, and I went in several times, and he wouldn't get up. Finally, I threw a shoe at him and hit him. He jumped up and shouted, 'Jesus Christ!' (Question: What happened then?) He got up and went over and sat on a chair. He did nothing to me."

Focus: "The shoe hitting him."

Feeling: Scared; I knew he was going to punish me. I felt between the devil and the deep blue sea." (Mom insisting that I get him up—Dad's anger)

Five years old: "I remember the first time I got hit. I was watching the end of 'Superman' and went into the bathroom and got a towel. I went down and started jumping off the couch. Dad kept calling me to dinner, but I wanted to play. Finally, I went upstairs, put the towel on the rack, and went downstairs; and Dad hit me."

Focus: "Him hitting me."

Feeling: "Angry because, in my own mind, it was unfair."

In the first recollection, Martin seems to be saying that the "stupid demands of others can force me to do idiotic things." In the second, the message is, "others will unfairly hurt me when I'm doing what I please."

This logic led Martin to develop strategies to insure that others would not be able to make demands of him and would not be in a position to punish him when he did not meet their expectations. Specifically, he became skilled at (1) thoroughly understanding every important issue and feeling that no one could teach him anything more, (2) showing others how stupid they were by finding every possible inconsistency in their logic, (3) confusing issues so that no one could pin him down, (4) "helping" others whom he felt were lost in ignorance (often those who were helped would then ungratefully "bite the hand that had fed them").

The counselor pointed out that the first three strategies were ones that clearly helped Martin in the courtroom, but when applied to his associates were obviously creating resentment. Martin recognized the above and realized that he wasted a great deal of time fighting with people from whom he really needed support. Martin and the counselor began to explore strategies whereby he could avoid alienating others and instead begin encouraging their cooperation. Martin recognized that his considerable skill would insure that he would, in the work setting, always be a "center of attention." He realized that he had convincingly demonstrated that no one could force him to meet their "unreasonable" demands (unless he so chose), and that it was unrealistic to expect that everyone would treat him as a special person (particularly colleagues who were as ambitious as he was). Thus, the idea that he should always be treated as a special person was placed in a better perspective. No longer was it as much of an obstacle as it once had been.

COMMENT: Martin's ERs epitomized his private logic. His professional life had been involved with correcting injustices. This concern for fairness is clearly reflected in his second recollection. He had great empathy with those who were caught in untenable positions (the first recollection). He had developed skills in fighting for those whom he felt were being oppressed. Regarding interpersonal relationships, his love life was dismal. He was attracted to women who had problems. He was an effective helper; but when his women became stronger, they would become angry with his superiority and would leave. Martin's strategies, while highly successful in his professional life, created great difficulties in his personal relationships. Counseling helped Martin recognize that he did not always have to be number one.

Conclusion

No longer can we simply prepare for a career or a job. Rather, it is likely that the majority of us during our lives will change jobs and perhaps even careers a number of times. This prospect of lifelong occupational change will lead to an increasing importance of career counseling. However, career counseling should be seen as part of the total therapeutic or counseling process. As illustrated above with James, a client may approach counseling with a career concern but investigation may reveal another more pressing problem. Likewise, career counseling may be the most appropriate approach to use with a client such as Rene who was referred because of other difficulties. The case of Martin, the civil rights attorney, illustrates that career counseling should be approached in a holistic manner. The new strategies that he learned to encourage his colleagues to help rather than attack him were useful in other areas of his life.

In helping individuals confront the challenge of work, the function of the counselor is to help clarify goals, articulate obstacles which stand in the way of reaching their goals, and finally to help the clients develop effective strategies to move them toward those goals. However, the ultimate focus of the entire process should be to teach the art of effective decision making and to provide encouragement that helps the clients implement their decisions. Clients who know how to process information in a commonsense manner and have the courage to act, will be able to develop new potentials for themselves and thus be prepared for the ever changing world of work.

References

Adler, A. *Problems of Neurosis: A Book of Case Histories.* New York: Harper & Row, 1964. (Originally published, 1929.)

Ansbacher, H. and Ansbacher, R. *The Individual Psychology of Alfred Adler.* New York: Harper & Row, 1956.

McCary, J. *Human Sexuality* (2nd edition). New York: Van Nostrand, 1973.

McKelvie, W. and Friedland, U. *Career Goals Counseling: A Holistic Approach.* Baltimore: F.M.S. Associates, 1978.

Mosak, H. and Dreikurs, R. "Adlerian Psychotherapy" in R. Corsini (Ed), *Current Psychotherapies.* Itasca, Illinois: Peacock Publishers, 1973.

Mosak, H. Personal communication. Chicago, June 1977.

O'Connell, W. and Hansoy, P. "The negative nonsense of the passive patient." *Rational Living*, 1971, 6(1), 28-31.

Orgler, H. *Alfred Adler: The Man and His Work.* New York: Capricorn Books, 1965.

U.S. Government Printing Office. *Dictionary of Occupational Titles.* Washington, D.C., 1977.

SECTION V

CLINICAL PAPERS

INTRODUCTION

ORGLER COMPARES ERs with the same basic theme, being bitten by a dog, from two different persons. She shows the differing styles of life of these two persons and demonstrates how life-style is reflected in the reconstruction and use each made of the dog-bite incident.

The balance of the papers in this section deal with ERs and a variety of clinical disorders.

Feichtinger presents a number of examples of ERs from neurotic patients and suggests how ERs can be used to assess life-style variables in neurotic disorders.

The Manaster and King study of ERs and homosexuality deals with the data from a limited number of subjects in a strictly clinical manner.

Friedman and Schiffman study the utility of ERs in distinguishing psychotic depression from paranoid schizophrenia.

CHAPTER 25

COMPARATIVE STUDY OF TWO
FIRST RECOLLECTIONS*

HERTHA ORGLER

ADLER USED TO SAY, "We are not at the mercy of our memories; we select them." He always emphasized the fact that it is the life-style that molds the memories. In his opinion people who have had the same type of experience in their childhood remember it in various ways according to their different life-styles. To prove the correctness of this conception we ought to carry out experiments in which we expose children to the same situation, and after ten to twenty years make tests to find out in what form they remember the original situations. This is unfortunately impossible, for we do know from observation that individuals who have had the same kind of experiences do not keep them as childhood memories, as they merely recall what seems important to *them*. This is why we have to rely on early memories discovered by chance, which show us that different people recall similar events in different form. Here are two such observations.

(1) Recollection of B.T.: "I was visiting some acquaintances with my sister. Suddenly a big dog jumped on me. I cried, and no one could calm me. My sister took me home to my mother. The doctor was fetched and I was ill for some time. The dog played an important role in my life. I said to my father, 'Go away, you are a bad dog.' I was then three years old."

(2) Recollection of J.R.: "When I was about five years old, I had been friendly for some time with a black Newfoundland dog, then on probation as a watchdog at Herne Hill. After one

* Reprinted by permission from the *American Journal of Individual Psychology*, 1952-53, *10*, 27-30.

of our long summer journeys my first thought on getting home was to go to see Lion. My mother confided me to the care of our one man servant, Thomas, and gave him strict orders that I was not to be allowed within reach of the dog's chain. To make sure of this, Thomas carried me in his arms. Lion was at his dinner and took no notice of either of us, on which I besought leave to pat him. Foolish Tomas stooped toward him that I might, when the dog instantly flew at me and bit a piece clean out of the corner of my lip on the left side. I was brought up the back stairs, bleeding fast but not a whit frightened, except lest Lion be sent away. Lion indeed had to go; but not Thomas. My mother was sure he was sorry and, I think, blamed herself most. The bitten side of the (then really pretty) mouth was spoilt forevermore, but the wound, drawn close, healed quickly. The last use I made of my movable lips before Doctor Aveline drew them into ordered silence for a while was to observe, 'Mama, though I can't speak, I can play on the fiddle.' But the house was of another opinion and I never attained any proficiency upon this instrument worthy of my genius. Not the slightest diminution of my love of dogs, nor the slightest nervousness in managing them, was induced by the accident." (John Ruskin, *Praeterita*, George Allen.)

In proceeding to interpret the two recollections, I shall limit myself only to that which appears to be essential for our present problem. B.T.'s recollection gives the following picture: Here is a youth who remembers the sad consequences the incident with the dog had for him; he was ill for a considerable time afterwards. His attention is focused on the hostility of life. The fact that the dog jumped at him holds a warning for him: "Don't leave home; danger lurks without. Security is where mother is." His crying proves that he is a spoilt child who has trained himself to reach his goal through weakness.

We find the same attitude in his second recollection. "I had been out with other boys and wanted to go home by myself. I lost my way and therefore cried. Then a woman came and showed me the way home." Again the movement in the same direction—home to mother. His recollections show a frightened, passive, and negative attitude. Does this interpretation conform with his life-style?

B.T., seventeen years old, was the youngest son of a very poor family. His sister was two years older; his brother, a well-known writer, was six years older than himself. His physician consulted me because his teachers thought he might be mentally deficient. He was extremely backward, had failed to move up in form several times, and was threatened with dismissal from school as a dunce. He was extremely unpopular with his teachers. They called him "Mephisto," as he was "the spirit that always said 'no.'" He was on bad terms with his father and elder brother, but was his mother's favorite. She pampered him. He liked to sit at home by the fireside and do nothing, and he led an isolated life. He disparaged the accomplishments of others. At the beginning of the treatment he said, "Well, who was Shakespeare after all!" He told me that he would commit suicide if he were dismissed from school. His mother told me that he had been a weak child, very often ill, and therefore she had always done everything for him. Even before the experience with the dog he had been a timid child, always clinging to his mother. It was possible to cure him by the methods of Individual Psychology. He lost his apparently inborn stupidity. Later he won a scholarship at a teacher's college and is now an excellent teacher.

Thus we find in B.T.'s life-style before the treatment the same attitude as was revealed in his first childhood-recollection.

The interpretation of J.R.'s recollection, on the other hand, shows an entirely different life-style. J.R. also remembers an experience with a dog. He does not experience the dog-bite as a hostile act, but pleads for the dog, although the dog's bite left a scar on his "then pretty mouth" forever. He does not recall pains or tears, but emphasizes the rapid healing. His mental attitude is a positive one, and is also shown by the remark which he made to console his mother, "Mama, though I can't speak, I can play on the fiddle." He makes "foolish" Thomas responsible for the accident against the strict command of his mother. We may conclude from this that he attached great importance to common sense. The emotional content of the recollection indicates a life-style full of courage and a positive attitude. This interpretation gains in strength by his second memory, which, summarized, runs as follows: He was alone in the same stable where he had been bitten. He went head-foremost into a large water-tub. He used the small watering-pot he had in his hand to give himself a good thrust up from the bottom and caught hold of the opposite edge of the tub with his left hand.

Courage, independence, and activity are even more striking here. From both these memories we may infer a courageous life-style. As a matter of fact, J.R. is the famous Englishman John Ruskin, who was professor of fine arts at Oxford, and who published books on painting, architecture, social reforms, ethics, education, political economy, and other subjects. As John Ruskin's great achievements tell us a great deal about his positive life-style, I shall give only a few details of his life. We learn that his parents brought him up to be independent and impressed on him that he must not attach too much importance to himself and to his troubles, but have interest in others and achieve something useful. John Ruskin was himself a great champion of courage. Thus he says in one of his most popular works, *Sesame and Lilies,* when discussing the education of girls, "Teach them also that courage and truth are the pillars of their being." His biography conforms with his early memories and shows the life-style of an active man. When we compare these completely different personalities, we find that though they both remember a similar experience, the recollection of the neurotic B.T. reveals lack of courage and lack of social interest, exclusion of all living creatures with exception of his mother and a tendency to see the hostile side of life, a passive and negative attitude, all corresponding to his life-style. In John Ruskin's recollection, on the other hand, we find courage, independence, and an active and positive attitude corresponding to his life-style. We see that two persons can remember similar events in quite different ways. I should, however, like to draw still another conclusion from these memories. The experience with the dog has the effect of a trauma, with a resulting neurosis on the anxious, spoilt child. In the case of John Ruskin, the shock—an unexpected dog-bite—is a much stronger one when considered objectively, and yet it has no injurious effect on his mental development and is not experienced by him as a trauma. It is clearly evident that the external event is of minor importance. It is the life-style which molds the experience.

The two recollections of incidents with dogs show clearly the immense importance of the life-style and provide proof for the correctness of Adler's conception that: (1) The life-style decides whether an event is experienced as a trauma or not. (2) The life-style molds the childhood memories.

CHAPTER 26

EARLY RECOLLECTIONS IN NEUROTIC DISTURBANCES*

FREDERIC FEICHTINGER

ALFRED ADLER WAS without any doubt the first psychologist to emphasize more than anybody else the totality, the unity, the entity of a person. Today psychiatry recognizes this important principle of totality. We realize more and more that taking things apart is always an artificial procedure, and do it only in order to have a better understanding and a better possibility of teaching. We can think only in terms of body *and* mind and never body *or* mind. We should never forget the constant and basic interrelationship between the two. Besides, we will learn more and more that we cannot even separate this body and mind unit from the social environment nor from the cosmic environment. Knowing little about that cosmic interrelationship does not excuse ignoring it.

When we begin to study this complex entity of personality, we have to study activities. The most subtle examination under the microscope of every existing organ, including the brain, still keeps us in complete darkness. Activities must be studied in two ways:

1. Direct study of activities, observing another person's activities.
2. Indirect study of activities, which are only recognized by the individual.

The patient has to tell us about his "inner" experiences. This includes thinking, feeling, desiring, understanding, dream-

---

* Reprinted by permission from the *Individual Psychology Bulletin,* 1943, 3 44-50.

ing, memory, etc. Alfred Adler says: "The greatest of all helps in gaining a quick comprehension of the meaning an individual gives to himself and to life comes through his memories."

It is fascinating to see how this simple method works when we have to examine cases in the clinic and in the ward, where we have not enough time to interview one person at length. Easier than explaining is to present a few examples; everyone can also experiment on himself and others.

Recently the students were called to the ward for their psychiatric study and examination of a patient. The patient, being a nurse, was very uncooperative and very indignant about the psychiatric interview. She felt she was really sick, complaining about her heart palpitations, sleeplessness, dizziness, shaky feelings, loss of appetite, and tremor. The 28-year-old patient had had a complete physical check-up; the result was negative, but the patient insisted that something must be wrong with her. As mentioned before, her unwillingness to cooperate gave very little possibility for diagnosing her psychiatric problems.

In order to come to a quick result, I asked the patient, "What is the very first thing you can remember about your childhood?" The patient answered, "I don't know, but my mother tells me that when I was about six years old, I wanted to go to school very badly, but when I went, I wanted to get out very badly." The students could not see very much in that answer. I told them, "You can be sure that this young lady is very poorly adjusted and she will prove to us that she always wants to get some responsible position; having achieved that, she wants to get out again."

The further interview proved that our guess was right. Becoming a nurse was her free choice. She liked it very much, but when she had to work in a hospital, in the ward, she felt it was too much of a strain on her, not enough pay, and she planned to take up some other occupation.

Shortly before giving up her position as a nurse, she complained of nervousness and palpitation and made these symptoms responsible for her leaving the hospital.

After a short period she got a job as a secretary, but she

did not like it too well either. Since her symptoms increased, she felt compelled to give this job up also. Now she was looking for still another occupation, but in the meantime her symptoms became so severe she claims she had to go to the hospital as a patient.

Asked about her interest in marriage, she said that she "fell in love quite often, but was always falling out again."

Without much explaining, the students could realize that the patient revealed her pattern of life through her early recollections: Going in—going out, wanting responsibility—running away from it. Furthermore it was quite obvious that her symptoms served as a very well-devised alibi for getting out, for running away from her responsibilities.

I would like to show now a few other examples of early recollections, in order to prove how easy it is to detect a patient's pattern of life.

A 38-year-old male patient suffers from anxiety neurosis. He has severe anxiety symptoms with palpitations, dizziness, sinking feelings, and intestinal disturbances whenever he goes away from home. He had to give up his occupation as a travelling salesman. His early recollection is: playing with a train together with his father.

Patient does not reveal very much interest in life; he enjoys playing with the train with his father. That his mother does not appear in his recollection is a very poor sign and indicates a feeling of having been neglected by her. He cannot forget it and his whole pattern of life is built around this experience. The fact is that the patient was very much attached to his father who died early. He never got along well with his mother and today he is still fighting and arguing with her. He usually sees her when he needs her financial support, since he is not too successful in life—which is not surprising when we know his first recollection.

A 35-year-old female patient was taken to the hospital after a suicide attempt and was diagnosed as a case of psychoneurosis with mild depression. Her early recollection was: "I always was a sickly child and I always wanted more than I had."

Her first recollection reveals that she has not too much courage, is very self-centered, shows a lot of self-pity, and has no social interest. She expects everything for nothing—a very typical picture of a neurotic pattern. Patient is today still constantly impressed by her weakness, is completely dissatisfied with life, especially her married life; the analysis reveals that her suicide attempt was executed as a revenge against her husband who, as she says, cannot give her the things in life she wants.

A 33-year-old male patient suffered from anxiety neurosis, phobia, and suicidal ideas. The patient was afraid of crowds and people, could not ride in a subway, a train, or in a tunnel. His early recollection is: "At the age of ten years I was terribly disappointed when my parents told me there is no Santa Claus. The whole world seemed to crumble."

This patient expresses: "You see how terrible life is in destroying my belief in Santa Claus. . . ." Patient, who is married, continued to be a daydreamer and was unwilling and unable to face reality.

A 20-year-old male patient, who was diagnosed as a case of maladjustment and schizoid personality, told me the following recollections: "Mother put soap in my mouth in order to curb my crying."

Through this recollection we can hear: "Even my mother makes life miserable and distasteful for me." Patient had severe difficulties in getting along with people, never participated in social activities. He was a typical autistic personality, and very seldom opened his mouth.

A 30-year-old female patient, a homosexual, remembers first: Playing with boys and tying down each other. She tied one boy and made heavy knots. But the boy had his legs pushed up, pulled his legs together and just stepped out of the rope. She felt very badly about being outwitted. The second of her recollections is: older boys chasing after her and other children. One big boy caught her and gave her a spanking. She felt terribly humiliated. Patient hates men, has no interest in the opposite sex, lives with other girls as though married.

"Only boys can be so mean and they just dominate and hurt you" is the expression of her first recollections.

A 26-year-old patient, suffering from compulsion neurosis and sexual neurosis, tells as follows: "When I was seven days old—you may not believe that I remember it—after being circumsized, I felt sleepy and lay on a huge pillow. Everybody was coming to look at me."

Through this recollection, the patient reflects his extreme interest in sex, especially his own sex-organ, and the isolation of his later life. He does not want to be bothered with responsibilities and enjoys being the center of attention. The fact is, the patient had no friends of either sex, was unwilling to face life, and used his sex-conflict, which he proudly considered an "Oedipus conflict," to excuse his constant failures.

A 40-year-old male patient, who was taken to the psychopathic ward after an attempted suicide by cutting his throat, told me as follows: "At about the age of three or four, I recall being struck in the head by a baseball bat while watching a ballgame. While this raised quite a lump and I was carried home a few blocks away and quite a fuss was made about it, I suffered, as far as I know, no ill effects." A second recollection is: "I also recall feigning a headache one day in school to avoid lessons I had not studied. On the way home from school I remember deliberately hitting myself on the head in order to really have a headache when I got home." The patient recovered very quickly from his suicide attempt, suffered no ill effects, and confessed to me later that he did not intend to kill himself, he just was fed up with his job and his marriage.

This patient shows complete lack of courage, a desire for being pampered, and he has not even the courage to shun his responsibilities openly. He has to hit himself on the head in order to have an alibi. In fact his suicide attempt was a bluff, an alibi, in order to run away from his marital responsibilities.

A 42-year-old male patient who was taken to a mental institution suffering from hysteria and severe obsessive ideas said: "When I was walking as a little boy behind my father's coffin, I got the greatest kick in my life out of it, realizing that the man I hated so much was dead." His main obsessive ideas have been to kill his wife and child and to yell "fire" in a crowded movie or theatre.

His whole pattern of life is built around hate and destructive feelings.

A 32-year-old female patient, who was taken to a mental institution after a suicide attempt and who was suffering from psychoneurosis and alcoholism, gave me the following recollection: "When I was three years old my mother gave a luncheon. The lady friends of my mother asked me how I felt. I said: 'I feel perfectly miserable.' Everybody laughed and thought it was cute from such a young child, but I felt terrible about it."

Her first recollection reveals that she enjoyed being a Cinderella since she could not be a princess.

A 35-year-old female patient, who suffered from a severe paranoia, recalls: "When I was two years old a sister was born and I threw her out of the cradle. My mother scolded me, but I said: 'You better throw her into the river.' When I was three years old, my mother went shopping and left me alone in the house. I remember seeing two mice running through the room, and I got scared. But then it looked to me as if the two mice were dressed like man and wife and were dancing in the middle of the room. Suddenly the whole thing disappeared."

Here we see a strong resentment against being dethroned and a jealous and aggressive character who wants to remove every competition. The second recollection reveals her phantasy. We are not surprised that later on this person develops a projected and delusional jealousy reaction called paranoia.

These are just a few examples to show how interesting and necessary it is to study the so-called inner experience of a personality. Not long ago heredity and environment were regarded as the main influence in the development of personality. But it was Alfred Adler again who stressed more than anybody else that experiences—and memories are past experiences—have a tremendous and far-reaching influence on the development of a total personality.

In the study of personality and neurotic disturbances, early recollection usually can give us a fundamental estimate:

1. of the beginning of a life history, the starting point of the personality development, his activities, relationship to others and ability to cooperate;
2. of problems which confronted the patient, how he solved them, and an indication how he will meet future problems;
3. of his pattern of life in its origin, his concept of himself, his main interest and purpose in life.

CHAPTER 27

EARLY RECOLLECTIONS OF MALE HOMOSEXUALS*

Guy J. Manaster and Marc King

According to Adler, early recollections (ERs) reflect important characteristics of a person's life-style. The purpose of this paper is to test this with male homosexuals. We shall report the ERs of five homosexual patients who were seen in therapy by the principal author, examine what their ERs have in common, and attempt to relate this to theory and research on homosexuality.†

Theoretical Position

Adler proposed five factors common in sexual perversion including homosexuality: (a) increased psychological distance from the opposite sex; (b) some degree of revolt against the normal sexual role, which is at the same time an unconscious device to enhance a lowered self-esteem; (c) compensatory tendencies to alleviate feelings of inferiority with respect to the opposite sex; (d) tendency to depreciate the normally-to-be

---

* Reprinted by permission from the *Journal of Individual Psychology*, 1973, 29, 1, 26-33.

† It is noteworthy that one of Adler's earliest statements about ERs was in connection with homosexuality. He wrote in 1917: "The full-fledged homosexual always appeals to his whole historically developed individuality. All his childhood recollections seem to him to justify his point of view. This uniformity in development has suggested to various authors the false thesis of an 'innate homosexuality.' But as Schrecker and I have pointed out, childhood recollections tend to falsify the past in accordance with the life plan. This understanding has completely eliminated a main piece of evidence for 'innate homosexuality' from the discussion" (1, pp. 273-274, translation modified from the German original). Paul Schrecker was a young co-worker of Adler who wrote the first paper on the significance of early recollections.

expected partner; (e) excessive sensitivity, personal ambition, and defiance, with a disinclination to "join in the game," and altogether "a strong limitation of social interest" (2, p. 424).

While the last four factors, although referring here to sex role and the sex partner, pertain otherwise to neuroses in general, the first factor is specific to sexual perversion. It also refers to a horizontal movement—increasing the distance from the opposite sex—while the other factors refer to vertical movements.

Kurt Adler, writing on the life-style of the homosexual states: "What is specific about the homosexual symptom, aside from a prolonged uncertainty as to gender identity in childhood, is fear of the opposite sex, or fear of inadequacy in one's proper sex role, or both" (3, p. 77).

Various other authors are in essential agreement with the Adlerian position. According to Judd Marmor, a prerequisite for male homosexuality is "impaired gender-identity" and "a fear of intimate contact with members of the opposite sex," as well as opportunity for homosexual behavior (16, p. 5). This is also the position of Sandor Rado, according to whom the most prominent factor leading to homosexuality is "hidden but incapacitating fears of the opposite sex" (20, p. 187). To these is to be added H. S. Sullivan who envisioned in homosexuals a "barrier" prohibiting intimacy with persons of the other sex, resulting from real experiences (23, p. 277).

In summary, these theorists agree in recognizing as basic to the development of homosexuality a barrier to, a fear of, or a distancing from the opposite sex. The last, the Adlerian formulation, is the most overt, most behavioral, least encumbered with assumed intrapsychic processes.

Research Findings

Research studies into the personality of the parents, family relationships, and child rearing practices do not, of course, all agree, but a pattern is evident which corroborates the theoretical position just presented.

As an example, Ullman (24) administered a questionnaire to 325 inmates at a California prison hospital with a record of sexual deviancy and to 311 control inmates. Homosexuals were found to have had different child rearing experiences than inmates with other sexual deviancies and than the controls. The homosexuals reported about their fathers: less attention, love, friendliness, affection, praise, and play. They stated significantly more often about their mothers: too much affection, criticism, unreasonable anger, success expectation, scolding, and physical punishment. Such a mother points, according to the author, toward a fear of women.

Bieber et al. (8), from most extensive data on 106 male homosexuals undergoing psychoanalysis in New York City, concluded that any son exposed to the following would be likely to develop homosexual problems: a mother who is close-binding and intimate with her son, and dominant and minimizing toward her husband, and a father who is detached and hostile toward his son. For us the most important statement of the study is that it "provides convincing support for a fundamental contribution by Rado. . . . A homosexual adaptation is a result of 'hidden but incapacitating fears of the opposite sex' " (8, p. 303).

Bene (7), comparing 83 homosexuals with 84 married men, found that the homosexuals expressed significantly more hostility and less affection toward their fathers as well as coming from their fathers. They also expressed more hostility and less affection toward their mothers. If they are more attached to their mothers, it is not because their relationship is better than that of nonhomosexuals, but because their relationship to their fathers is worse.

Other research of this type (6, 10-13, 15, 17-19, 21, 22, 25-26) similarly reports that homosexuals tend to perceive their mothers as having been intimate, close-binding, overpossessive, overcontrolling, seductive, and dominating. They tend to perceive their fathers as having been rejecting, hostile, indifferent, weak, ineffectual, and detached (4, 5, 9).

One contradictory study is that by Greenblatt (14). However, he used "well-adjusted" homosexuals. They described their fathers as good, generous, pleasant, dominant, and underprotective, and their mothers as good, generous, pleasant, neither dominant nor subordinate, and neither overprotective nor underprotective.

While these research studies are restricted to the influence of the parents, Kurt Adler points out that remembered "sibling relations must also not be forgotten, when one searches for factors which may have discouraged a child from pursuing his proper gender role." He reports that "one boy's earliest memory was that his twin sister, in their double perambulator, used to crawl over to his side and beat him." The boy "had been a promiscuous homosexual since the age of eighteen, and had never even dated a girl, which, with such an earliest memory, we can well understand" (3, p. 72).

Cases

A young man came to the first author with the complaint that he was extremely anxious about school, friends, his love life, everything. His first ER included: "She [mother] kicked me in the crotch. It hurt—but she apologized." He reported that he was homosexual, and his mannerisms confirmed this, which, to quote Kurt Adler again, "with such an earliest memory, we can well understand." In his second ER, his father pulled his legs out from under him in the water at the beach, and in a third ER his father caught him in a dress in a closet with a doll—themes often attributed to homosexuals. But it was the first dramatic ER which prompted the first author to look through his files at the ERs of the four other homosexuals he had seen. The ERs of all five cases are reported verbatim in Table 27-I.

Case B reports in ER 1, "I needed shots every other day. Grandma did it. . . . I cried and screamed. The first thing I wanted to do was run, but I didn't." He was an active homosexual who came to therapy in a crisis due to his inability to sustain an intimate relationship.

Case C said in his second ER, "Mother was cleaning the house. I picked a thing off the floor. I went to blow into it. I thought it was a balloon. She was furious and hollered." His fourth ER went, "Next door a woman had a garden and flowers . . . I can't remember whether I was picking the flowers or . . . smelling them. The woman came out screaming and screaming and screaming."

TABLE 27-I

EARLY RECOLLECTIONS OF FIVE MALE HOMOSEXUALS

Case A

1. Age 5-6. I was lying on the floor and made a caustic remark, and she [mother] kicked me in the crotch. It hurt—but she apologized. It was an enraged kick—but she immediately became soft.

2. Age 4. I was with my father at the beach and was standing in the water. Suddenly my legs were pulled out from under me. It was my father. I was scared.

3. Age 4. I was in a closet, in a dress, with a doll. My father opened the door. He caught me. [Question] I remember being caught in a compromising position.

Case B

1. Age 3-4. I needed shots every other day. Grandma did it. The first time, standing by the stove she got the hypodermic ready. She said, "Come here." I was crying. I held her legs, she was wearing a long dress, and she gave me the shot. I cried and screamed. The first thing I wanted to do was run, but I didn't. Then she rocked and held me, and said I was a good boy for not running away, and I felt real good.

2. Age 4. I was with grandma, and she was hanging clothes. I switched on the washing machine and tried to put some clothing through, and my arm went through. I screamed and grandma ran towards me. I was scared, and she turned the machine off, and I felt fine.

3. Age 4-5. I remember when my parents got married (when mother remarried). I hid their rings. The rings were above the mantle and I took them and hid them. Two hours later I sat and waited for them to find out. They asked me and I didn't respond. I said, "no." They asked again, and I said I wanted some boxes their presents came in, and I showed them. They gave me the boxes and left. . . . I remember holding grandma's hand as they went in the car. I felt like they were leaving me.

Case C

1. Age 5-6. I remember climbing up on the sofa where he [father] was lying and I lay on top of him. I knew I could do it. I'm almost positive there was something sexual about it. I felt wonderful but I don't remember what he did.

2. Age 4. Mother was cleaning the house. I picked a thing off the floor. I went to blow into it. I thought it was a balloon. She was furious and hollered. It seemed like a long time, on and on. I couldn't understand how, over a balloon, but I knew there was more to it. Now I know it was a prophylactic. Whenever they are mentioned I think of this.

3. Age 5. Sis and I were in bed. We had scarlet fever or measles. The room was very dark, the weather was warm, it was quiet and cozy. I looked out the screen door at where the kids whom I liked and wanted over, lived. But I couldn't go out of the house. [Question.] I liked the idea of both of us being sick, not able to scratch or rub, but getting great attention and care. It was a nice situation.

4. Age 5. Next door a woman had a garden, and flowers grew against our fence. I can't remember whether I was picking the flowers or standing and smelling them. The woman came out screaming and screaming and screaming. [Question.] I was scared. I remember mother coming out and they talked back and forth across the fence and then I went back into the house.

Case D

1. Age 4. During mother's pregnancy, I remember being resentful of her lack of attention. I told mother I wished she didn't have a baby in her stomach. She got very angry. [Question.] I suppose I felt it was unfair.

2. Age 5-6. I took some homework to the teacher and told her it made me nervous to work problems. She said, you are too young to be nervous. I pro-

TABLE 27-I (Continued)

EARLY RECOLLECTIONS OF FIVE MALE HOMOSEXUALS

tested, it makes me nervous. I don't know how it was resolved. I went back to my seat. [Question.] I felt anxious. I couldn't concentrate. I felt like she didn't know how nervous I was.

3. Age 6-7. I was trying to teach the maid English, to teach her the alphabet. She became frustrated and decided not to continue. She invented excuses and left. I felt she was giving up too easily.

4. Age 6-7. I was playing with Jimmy [brother], and I remember hurting him. He told Mom. I remember being scolded. She gave me a lecture, "Why are you always hurting Jimmy?" I protested, I hadn't meant to hurt him, and I really had. [Question.] I remember being passive, just sitting there.

Case E

1. Age 8. I was playing with a knife, whittling on an Indian. I slashed back and cut my fingers. I was holding them, looking at them, and I screamed. Father ran over, looked down and hugged my head and said it wasn't bad. [Question.] I needed someone; didn't know what to do.

2. Age 5-6. I was going over to a friend's house. I walked to the door, and his mother answered. She was tall, had black hair, and she screamed, "He can't play—not today—go home." And I walked away depressed.

3. Age 4. I was riding my sister's bike on the street. I'd just gotten off training wheels. Going down the street not using training wheels. At the end of the street I used the wheels to turn and come back. I remember my Dad saying "Great." [Question.] I felt great.

4. Age 4. At a carnival across the street, eating a candy apple and watching people and all. Everything seemed big, music, ferris wheel. [Question.] I felt strange and I was little; everyone else was big, and I was alone and the grass was tall.

Case D, a 22-year-old man who said he was a homosexual and was anxious because he had never had any physical contact with either sex and had never dated anyone, gave four ERs in which, in order, he was responded to angrily by his mother, his concerns were summarily dismissed by a female teacher, his constructive efforts were rejected by a maid, and his mother scolded and lectured him for hurting his brother.

Case E, a university senior who had considered himself heterosexual but had recently begun experimenting homosexually with a friend and was concerned that he was now homosexual, gave as his second ER "I walked to the door (of a friend's house), and his mother answered. She was tall, had black hair, and she screamed, 'He can't play—not today—go home.' And I walked away depressed."

Discussion

These cases have in common that in at least one ER there is a woman who hurt or was angry with the subject, or toward whom the subject showed a critical attitude. The ERs are thus in accordance with what one would expect from the theoretical positions of Adler, Sullivan, and Rado. They are also in agreement with the general research evidence that presents the mother, and one may assume women in general, in an unfavorable light.

The direct description by these cases of their mothers also reflects this negative, critical attitude. Briefly, they described their mothers as: Case A, "Nice enough most of the time but sometimes she was really mean"; Case B, "When she's in a good mood, she's the best person there is; when she's in a bad mood, she doesn't want to be bothered"; Case C, "She was kind and gentle until she started drinking"; Case D, "Pure bitch"; Case E, "Was a pushover, didn't respect her, but she was efficient." These descriptions are more general, like the findings of the research cited earlier, whereas ERs, by their very nature are concrete and idiographic. It should be noted that, significantly, four out of the above five descriptions of the mothers contain a contradiction, thus corroborating the double-binding behavior of the mothers reported in other research studies on male homosexuals.

In summary, a series of early recollections (ERs) from five male homosexuals were examined to test the hypothesis that the homosexual life-style characteristic of interposing a distance between oneself and the other sex is expressed in the ERs. We found indeed the presence of a hostile or aggressive female, or such attitude toward a female, in the ERs of our five male homosexuals. It remains for further studies to show whether this is a truly general finding, and if so, whether it applies also to the "well-adjusted" male homosexuals, or only to those in psychotherapy, as is suggested by the Greenblatt study (14).

References

1. Adler, A. The homosexual problem. *Alienist Neurol.*, 1917, *38*, 268-287. Original: *Das Problem der Homosexualität.* Munich: Reinhardt, 1917.
2. Adler, A. *The individual psychology of Alfred Adler.* Ed. by H. L. and Rowena R. Ansbacher. New York: Basic Books, 1956.
3. Adler, K. A. Life style, gender role, and the symptom of homosexuality. *J. Indiv. Psychol.*, 1967, *23*, 67-78.

4. Allen, C. Homosexuality: its nature, causation and treatment. In C. Berg and C. Allen (Eds.), *The problem of homosexuality.* New York: Citadel Press, 1958.

5. Apperson, L. B. and McAdoo, W. G., Jr. Parental factors in the childhood of homosexuals. *J. Abnorm. Psychol.,* 1968, *73,* 201-206.

6. Bell, A. P. The Scylla and Charybdis of psychosexual development. *J. Sex Res.,* 1969, *5*(2), 86-89.

7. Bene, E. On the genesis of male homosexuality: an attempt to clarify the role of the parents. *Brit. J. Psychiat.,* 1965, *111,* 803-813.

8. Bieber, I. et al. *Homosexuality: A psychoanalytic study.* New York: Basic Books, 1962.

9. Blaine, G. B., Jr. and McArthur, C. C. Basic character disorders and homosexuality. In *Emotional problems of the student.* New York: Appleton-Century-Crofts, 1961. Pp. 106-115.

10. Braaten, L. J. and Darling, C. D. Overt and covert homosexual problems among male college students. *Genet. Psychol. Monogr.,* 1965, *71,* 269-310.

11. Chang, J. and Block, J. A study of identification in male homosexuals. *J. Consult. Psychol.,* 1960, *24,* 308-310.

12. Edwards, H. E. The relationship between reported early life experiences with parents and adult male homosexuality. Unpublished doctoral dissertation, University of Tennessee, 1963.

13. Evans, R. C. Childhood parental relationships of homosexual men. *J. Consult. Clin. Pyschol.,* 1969, *33,* 129-135.

14. Greenblatt, D. R. Semantic differential analysis of the "triangular system" hypothesis in "adjusted" overt male homosexuals. Unpublished doctoral dissertation, University of California at Los Angeles, 1966.

15. Kolb, L. C. and Johnson, A. Etiology and therapy of overt homosexuals. *Psychoanal. Quart.,* 1955, *24,* 506-515.

16. Marmor, J. Introduction. In *Sexual inversion: The multiple roots of homosexuality.* New York: Basic Books, 1965. Pp. 1-22.

17. Mathes, I. Adult male homosexuality and perception of instrumentality, expressiveness, and coalition in parental role structure. *Dissertation Abstr., 28*(2-A), 811.

18. Miller, P. R. The effeminate passive obligatory homosexual. *AMA Arch. Neurol. Psychiat.,* 1958, *80,* 612-618.

19. O'Conner, P. J. Aetiological factor in homosexuality as seen in Royal Air Force psychiatric practice. *Brit. J. Psychiat.,* 1964, *110,* 381-391.

20. Rado, S. An adaptational view of sexual behavior. In P. H. Hoch and J. Zubin (Eds.), *Psychosexual development in health and disease.* New York: Grune & Stratton, 1949. Pp. 159-189.

21. Schofield, M. *Sociological aspects of homosexuality.* Boston: Little Brown, 1965.

22. Snortum, J. R. et al. Family dynamics and homosexuality. *Psychol. Rep.,* 1969, *24,* 763-770.

23. Sullivan, H. S. *The interpersonal theory of psychiatry*. Ed. by Helen
    Swick Perry and Mary Ladd Garvel. New York: Norton, 1953.
24. Ullman, P. S. Parental participation in child rearing as evaluated by
    male social deviates. *Pac. Sociol, Rev.*, 1960, *3*, 89-95.
25. West, D. J. Parental figures in the genesis of male homosexuality. *Int.
    J. Soc. Psychiat.*, 1959, *5*, 85-97.
26. Whitener, R. W. and Nikelly, A. Sexual deviation in college students.
    Amer. J. Orthopsychiat., 1964, *34*, 486-492.

Editor's Note

Friedberg also studied life-styles of homosexuals via ERs
and came to the following conclusions: The homosexual has
a weaker sense of identity, is more dependent and less hostile
and dangerous, and has more severely impaired gender identity
than the heterosexual. He found no difference in degree of
goal orientation or activity level.*

---

* Friedberg, R. L. Early recollections of homosexuals as indicators of their
life-styles. *J. Indiv. Psychol.* 1975, *31*, 1, 196-204.

CHAPTER 28

EARLY RECOLLECTIONS OF SCHIZOPHRENIC AND DEPRESSED PATIENTS

Joseph Friedman and Harold Schiffman

Early recollections (ERs) have long been of interest to clinical workers but have not received the systematic investigation afforded to similar data. Historically, there have been two major positions as to the significance of ERs. Freud (3) contended that they were but fragments which served to screen from awareness repressed experiences; thus the term "screen memories." This focus led to the bypassing of the manifest content and to the therapeutic effort of unearthing what lay behind it. Adler (1, 2) on the other hand, asserted that ERs were indicative of a person's style of life and so of worth in their own right. More recently a variety of investigators (4, 5, 6) have attempted to establish the relationship between early memories and such personality variables as emotional security, ego strength, the expression of hostility, etc.

This report is the first of a projected series aimed at demonstrating the diagnostic and dynamic utility of ERs. It focuses specifically upon those aspects which aid in differentiating between psychotic depression and paranoid schizophrenia. Preliminary study of such patients led to a series of nine hypotheses regarding the contents of their ERs, as shown in Table 28-I.

Procedure

From a carefully selected sample of 100 psychotic depressives (independently diagnosed by the hospital staff and two additional psychiatrists),

---

* Reprinted by permission from the *Journal of Individual Psychology*, 1962, *18*, 1, 57-61.

TABLE 28-I

HYPOTHESES REGARDING THE CONTENTS OF EARLY
RECOLLECTIONS (ERs) IN SCHIZOPHRENIC AND
PSYCHOTIC DEPRESSED PATIENTS

ERs of *schizophrenic* patients will show	ERs of *psychotic depressed* patients will show
1. absence of positive affects	5. positive affects
2. unmitigated fear, terror, and/or horror	6. if negative affects, then tragic ones, such as sadness, distress
3. concern with bodily harm other than that caused by illness or aging	7. concern with physical illness and aging but not with other bodily harm
4. absence of persons, or personal relations that are negative or neutral, at best	8. a strong but generalized desire to be emotionally close to others
	9. work and/or achievement orientation

twenty cases were randomly chosen. Ten paranoid schizophrenics were selected from the files of two institutions.†

The ERs were elicited from these groups by qualified psychologists using the following instructions: "Please think a moment and give me three of your earliest memories. I don't care what they are about, just as long as they go as far back as you can recall into your childhood." The age of the subject at the time of the recalled event and the associated affect were also elicited and recorded on cards.

These sets of ERs were presented to two judges to decide which was the product of a schizophrenic and which that of a depressive patient, using only the nine hypotheses as guides. The judges had no idea of the actual nosological proportions of the sample composition. In case the ERs of a set differed, the judges were to consider two out of three as decisive. If this was insufficient for reaching a conclusion, they were to weigh the first ER more. If the judges disagreed, there was a five minute discussion, based on the above rules. At the end of this period they could agree or remain deadlocked, in which case each judge's separate opinion was recorded. The judges were not informed as to their success until the entire task was completed.

It is to be stressed that the judges were psychologically naive; they were, in fact, secretarial workers. Their training in the present technique was limited to a fifteen minute explanation of the hypotheses and rules for decision making.

A replication of the experiment was conducted two months later with an additional nineteen depressives and seven schizophrenics, and two

---

† We are indebted to Dr. R. G. Ballard, Veterans Administration Regional Office, Philadelphia, for his aid in collecting the data.

new judges, also psychologically unsophisticated. This will be referred to as Experiment 2.

The results are shown in Table 28-II. The χ^2 values were computed using a 50-50 ratio of agreement-disagreement as the expected frequency, except in the last line. There the judges

TABLE 28-II

OBTAINED AGREEMENT OF JUDGES OF ERs WITH EACH OTHER (RELIABILITY) AND WITH THE CRITERION OF S's DIAGNOSIS (VALIDITY), COMPARED WITH AGREEMENT EXPECTED BY CHANCE

Exp. 1 (N=20 depr.+10 schiz.)		Exp. 2 (N=17 depr.+7 schiz.)	
	χ^2		χ^2
Judges 1 and 2	11.76**	Judges 3 and 4	14.71**
Judge 1 and criterion	4.04*	Judge 3 and criterion	3.38
Judge 2 and criterion	5.64*	Judge 4 and criterion	7.04**
Judge 1 and 2 agreed and correct	16.49**	Judges 3 and 4 agreed and correct	24.44**

* Significant at .05 level.
** Significant at .01 level.

were in accord with each other and the criterion, and the expected ratio was the conjoint occurrence of two 50-50 ratios of agreement-disagreement: hence the theoretical frequency was a 25-75 ratio.

The first line shows that in both experiments the judges achieved significant reliability on the basis of the given hypotheses which served as the guides for the judging.

Validity is here defined as the agreement between the judge's diagnosis and the independent psychiatric diagnosis as criterion. Of the four judges utilized in the two experiments three achieved significant agreement with the criterion and the fourth just failed, achieving the .07 level of confidence (lines 2 and 3). A second and more stringent assessment of validity was also carried out. This required the conjoint occurrence of both judges agreeing and being correct in each experiment. The last line shows the very significant χ^2 values which were obtained.

The following shows actual ERs obtained and how they were judged.

Case 5 (Depressive)

1. Being the oldest girl I did a lot with mother, taking care of kids.
2. First roller skates; I used to enjoy it very much. (E: Age?) Little kid; one of my aunts from Philadelphia sent them to us.
3. Used to take care of the kids and shop even as a little kid. (E: Age?) About 9, 10, 11. Enjoyable; the butcher always said I was a good shopper.

Positive affects are contained in the second and third ERs, the work and achievement orientations are contained in the first and third ERs, the desire to be emotionally close and in a positive relationship to others appears in all three. There is no fear, no bodily harm in this set.

Case 11 (Depressive)

1. Easter time; father got us chicks and rabbits for my sister and myself. (E: age?) Four years. (E: What were your feelings then?) Very happy.
2. First day of kindergarten; thrilled and happy to go to school. I always was chubby. Also, a little boy was quite fat. His mother came along with a big shopping bag full of food; she did not want Gilbert to become hungry before lunch. (E: Age?) Five-and-a-half. (E: How did you feel?) Very happy.
3. Chickenpox. I was kept away from my sister up on the third floor for two weeks. The very day I recovered, my sister got chickenpox. Grandmother took me to a movie, *Hit the Deck*, with Jack Oakie. Then we went to an automat. Big treat. (E: Age?) Seven. (E: And your feelings then? I only remember the thrill on going out.

The affects in two of the ERs are positive. Other persons are present and emotional closeness to them is displayed in all three. There is the memory of physical illness but not of bodily harm.

Case 8 (Schizophrenic)

1. I was frightened, didn't want to go to school, don't know why. Just feared it for a couple of days and weeks. My mother bought me a box of Chiclets® to pacify my fear. (E: Age?) Four-and-a-half.
2. In second or third grade I was upset. Mother would bring me milk and take me in the girls' room and practiced the stuff, then I'd get upset and throw up. Each Friday. Then I was tested and I would do well. (E: Age?) Six. (E: Your feelings?) I don't know.
3. I dropped my brother. He was two months old, I was seven. I loved him, I wanted to hold him and took him from someone, fell and dropped him. His eyes rolled back, all the white showing. They rushed him to the hospital. I got a licking that night. Very much scared.

In this set of ERs the affects of fear and terror are prominent, there is direct mention of body harm, and in two of the three ERs the personal relations are negative or lead to disaster in the single instance where they began positively.

Case 27 (Schizophrenic)

1. I can recall my aunt Mary caught me and my—all the sex, Christ—my niece, no, my cousin, her daughter in the bathroom. I was trying to insert my penis. I was about six. She told me she'd tell my mother. (E: How did you feel?) I was afraid and I wasn't.

2. When in Atlantic City, my mother and I found a chicken ring. I was four at the time. We argued over it. She took the ring. Made me feel pretty small, pretty bad. She felt she should have it. She was bigger than me.

3. Oh yes. We were living, I remember, in Point Breeze. I must have been three or four, not in school yet. Father was talking to somebody and I put chewing gum in his hair. He beat the living shit out of me and slapped me and scolded me. (E: How did you feel?) I felt I deserved it, I had no right to do it.

Here too, fear is prominent. The relations with others are uniformly negative. Physical harm is manifest and psychological harm is implied.

The judges were particularly effective in understanding and diagnosing depressives. In Experiment 1 they agreed and were correct on 16 of 20 depressive cases; in Experiment 2, on 15 of 19 cases. These findings imply a remarkable degree of characterization of depressives embodied in the hypotheses.

With regard to schizophrenics the judges' accuracy was much less. In Experiment 1 they were in accord and correct in but 3 of 10 cases; in Experiment 2, in only 2 of 7 cases. There were more occasions in which the sets of judges agreed but were in error (in 9 additional cases). The hypotheses led to reliable judgments but were not adequate validly to characterize schizophrenics.

Discussion

The results as a whole demonstrate that psychologically unsophisticated persons are able to distinguish reliably and validly psychotic depressives from paranoid schizophrenics on the sole basis of nine rules applied to their ERs. Further, the judges accomplished this with outstanding economy of time (approximately five minutes per decision).

The particular success in diagnosing depression lends support to the respective hypotheses. They thus seem relevant to a more general theory of that syndrome. It would appear that psychotic depressives are persons with strong needs, desires, or expectations to be with others. Also, they need or expect to work and achieve, probably as a means of implementing their need to be close to others. In illness they remember good times lost, and their attitudes and affects are those which typically evoke succorant responses from others and restore the emotional closeness. It is noteworthy that the affect of fear is absent in their ERs while it quite frequently appears in those of schizophrenics.

It would appear feasible to differentiate other nosological groups similarly through early recollections.

References

1. Adler, A. Significance of early recollections. *Int. J. Indiv. Psychol.*, 1937, 3, 283-287.
2. Ansbacher, H. L. Adler's place today in the psychology memory. *Indiv. Psychol. Bull.*, 1947, 6, 32-40. Also *J. Pers.*, 1947, 15, 197-207.
3. Freud, S. Screen memories. In *Collected papers.* Vol. 5. London: Hogarth, 1950. Pp. 47-69.
4. Langs, R. J., Rothenberg, M. B., Fishman, J. R. and Reiser, M. F. A method for clinical and theoretical study of the earliest memory. *AMA Arch. Gen. Psychiat.*, 1960, 3, 523-534.
5. Purcell, K. Memory and psychological security. *J. Abnorm. Soc. Psychol.*, 1952, 47, 435-440.
6. Saul, L. and Sheppard, E. An attempt to quantify emotional forces using manifest dreams: A preliminary study. *J. Amer. Psychoanal. Ass.*, 1956, 4, 486-502.

SECTION VI

CASE STUDIES

INTRODUCTION

$\mathbf{M}$osak and Kopp analyse ERs of three major leaders in modern psychological thought and relate the ER data with the life-styles of these men and the impact of their life-styles on their respective theories.

Rom discusses from an Adlerian perspective the recollection by Goethe analysed by Freud in his paper, "A Childhood Recollection from Dichtung und Wahrheit" (reviewed in the Annotated Bibliography). The Adlerian and Freudian interpretations are compared.

Thatcher in a very brief paper cites a case of an early recollection of a juvenile offender and how the judge made therapeutic use of this information.

Olson presents two cases, one of a wounded Vietnam veteran and one of a case of schizo-affective psychosis. The histories of these cases are thoroughly outlined with a series of ERs from each client analysed and annotated in detail. Ilgenfritz does the same with a case of dependency and depression.

CHAPTER 29

THE EARLY RECOLLECTIONS OF
ADLER, FREUD, AND JUNG[*]

HAROLD H. MOSAK AND RICHARD ROYAL KOPP

E ARLY RECOLLECTIONS (ERs) have a long tradition of interest and value for the clinical psychologist. Freud, in 1899, described his views on the subject in his paper on "Screen Memories" (11). While Adler began to develop his views, together with his general goal-oriented theory, around 1907 to 1913, he did not present them specifically until some twenty years later as chapters in several of his more popular books (2, 3, 4). Though both, Freud and Adler, observed that patients' ERs tended to be innocuous in content, their explanations of this fact reflected basic differences in their theories. Freud believed that the banality of the memories demonstrated their "screening" function, distorting presumed original traumatic experiences which are so threatening to the adult ego that they cannot be admitted into the consciousness. Adler, in contrast, felt that the apparent unimportance of remembered childhood events reflected the role of memory in the overall life-style—namely, that an individual selectively remembers only what is consistent with his present view of himself, the world, and other people (5, 15). Thus, ERs can be used as a tool for assessing the current subjective reality within which each person operates. Following Mosak (16), we have distinguished between a recollection and a report in choosing the memories reported in this paper. In order to qualify as a recollection, the memory had to be visualized by the informant, and it had to be an incident that could be described as a single occurrence.

---

[*] Reprinted by permission from the *Journal of Individual Psychology*, 1973, 24, 2, 157-166.

In this paper, we apply the Adlerian methodology to the ERs of Adler, Freud, and Jung. Our purpose is to illustrate this approach with three well-known subjects, and to see how well their recollections reflect their personalities and their theories. Our analysis will therefore concentrate on what seem to us to be the most salient features and trends in the memories. In an effort to achieve balanced presentation, we have omitted memories which repeated themes found in those included in our analysis.

Freud's recollections were found in Ernest Jones' biography of Freud (13) and Freud's *Interpretation of Dreams* (9). The sources of Adler's memories are the biography by Phyllis Bottome (7) and Adler's *Practice and Theory* (1). Jung's recollections are from his *Memories, Dreams, and Reflections* (15). We should point out that while Jung and Adler give their own ERs, most of Freud's are related by Jones and may therefore not accurately convey the ERs as Freud would have reported them.

In the following we are representing the recollections of our three subjects, each recollection set off in smaller type and followed by our interpretation in regular type.

Adler's Memories

ER 1. Age 2. I remember sitting on a bench bandaged up on account of rickets, with my healthy elder brother sitting opposite me. He could run, jump, and move about quite effortlessly, while for me, movement of any sort was a strain and an effort. Everyone went to great pains to help me and my mother and father did all that was in their power to do (7, pp. 30-31).

This recollection expresses Adler's attitude that he is deficient. He compares himself to others and finds himself wanting. The movement and actions of a person are important. There is a payoff for organ inferiority: Others become involved; others are showing social interest.

ER 2. Age 3. My parents left us two boys for a few days in the care of a governess. When they came back I met them, singing a street-song, the words of which are in my mind today, as is the melody to which I sang it. The song was about a woman who explained that she couldn't eat chicken because she was so hurt by the killing of her little hen. At this, the singer asks how she can have such a soft heart, when she thinks nothing of throwing a flowerpot at her husband's head (7, p. 32).

Actions speak louder than words; you can profess good intentions but you will be judged by your actions. We are reminded that Adler quoted Martin Luther's aphorism, "not to watch a person's mouth but his fists" (5, p. 18). There is also concern for good human relations. There is an interest in music.

ER 3. Age 4 or 5. I had pneumonia. The doctor, who had suddenly been called in, told my father that there was no point in going to the trouble of looking after me as there was no hope of my living. At once a frightful terror came over me and a few days later when I was well I decided definitely to become a doctor so that I should have a better defense against the danger of death and weapons to combat it superior to my doctor's (7, pp. 32-33).

Adler is incapacitated and this brings the concern of others. There is fear of dying. It terrifies him when people lose hope or are pessimistic. Adler resolves to compensate by learning appropriate skills. As he later stated: "The recollection of sickness or death is occasionally linked . . . with the attempt to become better equipped to meet them, possibly as a doctor or a nurse" (1, p. 354).

ER 4. Age 5 to 7. The father of one of my playmates, a lampmaker, asked me what I was going to be in life. "A doctor," I said. He answered, "Then you should be strung up at once to the nearest lamppost." This remark made no adverse impression upon my choice of a profession: I merely thought, "There's another who's had a bad time at the hands of a doctor. But *I* shall be a *real* doctor" (7, p. 33).

People's criticisms of him make no impact—in fact, they strengthen his resolve. A *real* doctor does not give his patients a hard time. He shows an interest in outcome, in the future.

ER 5. Age 5. Adler found that he could not quite believe in the Angel of the Passover visiting each Jewish home and being able to distinguish which was the leavened, and which the unleavened bread prepared for him. Adler therefore, one Passover night after the rest of the family had gone to bed, crept downstairs in his nightshirt and substituted leavened for unleavened bread, sitting up for the rest of the night in a cupboard with the door ajar, to discover through the crack the effect upon the Angel. "Nor was I altogether surprised," he told the writer, "when the Angel did not turn up" (7, pp. 33-34).

Adler is skeptical of the beliefs of others, especially in regard to religion, and he will experiment and observe, in an effort to find the truth. It is interesting to note that Adler joined the

Protestant Church in 1904, a small minority group in Austria at that time, which was considered most liberal (6, p. 331; 8, pp. 583-584).

ER 6. Age 5. I remember that the path to the school led over a cemetery. I was frightened every time and was exceedingly put out at beholding the other children pass the cemetery without paying the least attention to it, while every step I took was accompanied by a feeling of fear and horror. Apart from the extreme discomfort occasioned by this fear, I was also annoyed at the idea of being less courageous than the others. One day I made up my mind to put an end to this fear of death. Again, I decided on a treatment of hardening. I stayed at some distance behind the others, placed my school-bag on the ground near the wall of the cemetery and ran across it a dozen times, until I felt that I had mastered the fear. After that, I believe, I passed along this path without any fear (1, pp. 179-180).

Adler is afraid of death. He can overcome fear by taking action. Again—he compares himself to others and comes out on the short end. Fear inhibits one's movement.

It should be noted that the cemetery recollection turned out to be a fiction. Adler wrote: "Thirty years after that I met an old schoolmate and we exchanged childhood reminiscences. . . . He insisted there never had been a cemetery on the way to our school. Then I realized that the story . . . had been but a poetic dress for my longing to overcome the fear of death" (1, p. 180).

SUMMARY: Adler's memories express the attitude: I am inferior (ERs 1, 3). I don't measure up to others, and, although others show concern because of my inadequacies, I want to overcome in a useful way these deficiencies and fears, particularly my fear of death (ERs 1, 3, 6). I am indifferent to the criticisms of others and skeptical of their beliefs, religious and otherwise (ERs 4, 5). Furthermore, I am not deterred by their pessimistic attitudes—they only strengthen my resolve (ERs 3, 4). By focusing on my actions and movements and by experimenting on my own, I will be able to overcome these obstacles and thereby discover the truth (ERs 5, 6).

Actions speak louder than words, and I judge people by their actions and not their intentions (ERs 1, 2). If you don't have and show concern for others, it doesn't matter what else you feel (ER 2).

Freud's Memories

ER 1. Age 2. Freud would still wet his bed, and it was his father . . . who reproved him. He recollected saying on one of these occasions: "Don't worry, Papa. I will buy you a beautiful new red bed" (13, p. 7).

This recollection carries the message: Words speak louder than actions—don't look at my deeds, notice instead my good intentions. It also includes concern with a specific organic function and a father-son controversy, both of which became prominent in Freud's theory. The mention of color in a recollection is generally considered to indicate an aesthetic interest.

ER 2. Age 2½. Freud's Nannie disappeared . . . Having reason to suspect his brother's implication in the disappearance, Freud asked him what had become of her and received the . . . answer: *"Sie ist eingekastelt."* An adult would have understood this as meaning: "She has been locked up in prison," but Freud took it more literally as "she has been put in a chest" (13, pp. 9-10).

Freud is looking for answers, and upon receiving an answer, interprets it in an unusual way, which differs from the conventional meaning.

ER 3. Age 3. On the way to Leipzig the train passed through Breslau, where Freud saw gas jets for the first time; they made him think of "souls burning in hell" (13, p. 13.)

We might think of this as the forerunner of free association. There is an interest in symbolism and in religion.

ER 4. Age 6. I was expected to believe that we were all made of earth and must therefore return to earth. This did not suit me and I expressed doubts of the doctrine. My mother thereupon rubbed the palms of her hand together—just as she did in making dumplings, except that there was no dough between them—and showed me the blackish scales of *epidermis* produced by the friction as a proof that we were made of earth. My astonishment at this ocular demonstration know no bounds and I acquiesced in the belief which I was later to hear expressed in the words: "Thou owest Nature a death" (9, p. 238).

Freud is skeptical of statements made by others, but will acquiesce when shown "evidence." He is concerned with death, particularly with its inevitability. This recollection is consonant with his later theory of Thanatos.

ER 5. Age 7 or 8. Freud recalls having urinated (deliberately) in his parents' bedroom, and being reprimanded by his father, who said, "That boy will never amount to anything" (13, p. 16.)

Freud is deliberately provocative and evokes negative attention. Others will judge him negatively. In addition there are the organic function and the father-son controversy of ER 1.

SUMMARY: Summarizing Freud's memories, we construct the following picture: I am a skeptic and a doubter who is looking for answers (ERs 2, 4). I see and interpret things in a nonconventional, non-obvious way (ERs 2, 3). I am deliberately provocative (ER 5). I give meanings to things which others don't share. I will alter my ideas when they are contradicted by the "evidence" (ER 4).

People should judge me by my intentions rather than by my actions (ER 1). Through my natural urges I am likely to get into trouble with the authorities (ERs 1, 5). I am awed by the inevitability of death (ER 4).

This last point reminds us of Freud's death instinct hypothesis: "If we are to take it as a truth that knows no exception that everything living dies for *internal* reasons—becomes inorganic once again—then we shall be compelled to say that the aim of all life is death" (10, p. 70). The preceding point is a reminder of Freud's concepts of the Oedipus complex and of the repression of drives.

Jung's Memories

ER 1. Age about 4. Strangers, bustle, excitement. The maid comes running and exclaims, "The fishermen have found a corpse—came down the Falls—they want to put it in the wash house!" My father says, "Yes, yes." I want to see the dead body at once. My mother holds me back and sternly forbids me to go into the garden. When all the men had left, I quickly stole into the garden to the washhouse. But the door was locked. I went around the house; at the back there was an open drain running down the slope, and I saw blood and water trickling out. I found this extraordinarily interesting (15, p. 7).

Jung finds death interesting. Women try to prevent him from satisfying his curiosity. He doesn't give up. He is determined to have his way.

ER 2. Age 3 or 4. One hot summer day I was sitting alone, as usual, on the road in front of the house, playing in the sand. The road led past the house up a hill, then disappeared in the wood on the hilltop . . . Looking up the road, I saw a figure in a strangely broad hat and a long black garment coming down from the wood. It looked like a man wearing women's clothes. Slowly the figure drew nearer, and I could now see that it really was a man wearing a kind of black robe that reached to his feet. At the sight of him I was overcome with fear, which rapidly grew into deadly terror as the frightful recognition shot through my mind: "That is a Jesuit." The man coming down the road must be in disguise, I thought; that was why he wore women's clothes. Probably he had evil intentions. Terrified, I ran helter-skelter into the house, rushed up the stairs, and hid under a beam in the darkest corner of the attic. I don't know how long I remained there, but it must have been a fairly long time, because, when I ventured down again to the first floor and cautiously stuck my head out of the window, far and wide there was not a trace of the black figure to be seen (15, pp. 10-11).

Jung tries to reconcile discrepant observations. He corrects his conclusions on the basis of closer observations. His statement that he is alone "as usual" suggests that being alone is characteristic for him. When he is terrified, he runs and hides. There is confusion with respect to religion and perhaps masculinity and femininity. Either Catholicism, the confusion, or both frighten him.

ER 3. Age about 6. An aunt showed me the stuffed animals in the museum. We stayed a long time, because I wanted to look at everything very carefully. At four o'clock the bell rang, a sign that the museum was about to close. My aunt nagged at me, but I could not tear myself away from the showcases. In the meantime, the room had been locked, and we had to go by another way to the staircase, through the gallery of antiquities. Suddenly I was standing before these marvelous figures! Utterly overwhelmed, I opened my eyes wide, for I had never seen anything so beautiful. I could not look at them long enough. My aunt pulled me by the hand to the exit—I trailing always a step behind her—crying out, "Disgusting boy, shut your eyes; disgusting boy, shut your eyes!" Only then did I see that the figures were naked and wore fig leaves. I hadn't noticed it at all before. Such was my first encounter with the fine arts. My aunt was simmering with indignation, as though she had been dragged through a pornographic institute (15, p. 16).

Jung is observing again. A woman is interfering with his aesthetic searches. He focuses on the artistic beauty in things, where others may only see the erotic-sexual aspects. It will be recalled in this connection that Jung "de-sexualized" libido in his theory, saying that the so-called "primal" sexual libido should be considered a universal "life-urge" (7, pp. 49-50; 14, pp. 120-121). Some people make excessive fuss regarding sexual matters.

ER 4. Age 2 or 3. A lovely summer evening. An aunt said to me, "Now I am going to show you something." She took me out in front of the house, on the road to Dachsen. On the far horizon the chain of the Alps lay bathed in glowing sunset reds. The Alps could be seen very clearly that evening. "Now look over there"—I can hear her saying to me in Swiss dialect—"the mountains are all red." For the first time I consciously saw the Alps. Then I was told that the next day the village children would be going on a school outing to the Alps, near Zurich. I wanted so much to go, too. To my sorrow, I was informed that children as small as I could not go along; there was nothing to be done about it. From then on the Alps and Zurich became an unattainable land of dreams, near to the glowing, snow-covered mountains (15, p. 7).

Someone is opening the world to Jung. Becoming conscious of things is important. The mention of color suggests an artistic orientation again. He is little and is left out because of it; he does not get to the Promised Land.

ER 5. Age about 4. I am restive, feverish, unable to sleep. My father carries me in his arms, paces up and down, singing his old student songs. I particularly remember one I was especially fond of and which always used to soothe me. To this day I can remember my father's voice, singing over me in the stillness of the night (15, p. 8).

Others soothe him when he's uncomfortable. He is sensitive to voice quality and music. He is interested in contrast and opposites.

ER 6. Age about 4. Fourteen people were drowned and were carried down by the yellow flood water to the Rhine. When the water retreated, some of the corpses got stuck in the sand. When I was told about it, there was no holding me. I actually found the body of a middle-aged man, in a black frock coat; apparently he had just come from church. He lay half covered by sand, his arm over his eyes (15, p. 15).

While death horrifies others, it interests Jung. He is not afraid to look where others are afraid. Once again, color suggests an artistic sense. Can he be saying that church-goers can come to a horrible end?

SUMMARY: All of Jung's memories may be summarized as follows: I am a sensitive, curious observer, and I experience the world through all my senses (ERs 3, 4, 5). Becoming aware and conscious of things is very important to me (ER 4). I am interested in contrasts (ERs 2, 5), try to reconcile discrepant observations, and I will modify my conclusions if they prove wrong after closer observation (ER 2).

Life is wonderful when I can be alone with nature (ER 2), but people can come between me and nature (ER 3). I am infatuated by the artistic beauty in what I see (ERs 3, 4, 6), though others are attracted only to the erotic and sexual aspects (ER 3). Others can interfere with my aesthetic search and they may also try to prevent me from satisfying my curiosity (ERs 1, 3). They can also open my eyes to new horizons, however (ER 4).

I am interested in death, although it may horrify others (ERs 1, 6).

I am small and want others to do things for me and care for me (ER 5). Smallness can also be a liability in human relations, but it is not a handicap in relation to nature (ER 4).

Comparative Analysis

When we compare the portraits of these three men drawn from their memories, one similarity is that each of them emerges as a thinker and inquirer. Adler, Freud, and Jung draw conclusions from "evidence," and all three test and modify their beliefs in the light of facts. However, their style of inquiry distinguishes them from each other. Jung observes through his senses, Freud symbolizes and makes unique interpretations, and Adler observes and compares the actions and movements of people. Also, Freud and Adler display a generally skeptical stance toward traditional explanations.

Although all three show an interest in death, they differ in their approach to it. Jung is intrigued by death, Freud is awed by death's inevitability, while Adler resolves to work to overcome death. Also, Jung's interest in nature, art, and in the contrasting juxtaposition of things differs from Adler's preoccupation with people's actions and interactions, with deficiencies, and with overcoming obstacles; while Freud's main interest is in explaining things in nonconventional ways.

You will note that each man secured the involvement of other people, but in a different manner: Freud by being provocative, Adler by displaying and overcoming inadequacy, and Jung by being small and helpless, although there is the danger that being small and helpless could also result in his being left out. Though Freud anticipates that his provocative behavior may result in negative attention from others, he shrugs it off—

it does not bother him. Adler also anticipates criticism from others, but he is ready to respond to it with increased effort and resolve. Jung similarly anticipates trouble from others, expecting them to interfere with his attempts to get closer to the experience of nature and to satisfy his curiosity.

Reflections of each man's theoretical position appear in their recollections. Adler's ERs allude to organ inferiority (ER 1), to movement (ERs 1, 2), to inferiority feeling (ERs 3, 6), to compensation (ERs 3, 6), and to social feeling (ER 2). Freud's ERs allude to free association (ER 3), the oedipal situation (ERs 1, 5), symbolic interpretation (ER 3), nonconventional interpretations (ER 2), and the death instinct (ER 4). Jung's desexualization of libido, the reconciliation of opposites in his typology, his interest in artistic producton may all be discerned in his ERs.

Finally, the dominant life goals of each man emerge from their recollections. Adler's goal is to overcome inadequacy through effort and resolve. Freud strives to comprehend through analysis and interpretation, while Jung moves toward communion with nature through sensual awareness. Note also that feelings play a different role in the pursuit of each man's goal. For Adler, feelings facilitate and energize his movement; for Jung, feelings are another dimension of sensual experience; while Freud de-emphasizes the role of feelings, stressing intellectual understanding instead.

Summary

Early childhood memories recalled by Adler, Freud, and Jung are presented, interpreted, and summarized within an Adlerian framework. Similarities between the early recollection themes and each man's theoretical position are indicated. Finally, the three sets of memories are compared and the commonalities and distinguishing characteristics that emerge are noted.

References

1. Adler, A. *The practice and theory of individual psychology* (1920). Totowa, N. J.: Littlefield, Adams, 1969.

2. Adler, A. *Problems of neurosis* (1929). New York: Harper & Row, 1964.
3. Adler, A. *What life should mean to you* (1931). New York: Capricorn Books, 1958.
4. Adler, A. *Social interest: a challenge to mankind* (1933). New York: Capricorn Books, 1964.
5. Adler, A. *The individual psychology of Alfred Adler*. Ed. by H. L. and Rowena R. Ansbacher. New York: Basic Books, 1956.
6. Adler, R. *Superiority and social interest: A collection of later writings.* Ed. by H. L. and Rowena R. Ansbacher. 3rd ed. New York: Viking Compass Book, 1973.
7. Bottome, Phyllis. *Alfred Adler: A portrait from life.* New York: Vanguard Press, 1957.
8. Ellenberger, H. F. *The discovery of the unconscious.* New York: Basic Books, 1970.
9. Freud, S. *Interpretation of dreams* (1900). New York: Avon Books, 1967.
10. Freud, S. *Beyond the pleasure principle* (1928). New York: Bantam Books, 1967.
11. Freud, S. Screen memories (1899). In *Collected papers.* Vol. 5. London: Hogarth, 1950. Pp. 47-69.
12. Harper, R. *Psychoanalysis and psychotherapy: 36 systems.* Englewood Cliffs, N.J.: Prentice-Hall, 1959.
13. Jones, E. *The life and work of Sigmund Freud.* Vol. 1. New York: Basic Books, 1953.
14. Jung, C. G. *Modern man in search of a soul.* New York: Harcourt, Brace and World, 1963.
15. Jung, C. G. *Memories, dreams, and reflections.* New York: Vintage Books, 1963.
16. Mosak, H. H. Early recollections as a projective technique. *J. Proj. Tech.*, 1958, 22, 302-311. Also in G. Lindzey and C. S. Hall (Eds.), *Theories of personality.* New York: Wiley, 1965. Pp: 105-113.

CHAPTER 30

GOETHE'S EARLIEST RECOLLECTION*

PAUL ROM

G OETHE BEGINS HIS autobiography (4) with an early recollection. We shall in the present paper interpret this recollection in the Adlerian sense (1, pp. 351-357), and in the manner in which Adler would have done it, and then make a brief comparison with an interpretation by Freud.

The third paragraph of the autobiography begins with the words:

When we attempt to recall what befell us in the earliest period of youth, we are apt to confound what we have been told by others with what we remember from our own experience.

This is very true but irrelevant when we intend to work out the narrator's style of life, which is our purpose here. Goethe continues:

Without, therefore, attempting an exact investigation of the sources of my recollections—in any case a profitless task—I know as a fact that we lived in an old house, which really consisted of two adjoining houses that had been thrown into one.

The narrator does not yet come to the real point, but the fact which he chooses to mention lets us understand that his early existence was favored by material well-being. We shall look out for persons and movements to be mentioned.

A turret-like staircase led to rooms on different levels, and the unevenness of the storeys was remedied by steps.

Here a movement is implied: an easy going from one story to another.

For us children, . . .

The previously used pronoun "we" referred to all the family who lived in that large house; now the account narrows down

---

* Reprinted by permission from the *Journal of Individual Psychology*, 1965, *21*, 189-193.

to the children. So he was not an only child. He goes on to say:

. . . a younger sister and myself, the favorite resort was the spacious entrance-hall where, by the side of the front door, was a large wooden lattice through which we had direct communication with the street and the open air.

This description of things visible indicates that the author is a visual type and is looking outwards. There seem to be no harsh conflicts with members of the family, or they would have been expressed or hinted at in some way or another.

Of . . . our neighbours . . ., three brothers von Ochsenstein, the surviving sons of the deceased Schultheiss [chief magistrate of the town], lived opposite us; they became fond of me, and frequently showed their interest by playing with me or poking fun at me.

All this is not yet a particular early recollection. Goethe notes, however, the attention which he received from grown-up neighbors. This must have been important for him. Beginning with "our" neighbors he ends this sentence with "me," this word occurring three times. Had he lost some attention of his mother when after having been the only son a sister was born? He goes on:

My relatives . . .

So there must have been grandparents or uncles and aunts as a fortunate extension of the narrower circle of the family.

. . . were fond of narrating all sorts of pranks which these solitary and otherwise sober-minded men put into my head. I will give an instance.

The responsibility for initiating pranks is put upon the others; however, it seems that now we come to a point which may reveal more of the author than that he is a well-to-do visual type who seems to have developed his social relationships without particular conflicts and who adopts the quasi-scientific attitude of an observer and reporter, aware, however, of his own importance.

The Particular Incident

A crockery fair had just been held, and not only had the immediate needs of the kitchen been supplied, but miniature articles of the same ware had been purchased as playthings for us children.

This confirms what we already guessed about a certain harmony in the family atmosphere.

One fine afternoon, when everything was quiet in the house . . .

This quietness may have been perceived as a contrast to the usually prevailing conversations and noises. Its being mentioned here suggests that the writer also has acute hearing. He seems to be alone in that vast house. Goethe goes on:

. . . I was amusing myself with my pots and dishes . . .

The pots and dishes were first mentioned as "playthings for us children." We should think they were more particularly toys of the girl training for her later function as a housewife. Now we read, "my pots and dishes"!

. . . and not knowing what to do next, I hurled one of my toys into the street.

Again, "my toy." And why does he hurl *his* piece of crockery in the street and thus break the object with which he had just been amusing himself? This might make sense if he felt neglected, the mother having perhaps gone out with the younger sister. So in breaking a toy which was rather *hers* he would get even with her. We read on:

The von Ochsensteins, who saw my delight at the fine crash it made, and how I clapped my hands for joy, cried out, "Another!"

These men saw his delight at the fine crash; again, the poet's acute awareness of both visual and acoustic events is expressed.

Now the boy had secured both the missed attention and a desired applause. Would he follow the suggestion and break more of "his" toys? As they may rather be those of his sister he might not mind; indeed, Goethe goes on:

Without delay I flung out a pot, and as they went on calling for more, by degrees the whole collection, platters, pipkins, mugs and all, were dashed upon the pavement. My neighbours [who had before been "our" neighbours!] continued to express their approbation, and I was highly delighted to give them pleasure.

To gain applause for giving pleasure appears here as the narrator's main purpose. We read on:

But my stock was exhausted, and still they shouted, "More!" I ran, therefore, straight to the kitchen, and brought thence the earthenware plates which as they smashed naturally afforded a still more lively spectacle; . . .

Suppose that either the von Ochsensteins or the Goethes were very poor people; then what is related here as a funny event would be tragic.

. . . and so I kept running backwards and forwards, fetching all the plates I could reach from where they stood in rows on the dresser.

We note here the intensity of the movements, to and fro, which suggests that the narrator enjoyed movement as a means to see, hear, and get applause for extraordinary actions. We remember that Goethe became a great traveler in search of visual beauty, in Dresden, Strasbourg, and Italy, as he reports later in great detail.

But as that did not satisfy my "audience" [a word from the vocabulary of the dramatic poet and theater director], I devoted all the ware that I could lay hands on to similar destruction.

These words remind us of the director's lines spoken to the poet in the "Prelude in the Theater" to *Faust, Part I.*

> . . . take occasion by the hair,
> For, once involved in the affair,
> You'll carry on because you must.
> The German stage lets each try what he may;
> Then spare me nothing, on our special day (3, p. 27).

Goethe concludes the report of what he has selected to tell us as his first recollection by saying:

Not till later did any one appear to hinder and restrain. The mischief was done, and to compensate for much broken crockery, there was at any rate an amusing story, in which the mischievous authors took special delight to the end of their days.

Once more the narrator thus expresses his satisfaction of having greatly delighted his public. This is the guiding fiction behind the behavior pattern in which seeing, hearing, and moving about are outstanding features.

The writer believes that his interpretation of Goethe's first recollection would have been the same even if he had not since his teens known and loved Goethe. It can be shown that the life-style revealed here prevails in all the writings, autobiographical, epic, dramatic, and lyric, of the sage of Weimar.

Freud's Interpretation

As early as 1917 Freud (2) wrote a paper about this childhood recollection of Goethe. Freud held that for a depth-psychologically uninformed reader, "A mischievous trick with bad results for the household economy, carried out under the spur of encouragement by strangers, is certainly not a fitting vignette for all that Goethe has to tell us of his full life" (2, p. 359).

For Freud this is a screen memory. The Adlerian approach which takes the incident as a significant sample of behavior uses all that is given in the recollection and tries to empathize with it as fully as possible. Freud does not do this. He is quite detached, uses only those parts of the recollection which are important for his hypothesis, generalizes from what he believes to have noted in some other people, and adds to this some further outside information. In this way he arrives at the conclusion that Goethe in this recollection actually expresses the wish to get rid of a baby brother by a magic action, probably the brother born when Goethe was a little over three years old. As is well known, Goethe had a sister, Cornelia, born fifteen months after him. But four additional siblings were born after her, none of whom survived. Freud explains:

This "Out with it!" seems to be an essential part of the magic action and to arise directly from its hidden meaning. The new baby must be *thrown out* through the window, perhaps because he came through the window. The whole action would thus be equivalent to the familiar things said by children who are told that the stork has brought a little brother or sister. "Then the stork is to take it away again" is the verdict (2, p. 363).

To fit this notion of sibling rivalry, Freud concentrates on merely the act of throwing crockery out of the window and disregards the manner, the spirit, and the setting in which this was done—all aspects which we have pointed out in the preceding. Many people are jealous of their siblings. Having found that a number of his patients who were jealous in this way had indeed thrown things out of the window, and having interpreted this as a symbolic act of getting rid of the rival, Freud put Goethe's recollection in the same bed of Procrustes while there was actually no evidence of an existing rivalry.

Adler in his individualizing approach always insisted that when two people do the same it does not necessarily mean the same. He treated a recollection as a sample of the individual's behavior and tried to see it as completely as possible with all its concrete interrelations and interactions, as we have attempted to do here. Thus our interpretation is individualizing, or idiographic, whereas Freud's is, within the framework of psychoanalytic theory, generalizing, or nomothetic.

Summary

The earliest recollection given by Goethe in his autobiography reveals an interest in delighting an audience, and emphasis on visual, auditory, and kinetic activity, all of which seems quite consistent with the life of the great poet, statesman, and dramatist. Comparing this Adlerian interpretation with that by Freud of the same recollection brings out the difference between the two approaches.

References

1. Adler, A. *The individual psychology of Alfred Adler.* New York: Basic Books, 1956.
2. Freud, S. A childhood recollection from *Dichtung and Wahrheit* (1917). In *Collected Papers.* Vol. 4. London: Hogarth, 1925. Pp. 357-367.
3. Goethe, J. W. v. *Faust.* Part 1. Translation by P. Wayne. London: Penguin Books, 1949.
4. Goethe, J. W. v. *Poetry and truth from my own life.* Revised translation by Minna S. Smith. London: Bell & Son, 1913.

CHAPTER 31

EARLY RECOLLECTION IN A CASE OF JUVENILE DELINQUENCY[*]

PAUL THATCHER

T HIRTEEN-YEAR-OLD JIMMY was referred to the Juvenile Court because of auto theft. He had run away from home several times, after quarrels with his parents, and on the last occasion he had stolen a car for transportation. When, after several days, he was not apprehended, he drove the car home and frankly told his parents what he had done.

Jimmy was the third of four children—two girls and two boys in that order. He was about four years older than his baby brother, who was "the sweetest child." He talked readily, especially about his grievances, but seemed somewhat reserved and distrustful of court personnel in discussing motives for his behavior. He claimed that his mother and father "put up a good front," but "weren't nearly as good as they pretended." He said that they quarreled a good deal. The family lived on a farm. Jimmy felt very strongly that he was the object of unfair discrimination. Too much work was expected of him, and the other children were given more privileges and advantages than he. His parents didn't really love him. He didn't know why he had offended, but was sorry for the act.

The entire family was talented musically. Jimmy was a prize-winning musician.

Against the recommendations of the police, who said the family was "no good," the boy was placed on probation. However, three weeks later he was again arrested several hundred miles from home in possession of a stolen car, and was returned

[*] Reprinted by permission from the *Individual Psychology Bulletin*, 1944-45, **4**, 59-60.

to court, where he was placed in detention pending notice to his parents.

After lunch the judge went to the detention room for an informal interview. The door, fitted with a spring lock, was blown shut by the wind when the judge carelessly left it unblocked. This accident forced the judge to spend the afternoon "in detention" with Jimmy.

The common plight of imprisonment seemed to shorten the distance between them, and Jimmy talked more freely, even mentioning his shortcomings in the family group effort. Very shortly the judge was in the role of a comrade in distress.

Jimmy related his earliest recollection. When he was about five years old he ran away to play with a neighbor boy. The boys had a fight and Jimmy was knocked down and his nose bloodied. He went home crying. His mother put the baby brother down in the crib, took Jimmy in her arms and washed his face—"and did she give that kid heck!"

It occurred to the judge that this was typical of his pattern—Jimmy's efforts were devoted to compelling his parents to give him what he deemed to be the solicitous attention without which he felt defenseless and which he believed was stolen from him by his brother. Getting in trouble was his only sure weapon when his position of safety as the "son and heir" in the bosom of his father's family was threatened by preference for little brother's angelic behavior.

An attempt was made to explain to him this possibility. He admitted that he would really feel insulted if anyone should openly assert that he was capable of no more work and responsibility than his nine-year-old brother, and it was suggested that his parents in giving him more tasks merely recognized his superior abilities and in no way showed lack of parental affection. He was told that, after all, his safety and welfare depended on himself and not on his parents' protective regard, and that at age thirteen he should want to begin to stand on his own feet instead of running to mamma whenever he had a bloody nose.

Jimmy also said that when running away he often thought that his parents would be sorry when they realized their favoritism had driven him away. As he was apparently an aural type, an attempt was made to reach him by saying that this behavior reminded one of the old folk tune with the words, "Nobody loves me, everybody hates me; I'm going in the garden and eat worms!" The song was sung to him so he could fix the "catchy" tune in his mind. He showed a sheepish interest in the song.

He was told that one could be excused for such behavior so long as he was a little child and did not understand why he acted so, but that as one approached manhood and understood the matter, the full responsibility could not be avoided.

In conclusion the judge told Jimmy that now since he had in mind both his responsibilities and the reason for his past difficulties there was no reason why he should not live a useful life, and that he was therefore going to be returned to his home.

If things grew too "tough" there, he could come and tell his troubles to the probation officer, who would consider with him the best and most useful way to solve the difficulty. It was suggested to him that the next time he got the feeling that he must run away from his unfair home, the little song "Nobody loves me . . ." would suddenly pop into his mind and make him laugh. Then he would no longer have the desperate feeling that he had to run away, and would be able to make allowances and bear his difficulties because his sense of humor would save him.

Three years later, although Jimmy was discouraged about his lack of scholastic achievement and he had in that period received a traffic ticket for driving his father's car without a driver's license, he had not run away and he had not stolen. He had been subjected to very little supervision during a short period of probation. Notwithstanding his discouragement about school, he was plugging away at it.

CHAPTER 32

TOM: A WOUNDED VIETNAM VETERAN*

HARRY A. OLSON

Tom is a twenty-nine-year-old married veteran. Although ambulatory, he has 100 percent service connected disability due to wounds received in Vietnam when he was twenty-one. He was accidently shot by another GI who supposedly became confused while fighting for a dugout. It is unclear whether Tom and the other GI were fighting each other for the same shelter. Tom sustained severe injury in both legs from two shots of an M-16 rifle. Now Tom receives a sizeable Veterans Administration check plus Social Security disability benefits monthly. In addition, he has vocational rehabilitation services for himself, educational benefits for his wife, a specially adapted automobile, a clothing allowance, and other insurance and medical benefits. Tom's wife is a nurse. The couple have no children.

Since 1971, Tom has been enrolled in several vocational rehabilitation training programs, including a college preparatory course, a business administrative program, and a motel management program. In every case, Tom had many interruptions for medical and personal reasons, and he completed only the college prep course. He attempted 138 credits but completed 67. His pattern is one of initial enthusiasm followed by panic and failure. He currently has little apparent motivation to continue training and prefers to socialize with some close friends and old army buddies. He also plays in a musical group which he organized.

This case raises some interesting questions. Why does Tom not follow through on training? It may be argued that if he

* Grateful acknowledgement is given to James P. Jarvis, Jr. who supplied the raw data and history material for this case.

were gainfully employed he might lose his benefits. Even so, that argument is insufficient. Some persons respond to similar adversity with renewed vigor while others succumb and continue to remain dependent on disability income even when they may have the potential to do otherwise. Secondly, could there be any significance to the fact that he was wounded by one of his own buddies? This is not to suggest foul play or conscious planning, but could it be that his accident was a bit *more* than accidental?

Delving into Tom's life-style, particularly his early recollections, reveals valuable insight into Tom's current situation and offers a prognosis for his future.

Tom is the third-born child in a family of nine children. He is also the oldest male. He found his place in the family by demanding and getting his way, rebelling, being athletic, and wanting to be the center of the action. He also had a hot temper and was quite critical. He strongly identified with his father who was very authoritarian, masculine, and "a man's man." Yet his father liked children, had a good sense of humor, and was a good father in the client's estimation. While Tom considered himself the least considerate of the family, he managed to have a number of friends.

Tom's mother was strict but overprotective and cautious, with a strong sense of right and wrong. Tom was manipulative and became quite adept at playing mother and father against each other to get his way.

Although the family placed the highest priority on getting a good education, Tom feels that he lived up to family standards the least. He perceived himself as less intelligent, got the worst grades in school, and was the least industrious. He was not helpful at home, but rather preferred to make mischief and do daring things, causing him to be involved in a number of accidents. As a result, he was punished quite a bit and finally thrown out of the house at eighteen.

At school, Tom was a continual discipline problem. He did not get along with teachers and fought with a number of his fellow students.

Today, Tom is a verbal and friendly man. He likes people and is concerned for their welfare. It would also appear that

Tom likes to take chances and risks, but this is apparently inconsistent with shying away from preparing for a career. Underneath, Tom views himself as inferior, underestimates his abilities and talents, and has a self-fulfilling prophecy of failure.

A close examination of Tom's early recollections reveals the solution to some inconsistencies. They are reproduced here as they have been recorded by Mr. Jarvis. This author's interpretations follow each recollection.

ER 1. Age 4 or 5. There was an open field between two houses which had a bridge and a little stream. He left his house and went across the field to his aunt's house. He wanted to see what was beyond the open field. His family was surprised he had gone so far. The aunt took him home.

Vivid: The bridge, which was made of railroad ties. The field appeared very large.

Feelings: Apprehensive about leaving the security of his own yard.

Change: He would not change the recollection in any way.

Interpretation: "I am curious about what's ahead, and I (like to) do adventurous things that surprise others, even though I have inward apprehension about moving beyond a safe situation. "When I do go out on my own others finish the job" (his aunt brought him home). "I take an observing stance. I notice what goes on and exists around me." (He noted that the bridge was made of railroad ties.)

ER 2. Age 4 or 5. He was playing in the front of his house on a tricycle with a wiggly front wheel. His older sister came out dressed for a confirmation service for his oldest sister, and first Holy Communion for Paulette. They were both dressed in white with veils. They got in the car and left to go to church. After being told he could not go, he waited a few minutes and decided to go to church on his tricycle. He got lost and was crying. A lady in a florist shop asked him what was wrong and called the police. He had the police take him to his grandparents' house.

Vivid: Sitting in front of the florist shop crying.

Feelings: Left out because he couldn't go along, alone, frightened.

Change: He would not change the recollection in any way.

Interpretation: "I feel alone and left out when I'm not part of the action. The world often goes by, leaving me behind. People can't tell me, 'no'; if they do, I'll do it my own way. Yet when I try to do it myself, I blow it and must get assisted by others. I'll create some action of my own, even if it happens through mistakes."

ER 3. Age 6. It was the first day of school, and he didn't want to go. School seemed like a long way from home, and he was bewildered by all the strange children.

Vivid: Mother left and the teacher was holding his hand. He kicked the teacher.

Feelings: Afraid of being left there alone.

Change: He would not have kicked the teacher.

Interpretation: "I become frightened and confused in strange, new situations when my familiar support is gone. When I feel this way I may act out my fear in anger (against the wrong person), and make mischief."

ER 4. First grade: He was examined by the school doctor who was a female. He refused to take his clothes off, so his mother came into the examination stall with him and convinced him to cooperate.

Vivid: Mother trying to talk him into being examined. Hearing the other dressing room stall doors being opened and closed.

Feelings: Felt dumb, embarrassed.

Interpretation: "My image is extremely important, and it embarrasses me if I get 'caught with my pants down.' I get others into my service through obstinance. I'm very aware of my surroundings."

ER 5. Age 7 or 8. He kicked a piece of a broken glass bottle against a building. It bounced back and hit him on the leg, requiring him to go to the doctor and have stitches.

Vivid: Lying on the doctor's table, seeing a "fishing hook" type needle he was to be sewn up with.

Feelings: Scared, angry with himself, frightened of the doctor.

Interpretations: "My actions backfire and I get hurt. When I do, I berate myself. I'm afraid of situations in which I'm out of control or at the mercy of others."

ER 6. Age 6 or 7. Mother had a pet owl which she kept in an oval cage in the coal storage bin. He liked watching him. The owl escaped several times. Mother would take the cage and he would fly back in.

Vivid: Owl flying back into the cage.

Feelings: Pleasing to watch the owl.

Interpretation: "I like animals. I also take pleasure in an observer role, watching the action." (At a symbolic level it may be suggested that he prefers a position of safety and security—the owl escapes but comes back to the cage.)

We see via Tom's recollections, that he is less truly adventurous than he gives himself credit for. He is willing to take risks only in situations that he figures in advance that he can handle. His lack of self-confidence comes through in recollections where he begins on his own but his actions backfire and he ends up being taken care of or rescued. In this vein, it is interesting that he indicated that he would not change the second recollection (getting lost) in any way, even though to the reader the content seems negative. This may reflect Tom's system of payoffs; he muffs it and gets rescued.

The people who are close to Tom seem to reject or leave him behind, whereas it is often those less close or responsible that help him in the end. This is true of mother as she is portrayed. Mother becomes involved with him only through his obstinance. We could guess that much of Tom's misbehavior was designed to force parental and family involvement as well as a reaction to feeling left out. Apparently, Tom's misbehavior got to such a pitch that he was eventually thrown out of the house, a situation that he in part engineered via his behavior.

ER 4 (physical exam at school) seems to be a correlate of his vocational rehabilitation training experience. He is afraid to expose himself—in training, to possible failure or criticism—and he refuses to follow through. We could imagine how much agency time was spent trying to counsel and convince Tom to finish.

Tom's Vietnam accident has two antecedents in his ERs. Number 5 (broken glass) and number 2 (getting lost) both indicate how his assertive action backfires to his own detriment. Given his history of accidents and ER 5, we could guess that

Tom is accident prone. Getting shot in Vietnam was a high probability in hostile action. For Tom, the probability was even higher, and we find he got shot by another GI. Through it all, the overriding pattern in his ERs is acted out in life: Tom engages in daring action only to muff it, and he ends up being taken care of by others, which for Tom, based on his ERs, may be his ultimate payoff. It is no accident that Tom married a nurse!

CHAPTER 33

ROBERT: A CASE OF
SCHIZO-AFFECTIVE PSYCHOSIS

HARRY A. OLSON

ROBERT WAS A twenty-two-year-old single young man who was
in therapy with two therapists for about three years since he
was eighteen. He was diagnosed as schizo-affective psychosis
and came to his first therapist with visual hallucinations, a hand-
washing compulsion and threats of suicide and occasional minor
physical attacks on his younger brother. He was treated by his
first therapist for two years with psychotherapy and antipsychotic
medication. Rapport was good but began to deteriorate. His
parents were paying for his therapy but made it contingent upon
his changing his behavior. This enabled Robert to passively-
aggressively attack his parents by not responding in therapy.
At that point, when Robert was twenty, his parents and he
decided to change therapists.

When Robert came to the second therapist, he was no longer
actively psychotic. Hallucinations were gone and he was not
carried on medication. He was still occasionally threatening
suicide and hitting his younger brother, and was in the height
of his hand-washing compulsion. He also had "special food
requirements" (his option for natural foods—no medical basis)
which served to interfere with living outside his parents' home.
He had a job as a warehouse stockman, was thoroughly bored,
was in the process of quitting, and was into a pattern and mood
of apathy and failure. He was also given to excessive rumina-
tion and marijuana use. He saw himself as interested in "essential"
things rather than outward social trappings and obsessed about
lofty ideals.

Robert was in therapy for eight months at that point, during

313

which he went to work in his father's business, which caused additional problems. He moved out of his parents' home and went to college and passed one semester. He terminated therapy at the end of the school year because he felt he was doing well. One year later, his parents had initiated therapy for him again in a state of crisis. That past fall he had dropped out of college, he was taking drugs, and his relationship with the people with whom he shared an apartment had deteriorated. One night he appeared on his parents' doorstep. They took him in for the night, a night which was to last almost a year.

While living at at home, he did no chores, demanded service, and began to threaten suicide. His parents, particularly his mother, were at their wits end but took little assertive action. Robert was talking continually about how bad his home was and that he wanted to move to a commune. He took no action on this move, however. All the while his anger at his parents increased. He was in therapy for four months then, with little success, when his parents removed him from therapy and took him to a physician who treated schizophrenia with vitamin therapy.

By way of history, Robert was a sickly child who was often crying and uncomfortable. He had a closed stomach at birth and could not keep food down. Operations were performed at age two and three. His mother pitied and spoiled him, refusing to push him into taking on responsibility. Robert's only sibling was a brother four years his junior. He apparently took the birth of his brother quite hard and their relationship was marked by fights. Whereas Robert was afraid of other children, he could be at ease with his brother because he could dominate him.

In school and socially, Robert did not adapt well. He was teased for being somewhat of a sissy. When asked to describe himself as a child, Robert first identified his fearfulness. He was afraid to socialize, although he wanted to make friends, and was very afraid to try the unknown. He had imaginary friends that would accompany him to school. He also had an imaginary dog. Robert was wrapped up in his fantasies and stayed to himself. His parents responded to this by being sheltering and overprotective. As a result, Robert stated he could not trust his own decisions but constantly asked his mother about what he should do. He and his mother were very close and he worked hard to keep her involved with him through his problems. He stated, "I would cry to keep her busy with me. She wanted to appease me." Father, on the other hand, was more distant and Robert felt he did not understand. Overt and covert power struggles and rebellion characterized Robert's relations with his parents. He developed much anger toward his parents over the years and unconsciously wanted to get back at his parents. In therapy it was very difficult for him to acknowledge this anger.

With an IQ of 119, Robert found schoolwork easy. He received high grades with little effort, although as he went into high school his attitude deteriorated. He started to play hockey, was apparently very good at it, and soon made it the central goal of his life. All other activities, school and social, were subordinated to hockey. The interest in hockey, like so much else in his life, was taken to excess and admittedly served as an excuse to avoid social and school activities in which he felt inferior.

An affable young man, Robert got along with people on the surface. He confided in no one, and those he called his "friends" would be more properly classed as acquaintances. In school he never dated, and he had his first date at age twenty. He went with a girl for two and a half months and only rarely dated after that time. The relationship broke up over "differing values." They did not get along and he never learned to know her well. Up to that time Robert never had sexual intercourse.

Robert went to a large university and lived in the dorm. In college he "fell apart" and dropped out before the end of his second semester. He became preoccupied with the badness of people, would "forget" his homework assignments, and engage in long, boring philosophical discourses. During or prior to this time he also developed his hallucinations. He would be driving along and imagine he had run over someone. He would visualize the body lying in the street and would back up or stop the car to see if indeed he had run over someone. He became increasingly afraid to socialize and more and more moved his social experiences into the drug culture. He then took his job as a warehouse stockman. He was in therapy with his first therapist and his hallucinations were controlled through medication.

During the following September, when he was twenty, he began therapy with his second therapist. In the course of taking a life-style analysis the following recollections were given. Robert's therapist's interpretations follow each ER.

ER 1. Age 2. I was playing with all my toys strewn all over the place. I was lying on my side on the floor in a hall. Mom came in and put them all away, putting away particularly the plastic donuts. I was lying there not doing anything.

Vivid: Watching the rings being put back on the loop.

Feelings: Happy to sit there and watch it happen and not do anything.

Interpretation: "I want to be taken care of, to have others in my service. Others should take care of me, clean up after me, I am special." (Notice the character of the relationship with Mother. It is one of servitude. No interaction is referred to—he plays and lies on the floor while she cleans. In this ER Mother and he do not relate but coexist. This is a paradigm of his relations with others, and especially his parents at the time this ER was elicited. Even then his mother took care of him and he did no chores around the house, even for himself. He has a passive, visual orientation to life. He will notice things but not act on them.)

ER 2. Age 2. My room, I remember seeing a tremendous blue rocking chair with polka dots, also a red toy box. These seemed huge. The rest of the room seemed out of focus, hazy and black-like. No light from outside, space that seemed consumed, as if there were no doors or windows. Remember being there, not wanting to know what was on the outside, not caring.

Vivid: I would think the brightness of the two objects, but actually the nothingness, not caring about the outside. Hazy darkness outside.

Feelings: Warm, feeling secure. There was a hazy tone. Everything frosted over. Looking at the window and not seeing anything out of it.

Interpretation: "I am small." "I want to stay by myself,

with that which is familiar and comfortable." By inference: "I am inadequate and I don't wish to face the tasks the world provides. Life outside is dark, hazy, and vague and I can't get a grasp on it. I'm afraid, but I cover my fear by not caring and saying life outside isn't important." (Note the total absence of interpersonal contact. In fact no other person is even mentioned. This is typical of psychotic and schizoid people, although not exclusive to them. Interpersonal relations are highly threatening and avoided. The self-boundedness of these people is reinforced through barren memories. The implication is that isolation is comfortable, contact is uncomfortable or threatening. Persons into drugs often have similar ERs. The drugs and their effects serve as a substitute for the gratifications available in the social realm.)

ER 3. Age 10, recurring dream. Seems like a dream, sometimes I think it really happened. Being in a car, looking over to the right. There was an edge of a cliff, the other side was in the distance. This side was white granite, rough, jagged, with black lines in it. All over the other side was creeping green foliage, soft, inviting looking, something you'd want to go into. I wanted to get over to it, but the footbridge was broken. I didn't know the depth of the chasm, but couldn't get across. Shacks were on side I was on, built into the cliffs; the other side had only trees and foliage. I wanted to cross. I was driven away and never found out what was on the other side, but wondered, but pulled away passively, was driven away in the car. Wanted it but gorge so forbidding, not safe to get near it.

Interpretation: "My life is barren, lifeless, and rough. Real life on the other side is inviting and alive, but I'm scared to go over to it. I want to go, but there is no way; I'm irrevocably separated. I'm passive and forces beyond my control pull me away, but I'm curious about life in the real world. I am a victim, don't expect me to make it."

(Again a barren, lifeless image. On the other side it was inviting, but there were no people. The only implication of people is the driver of the car, with whom he has no relationship but only coexists, whose role is to further separate him from the object of his pseudodesire. We find a neurotic, *yes—but* pattern of good intentions followed by impossibility of follow-through due to external circumstances. In his everyday life, Robert was full of plans and desires but had a myriad of excuses based on other persons, circumstances, and lack of will-power which successfully blocked his accomplishment. No affect was reported in this dream, but one could readily imagine that he would feel angry with others and life for being thwarted. His color descriptions suggest artistic tendencies.)

ER 4. Age 2. In the den of ours, playing with boxes of medicine, aspirin, etc. The room looked bare. There was a big TV and other things in the room, but I didn't notice them. I got so into playing that I forgot everything else. *Vivid*: The emptiness of the room. Like I was looking straight down on the floor. I don't remember seeing anything else, just the bare floor.

Feeling: Remoteness, except for the center of attention which was me playing with the boxes. It was a small room but it seemed like a big expanse.

Interpretation: "I get wrapped up in my own actions and ideas and shut out the rest of the world. I feel alone, apart, and small and my life is empty." (Again the theme of remoteness is carried through, but this time it is picked up in the feeling description, which may imply personal dissatisfaction with this state of affairs. Underlying depression is implied in spite of his being the center of attention. Whose attention? He does not say. This style bespeaks extreme social distance—when people are absent, or vaguely implied but not mentioned.)

ER 5. First grade. First thing in the year we were asked to do something with colors. Directions indicated only one way to do it. When teacher was giving directions, I got worried (apprehensive) about directions, being told to do it that way. I lost track of what I was thinking. Worrying kept me from concentrating on her directions. I looked around; everyone else was doing it right. I was scared to raise hand, not wanting to make a fool of myself. I asked teacher later to come over to me to give directions. Then I got it right.

Vivid: Worrying, I said "I can't get it, she'll have to come over to me." Afraid of being embarrassed in front of the class, so I called her over.

Feelings: Confusion, worrying that I couldn't follow directions, embarrassment.

Interpretation: "I worry that I just can't do what is expected and I don't want others to find out. I impede my learning and growth by worrying about my performance. Then I never learn how to do the task at hand. I must be perfect; to make any mistake is embarrassing. If I make a mistake I will be labeled a fool and that is utterly terrible. (Relating the ER to his purposes and behavior, we see that the pattern provides him special attention through ineptitude and fear. By feeling embarrassed and worrying he creates a sideshow that (a) effectively removes him from the competition—other class members—and (b) keeps the teacher thoroughly busy with him in his service. Notice that he did not engage the teacher through *demonstrated* failure—he didn't try and *then* find difficulty. Rather, he had her show him how from the beginning; he didn't hear or understand the directions. In so doing, he sidesteps the main task and his ability or disability is not demonstrated until he can feel sure *a priori* that he can succeed. Likewise we see a basis for his tremendous avoidance; he will be thought a fool—rejected— if he is not perfect.)

When we compare the ERs to Robert's current behavior, we see the attitudinal underpinning behind his actions. We can also see that, at the time the ERs were given, Robert was entrenched in his isolation and fear of rejection. This further reduced the likelihood of a successful brief therapeutic encounter even though he was no longer exhibiting psychotic behavior, was holding a job, and had good intentions and plans of going back to college. Indeed when he went back to college the second time, he "fell apart" and subsequently withdrew. We can observe a parallel with this in his last ER and his recurring dream. He eventually came back to the homestead where his parents, in concern and desperation again, took up their caretaking. (See his first ER.) His ERs mirror his actions.

A year and a half later, when he returned a second time

to his second therapist, he gave the following recollection:

ER 1. I have a set of rings from bigger to smaller. I was lying down in the hall looking at the rings. Mother comes along. She tells me to put them away, but she starts putting them away herself. All the rings are back on the peg.

Vivid: Watching the rings get put back on the peg.

Feelings: At ease watching someone else do it. Nice, lazy feeling watching her.

Change: I would have gotten up and put the rings on.

Interpretation: (Note the remarkable consistency and absence of change between this ER and his first one in the previous series. His "change" statement is reflective only of surface good intentions; there is nothing given in the ER itself that would suggest any reason why he should want to change, yet it reflects superficial activity.)

ER 2. Mother said I couldn't go out of the yard. Going out of the yard was fearful. I didn't want to venture out. When asked to leave the yard, it made a knotting tension, therefore I did not venture out, I avoided.

In these two recollections, we see previous patterns basically unchanged. This second ER was given at the time Robert was talking about going to live in a commune, but he was afraid that, among other things, he would not like the food there. His ERs tell his true goal. They also reflect that real progress, i.e. life-style changes, in the latest therapy had been very limited. Truly he had made changes—holding a job a while, starting school, living away from home, travelling across country, not hallucinating nor excessively washing his hands—but his basic approach to and apperception of life, i.e. his life-style remained virtually unaltered.

CHAPTER 34

ANN: A CASE OF
DEPENDENCY AND DEPRESSION

CAROLYN W. ILGENFRITZ

ANN IS A young woman in her early twenties who is suffering
from recurrent depressive symptoms. She complains that life
is empty, meaningless, and almost unbearable. Ann lives in
the home of her parents in a situation she intensely dislikes, yet
she does not plan to move. She works at a job she says is dull,
boring, and dead-end, yet she is making no changes. Ann complains of loneliness and social isolation, but when opportunities
to socialize do arise, she withdraws into herself. Although Ann
has completed two years of college, she is convinced that her
brain is dysfunctional to the point that she is uniquely different
from and inferior to others.

Ann is refusing to take responsibility for herself and for
her own growth and change. She is assuming a *poor me* position
in life and insisting that she is incapable of change. Ann presents
a clinical picture of massive passivity and dependence, and her
case offers the opportunity to study how the knowledge of
life-style and early recollections can broaden our understanding
of her present life situation.

Ann is the oldest child in a middle-class family of two
children. Since she is five years older than her brother, she was
a psychological-only child and the center of her parents' attention until the birth of her brother, whom she accepted and related
to in a caretaking big-sister role. The family values focused on
conformity, fulfilling social roles, and presenting the image of a
perfect family to the community. There was a lack of emotional
warmth in the family, and the members did not share their
personal thoughts and feelings. Ann was showered with presents

and material advantages, but felt close to no one. Her mother was emotionally distant, yet very possessive of her children whom she tended to treat infantilistically. Ann was not encouraged to think for herself, set her own goals, or carry through with them. Her father was more supportive and encouraging, but he was quite passive and deferred to his wife in the making of family decisions.

Ann found her place in this family by being obedient and trying hard to please; yet she did not succeed in gaining the positive praise and encouragement necessary for the development of a sure sense of personal worth. She developed a very poor sense of self-identity, so that she was often confused about who she really was and what she wanted. Ann tended to go along with the crowd in making decisions and to be overly concerned with others' opinion of her because she was unsure of herself.

Ann did not learn to acknowledge and deal directly with feelings of anger. She turned her anger inward, directing it against herself, thus reinforcing her low sense of self-esteem and developing the depressive symptoms which trouble her. Today she discounts her attractiveness, value, and worth as a person and is refusing to take responsibility for her own growth and change. She has a narrow sphere of social interest and little feeling of being part of any community. She is wrapped up in herself and thinks she is empty and uninteresting to others. Ann believes she is a victim of her family environment and is using her depressive symptoms to demonstrate to others how she has been victimized. This gains her sympathy and attention and allows her to maintain her dependency on others and her belief that other people are responsible for her happiness and her unhappiness.

Ann was able to produce four early recollections, which are reproduced here as they were recorded in therapy sessions. The author's interpretations follow the recollections.

ER 1. Age 6 or 7. When my brother was little, walking with him.

Vivid: Walking, just walking.

Feelings: Happy because I was walking with him.

Interpretation: "Relationships with people are important

to me. I like to keep moving along in my relationships."
"I like to take the helper role in my relationships." (At a
deeper level, this recollection suggests discomfort in equalitarian relationships and a tendency to structure all relationships in a helper-helpee mode. It also points to an interest
in working with children, a vocational interest which she is
indeed considering.)

ER 2. Age 5. I went to the hospital for my tonsils. I didn't
want to leave home but once I got there, I was okay. I had
a crib; everybody else had a bed. That really bothered me.
Vivid: I didn't want to leave home.
Feelings: Scared.
Interpretation: "I'm afraid to leave the security of my home;
but once I've taken that step, I'll probably be okay." "I feel
less than or different from other people. I feel smaller.
Others have more and better than I have." (This recollection
closely parallels Ann's current living situation, her fear of
leaving home, and her feelings of inadequacy. Again, there
is the focus on inequality in personal relationships, with her
presenting herself here as the person needing help, rather
than as the helper as in her first recollection. This apparent
discrepancy is resolved when we recognize that the one with
whom she felt comfortable was her five-year younger brother,
while she felt inadequate with peers. She can only feel
competent with those younger or weaker than herself. Note
also that in the ER she ended up okay yet in the *Vivid* and
Feelings this is underplayed. She becomes frightened at the
prospect of a new situation and builds up negative feelings,
not giving enough credit to her ability to come out okay.)

ER 3. Age 5. When I went to Florida to my grandparents' I
fell in the creek. I couldn't swim so I don't know how I
got out. She (grandmother) told me crocodiles and alligators
were in there. I was scared.
Vivid: When I was crying, and she was hugging me saying,
"I'm glad you're okay."
Feeling: Scared, plus knowing somebody cared.
Interpretation: "I get myself into all kinds of binds, and
then I confuse myself as to how to get out. When I do things
on my own I get in trouble by goofing things up. When I

goof, people give me attention. I like that. Other people are responsible for my happiness and my unhappiness." (Here is an expression of Ann's massive dependency and passivity. She was prepared to live as a child, not as an adult, and is still insisting that others pull her out of trouble.) The following is a spontaneous recollection produced during a discussion of her school experiences.

ER 4. Age 6. My first day of kindergarten at public school. All I can remember is having my picture taken on the front porch before I left for school. I was very dressed up.

Interpretation: "My appearance is very important. I try to make a good impression on other people, especially at the beginning of relationships."

This spontaneous recollection, focusing on the importance of appearances for Ann, gains additional significance when it is viewed as part of a larger family pattern of emphasis on making a favorable impression on others and getting into difficulty when one acts on one's own. Following is the partial reproduction of an early recollection of her father, who was also in treatment with the same therapist.

My first Holy Communion. I wore a white shirt, stove-pipes, and shoes. I went out to play in my clothes near a chemical plant. A big puddle! Someone threw a rock! Red spots all over!

Vivid: Knowing that my mother would holler.

Feelings: Afraid to go home.

Interpretation: "Appearances are important." "If I do it myself (I went out to play) I will get into difficulty."

Across the generations, these messages remain the same: it is important and necessary to please others by looking good, and others mess it up for me, get me in trouble. Here we see where Ann may have developed her fear of the outside world. Other themes, such as lack of trust in self, problems in equalitarian relationships, and fear and refusal of responsibility for self are clearly identifiable in her early recollections and remain basic attitudes underlying her present life-style where depressive symptoms serve the purpose of allowing Ann to continue to avoid personal responsibility for her own growth and positive change.

READER PRACTICE

INTRODUCTION

H ERE IS YOUR chance to test your skill. On the following pages, you will find a number of ERs from actual clients representing a broad spectrum of age, sex, and presenting problems. You will be presented with one or more ERs from each client. In certain cases, you will also be asked to make guesses as to history, assets, or problems of the client based on the ER data you receive.

You are requested to study the recollection and write out interpretive statements in the first person; for example, "When I try to do things by myself, I fall on my face." Where more than one ER is presented, try to formulate a gestalt or overall picture of the client's attitudinal frame of reference. In the interpretation section which follows, you will find the statements which the clients' therapists made about the ERs and the answers to the questions which are asked. You may use this section to test out your hypotheses. The therapists' statements are not presented as the best of all possible conclusions, but rather as what the therapist actually deduced from his clients' ERs. Their responses, however, are accurate. You may find nuances, however, which the therapist missed or not did not comment on. This invalidates neither your conclusions nor those of the therapist.

CASES

Miss A

Nineteen-year-old single woman living at home with her parents, employed as a secretary.

ER 1. Age 4. I can't think right now, I guess. This isn't the

earliest memory. My dog broke her leg. I was in kindergarten and we had just gotten her (the dog). I took her to
kindergarten for show-and-tell on a leash. I was going
downstairs, but she didn't want to go. I pulled on the leash
and she fell and broke her leg and she cried. I remember
Dad carrying her up and looking up a vet. I remember the
cast on her leg. Before brother and I went to school we
would make her walk across the living room.

Vivid: My father holding her and looking through the
phone book. Tears in the dog's eyes. Dad was crying, too,
I guess.

Feelings: Guilty. I caused her to fall. To this day she (dog)
doesn't like or trust me. It was my mother's dog. It hurts
because I love that dog. I would make up on her, dress her
up, etc.

ER 2. Age 5. My mother was mad at my brother, and she came
after him with her hairbrush. He ran upstairs, yelling, "No,
no!" She kept after him and got him. When we were real
bad, we got hit with the hairbrush.

Vivid: Her chasing him, yelling.

Feeling: Scared. I jumped out of the way.

ER 3. Age 8-14. Playing with kids in the neighborhood, I had
a bad time in elementary school. Three girls were friends
with me when they wanted me, and when not, they would
gang up and not talk to me. In the neighborhood I was
not allowed to do what others would do. I felt like an
outcast and they probably thought I was weird. They could
go places I couldn't, they could stay up later, etc. I felt
I didn't fit in, felt their parents thought I was overprotected.
Mother wouldn't allow me to swim in their pools because
we couldn't take them to the pool we belonged to.

Vivid: So many things.

Feelings: Resented the way my mother treated me; she
did more harm than good.

ER 4. Age 6 or 7. C and I were bratty sometimes. We went
to this kid's house. He built cities in the dirt under his porch.
We went over and messed it up. As we got done, his mother
caught us. She told us not to move but we ran off; C to her
house and I to mine. I was scared. I asked Mom to take

me to the store to get away. Mom knew something was up and didn't take me. Five minutes later the kid's mother came to the door. I was in the other room and heard them raise their voices. Mom didn't like her attitude. She (kid's mother) said, "I want A to come down to clean it up." I don't remember whether I went.

Vivid: Being caught and running home scared.

Feelings: Scared I'd get in trouble. Also Mom and kid's mother broke their friendship over this. I thought it was my fault.

ER 5. Age 8 or 9. I fell off my bike. There was a big hill. All the kids ride down with their hands off the bars. I rode down with my hands on my hips. A dog came into the path. I hit the dog and it ran off yelping. I fell off and the bike flipped around in the air. I was sitting on the curb crying and my friends came over and said, "Are you alright?" A guy about 20 came over. He was nice to me. He walked me and my bike home and bought me ice cream.

Vivid: Sitting on the curb, not hurt but shaken.

Feelings: Frightened about hitting the dog. Everyone wondered, "Are you alright?" (family and everyone in the neighborhood).

ER 6. Age 9. My grandmother lived with us. She spoiled me so bad. Once I did something, probably talked mouthy. She got angry and I slapped her face. Then she smacked me. I remember lying in bed that night crying. I felt so bad about it. I can still see the look on her face; startled. I wondered, "What will I do? She'll die someday and I'll feel bad because I smacked her."

Vivid: The look on her face when I smacked her.

Feelings: Bad; ashamed of myself.

(Interpretations on page 336.)

Mr. B

Twenty-seven-year-old single man hospitalized as paranoid schizophrenic. Physically short (about five feet four inches).

ER 1. Age 11 or 12. I tried to have sex with this girl. My dick wasn't big enough. Jimmy (fifteen-year-old brother) was

with. He got it (intercourse), I didn't. She was willing. QUESTIONS: Guess what some of his difficulties might be, what kinds of people they may center around.
(Interpretations on page 338.)

Miss C

Forty-year-old single female, nursing chief in a general hospital. She gave this ER four months into individual therapy.
ER 1. I remember getting a bath in a tin tub in the dining room. Ours was a three-story house; it was cold upstairs but fairly warm on the first floor. Mother heated the water downstairs and poured it into the tub. I was in the tub looking down at my round belly. It looked like a baby with a round belly. I remember putting soap on it and rubbing it. It felt good.
Vivid: Being in the tub and getting soaped down, dried, and hugged by mother.
Feelings: Pleasant. I liked getting/being given a bath.
QUESTIONS: In addition to providing first-person interpretive comments, try guessing the answers to the following:
1. What problems did she present at the outset of therapy?
2. What kind of difficulties might she have on her job?
3. What is her basic goal at this point?
4. What assets does she have?
(Interpretations on page 338.)

Mrs. D

Fifty-one-year-old divorced woman contemplating remarriage.
ER 1. Age 5. I had an urge to see the outside world. We had a store in a small town. I ran away and wandered around town till people brought me home. One day I got spanked hard for this. I was still smarting, went up to the screen door and out again.
Vivid: Me sniffing and snivelling at the door but deciding "to hell with it," and going again.
Feelings: Angry they spanked me, I guess. I really don't know. I probably didn't think it so terrible if I went for a

walk.

ER 2. Age 8, third grade. I was asked to spell "stall." I couldn't. I was asked to write it on the board, but I couldn't. The teacher wrote it and erased it and demanded I write it. I couldn't. Teacher was furious, she shook me hard and told me, "You think you're so smart just because you've got a yellow ribbon in your hair." (I forgot about that yellow ribbon that day.)

Feeling: Hurt. I never spoke in front of large groups since.

ER 3. No age given. I was in the car alone in the city while Father and Mother conducted business. An older man was trying to get into the car. He was drunk. Mother came out and was hysterical and began screaming.

Vivid: Her screaming.

Feelings: I don't know why she got so upset. I was in the car, the window was up, and the car was locked.

(Interpretations on page 339.)

Mrs. E

Forty-two-year-old housewife, youngest of four girls.

ER 1. Age 3. The big storm in 1933. Being in the car with water all around us. Sister saw a lifeboat. My middle sister cried before I did. I can picture the inside of the car.

Vivid: Seeing the water. The story about my sister and me.

Feelings: I felt safe with my parents in charge. I don't remember fear. Proud of myself that my older sister cried first. It made me feel grown-up.

ER 2. Age 4. Mother went into the hospital. Being in the car after we left her. I cried. Bigger sister said, "Aw, she misses her mother." She was sympathetic. It was the only time they were sympathetic with me.

Vivid: What sister said.

Feelings: Lonely.

ER 3. Age 4. When I had my tonsils out. I was unhappy. I had poison ivy which kept me in awhile. I didn't like being alone. Another child was in the room. The nurses threatened, "If you don't stop scratching, we'll tie your hands." No one came to visit me for at least a week. They never came.

(Years later I found out a measles epidemic was on so no one could have visitors.) The nurses were businesslike. They should have told me, but they didn't. People don't treat children like they're intelligent enough to understand.
Vivid: Wondering why nobody came.
Feelings: Hurt . . . not hurt but baffled. I figured they'd come tomorrow, but they never did.

ER 4. Age 5 or 6. The venetian blind cracked. Father didn't know how to fix it. I gave him the idea. He thought I was clever to think of that.
Vivid: That he thought I was clever.
Feeling: Proud.

ER 5. Under 9. When I broke something. I was very afraid to tell father, but I did. He was touched that I told him.
Vivid: Scared. He was strict with my sisters. He was flabbergasted that I volunteered the information.
Feelings: Don't know. I knew he was pleased. I was relieved that I didn't get punished.

ER 6. Age 9. Lots of things like this happened. My parents were divorcing. My sisters were in their teens and had a terrible time with Father. Mother was in the hospital (chronic arthritis). Sisters wanted her to get a divorce. Father had a millionaire brother, and sisters wrote him to settle it. Then Father went up to see him. He was not supposed to bring me, but I talked him into it. The world's fair was there. I knew exactly what was going on so I shouldn't be left out. When we got there, my uncle said, "You were not supposed to bring her." I was shunted aside. Sisters said I was a spoiled brat. I was the age you'd like a child, they were the age they'd give him hell. I knew what was going on.
Feelings: Resented being left out. They didn't give me credit for knowing.

(Interpretations on page 340.)

Mr. F

Thirty-year-old married man.

ER 1. Age 4 or 5. I woke up one night and discovered that neither of my parents were home. I began crying and scream-

ing out the window and a neighbor (I think) came in the house, comforted me, and stayed until my parents returned.
Vivid: I guess the darkness.
Feelings: Scared, alone.
ER 2. Age 4 or 5. One winter we went for a ride in a horse-drawn sleigh that someone was driving in the field behind our house. It seems that the field was icy rather than snow covered.
Vivid: Horse galloping in front, bright moon.
Feelings: Exhilaration, excitement.
ER 3. Age 4 or 5. The stream behind our house overflowed and water came up past the houses. We had to evacuate and were standing in the street watching firemen chop holes in the front of the housing unit to let the water pass through.
Vivid: Magnitude and force of the water.
Feelings: Don't remember being scared—more fascinated by the power of the water.
ER 4. Age 4 or 5. Before Christmas one year, my father sat down with my sister and me and explained about Santa Claus. He mentioned that Santa Claus was watching everything that we did and would know if we were good or not.
Vivid: Sitting in the living room, also the closet (for some reason I can't remember).
Feelings: Impressed by Santa's ability, a bit wary and uneasy.
ER 5. Age 4 or 5. There was a bit of a clearing in a woods near our house. I can't remember if I discovered it or was shown it by a friend. It was a good play area where we exercised our fantasies of a hideaway.
Vivid: Aspect—a neat place, all our own.
Feelings: A kind of independence, maybe security.
(Interpretations on page 341.)

Mrs. G

Woman in her mid-thirties. She was the subject of a student of the author's in a class assignment and no first hand data was available other than the following recollection:

I was drinking a soda. I accidently swallowed an ice cube.

It hurt.

(Interpretations on page 342.)

Mr. H

Twenty-eight-year-old single male with a masters degree in one of the helping professions; an only child.

ER 1. Age 2 or 3. Walking in a back alley. The gutter in the middle had water coming down it. I was walking barefoot in the water. The water covered my feet. I was walking up the alley by myself. I got spanked for it later. I don't know why.

Vivid: Water running over my feet.

Feelings: Fascination and sensation of it. Freedom.

Change: Nothing.

ER 2. Age 4 or 5. I was at the hospital. They thought I had leukemia. I was in isolation by myself. It was nighttime. Looking out of the window I saw the green and red lights at the oil company flashing back and forth. It (oil company) was over by my aunt's; we would always drive by it.

Vivid: Lights flashing back and forth.

Feelings: Alone, sad that I was in complete isolation from the other children.

Change: Not being alone.

ER 3. Age 5 or 6. Down on my cousin's farm on a summer night. I remember looking out the window going upstairs. Older cousin Marlene looking out the window with me, looking at the stars. She pointed out the Big Dipper to me.

Vivid: Looking up at the stars, being with my cousin.

Feelings: I don't remember any feelings. Maybe fascination with looking up at the stars and having them explained.

Change: Nothing.

ER 4. Age 6 or 7. Mom got into this big argument with me at 9 or 10 at night. She threatened to send me off to boarding school if I didn't behave. I didn't behave, so she packed my bags, put me in the car, and took me under a train trestle. She let me out of the car under the trestle. She told me someone from the school would pick me up. I waited and cried. She drove off. Later she came back, asked me if I would behave. I said I would so I got back in the car.

Vivid: Standing under the streetlights with my little suitcase in front of me, alone.

Feelings: Extremely unhappy, scared, crying.

Change: Not being left there, let out of the car.

ER 5. Age 5 or 6. Sitting in the living room with my legs flopped on the edge of the chair watching an old TV, a big one. Mother came in and showed me brochures from kindergarten, showing me how nice it was to go to school.

Vivid: That I was nonchalant when she came in. I didn't move too much.

Feelings: Just blasé about it. It (going to kindergarten) happened to all my friends; it would happen to me, too.

(Interpretations on page 342.)

Miss I

Twenty-two-year-old woman, a middle child, college graduate.

ER 1. Age 7. I remember listening to this Sunday School teacher saying, "Fear God." We were reading the Bible. "You must fear God."

Vivid: That's what I had to do to earn God's attention. Then I had to set about doing it.

Feelings: Fear of not having done it and not knowing what fear meant, except to be afraid.

ER 2. Age 5 or 6. My aunt called me and wondering why I was home and not in kindergarten. I said mother didn't want me to go to kindergarten because I could learn it at home. I was waiting for the kids to come home so I could play.

Vivid: I felt bad because I couldn't do what everyone else was doing. I was mad about it. I was defensive, trying to justify to my aunt being at home when I disagreed with it (mother's keeping me home). My aunt was critical in the way she asked me.

QUESTION: In addition to the ER interpretations, take a guess as to what her occupational goal might be.

(Interpretations on page 343.)

Mrs. J

A forty-eight-year-old married woman.

ER 1. Age 2½-4. Remember being wrapped up in blanket, it was the only way to control me. Doctor put thermometer in my rectum, finally. I was screaming and carrying on. Mother was watching—stood by, didn't help me.

Vivid: Being wrapped in blanket.

Feelings: Boy, was I upset, angry that he would do this to me and mother that she let him do that.

ER 2. Age 7 or 8. I remember Father having terrible car accident. He was hit by a train. He didn't want to talk about it. Went to movies twice because he was so happy to be alive. I never found out details, Dad was not injured.

Vivid: My reaction to his reaction, that he wanted to go to movies and do pleasant things. It was an interesting, different reaction. Accident must have been his fault. He didn't want to talk about it. He was a bad driver.

Feelings: Don't know, hard time with feelings. Glad to be alive. Nice to go to movies.

ER 3. Age 8 or 10. Mother and Father had a terrible fight. They were very upset with each other. Mother made me come in bed with her and Dad slept in other room. I was terribly upset, shaking—my knee would not stop shaking. First time I heard them fight like this. Father retaliated. Heard words I never heard before.

Vivid: My shaking from head to toe in that bed. Mother did not appear concerned. Probably she was upset herself. Didn't console me because of shaking.

Feelings: Not happy—concerned what results would be. I threatened. Mother rejecting my father. Don't know what the argument was about. It was violent, but with words.

ER 4. Age 11. Going to camp, which I hated. It was there during visiting day I received a letter from Mother saying Dad was not going to come and my uncle was driving her up. When Mom came, I panicked, feared something happened to Dad. Mom said, "I told you in the letter that Dad would not come." She did, but I hadn't read it.

Vivid: Seeing them drive up in the car thinking "What happened to Dad?"

Feelings: Terrible time with that—fear, fright—I can't articulate my feelings.

ER 5. Age 10 or 11, fifth grade. In a school play in elementary school. I was a rabbit, Flopsie. Grandmother came to see me. It wasn't really important, but it was important at the time. Mother was proud, I was proud. It was an operetta and I sang in it.

Vivid: Really vague—dressed in white bunny suit with big ears.

Feelings: Proud to be in it. Competitive in that you have to be cast; I made the first move and got chosen.

(Interpretations on page 344.)

Miss K

Fifteen-year-old freshman girl with a twin brother and one older brother. She was referred by her school for being withdrawn and shy.

ER 1. Age 4. I was in kindergarten. I did not say my prayers. Mom and Dad hollered. The teacher had to run after me. She told my parents.

Vivid: When she had to chase me.

Feelings: Probably terrible, because the other kids were saying them and I was the only one who wasn't.

ER 2. Age 5. In first grade. Teacher really took a yardstick and swung me around and hit me.

Vivid: When she swung me around.

Feelings: I forget . . . not so hot, terrible. Afraid she probably would really hit me.

ER 3. Age 6 or 7, second grade. Sister let me, gave me presents —a rosary and a party tea set, all wrapped up; a child-sized party set.

Feelings: Okay, I guess. I felt she liked me or something.

ER 4. Age 10 or 11, sixth grade. Sister said that if I passed my science test it would snow and it snowed. I passed.

Vivid: I passed it.

Feeling: Happy because I passed it.

ER 5. Probably kindergarten. I remember walking in the May procession. I had this long dress on. I remember carrying flowers and red roses.

Vivid: Carrying the flowers.

Feelings: Happy. I felt like I was in a parade.

ER 6. (She was asked what she recalled of her first day of school.) I was afraid. I think it was because I never went to school before. I went. I think I cried. It took all year to settle down.

(Interpretations on page 345.)

Mr. L

Thirty-year-old married man, oldest child.

ER 1. Age 5. Sitting in the bathroom area, Jon is an infant coming home from the hospital (when he was born). Sitting, getting to rock him for awhile.

Vivid: Jon in my lap, the sun, it was a bright sunny day. The room had windows all around.

Feelings: Pride, happiness that Mom and Jon were okay. Felt good that they trusted me to hold him.

ER 2. Age 5 or 6. The night my great-grandmother died, when my parents got the call she had died. I was sitting in the kitchen with Mother, Dad, Grandmother, and Grandpa. They were talking about arrangements.

Vivid: Mom taking the phone call and sensing from her words that my great-grandmother had died.

Feelings: Confusion, not understanding what was going on. I knew she had died but had no grasp of death, not understanding why they behaved as they did.

QUESTION: Guess what this person chose as an occupation. (Interpretations and answer on page 346.)

INTERPRETATIONS

Miss A

ER 1. "One little slip screws it up for ever." "I cause pain." "The world must do what I want." "I am deeply sensitive to the pain others feel and feel guilty for causing it." "I make excuses for real or anticipated mistakes." (She starts out saying, "I can't think right now." In other words, "Don't hold me accountable for what I may come up with.")

ER 2. "Angry conflict is dangerous and scary—avoid it at all costs." (She also is probably saying that adult authority figures, and/or especially mother, are volatile and will hurt you if you cross them.)

ER 3. (This is actually not an ER, but a report. Yet it has great significance in its revelation of her self-perception and view of her mother with whom she lived at the time this report was given.) "I am a victim—poor me. I feel less than others." "I resent it when others stand in the way or deprive me of what I believe is my right." "People are fair-weather friends—unfair, fickle, and can't be trusted." "I'm sensitive and easily hurt." "Appearances are important. I'm very concerned over how others evaluate me." ("Felt their parents thought I was overprotected.") "Others, especially my mother, are responsible for my difficulties."

ER 4. "I cause trouble, but am afraid to pay the consequences. Therefore, I try to manipulate others to cover for me. They don't always fall for it, but I still get protected." "I feel responsible, possibly guilty, when others experience difficulty over what I do."

ER 5. "When I hurt myself, people show they care." (This is a central dynamic to this client's current behavior.) "I enjoy the attention I get." ("I enjoy people, especially men, feeling sorry for me. I cry and they become tender.") "I have to be able to do what others do." (Submit to peer pressure, right or wrong.) "The hurt I produce frightens me."

ER 6. "I shouldn't act out my anger on people close to me. If I do, I feel guilty and overreact with excessive worry." "I act on impulse and think later of the consequences." "Others are responsible for the way I am today." (This is a loose interpretation based on "*She* spoiled me so bad," a phrase which was not necessary for her to insert in order to tell the story. This ER reflects her pampering and her temper.)

Miss A was an attractive but manipulative young woman who used sexual acting out to punish her parents, avoid intimacy, and gain attention and concern. In therapy, she gave the appearance of being ridden with guilt and denied the otherwise obvious anger at her parents, especially mother. Actually, her display of guilt was quite superficial. She presented a "poor me" image and expressed the countenance of a whipped puppy, all the while being very strong and highly resistant to change. She became increasingly angry at her therapist and prematurely left therapy at a point when the focus in therapy was upon her taking specific action in her life.

Mr. B

ER 1. "I'm not enough. When I try, I can't pull it off, can't accomplish." "Women want sex. They are to be used." (This is based on the role the girl plays vis-a-vis he and Jimmy in the ER.)

HISTORY: The client, short of stature, admits he has always felt inferior. He views women as "causing you trouble," and as a result he rarely dated. "I didn't talk to too many girls; I was afraid they'd say 'no.'" Also, he blames his stepmother for breaking up his family through drinking and affairs, but also believes she wanted him to rape her. At seventeen, he beat up his stepmother and was placed in a mental hospital. While there at twenty-two, he beat up a nurse he believed was in love with him and was transferred to a facility for the criminally insane. He was released at age twenty-seven, sent to live at a rescue mission for five days, and was again placed in a psychiatric hospital because he couldn't adapt to life on the outside.

VOCATIONAL GOAL: Heavy equipment operator.

Miss C

ER 1. "I want to be taken care of and kept comfortable." "Close contact with others is pleasurable and desirable, especially when they are ministering to my needs." "I will create my own pleasure." (Based on the statement, "rubbing my belly," this was a new feature in her recollection. Within a relatively passive context, she was beginning to take action herself to meet her own desires.) "Its 'colder' at the top of the status hierarchy." (This may be a rather symbolic interpretation for her description of the house, but she included the house for a purpose, possibly to reinforce the feeling of comfort and warmth. The client was in a high-status position at the time, was having difficulties with subordinates, and related well to this interpretation.)

This recollection was given by the client at a transition point in her therapy in which she was developing more assertive behavior with her mother and also on the job. The client was still wrapped up with herself; others (should) provide her service.

ANSWERS TO QUESTIONS:

1. Occasional depression, low self-esteem, inability to be assertive, low productivity, obesity (weighed 278 pounds at outset of therapy). Diagnosis: Asthenic Personality.
2. The client presented herself in general as knowledgeable but childlike. She had difficulty obtaining the administrative respect of her subordinates, although she was well liked. Another nursing chief felt in competition with the client and tried to undercut her which disturbed Miss C deeply.
3. Goals: Maintaining physical, emotional, and interpersonal comfort, also getting her way (via passive means).
4. Assets: Bright, verbal, very likeable, and a good diplomat. Very pretty in spite of her weight and looks much younger than forty.

Mrs. D

ER 1. "I am active and will meet my needs regardless of the consequences." "People misunderstand me and overreact. This confuses me." ("Not so terrible if I went for a walk.") "Authority figures are hostile." "The world demands obedience, but I will show them!"

ER 2. "I must meet the expectations of the authority." "I must not make mistakes or I get ridiculed, and this is catastrophic in its hurt." "Authority figures are hostile."

ER 3. "Strange men can be dangerous." "The world is a jungle, but you're okay if you keep control." "People overreact unnecessarily and this confuses me. They just don't consider the facts" (windows up, car locked).

Authority figures who overreact or threaten and hurt run through her recollections. The role assigned to emotions is one of nuisance, confusion, and loss of control. The preference is on keeping calm and considering the evidence. She expects to be misunderstood and to be ridiculed if she makes a mistake.

Mrs. D. is a very responsible, careful, active, and self-determined woman with a responsible managerial position. She is very detailed and competent in her work. Her philosophy is, "My mind is made up, don't confuse me with feelings." and she is emotionally constricted. Her first husband was dependent and an alcoholic. She subsequently married a loving but exceedingly deferent man whose goal in life was to make her happy.

Mrs. E

ER 1. "I must appear strong and grown-up." "I should be better than others." "I can be brave in the shadow of someone else who is in control." (This is a passive ER. Note that her feeling of self-worth, i.e. grown-up or not, depends on what *others* do. We would suspect that she easily slips into feeling like the victim, as the "others are responsible" mentality is subtly evident here.)

ER 2. "The world is cold. It's rare to get sympathy and concern. Crying (sometimes) works to get the concern of others."

ER 3. "People are cold, not there when I need them." "People discount my intelligence." "I keep hoping, but my hopes are never realized."

ER 4. "I am proud of my cleverness, and others should recognize it also. Others benefit from taking my advice." (The implication is, "The world would be a better place if people listened to me.")

ER 5. "Honesty is the best policy, even in the face of dire consequences. I have the courage to act on my convictions."

ER 6. "I must get my way." "The world is unfair." "I resent being (unfairly) left out and not being given enough credit for intelligence."

Several themes run through her ERs. The world is unfair and cold, my intelligence is discounted although it would be better if they listened to me, I will get my way by crying or manipulation, but others are responsible for my feeling of worth.

Mrs. E is a lonely and depressed woman with high moral

values. She tries desperately to force them on her family who will not listen. She had frequent episodes of hysterical crying in which her son and husband are blamed outright for all the evils she endures. As she is highly critical and frequently trying to correct them, her family considers her a nag and tune her out, reinforcing her loneliness. She desperately wants them to change because she holds them, and not herself, responsible for her happiness and peace in the home. Basically passive, she wanted a husband to take the lead, yet she married one who is more passive than she and in many ways irresponsible. The parallels between her ERs and overt behavior are clear.

Mr. F

ER 1. "It's frightening to be left alone in a strange situation, beyond my control. Then I feel helpless. When this is the case I may take (passive) action to get others involved to provide help and comfort." (He may also play the victim-martyr role—"poor me.") (There is also a concern for correctness revealed in the words, "I think." He won't commit himself to that of which he isn't sure.)

ER 2. "I like excitement" (with others—"we"). (In this ER, he is along for the ride. He is a passive observer here. Another person initiates the activity.)

ER 3. "When I'm with others, I needn't be afraid" ("We). "I appreciate and am fascinated by nature and its power." (His fascination may reflect curiosity and a bent for the philosophical. While the firemen work, he seems to ponder the water's force.)

ER 4. "You'd better be good . . . or else." (We see the emphasis on a moral code, possibily a retributive code. Again he is impressed with extraordinary powers and ability.)

ER 5. "I long for peace, away from the pressures of the world." (We suspect an active fantasy life and an emphasis on the value of fantasy.)

Throughout his ERs, Mr. F is safe and secure as long as others are around, close at hand. It is catastrophic for him to feel left alone, out of control of a situation, especially since he values strength, power, and ability. He also has a strong emphasis on doing right, and when others do wrong or disappoint him, he may play a victim-martyr role. In fact, when his wife was having an affair, he did indeed drink to excess and play "poor me." His wife is quite mischievous and flighty, and their marriage is not dull. He has the excitement, but it has backfired. All five ERs reflect passivity and his concern for detail. Several portray him in a role as a visual type, an observer rather than an actor. He will need prodding to take assertive action in potentially uncomfortable situations. He is a successful engineer, which fits his attention to detail.

Mrs. G

The class agonized over an interpretation. Finally we came up with the following:

"I bite off more than I can chew."

The student who presented the subject's ER stated, "That's it!" The subject was overextended in various activities. Her pattern is to get overinvolved and then complain about the excessive pressure.

Mr. H

ER 1. "I enjoy my freedom, but I am confused when others can't accept my activities—the world is unfair." "I am fascinated by novel experiences and things."

ER 2. "I can make the best of adversity (or at least keep occupied)." "It's particularly bad to be caught in situations I don't like which are beyond my control. Then I don't want to be alone." (We can reconcile the feelings attached to being alone in these two ERs when we notice that in the first, he is apparently alone by choice, whereas in the second, his isolation is being done to him. The key variable appears to be *his choice* in whether or not to have others around him. Also the theme of *looking* appears here and reoccurs in subsequent recollections.)

ER 3. "It's very important that people take an interest in me." "I must be careful how I acknowledge or express my feelings." (Based upon the *Feelings* statement in an obviously pleasant situation.)

ER 4. "When there is trouble, others will usually cause it." "I will do what I want and face the risks." "Being rejected and cast aside (by people who are supposed to love me) is one of the worst, painful things that can happen." "Therefore: You can't trust people."

ER 5. "I face the inevitable with resigned acceptance."

This young man keeps definite emotional distance with a chip on his shoulder and has definite loner tendencies. We find that he believes close people will reject him. (His mother categorically denies the truth of the fourth ER). Thus he insulates himself from intimate relations. In dating, as soon as the girl would fall for him, he would lose interest and end the relationship. Peers feel anxious in his presence if the conversation goes below a surface level. He would like to be accepted by people but he is afraid to take the first step. As a result, he feels on the outside of things, but places himself on the periphery. After several brief jobs in a helping profession in which he felt very uncomfortable, he quit, moved to a different part of the country, and went into marketing. He is a bright and strong young man who can make the best of adversity, but must maintain personal control to feel secure.

Miss I

ER 1. "I must do what I'm supposed to." "I must earn any favors, even attention, even from God." "It frightens me to be in situations in which I don't know what to do." (The recollection, especially the statement "then I had to set about doing it," implies a driven, obsessional quality about meeting standards, possibly self-imposed standards that are unreasonably high. We could suspect an active, sensitive girl who may catch one piece of the total content and then overreact emotionally; active even though the primary activity is listening because of the statement quoted above. Implied in the ER and in the interpretive comments is that this young woman devalues herself, she is not worthy or good, *unless* she meets standards.)

ER 2. "Life is unfair." "People are critical and nongiving (especially authority figures)." "I get angry when I feel my rights are being denied." "I get defensive when asked to justify my behavior." (Again we see the sensitivity to criticism. She took it personally even though she basically agreed with the aunt—she should be in school with the other children—and her staying home was mother's idea. This sensitivity makes sense in light of the interpretations above regarding her self-esteem. We would suspect that she is a girl of high moral calibre but one who is discouraged and tends to blame others for her difficulties.

ANSWER TO QUESTION: This girl was interested in pursuing the ministry. Apart from the fact that she might be virtually "self-employed" in that she could have a great deal of freedom to structure her time on the job, she admitted that she does fear God and wants to prove herself acceptable to Him and worthy of His love. She feels that maybe a minister has an "in" in this regard.

Mrs. J

ER 1. "The world is hostile." "I strongly resist being controlled, but often lose." "The people close to me don't protect or help me when I need them. (You can't depend on them.)"

ER 2. "I judge others (even getting saved from death and happiness over it does not save father from my judgment). If one gets into difficulty, it is obviously his own fault." "I am curious and interested in the reactions of others." "Being alive is to be appreciated." "I have difficulty expressing my feelings."

ER 3. "Anger and fights are painful and to be avoided. They upset me greatly." "Others (those who should) don't take my needs and feelings into consideration." "I can't control myself in deep stress and should be taken care of. (I try to get my way through anxiety and appearing out of control.)"

ER 4. "I jump to immediate conclusions without checking the data." "I become very frightened at the thought of danger or loss, or when things happen unexpectedly."

ER 5. "I am proud of what I do well." "It's necessary to be noticed, recognized." "I get my way."

Mrs. J was an only child who was spoiled by an extended family without other children. Consequently she was the apple of their eye. She was also rebellious as her parents were strict and she felt she could never satisfy them. She suffered from depression. We can see from her ERs that she expected to be taken care of but perceived those close to her, who should take care of her, as nonsupportive and undependable—at times hostile. She had tremendous difficulty expressing feelings openly but rather used anxiety and loss of control to influence others. She was judgmental and had a strong need to be right and in control in her adult life, and plagued herself with gnawing feelings of self-dissatisfaction.

Miss K

ER 1. "I rebel and get everyone upset and busy with me; even if the consequences are negative." (Her use of "probably" when reporting her feelings may indicate that she is not sure but may be saying what she feels is expected.)

ER 2. "Authority figures are hostile." (We might guess that she also feels they overreact. Again she has difficulty expressing her feelings.)

ER 3. "I am special."

ER 4. "I am special." (Even the weather falls in line!)

ER 5. "I am special."

ER 6. "I am frightened in new situations." (She overreacts and takes too long to calm down. This suggests she uses fear to excuse misbehavior.)

The theme of specialness pervades all ERs. She is either special in a positive way or she acts out and keeps everyone involved with her. Her first ER is particularly noteworthy. The *Vivid* is that teacher chases her. Her primary behavioral symptoms were withdrawal and elective mutism. The effect was very provocative. She would not talk and withdrew noticeably, whereupon everyone would try to get her to talk. In response she would usually remain quiet. She would passively provoke others to attend to her, then defeat their efforts. She got everyone to "chase" her.

Mr. L

ER 1. "I am proud when others have faith in me." "I care for people, am concerned for their well-being.

ER 2. "Death and people's reactions to it confuses me. "I am a sensitive observer of people."

OCCUPATION: Clergyman.

MANASTER-PERRYMAN MANIFEST CONTENT EARLY RECOLLECTION SCORING MANUAL*

Guy J. Manaster and Thomas B. Perryman

T HE SCORING VARIABLES for ERs are listed below. Explanations and examples will appear after each item and/or category where necessary in order to clarify the meaning and method for scoring the variable.

A. Characters (Persons mentioned in the ER)
1. Mother
2. Father
3. Siblings
4. Other family members (uncles, aunts, grandparents, etc.)
5. Non-family members (individuals specifically mentioned in the ER, but not members of the family: e.g. "My friend and I . . .")
6. Group (references to a group or groups of people: e.g. "My class went on a field trip.")
7. Animal
8. Number of character types mentioned in ER (may range from 0-7).

(Category A concerns the characters mentioned in the memory, whether they played an active role in the memory or not. The fact that they are mentioned by the subject indicates their salience for him. Score "character" variables on a presence or absence basis, except for No. 8 which received a numerical score.)

* Reprinted by permission from "Early Recollections and Occupational Choice," paper presented at the Twenty-First Annual Convention of the American Society of the American Society of Adlerian Psychology, Toronto, Canada, May 1973. Cited in the *Journal of Individual Psychology*, 1974, 30, 232-237.

B. Themes (What the memory is about)
  9. Birth of a sibling ("I remember when my brother was born we. . . .")
  10. Death (of a person or animal)
  11. Illness/Injury (to self, another person, or an animal: "My brother was hit by a car and we took him to the hospital.")
  12. Punishment (of the subject or another person)
  13. Misdeeds (acts committed by the subject which he knew to be wrong.)
  14. Givingness (generosity or kindness, either overt or covert felt by the subject toward another: e.g. "The old lady looked very ill and I wanted to help her.")
  15. Mastery (attempts by the subject to gain control of himself, others, or the environment by psychological or physical acts: e.g. "I knew he was going to hit me so I played dumb." "I tried to reach the cookie jar, but couldn't quite make it.")
  16. Mutuality (a friendly, socially reciprocal, or cooperative experience with othrs: e.g. My family went to the beach and everyone had a good time.")
  17. Attention-getting (the subject receives or wants special attention: e.g. "I screamed and yelled when mother wouldn't take me skating." "I remember getting lots of presents.")
  18. New or unfamiliar situation causing excitement (e.g. "I remember the first day of school." "We got caught in a storm and it was very exciting.")
  19. Fear or anxiety provoking or threatening situation (e.g. "The old man chased me and I was badly scared." "My mother was late coming home and I was afraid she had left me.")
  20. Open hostility (e.g. "I remember a fight my parents had.")
  21. Other (list other themes separately)
  22. Number of themes in the ER (may range from 1-13)
  (Category B concerns the theme or plot of the ER. Score "theme" variables on a presence-absence basis, except for No. 22 which receives a numerical score. More than one theme may be scored.)

C. Concern with detail
23. Visual (attention given to describing color, size, shape, etc. of a person or object, e.g. "I remember my pink and yellow swimsuit.")
24. Auditory (attention given to describing volume, quality of sound, or something heard)
25. Motor (attention given to describing some vigorous physical movement, e.g. "We ran and jumped around the yard.")

(Category C concerns the attention the subject gives to describing something seen, or heard, or to describing vigorous physical movement. Score "detail" variables on a presence-absence basis. More than one variable may be scored.)

D. Setting (where the situation remembered took place)
26. School (inside or out)
27. Hospital/doctor's office
28. Inside the home—family or relatives
29. Outside in the subject's neighborhood
30. Traveling (in a car, airplane, boat, etc.)
31. Inside the home of a non-family member
32. Outside, away from family home or neighborhood
33. Unclear (no clear indication is made in content of ER)
34. Others (list separately)
35. Number of settings in the ER (may range from 1-9)

(Category D concerns the place the situation remembered took place. Score "setting" variables on a presence-absence basis, except for No. 35 which receives a numerical score. More than one setting may be scored.)

E. Active-Passive
36. Active (subject initiates action; he acts rather than is acted upon: e.g. "I remember when I tried to drive dad's car to see what it was like.")
37. Passive (subject initiates little or no action; he is acted upon rather than acts; e.g. "I watched the workmen building the house next door.")

(The "active-passive" category is concerned with the degree of initiation the subject has with regard to what happens in the memory. Does he decide to do something (active), or is his action the result of decisions or actions of others (passive).

Score "active-passive" variables on a presence-absence basis. One or the other, but not both, variables should be scored.)

F. Control

38. Internal (subject accepts responsibility for what happens in the ER)

39. External (subject disassociates himself from any consequences or outcomes of the ER)

(The "control" category is concerned with whether the subject assumes responsibility for what happens in the ER. Score "control" variables on a presence-absence basis. One or the other, but not both, variables should be scored.)

G. Affect

40. Positive (overall feeling tone of the ER is pleasant)

41. Negative (overall feeling tone of the ER is unpleasant)

42. Neutral (no indication of affect in the ER)

(The "affect" category is concerned with the pleasantness or unpleasantness or lack of these the subject felt about what happened in the ER. Score "affect" variables on a presence-absence basis. Only one of the variables should be scored.)

INSTRUMENTS—FOR USE WITH THE MANASTER-PERRYMAN MANUAL

EARLY RECOLLECTIONS

Part 1: Personal Information
1. a. age:_____
   c. sex:_____male
      _____female
b. major:_____
d. marital status:
   _____single   _____engaged
   _____married   _____divorced
2. a. Where were you born? city_____
                           country_____
   b. Where did you go to high school? city_____
                                       country_____
   c. Have you attended other colleges:
                    name_____
                    when_____
3. What is your father's principal occupation? (If he is retired or not living, what was his occupation?)_____
_____
4. How many years of school has your father had? Indicate by a number: 1-6 elementary; 7-12 secondary; 13+ higher_____
5. How many years of school has your mother had?_____
6. How many brothers and/or sisters have you?_____
   How many older brothers?_____
   How many older sisters?_____
   How many younger brothers?_____
   How many younger sisters?_____
7. How would you characterize your present physical condition?
   ____excellent ____good ____fair ____poor

351

8. What job do you want to have after graduation?_____

9. What will you do on that job? Describe it:_____

_____

10. Do you think you will get the kind of job you want?

_____yes   _____no

11. If "no," what job do you think you'll get?_____
    Describe it:_____

12. If you plan to go to graduate school, what type of department will
    you enter?_____
    What will be your area of specialization?_____

_____

___ ___ ___ ___ ___ ___ ___ ___ ___ ___ ___ ___ ___ ___ ___ ___ ___ ___ ___

If you would be interested in knowing the results of this study, write
your name and address below:

Part II: Early Memories—Instructions

On the following three pages we want you to describe in detail three
early memories. Try to think back to the earliest event or scene that
you can remember. Do **not** describe an event that someone told you
about ("My mother said when I was four I . . .") or a recurring event—
something that happened again and again ("We always used to . . .").

Describe a scene that happened once, say, when you were four,
five, or six years old, and that you can clearly remember. Tell what
happened, who did what, how it came out, and how you felt about
what happened,

Please be as detailed and descriptive as you can, but only write
down what you actually remember, what you can see in your "mind's eye."

If you have any questions or are unclear as to what is being asked,
please raise your hand and the experimenter will come to you.

If not, please turn the page and proceed.

ER 1

Describe a scene that happened once, say, when you were four,
five, or six years old, and that you can clearly remember. Tell what
happened, who did what, how it came out, and how you felt about
what happened.

Please be as detailed and descriptive as you can, but only write down what you actually remember, what you can see in your "mind's eye." How old were you when this occurred?_____
(These instructions may be repeated on two additional pages for ER 2 and ER 3.)

PROTOCOL FOR HYPNOTIC RETRIEVAL OF EARLY RECOLLECTIONS

Harry A. Olson

(Note: The client is first put through an induction procedure. When the client is in a trance state, the following instructions may be given to the client. The hypnotist should tape or record responses verbatim.)

The time is the present but you notice that your memory is becoming clearer and clearer. You are coming in touch with your childhood.

Think back now to the very earliest single incident you can recall. It will seem to you as if you are watching it on a movie screen. You need not tell me what the incident is, but when you have captured it in your mind, raise the index finger of your right (left) hand.

Good. We are still in the present. How old were you when that incident took place? (Client answers.) You are watching the incident take place in your mind's eye as if it were on a movie screen. Now tell me what you see from the beginning. (Client tells ER.)

That's fine. When one remembers an early incident, usually one part of the memory stands out in clearest focus, or is the most vivid or significant part. Now review the incident you just told me from the beginning as if you are watching it as a film on a movie screen. Stop the movie at the frame or point which is in clearest focus and tell me what that point is. (Client tells the focus. If necessary, ask questions for clarity such as "Where are you?" "What are you doing?" "What are you thinking?") Fine. What feelings do you recall having had at that time? (Client tells feelings.)

Very good. Now we are going to take a journey back in time, but before we go, I want to let you know what will happen. You will drift back in time and space until you are at the exact age and place that your earliest memory took place. You will be and act___years old. We will go back to the beginning of the earliest memory you have just told me and you will relive it in your mind as if it were actually happening.

We will now go back in time and space. I will count from one to ten. When I reach ten you will be at the time and place of the earliest memory you have described. One—it is no longer (*current year*), you are going back. Two, three—you are___ years old. Four, five, six— you are going back farther and farther, you are___years old. Seven, eight—you are going back, aproaching___years old. Nine, ten! You are now___years old, and are at the scene of your memory which you described before. Describe the scene as you are reliving it in your mind's eye. Where are you? Is anyone with you? If so, who? What are you doing? What is going on?

You are___years old and you will now relive the incident in your mind's eye as if it is actually happening to you. Please describe to me what is taking place. (Client describes the incident.)

That is fine. How are you feeling now? (Client tells feelings.)

What is the most vivid or important part of this incident as you have just described it? (Client tells.)

That's fine. In a little while I'm going to ask you to relive the incident again. You are___years old, but you have the knowledge of life of a (*client's age*)—year-old man/woman. This time, as you relive the incident, you will be free to change any or all events and/or outcomes that are undesirable or that you wish you could have changed. You are the director and you may do the incident in any way that you please. Ready?

You will now relive the incident again, this time making any changes you wish. Please describe what is taking place. (Client describes the incident.) That's fine. What is the most vivid or important part of this incident as you have just described it? (Client tells vivid portion.) How are you feeling now? (Client tells feelings.)

That's fine. We are now going to go up to (present year) again. When we return you will remember this incident which you have just recreated with all the detail and feelings you have just described. I will count backwards from ten to one. When I reach one, you will be___years of age. You will be in my office at (*time*) on (*date*). Let's go. Ten—you are moving forward in time. Nine, eight—you are coming back to the present. Seven, six, five, four, three—you are approaching (*present year*)___years old, two, one. It is (*time*), (*date*) and you are in my office. You are about to wake up. When you do you will have complete recall of the incident and feelings you recreated when we went back to age___, but you will have no memory for the original incident you saw on your movie screen. You will replace the original incident with the one you recreated today when we went back to age___. Neither will you remember going back in time. If anyone asks you for your earliest memory this one is what you will offer. I will count from one to five. When I reach three you will open your eyes; when I reach five, you will be fully awake and alert. You will feel calm and at peace, with a sense of well-being and accomplishment. Ready. One, two, three—open your eyes, four, five.

Post-hypnotic questioning:
How do you feel?
What do you remember?
What is the earliest incident you can recall?

APPENDIX D

DATA FORM FOR STRUCTURED EARLY RECOLLECTIONS TECHNIQUE

	E.R. HOW LIFE IS (HAS TO BE)	CURRENT SITUATION HOW I LIVE	RESTRUCTURED E.R. HOW LIFE SHOULD BE (IDEAL)
AGE			
SITUATION			
FOCUS			
FEELING			
REASON FOR FEELING			
"I WANT" STATEMENT			
FACILITATORS			

ANNOTATED BIBLIOGRAPHY

THIS SECTION PROVIDES a listing by category of almost every article, not included in this book, written specifically on early recollections. Citations of literature which is related but peripheral, e.g. the psychology of memory, are not included. Following each citation is a review of the content and/or findings so that the researcher interested in ERs has at his fingertips a virtually complete summary of the ER literature.

Articles are listed alphabetically by author under the following categories:

> THEORY
> CLINICAL
> TESTING
> VOCATIONAL CHOICE
> RESEARCH
> LITERATURE REVIEW

THEORY

1. Ansbacher, H. L. Adler's interpretation of early recollections: Historical account. *J. Indiv. Psychol.*, 1973, *29*, 135-145.
Ansbacher presents a fascinating and useful history of the development of Adler's theory of ERs tracing the theory through Adler's writings. He cites the work of Paul Schrecker (whose paper on ERs is also reviewed in this book) and the influence of Henri Bergson on Adler's thinking.

2. Ansbacher, H. L. and Ansbacher, R. R. (Eds.) Early recollection and dreams. In *The individual psychology of Alfred Adler*. New York: Harper and Row, 1967, 350-357.
This book is a selection of Adler's major writings arranged topically with commentary by the editors explaining Adler's meaning and comparing his views with his contemporaries, notably Freud and Jung. This chapter presents selections from Adler on ER theory and also provides example case material, one case of anxiety neurosis and a case of good adjustment. The section on ER interpretation, although brief, is a helpful guide. This book is one of the best scholarly works yet published on the theory and background of Individual Psychology.

358

3. Chess, S. Utilization of childhood memories in psychoanalytic therapy. *J. Child Psychiat.*, 1951, *2*, 187-193.

The paper makes the following point through theoretical discussion with clinical examples:

The formation of the memory is related to the needs of the child's personality at the time that the incident occurs, and secondly that the nature of the memory as it is recalled at some subsequent time, is dependent upon the needs of the personality at the time of recall (Chess, p. 193).

4. Freud, S. Childhood and concealing memories. In *Psychopathology of everyday life.* New York: Macmillan 1914, 57-68.

In this chapter Freud clearly and succinctly spells out his view of ERs as a purposive, yet unconscious, displacement of significant but repressed material by an impression (the ER) which is relatively innocuous or indifferent. He concludes, "They (ERs) do not owe their existence to their own contents, but to our associative relation of their contents to another repressed thought" and thus earn the title of "concealing memories" (p. 58). He then discusses several forms of displacement and continues his discussion of the nature of ERs with an analysis of one of his own early memories.

5. Freud, S. Screen memories. In *Collected papers, vol. 5.* London: Hogarth, 1950, 47-69.

In this paper written in 1899, Freud spells out his theory of ERs as screen memories in that they represent displacement for associated but repressed material. A lengthy analysis of a colleague's ER is described to demonstrate the theory. This paper, like the one cited above, is clearly written. Both papers are logically written and are relatively free of traditional psychoanalytic terminology which might confuse the novice to psychoanalysis.

6. Greenacre, P. A contribution to the study of screen memories. *Psychoanal. Stud. Child.*, 1949, *3-4*, 73-84.

Greenacre discusses screen memories from the standpoint of visual stimulation and stress in the course of superego development. She states the salient and shocking events from childhood which carry strong visual components may be reactivated later in life under similar conditions of stress. She discusses the structure of screen memories and then deals with a special type of screen memory which incorporates stubborn persistence but without brightness, and in which the manifest content is disturbing but vaguely or sparsely elaborated. These memories, she contends, reflect the central core of the neurosis and are highly resistant to analysis. A detailed case report is included.

7. Hall, G. S. Note on early memories. *Pedag. Sem.*, 1899, *6*, 485-512. This is one of the oldest articles written specifically about early recollec-

tions and is of interest from a historic point of view. Hall cites and reminisces over his own early experiences with ongoing commentary. The paper is designed to note his experiences rather than to draw any firm conclusions about the psychology of memory. The article is thus an experimental odyssey and, though old, is still unique in the ER literature.

8. Ivimey, M. Childhood memories in psychoanalysis. *Amer. J. Psychoanal.*, 1950, *10*, 38-47.

The author presents a neoanalytic discussion of ERs, *a la* Horney, and compares Horney and Freud in the role of past experiences for the client. The past is seen as part of the present because of the emotional investment of past experience which is carried into the present and may even link into the future in the form of self-fulfilling prophecy. Various expressions and uses of ERs in neurosis are outlined with several examples, including Adler's cemetery recollection (cited without reference to Adler). Memories are presented as having both inhibitory effects on therapy and constructive value for the patient's growth and can be used to consolidate changes in the client's life.

9. Kris, E. The recovery of childhood memories in psychoanalysis. *Psychoanal. Stud. Child.*, 1956, *11*, 54-88.

This paper is a theoretical discussion, with clinical examples, of advances in ego psychology and increased understanding of childhood conflicts, as they relate to early memories and the role of repression.

10. Nikelly, A. G. and Verger, D. Early recollections. In A. G. Nikelly *Techniques for behavior change.* Springfield: Thomas, 1971, 55-60.

This chapter outlines the basic theory behind ERs from the Adlerian point of view. Instructions for collecting ERs are briefly given and a number of interpretive hints are supplied, which makes the chapter of value to the clinician. A major point of the chapter is that ERs do not predict how a client will behave or wishes to do things or be something in the future, but rather they reflect his convictions, his fundamental attitude about himself, life, and the world around him.

11. Saul, L. J., Snyder, T. R., Jr., and Sheppard, E. On earliest memories. *Psychoanal. Quart.* 1956, *25*, 228-237.

This paper is an excellent theoretical discussion of the diagnostic and structural nature of early memories from a psychoanalytic point of view. Several of the points made in the paper are that (a) ERs are the same in nature and structure as dreams and are used in the service of basic personality forces, (b) every ER detail is significant, and (c) these details reflect the central emotional constellation quite directly. There is much in this paper that parallels the Adlerian understanding and use of ERs, and psychoanalytic language is kept to a minimum.

12. Schmideberg, M. Infant memories and constructions. *Psychoanal. Quart.*, 1950, *19*, 468-481.

The paper casts doubt upon the "popular tests" of the accuracy of infantile memories and cites a number of reasons why people might not remember, including immature development of the memory function, mental economy, and disturbing unconscious factors. The psychodynamic nature of ERs is thoroughly discussed with clinical examples.

13. Schrecker, P. Individual psychological significance of first childhood recollections. *J. Indiv. Psychol.*, 1973, 29, 2, 146-156.
This paper was written originally in 1913 by a twenty-four-year-old law student and is the first paper on ERs from the Adlerian position. The paper presents a theoretical overview of ERs within the context of the psychology of memory and life-style. Several case examples are cited, including ERs of Richard Wagner, the sculptor Ernst Rietschel, St. Augustine, and Friedrich Hebbel, a German poet and playwright. These recollections are analysed in terms of the influence of the ER on the individual's subsequent development. Schrecker draws the conclusion that "what is reported as a first childhood recollection serves the function of supporting the life plan, be it directly or by detours." The paper is well written and of historical as well as current interest and value.

14. Verger, D. M. and Camp, W. L. Early recollections: Reflections of the present. *J. Counsel. Psychol.*, 1970, 6, 510-515.
The authors introduce ERs to the reader who is uninitiated to this method and discuss some basic considerations and techniques in interpretation.

CLINICAL

15. Crook, G. H. Memory of infantile life—A scrap of personal experience. *J. Abnorm. Soc. Psychol.*, 1925, 20, 90-91.
Crook contested the statement made in another article of the time that a memory going back to infancy is undoubtedly hallucinatory. He presented an ER of his own as an example. The article is of little value for either the researcher or clinician.

16. Eisenstein, V. W. and Ryberson, R. Psychodynamic significance of the first conscious memory. *Bull. Menninger Clin.*, 1951, 15, 213-220.
The paper demonstrates through clinical examples and discussion the correlation between ERs and psychodiagnosis, particularly in the relationship of ER themes and organ dialect in psychosomatic disorders. A brief example of correlation of an ER with some Rorschach data was given. The paper was written from a psychoanalytic point of view and presupposes elementary knowledge of that terminology. Unfortunately, the clinical material was presented in segments, not in its entirety, so that a wealth of ER use suggested by the paper is lost to the reader. The apparent purpose of the paper, however, was just to make a case for using the first memory as a routine part of the diagnostic interview.

17. Freud, S. A childhood recollection from "Dichtung and Wahrheit." In *Collected papers, Vol. IV,* London: Hogarth, 1946, 357-367. In this paper, Freud provides an analysis of one of Goethe's ERs as a basis for a discussion of sibling rivalry and its symbolic sublimation in memories and such behaviors as throwing things out of the window. The reader is directed to the paper in this book entitled "Goethe's Earliest Recollection" which discusses the same recollection from an Adlerian point of view.

18. Friedman, A. First recollections of school. *Intl. J. Indiv. Psychol.,* 1935, *1*, 1, 111-116.

The author suggests that the first memory of school has particular diagnostic relevance for understanding the life-style of a person. School is the first major situation which requires cooperation outside of the family and relation with nonfamilial authority figures. School is also viewed by most people as an opportunity for and assessment of achievement. Thus in the school memory, we obtain a prototype of how the person responds to the task of occupation as well as community. The author points out that school ERs seem to have a quality of their own, and that persons who have difficulty producing other ERs often open up when asked to recall their school days. This might reflect the vast impact school has on us all. The paper uses a clinical approach; empirical data is lacking. Numerous clinical examples are given with a general analysis and theoretical exposition regarding the diagnostic value of ERs.

19. Friedman, A. R. Early childhood memories of mental patients: Preliminary report. *Indiv. Psychol. Bull.,* 1950, *8*, 111-116.

(This paper was also published, with only minor revisions of wording, in the *Journal of Child Psychiatry,* 1952, *2*, 266-269.) This study analysed ERs from one hundred psychiatric patients to assess the affinity between the ER and the diagnostic characteristics of the case in terms of personality organization. Several conclusions were cited:

A. Social interaction appears more frequently and positively in neurotics' ERs as opposed to the ERs of psychotics.

B. ERs of a psychotic may sometimes reflect the fear of losing or having lost his own self. Neurotics do not exhibit this theme.

C. Sickness appears in neurotic ERs as a scene of overprotection and acceptance of that situation, whereas in psychotics, illness is a scene of neglect and confusion.

D. Memories of death for neurotics often represent a scene of despair and sorrow over loss of love. Schizophrenic ERs of death lack these human qualities and appear more bizarre.

20. Glover, E. The "screening" function of traumatic memories. *Intl. J. Psychoanal.,* 1929, *10*, 90-93.

This paper presents a case to illustrate that, when dealing with screen memories, a recollection that is particuluarly traumatic may be too readily accepted at face value rather than being analysed in terms of its defensive value.

21. Hadfield, J. A. The reliability of infantile memories. *Brit. J. Med. Psychol.*, 1928, *8*, 89-111.
The paper discusses the reliability or truth of ERs and suggests several ways to test their truth. These include not only objective verification and corroboration from early childhood, but also subjective factors such as (a) a subjective certainty on the part of the client that the experience happened, (b) the emotional tone of the ER, (c) that the ER may produce symptoms, (d) that discovering the ER may produce a new reaction and hence a symptomatic cure, and (e) the ability of the ER to fit into the whole personality pattern. The author provides lengthy clinical material in evidence of his tests. He accepts a cause-effect theory of ERs in regard to symptoms (c and d) which, while consonant with psychoanalytic theory (which is the author's frame of reference), is at variance with Adlerian theory. His belief that ERs can be thoroughly validated is also contradictory to the psychology of memory as reconstruction. Much has been learned since 1928 when this paper was written.

22. Kahana, R. J., Weiland, L. H., Snyder, B., and Rosenbaum, M. The value of early memories in psychotherapy. *Psychiat. Quart.*, 1953, *27*, 73-82.
The paper makes the point that ERs can be a vital part of the diagnostic interview because they reflect major unconscious conflicts and defenses and may also suggest transference issues. They are especially valuable in brief psychotherapy planning because they can provide significant data very quickly and economically. Six case examples are provided and analysed from a psychoanalytic frame of reference.

23. Mayman, M. Psychoanalytic study of the self-organization with psychological tests. In *Recent advances in the study of behavior change: Proceedings of the Academic Assembly on Clinical Psychology.* Montreal: McGill University Press, June 1963, 97-117.
From a psychoanalytic ego-psychology frame of reference, the author discusses the use of early memories in diagnosing a person's identity structure and relationship paradigms. Tables are presented which show some of the questions one can answer in analysing early memories and a breakdown of common ER themes according to traditional stages of psychosexual development. A case example is also presented. The paper is highly psychoanalytic in language and the reader would require a prior knowledge of psychoanalytic terminology. The tables are helpful and can serve as a basis for a scoring system based on psychoanalytic concepts.

24. Mayman, M. Early memories and character structure. *J. Proj. Tech.*, 1968, *32*, 303-316.

The author presents a discussion of ERs from a psychoanalytic point of view. Clinical material from adolescents is presented and analysed, and a table of prototypical interpersonal themes is displayed categorizing these themes according to the standard psychoanalytic stages of psychosexual development. A second table provides a number of questions or interpretation guides which the clinician may use to analyse ERs. The article presupposes a working knowledge of psychoanalytic language and concepts. The tables, especially the second one, are very helpful.

25. Mayman, M. and Faris, M. Early memories as expressions of relationship paradigms. *Amer. J. Orthopsychiat.*, 1960, *30*, 507-520.

The authors studied the possibility of inferring interlocking identity patterns of a subject and his parents from the perception all of them had of the subject as a child, as expressed in the content and form of their recollections of him. Clinical material was presented, with verbatim sets of ERs, to show how the ERs revealed transference patterns which were carried into each new interpersonal encounter. They assume that ERs mirror early relationships in the formative years, when he was most open to others' influence.

26. Mosak, H. H. Early recollections as a projective technique. *J. Proj. Tech.*, 1958, *22*, 3, 302-311.

(This paper is also reprinted in Lindzey, G. and Hall, C. S. (Eds.) *Theories of personality: Primary sources and research.* New York: Wiley, 1965, 105-113; and Mosak, H. H. *On purpose.* Chicago: Alfred Adler Institute, 1977; and as a separate monograph published by Alfred Adler Institute, Chicago.)

This article presents a thorough discussion of ERs from the Adlerian perspective, including history, theory, interpretation, and applications. Numerous examples are provided, with interpretations in terms of the client's characteristic outlook and/or behavior.

27. Niederland, W. G. The role of the ego in the recovery of early memories. *Psychoanal. Quart.*, 1965, *34*, 564-571.

The recovery of memories is therapeutically effective not only because of the discharge of affect, but also through the re-emergence of the specific state of the ego which was repressed at the time of traumatic experience. The regressive features which often accompany the recall may approximate forms of thinking and feeling close to the primary process. . . . With the release of forces that were bound in the psychic structure, the synthetic function of the ego makes possible its reorganization and restructuralization. . . . Content and affect of memory can be dealt with in a revised fashion by both the ego and superego functions, permitting a more realistic solution of the conflict (author abstract). Two detailed cases were presented as examples.

28. Oberholzer, E. An infantile cover-memory: A fragment of an analysis. *J. Nerv. Ment. Dis.*, 1931, *74*, 212-213.

The author presents a memory of a twenty-five-year-old schizophrenic male and demonstrates the screen function of that memory in terms of the repressed material to which the innocuous memory related.

29. Opedal, L. E. Analysis of the earliest memory of a delinquent. *Intl. J. Indiv. Psycho.*, 1935, *1*, 3, 52-58.

Opedal uses the earliest recollection of a twenty-four-year-old man who was charged with counterfeiting as a basis for discussion of basic principles of ER theory and use. The author made the following points: (1) The ER shows the client's style of handling his problem, (2) Pampering or neglect is often reflected in the ER, as is (3) ability to cooperate, (4) the extent of his independence, (5) his relationship to his family, and (6) his self-concept.

30. Orgler, H. First memories. In *Alfred Adler: The man and his work.* New York: Mentor, 1963, 38-53.

Orgler's book is both a biographical portrait of Adler and an exposition of his theories. The chapter reviewed here presents Adler's ideas regarding ERs and cites a number of ERs with Adler's interpretations. Two of Adler's own recollections are cited, including his cemetery recollection, as are the two dog-bite recollections described in Orgler's paper in this book.

31. Reider, N. Reconstruction and screen function. *J. Amer. Psychoanal. Assn.* 1953, *1*, 389-405.

The author hypothesizes that the associative connection between constructions and recollections of derivative screen material results from the fact that the reconstruction offered by the analyst serves as a command to remember following the mechanisms described by Fenichel on the inner injunction to remember. The reconstruction, when it has the double effect described, then permits, by its approximate accuracy, unconscious material to reach consciousness, but via derivatives which serve as a screen. The other effect is in the aggravation of symptoms, which likewise serves a resistance function. Coupled together, the double effect may be understood as a compromise solution to a disturbance in economic relationships precipitated by a reconstruction (author summary).

TESTING

32. Hedvig, E. B. Stability of early recollections and thematic apperception stories. *J. Indiv. Psychol.*, 1963, *19*, 1, 49-54.

Hedvig attempted to determine whether ER and TAT changes take place as a result of experimentally manipulated experiences of success-failure and hostility-friendliness. The hypothesis tested was that, in each of the experimental conditions, ERs would not be significantly influenced but TAT stories would be significantly affected.

Results confirmed the initial hypothesis—ERs remain relatively stable whereas TAT stories change when immediately following experimental conditions of friendliness-hostility and success-failure. The results "provide additional support for their (ERs) clinical validity as a projective technique in revealing permanent personality characteristics" (Hedvig, 1963).

33. Lieberman, M. G. Childhood memories as a projective technique. *J. Proj. Tech.*, 1957, *21*, 32-36.

The study tested the hypothesis that there is a significant relationship between data shown by ERs and a test battery including the Wechsler-Bellevue, Rorschach, Bender-Gestalt, and the House-Tree-Person. Results indicated a "significant similarity between the type of content obtained by using the two procedures, although quantity of information was more extensive on the test battery" (Lieberman, 1957). She also noted differences between her psychotic and nonpsychotic samples but, due to insufficient N, she did not analyse those differences stastistically. The author cited as advantages of the technique the ease and rapidity of obtaining ERs and their function as serving as a check on other projective data.

34. Naschke, Arlene. First memory and graphic explication: A method for determining a child's self-image. Unpublished research paper.

The author hypothesizes that the human drawing reflects a child's life struggles and that first memories are consistent with and reflect how the child feels about himself in the world. In her paper, the author combines the two techniques to assess the level of self-esteem. The paper presents three cases and includes history data, three ERs, and figure drawings. The paper is of interest because it deals with two projective techniques with children. Reports on the use of ERs with children is virtually absent in the literature.

VOCATIONAL CHOICE

35. Attarian, P. J. Early recollections: Predictors of vocational choice. *J. Indiv. Psychol.*, *34*, 1, May, 1978, 56-61.

Attarian's study tested four hypotheses: (A) that Adlerian-trained judges can each predict educational preferences on the basis of ERs alone, (B) that a consensus of two out of three judges can predict educational preferences of S's by using ERs, (C) that the judges will agree in the interpretation of ERs for purposes of determining educational preferences, and (D) that the Self-Directed Search can be used to determine present educational preferences (college major). Hypotheses C and D are not supported, hypothesis B was supported as was A for two of the three judges. The article also describes similarities between Adler and Holland, and suggests areas for future research.

36. Holmes, D. S. and Watson, R. F. Early recollection and vocational choice. *J. Consult. Psychol.*, 1965, *29*, 5, 486-488.

The study tested the Adlerian hypotheses that (a) the manifest content of freely associated early recollections (ERs) was related to the person's vocational choice (a measure of the style of life) and that (b) the vocationally related ERs would have a more negative affective tone than similar ERs offered by another occupational group. The groups were equivalent on measures of socioeconomic class, medical history, and security feelings. The first hypothesis was supported in comparisons of the freely associated ERs offered by teachers, nurses, and controls. When considering the affective tone of vocationally related ERs of teachers, significant results were found which were in opposition to the Adlerian prediction. Nurses did not differ from controls on this measure. The affective tone of ERs associated with vocationally related stimuli did not differentiate between the groups (authors' abstract).

37. Manaster, G. J. and Perryman, T. B. Early recollections and occupational choice. *J. Indiv. Psychol.*, 1974, *30*, 2, 232-237.

The authors developed a manifest scoring guide for ERs (reproduced in Appendix A) and indicated that ERs are indeed helpful in vocational counseling. Studying ERs for teachers, counselors, nurses and physicians, biologists, and businessmen and accountants, the authors came to a number of statistically significant conclusions:

A. Nursing/medical and counselors mentioned "mother" characters more than those in other groups.
B. Teaching and nursing/medical groups recalled "nonfamily" members more than other groups, indicating an orientation toward working with larger numbers of nonfamily members on a one-to-one basis.
C. Those entering the helping professions live in a more emotional world, and hence see and respond to life in more emotional terms.

The authors indicate the value of using a standardized scoring guide for counseling and research purposes.

RESEARCH

38. Bach, G. R. Some diadic functions of childhood memories. *J. Psychol.*, 1952, *33*, 87-98.

This paper challenges the assumption that the brain is a warehouse of past experience ready to be reproduced in an unmodified fashion, but rather suggests that, from psychodynamic and neurological standpoints, such an assumption is totally untenable. Bach states in this article:

> Because of the interpersonal aspect of childhood memories of adults and because of their functional role in achieving adult tension reduction, it is systematically impossible to reconstruct the childhood life space from retrospective reports by adults, for such retrospections are geared to the social adjustment requirements of the situations in which the retrospection is made.

Bach suggests that more research be done on the interpersonal variables in actual child-adult relations rather than determining aspects of childhood psychopathology or precursors on the basis of memories by adults in therapy.

39. Burnell, G. M. and Solomon, G. F. Early memories and ego function. *Arch. Gen. Psychiat.*, 1964, *11*, 556-567.

This study attempted to study the predictive and thematic significance of ERs for 100 patients at an Air Force mental health clinic and 100 controls with the following results:

A. It was possible to predict success or failure in basic military training at a statistically significant level from ERs alone.

B. The prediction criteria for the above were derived from a clinical approach and were able to be used by others.

C. ER themes in young people undergoing the stress of basic training centered around conflicts of dependency and aggression.

D. Systematic psychoanalytically-oriented ER analysis was useful in identifying theme types, whereas more impressionistic methods were more helpful in assessing the degree of complexity and regression present in the content.

E. Controls showed more themes of regressive dependency, whereas more patients exhibited themes of regressive aggression.

F. The authors concluded that ERs, like dreams, represent expressions of the ego's synthetic function.

This study is the only one that could be found which deals with prediction of success or failure in training or any program based solely or primarily on ERs.

40. Crook, M. N. and Harden, L. A quantitative investigation of early memories. *J. Soc. Psychol.*, 1931, *2*, 252-255.

The authors tested the hypothesis that repression of ERs is associated with neurotic or unstable personality traits. They found that Pressey X-O test scores correlate negatively with the wealth of ERs reported by their sample. A genuine relationship was suggested even though the correlations were not highly reliable. There was also a negative correlation between Pressey scores and age at the time of the earliest memory, and the subject's certainty of the time the ER took place. Alternative interpretations of the findings are briefly mentioned.

41. Friedberg, R. L. Early recollections of homosexuals as indicators of their lifestyles. *J. Indiv. Psychol.*, 1975, *31*, 1, 196-204.

Friedberg reviews the Adlerian and some other literature regarding personality traits and world views of homosexuals. He concluded that the homosexual and heterosexual styles of life differ in terms of the following characteristics: The homosexual has a weaker sense of identity, is more dependent and has less social interest, views the world more as a hostile place, and has more severely impaired gender identity than the heterosexual. The author found no difference between homosexuals and heterosexuals in degree of goal orientation or activity level. He discusses briefly the development of a homosexual life-style from the Adlerian perspective. ERs were found to be an aid in identifying homosexual and heterosexual life-styles.

42. Dudycha, G. J. and Dudycha, M. M. Some factors and characteristics of childhood memories. *Child Dev.*, 1933, *4*, 265-278.

The Dudychas analysed the written ERs of college students for memory characteristics. They found the following results: (a) Students in the top quartile of intelligence tended to report earlier memories although the correlation between age of first memory and IQ was practically zero. (b) Most ERs date back to the third and fourth years of life. (c) Fear, joy, and anger appear most frequently. (d) More women remembered joyful and angering experiences whereas more men than women remembered fearful events. A number of ERs were reproduced verbatim but no clinical interpretations were drawn.

43. Ferguson, E. D. The use of early recollections for assessing life-style and diagnosing pathology. *J. Prof. Tech.*, 1964, *28*, 402-412.

The study sought to demonstrate whether life-style formulations based strictly on ERs were reliable. ERs were obtained from psychotics, neurotics, and normals. Three Adlerian clinicians then wrote life-style summaries for each subject based only upon the ERs. Those clinicians plus seven others then matched ER protocols to the life-style summaries beyond a .0001 significance level. However, clinicians were not able to make accurate, specific statements of diagnosis above a chance level. The relationship of life-style to manifest psychopathology is briefly discussed and the three life-style statements for one client were presented verbatim.

44. Gordon, K. A study of early memories. *J. Delin.*, 1928, *12*, 129-132.

This study attempted to determine if affective tone of an experience alters our recollection of that experience. In a sample of college students, unpleasant memories were recalled about almost twice as often as pleasant ones. The author indicates that this disproves the theory that there is a tendency to forget unpleasant experiences.

45. Hanawalt, N. G. and Gebhardt, L. J. Childhood memories of single and recurrent incidents. *J. Genet. Psychol.*, 1965, *107*, 85-89.

The authors, interested in single-trial learning, compared early memories for single and recurring events. The authors found that single incidents (SI) are recalled to a significantly greater degree than recurring incidents (RI). The authors suggest that the higher "recall of SIs poses a paradox for a frequency theory of learning."

46. Hedvig, E. B. Children's early recollections as a basis for diagnosis. *J. Indiv. Psychol.*, 1965, *21*, 187-188.

The study investigated the ability of Adlerian clinicians to determine from children's ERs whether the subjects have been diagnosed by a clinical team as psychoneurotic, or adjustment reaction, conduct disturbance. Two of three judges were able to make this distinction to statistically significant levels. It was concluded that experienced clinicians can in a limited way make accurate diagnoses on the basis of ERs only, but that ERs should be included in a battery of projective tests.

47. Henri, V. and Henri, C. Earliest recollections. *Pop. Sci. Mon.*, 1898, *53*, 108-115.

The Henris' study of ERs, perhaps the first empirical one, arrived at several conclusions. Among these are (1) that the average ER dates from three years of age, (2) that visual images are predominant and auditory images are weaker, (3) that the earlier the recollection, the more greatly the event affected the person recalling it, and (4) that most ERs relate to brief scenes. They review Taines' theory that attention is the key function in recall—that the event must have been especially delightful, horrible, surprising, or novel in order to be remembered. Current findings discount attention as the primary factor. Emotional images are briefly discussed. Seveal ERs were reprinted as examples, although no attempt was made at interpretation.

48. Holmes, D. S. Security feelings and affective tone of early recollec-
     tions: A re-evaluation. *J. Proj. Tech.*, 1965, *29*, 314-318.

The aim of this study was to evaluate the relationship between feelings of psychological security and affective tone of early recollections . . . Data was reanalzyed using the more sensitive continuous measure of affective tone and analysis of variance to compare the ER tone of High, Middle, and Low Secure Ss. On the first ER there was a curvilinear relationship between affective tone and security with Middle Secure Ss offering the more pleasant ERs. There were no significant differences among the groups on later ERs. When the affective tone of ERs associated to stimuli by these groups were compared, significant differences were found on "social" stimuli, again with the Middle Secure Ss offering more pleasant ERs. A defensive selective recall hypothesis was suggested to explain the results (author abstract).

49. Jackson, M. and Sechrest, L. Early recollections in four neurotic diagnostic categories. *J. Indiv. Psychol.*, 1962, *18*, 1, 52-56.

ERs of patients exhibiting anxiety and depressed, obsessive-compulsive, and gastrointestinal distress were studied. The hypothesis tested was that certain categories of neurotics would exhibit certain ER themes. Results were hampered by small absolute frequencies of themes but suggested that, more than for other groups, anxiety neurotics produced themes of fear and depressed clients showed themes of abandonment. Gastrointestinal patients indicated themes of gastrointestinal distress, illness, accidents, and trauma. The latter three were also more frequent in normals and anxiety neurotics. Sexual themes were more frequent in the obsessive-compulsive group. (See Taylor's paper in this book for further review.)

50. Kopp, R. R. and Der, Du-Fay. Level of activity in adolescents' early recollections: A validity study. Unpublished research paper under support from a grant from USPHS, NIMH. (For further information, contact the senior author at the California School of Professional Psychology.)

The authors conclude that "the degree of activity and type of role that an individual plays in his/her ERs correlates with the clinical assessment of his/her behavior based on descriptions by his/her parents along with an activity dimension." Therefore, the Role Activity Scale for ERs is a valid indication of current activity level in adolescents' behavior. Additionally, they discovered that while the clinically active adolescents were mostly firstborns, the clinically passive group contained more youngest children.

The following four studies by Langs report on varying aspects of the same research project, i.e. the effects of LSD-25. Subjects and basic screening procedures were the same in each of the studies cited.

51. Langs, R. J. Earliest memories and personality: A predictive study. *Arch. Gen. Psychiat.*, 1965, *12*, April, 379-390.

The hypothesis tested was that the manifest content of first memories is predictive of and has a significant relationship to personality. The ERs of forty-eight male actors were scored according to manifest content and compared to personality measures obtained from clinical interviews, Rorschach, TAT, Wechsler-Bellvue, and autobiographies. Results indicated a significant relationship between personality and first memories. Specific personality correlates for selected early memory scores were discussed, as was the role of ERs in psychoanalytic research and theory.

52. Langs, R. J. First memories and characterologic diagnosis. *J. Nerv. Ment. Dis.*, 1965, *141*, 318-320.

Subjects were placed in four categories: obsessive-compulsive, inhibited obsessive-compulsive, hysterical, and narcissistic. Definitions of the categories were supplied. Results indicated that first memory analysis was highly consistent with clinical observations. Obsessive-compulsives' ERs reflected problems with aggression and fear of loss of control. Hysterics' ERs revealed themes of relationships with women and were energetic, reflecting activity and heterosexual concerns. Narcissistics' ERs reflected separation and loss. The author concludes that ERs not only help reveal early experiences but predict present functioning and personality.

53. Langs, R. J. Stability of earliest memories under LSD-25 and placebo. *J. Nerv. Ment. Dis.*, *144*, 3, 171-184.

This study focuses upon the stability of ERs under LSD-25 as compared to a placebo, and the relationship between stable and altered recall and the subject's personality and reaction to the drug. Some studies have shown that an archaic ego state can be produced by LSD-25 with certain people. Results indicated that LSD produces regressive ER changes in schizoids or those with poor personality integration, whereas it constricts or does not alter ERs of impulsive, rigid, or obsessive persons who show minimal drug reaction. With the placebo, stable or altered ER recall was found to be unrelated to personality organization or placebo reaction. The conclusion was that ER stability is probably a function of the ego's ability to maintain overall stability.

54. Langs, R. J., Rothenberg, M. B., Fishman, J. R. and Reiser, M. F. A method for clinical and theoretical study of the earliest memory. *Arch. Gen. Psychiat.*, 1960, *3*, 523-534.

The authors begin with a discussion by Freud and Adler of the differing use of ERs and cite several research studies. The purpose of the research was to glean a large number of ERs from a variety of clinical categories of patients and categorize them, and to demonstrate their "Manual for the Scoring of the Manifest Content of the Earliest Memory." Their results attest to the psychological value of the manifest content of ERs. Significant differences were found between memories of women diagnosed as being hysterics as opposed to those diagnosed paranoid schizophrenic. Two appendices are included, the first an ER record sheet and the other a list of section headings in their ER manual.

55. Levy, J. Early memories: Theoretical aspects and application. *J. Proj. Tech.*, 1965, *29*, 3, 281-291.

Early memories from an out-patient psychiatric population are analyzed according to a specifically devised scoring system. The units of analysis are referred to as modes and are defined as the individual's approach to emotional areas such as "givingness," "mastery," and "mutuality." An inter-judge agreement of about 74 per cent resulted from scoring the early memories by three judges. On the basis of the various combinations of modes, three types of early memories are constructed and compared with certain aspects of psychological reports. The types seem to distinguish between relatively adequate and inadequate level of ego integration (author abstract).

56. Levy, J. and Grigg, K. A.   Early memories: Thematic-configurational analysis. *Arch. Gen. Psychiat.*, 1962, 7, 57-69.

The authors suggest the use of theme analysis in the interpretation of ERs. A theme is a focal point which captures an essential emotional state of the client. Single themes or a configuration of themes present themselves in ERs. They assert that thematic change in ERs reflects dynamic changes in the ego's synthetic function. Three categories of themes were developed which were Dependency-Independency, Destructive Aggression-Constructive Aggression, and Sexuality. Scoring criteria for each theme were devised. Memories of twenty-one patients were analysed according to their scheme, producing significant results for interrater reliability. They conclude that preconscious themes can be predicted from ERs, but that when the patient is using denial as a major defense, the task of prediction becomes more difficult, and that the thematic configurational method is reliable and communicatable. Several clinical examples are presented and an appendix produces the scoring criteria in entirety, with examples.

57. McCarter, R. E., Schiffman, H. M., and Tomkins, S. S.   Early recollections as predictors of Tomkins-Horn Picture Arrangement Test performance. *J. Indiv. Psychol.*, 1961, *19*, 2, 177-180.

The authors hypothesize that certain ER characteristics could predict performance on several scales of the Tomkins-Horn Picture Arrangement Test (PAT). ERs did so to a significant degree in the areas of strong superego in work orientation, inertia in work orientation, sociophilia, high-activity level of expression, fantasy level of expression, superego in social orientation, and low general work orientation. The authors state that these variables have the factors of social interest and degree of activity in common. They conclude that ERs is a valid technique for appraising these two factors. EDs did not however predict optimism-pessimism in this study. They state that optimism-pessimism is probably present in ERs but that factor in ERs has a nonmonotonic relationship to how optimism-pessimism is measured in personality tests.

58. Miles, C. A study of individual psychology. *Amer. J. Psychol.*, 1893, 6, 534-558.

The author directed a specific questionnaire to female college students and tabulated the results. Among the numerous questions asked was, "What is the earliest thing you are sure you can remember?" The most common themes were a birth or death in the family, being frightened or hurt, and an illness of self or family. Of the ninety-seven responses, seventy show attention to the outside world, whereas twenty-seven show attention to self. The person is more likely to recall incidents of being a victim rather than as an agent making things happen. She concludes that the child's world is superficially more one of sensation than of feeling, but suggests that conclusion is in error because it was an emotion of some sort that made the experience initially impressive.

59. Pattie, F. A. and Cornett, S. Unpleasantness of early memories and maladjustment of children. *J. Pers.*, 1952, 20, 315-321.

Two hypotheses were tested: (1) More unpleasant ERs will be remembered by children living in highly unfavorable environments (slums, poverty areas) and (2) The more maladjusted children in a given environment will remember more unpleasant memories. In a study of three groups of thirty-six boys each (mean age 12), the first hypothesis was confirmed. Boys reared in unfavorable environments produced over twice as many unpleasant memories as those raised in favorable environments (52% vs. 24% unpleasant). There was a slight tendency for maladjusted boys to remember unpleasant memories but the results were not statistically significant. It was concluded that the violence, poverty, and neglect which is experienced in early life is mirrored in ERs.

60. Plottke, P. First memories of "normal" and of "delinquent" girls. *Indiv. Psychol. Bull.*, 1949, 7, 15-20.

This study attempted to compare the ERs of fifty "normal" and fifty "delinquent" adolescent girls. The "delinquent" girls were housed in a Catholic institution for reeducation. Results indicated that the ERs of the delinquent girls were more active, pessimistic, and involved more punishment. They revealed less emotion and were richer in social relations although not necessarily harmonious in those relations. The "delinquents'" ERs also occurred later in childhood and showed a greater feeling of parental abuse through deception. The latter finding, parental deception, was briefly discussed.

61. Potwin, E. Study of early memories. *Psychol. Rev.*, 1901, 8, 596-601.

This study categorized memories of one hundred college students under seventeen headings and described the percentage of men's versus women's memories in each category. No statistical tests were carried out. There is no summary, discussion of results, or bibliography.

62. Purcell, K. Memory and psychological security. *J. Abnorm. Soc. Psychol.*, 1952, 47, 433-440.

The study attempted to determine the relationship between affective characteristics of memory and security feelings, and to determine whether childhood memories are as significant as adult memories when analysed superficially. ERs were taken from 126 subjects for various periods of their life from childhood to adulthood. The Maslow Security-Insecurity Test was used to determine security scores. Results indicated that affect in both child and adult memories was significantly related to security, as was memory, optimism-pessimism, and frequencies of joy versus fear memories. The results challenged the idea that the screen memory is the typical early recollection. Adler's idea of the special significance of the very earliest recollection was also challenged.

63. Quay, H. The effect of verbal reinforcement on the recall of early memories. *J. Abnorm. Soc. Psychol.*, 1959, 59, 254-257.

The hypothesis under question was that a verbal reinforcing stimulus increases the frequency of certain types of ERs over their baseline frequency level prior to reinforcement. The verbal stimulus was simply an "uh-huh" given by the experimenter to reinforce certain ER themes. Results indicate that very emotional and personal memories can indeed be manipulated by another person with minimal reinforcement. The implications for selective reinforcement in therapy were briefly discussed, questioning whether changes in patients' verbal behavior during therapy actually reflect personality change or are an artifact of selective reinforcement.

The following three articles by Reimanis study the relationship of anomie and early experience revealed through ERs. All three studies establish ERs by means of a rating questionnaire. ERs are not directly elicited.

64. Reimanis, G. Relationship of childhood experience memories to anomie later in life. *J. Genet. Psychol.*, 1965, 106, 245-252.

The author hypothesizes that childhood experiences which do not aid in the development of basic socially positive goals and values are related to a tendency toward anomic life-styles. Fifty subjects were given the Srole anomie scale and the Life Experience Questionnaire which asked how truly several items fit the subject's childhood experiences. The hypothesis was confirmed. The following themes had a significantly positive correlation to anomie. (a) Ss brought up in socially disorganized homes with much anxiety-provoking parental discord, (b) inability to identify with rejecting parents, (c) high rate of residential mobility and lack of acceptance in the community, and (d) failure to develop a satisfactory relationship with siblings.

65. Reimanis, G. Childhood experience memories and anomie in adults and college students. *J. Indiv. Psychol.*, 1966, *22*, 1, 56-64.

Reimanis discusses anomie as synonymous with the Adlerian concept of social interest, and reviews the results of his 1965 research (see above) as his hypotheses for the current study. Again the Srole anomie scale and a Childhood Experience Questionnaire were used, this time on a sample of 184 VA employees and 113 college freshmen. It was found that ERs which do not foster or which interfere with the development of social interest relate positively to anomie, whereas those ERs which reflect social interest development relate negatively to anomie.

66. Reimanis, G. Anomie, crime, childhood memories and development of social interest. *J. Indiv. Psychol.*, 1974, *30*, 1, 53-58.

Again the results of Reimanis' 1965 research served as hypotheses for this study, which utilized the Srole scale and childhood experience questionnaire scores on 103 convicted male offenders from sixteen to twenty-one years of age. Results indicate that convicted youths, more so than control youths, show a higher level of anomie and more ERs which could be expected to interfere with social interest development.

67. Smith, M. E. Childhood memories compared with those of adult life. *Genet. Psychol.*, 1952, *80*, 151-182.

This study focused primarily on the recollections of a sixty-two-year-old subject recalled from all periods of life. The characteristics of her memories at various age levels were noted, and the memories were topically categorized. A number of results were gleaned. The subject remembered over 6,000 incidents across her life span. Most early memories (before age four) were visual and of novel experiences and of neutral affective tone. Overall, 38 per cent were of unpleasant experiences, whereas 36 per cent were pleasant memories, and there was a greater variety of emotions attached to the unpleasant ones. Unpleasant memories at early ages were usually of physical pain or discomfort, while those at the teen years primarily had themes of embarrassment or some other felt inadequacy. This study is unique in the ER literature; it had primarily a N of one and focused on the recollection of incidents over a life span. Unfortunately, the research conclusions do not warrant laboring through the lengthy article.

68. Tobin, S. S. and Etigson, E. Effect of stress on earliest memory. *Arch. Gen. Psychiat.*, 1968, *19*, 435-444.

To investigate the effect of stress on the reconstruction of the earliest memory, the earliest memory was gathered before and after the severe stressor of institutionalization in the aged. A significantly greater percentage of respondents in the experimental sample introduced more extreme loss in the reconstruction of their repeat earliest memory than respondents in four control samples from whom two earliest memories were gathered at a comparable time interval. Thus, the latent affective experience of the current environmental transaction appears to be actively incorporated into the reconstruction of the past; as reflected in the present study by an increase in theme of mutilation and death associated with the impact of institutionalization in the aged (from author's summary).

69. Vogel, W., Lauterbach, C. G., Livingston, M., and Holloway, H. Relationships between memories of their parents' behavior and psychodiagnosis in psychiatrically disturbed soldiers. *J. Consult. Psychol.*, 1964, 28, 126-132.

Presence or absence of psychopathology and psychodiagnosis were investigated in their relationships to adult Ss' memories of their parents' childrearing behavior on Schaefer's Recollections of Parent Behavior Inventory (RPBI). Ss were 80 neuropsychiatric soldier patients (24 schizophrenics, 20 neurotics, 36 character and behavior disorders) and 117 normal Ss. Normal Ss did not remember their mothers signficantly differently than did neuropsychiatric Ss, but did remember their fathers to have been relatively more supportive, giving, and encouraging of intellectual and social growth than neuropsychiatric patients remembered their fathers as having been. Within the neuropsychiatric sample, neurotics remembered their parents' behavior more favorably than did character and behavior disorders or schizophrenics (authors' abstract).

70. Wagenheim, L. First memories of "accidents" and reading difficulties. *Amer. J. Orthopsychiat.*, 1960, 30, 191-195.

The study was carried out to test the hypothesis that accidents were frequently recalled in the earliest memories of poor readers. Results indicated that boys of lower intelligence and poorer reading ability produced significantly more accident themes, but for girls, accident themes were relatively equally distributed across IQ and reading difficulty levels, yielding no significant results for girls. Boys in the lowest deviation group mostly remembered accidents to themselves without an identified aggressor—such as falling or cutting oneself. No definite conclusions were drawn by the author except a correlation between intellectual inadequacy and preoccupation with physical inadequacy and aggression. The role of body image was also hypothesized.

71. Weiland, I. H. and Steisel, I. M. An analysis of manifest content of the earliest memories of children. *J. Genet. Psychol.*, 1958, 92, 41-52.

The authors analysed first memories from ninety-five emotionally disturbed children (mean age 11.9) according to seventeen characteristics. Results indicated that the sample had few ER characteristics in common. The greatest consistency was that, by far, most ERs from this group took place during oedipal years. The other results were negative. The authors conclude that the significance of ERs should be determined in relation to the subject rather than to analyse the detailed aspects of ERs out of context. This article is one of the few which reports the collection of first memories from children as opposed to adult subjects.

72. Winthrop, H. Written descriptions of earliest memories: Repeat reliability and other findings. *Psychol. Rep.*, 1958, *4*, 320.

In an attempt to assess the stability of ERs over time, the author studied two sets of ERs of students taken eight weeks apart. Whereas 32 percent of his subjects demonstrated some variability across inquiries, only three of the sixty-nine subjects produced entirely different recollections on the second recall. Memories from ages one and two are more likely to be produced by self-labeled introverts.

73. Wolman, R. N. Early recollections and the perception of others: A study of delinquent adolescents. *J. Genet. Psychol.*, 1970, *116*, 157-163.

This study attempts to demonstrate the interrelationship of early recollections and the perception of significant others during adolescence. It was hypothesized that early memories of a succorant need-fulfilling nature coupled with early memories of self-abasement and abnegation would impair the objective perception of significant others. Similarly, it was predicted that early memories of independent activity and confrontation would enhance objective, "mature" perception. Both hypotheses were supported. The sample comprised adolescent "delinquent" males and females from correctional institutions. This group represents an extreme highlighting the conflicts of adolescence which apply to the normal adolescent process as well. Suggestions were made for recognizing this process in adolescents and using it as a constructive force in work with them (author summary).

74. Wynne, R. D. and Schaffzin, B. A technique for the analysis of affect in early memories. *Psychol. Rep.*, 1965, *17*, 933-934.

The authors briefly describe a scoring technique for ERs based on Plutchik's theory of emotions. They have developed a manual which may be obtained from the ADI Auxiliary Publications Project, Photoduplication Service, Library of Congress, Washington, D.C. 20540. The manual is Document Number 8634. The authors' description is scant, so the technique cannot be replicated without the manual.

LITERATURE REVIEW

75. Dudycha, G. J. and Dudycha, M. M. Childhood memories: A review of the literature. *Psychol. Bull.*, 1941, *38*, 668-682.

The authors review and evaluate empirical studies done on the nature of early memories and summarize their data under such headings as "Age," "Sex Differences," "Sense Modalities," "Intelligence and Early Memories," "Racial Differences," and "Affective Experiences." Most of the thirty-five studies reviewed are more concerned with the psychology of memory, but the article does devote a section to early memories and psychoanalysis. Suggestions are made for further research. There is little in the paper which is relevant to the clinical use of ERs.

76. Mosak, H. H. Early recollections: Evaluation of some recent research. *J. Indiv. Psychol.*, 1969, *25*, 56-63.

The paper provides a critical review of four psychoanalytically-oriented studies by R. J. Langs, which are also reviewed in this bibliography, and gives a detailed summary of the results.

77. Titchener, E. B. Early memories. *Amer. J. Psychol.*, 1900, *11*, 435-436.

Titchener provides a very positive review of G. S. Hall's paper of 1899 entitled, "Note on Early Memories," also reviewed in this bibliography.

INDEX

NOTE: Text material and the annotated bibliography are indexed below. Specific clinical examples, case material and interpretations, and names have not been indexed.

381

Date Due